D1249836

The Practical Student

Career-oriented Success

New Port Richey
Public Library

DISCARD

Donated by
Rasmussen College

DISCARD

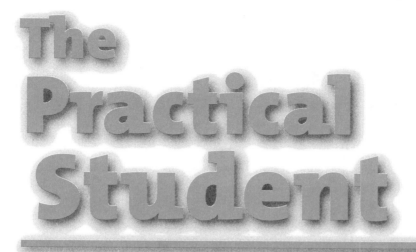

The Practical Student

Career-oriented Success

Carl Wahlstrom
Genesee Community College

Brian K. Williams

Casandra Kelly Dansby
Florida Metropolitan University, Tampa College Brandon

Student photographs by Michael Garrett, *Genesee Community College*

 Wadsworth Publishing Company

I(T)P® An International Thomson Publishing Company

Belmont, CA ▪ Albany, NY ▪ Bonn ▪ Boston ▪ Cincinnati ▪ Detroit ▪ London ▪ Madrid
Melbourne ▪ Mexico City ▪ New York ▪ Paris ▪ Singapore ▪ Tokyo ▪ Toronto ▪ Washington

Publisher: *Karen Allanson*
Editorial Assistant: *Godwin Chu*
Director of Marketing: *Lauren Ward*
Marketing Manager: *Chaun Hightower*
Production Management: *Stacey C. Sawyer, Sawyer & Williams, Incline Village, NV*
Interior Design: *Seventeenth Street Studios, Oakland, CA*
Print Buyer: *Barbara Britton*
Permissions Editor: *Susan C. Walters*
Copy Editor: *Patterson Lamb*
Cover Design: *Seventeenth Street Studios*
Cover Photos: *Clockwise from top: PhotoDisc; Chip Henderson/Index Stock Photography, Inc.; PhotoDisc; Richard Shock/Tony Stone Images*
Compositor: *Seventeenth Street Studios*
Dummy: *Sawyer & Williams*
Printer: Courier, Kendallville, IN

COPYRIGHT © 1999
By Wadsworth Publishing Company
A Division of International Thomson Publishing Inc.

I(T)P® The ITP logo is a trademark under license.

Printed in the United States of America.
    4 5 6 7 8 9 10

All rights reserved. No part of this work covered by the copyright hereon may be reproduced or used in any form or by any means—graphic, electronic, or mechanical, including photocopying, recording, taping, or information storage and retrieval system—without the written permission of the publisher.

Library of Congress Cataloging-in-Publication Data

Wahlstrom, Carl.
    The practical student : career-oriented success / by Carl Wahlstrom, Brian K. Williams, C. Kelly Dansby
        p. cm.
    Includes index.
    ISBN 0-534-53406-6
    1. Study skills—United States. 2. College student orientation—United States. 3. Vocational guidance—United States.
    I. Williams, Brian K. II. Dansby, C. Kelly. III. Title
LB2395.W34   1998
378.1 ' 7 ' 0281—dc21   98-23190

For more information, contact Wadsworth Publishing Company:

Wadsworth Publishing Company
10 Davis Drive
Belmont, California 94002 USA

International Thomson Publishing Europe
Berkshire House 168-173
High Holborn
London, WC1V 7AA, England

Thomas Nelson Australia
102 Dodds Street
South Melbourne 3205
Victoria, Australia

Nelson Canada
1120 Birchmount Road
Scarborough, Ontario
Canada M1K 5G4

International Thomson Editores
Campos Eliseos 385, Piso 7
Col. Polanco
11560 México D.F. México

International Thomson Publishing GmbH
Konigswinterer Strasse 418
53227 Bonn, Germany

International Thomson Publishing Asia
221 Henderson Road
#05-10 Henderson Building
Singapore 0315

International Thomson Publishing Japan
Hirakawacho Kyowa Building, eF
2-2-1 Hirakawacho
Chiyoda-ku, Tokyo 102, Ja

Brief Contents

Preface to the Instructor   viii

Detailed Contents   xv

- **1. STARTING UP:**
  Challenges & Rewards for the Practical Student   1

- **2. TARGETING SUCCESS:**
  Why Are You Here? What Is Your Fear?   23

- **3. TIME MANAGEMENT:**
  How to Find Time to Handle Everything   49

- **4. LEARNING & LECTURES:**
  Learning Styles & Note Taking   77

- **5. RECALL & READING:**
  Better Memorizing, Reading, & Study Techniques   99

- **6. EXAMS:**
  Taking Tests with Confidence & Integrity   135

- **7. WRITING & SPEAKING:**
  Making Powerful Written & Oral Presentations   169

- **8. THINKING SMART:**
  Critical, Creative, & Other Kinds of Thinking   207

- **9. INFORMATION TECHNOLOGY:**
  Using Computer & Communications Tools   227

- **10. PERSONAL GROWTH:**
  Managing Stress, Conflict, & Money   251

- **11. CAREER & WORK:**
  Vocational Direction, Job Hunting, Résumés, & Interviewing   285

- **12. RESOURCES:**
  Assistance, Opportunity, & Diversity   309

Sources & Credits   339

Glossary/Index   340

About the Authors

CARL WAHLSTROM is Professor of Intermediate Studies and Sociology at Genesee Community College, Batavia, New York. He has been the recipient of the State University of New York Chancellor's Award for Excellence in Teaching, the National Freshman Advocate Award, and several other teaching honors. He is past president of the New York College Learning Skills Association and a member of the State University of New York College Transition Course Development Council. He is an active presenter and educational consultant at the national, state, and local level.

Besides developing and teaching First-Year Experience courses, he has taught courses in human development, learning strategy, sociology, psychology, and human relations. He has a B.S. in Sociology and an M.S. Ed. in Counselor Education from SUNY Brockport and an M.A. in Sociology from the University of Bridgeport.

He lives with his wife, Nancy, an employee benefits consultant, in the Finger Lakes area of New York. He enjoys running, skiing, tennis, boating, mountain biking, karate, motorcycling, music, travel, and getting together with friends and students.

BRIAN K. WILLIAMS has a B.A. in English and M.A. in Communication from Stanford University. He has been Managing Editor for college textbook publisher Harper & Row/Canfield Press in San Francisco; Editor in Chief for trade book publisher J. P. Tarcher in Los Angeles; Publications & Communications Manager for the University of California, Systemwide Administration, in Berkeley; and an independent writer and book producer based in San Francisco and in Incline Village (Lake Tahoe), Nevada.

He has co-authored 17 books, including such best-selling college texts as *Computers and Data Processing* with H. L. Capron, *Microcomputing: Annual Edition* with Tim and Linda O'Leary, *Invitation to Health* with Dianne Hales, and *Using Information Technology* with Stacey Sawyer and Sarah Hutchinson.

He is married to author/editor and book producer Stacey Sawyer, and the two have a passion for travel and for experimenting with various cuisines. He enjoys reading four daily newspapers and numerous magazines and books, hiking in the Sierra, playing blues on the guitar, and getting together with his family, including two grown children, Sylvia and Kirk.

CASANDRA KELLY DANSBY is Dean of Academics at Florida Metropolitan University, Tampa College Brandon. She has received many awards, including the FMU Presidential Distinguished Service Award, Faculty of the Year Award, and two Student Appreciation awards from FMU-TCB. Dean Dansby received her B.A. in Psychology and her M.S. in Counseling Psychology from the University of Southern Mississippi. She taught undergraduate students while completing doctoral coursework in Communication at USM.

Divorced at 22, with two young children, she worked at various odd jobs before beginning college at age 27. Later she volunteered for various community and social service projects. She has served as director of a halfway house for the mentally ill in Mississippi, a substance abuse specialist in Texas, a public relations specialist for a Louisiana private drug treatment hospital, and a deputy sheriff in Louisiana. In addition, she has served as a college instructor since 1988. At FMU, she has served as departmental chair, counseling psychologist, Associate Dean of Faculty Development, and Dean of Faculty and is now Dean of Academics.

She is married to small business owner/student Grant Dansby and has two grown children, Natasha and Kyle, as well as a step-daughter, Camille. Besides canoeing and working with visual/tactile arts, she enjoys singing and playing blues, gospel, and Celtic/Irish music on a variety of musical instruments.

Foreword

by Omer Waddles
President
The Career College
Association

Where are the workers? the skills? the training?

Newspapers and magazines have raised the alarm about the serious problem of a national "skills gap":

- Two-thirds of the companies belonging to the National Association of Manufacturers report they cannot find employees with the right skills.

- About 190,000 information technology jobs remain vacant because of a lack of qualified workers. The demand for computer engineers, for example, is expected to increase 90% by 2005, for systems analysts 92%.

- Demand for health-care workers—physical therapists, medical assistants, dental hygienists, surgical technologists—is expected to surge 224% by 2005. The number of jobs in home health care services is projected to jump 120%.

Some companies have launched their own training programs to try to meet their needs. For most, however, the difficulties are too great. The solutions must come from elsewhere—from education. In particular, they must come from institutions offering career education.

But future job applicants must also do their part. It is not enough to have acquired technical training. To get the job you want—and then, even more important, to be successful on that job—you also need to have mastered communications skills, interpersonal skills, the skills of perseverence and adaptability. This mix of hard and soft skills—of the technical and the personal—represents the winning combination for success in today's marketplace.

Whether it's in business, health care, computers, graphic arts, or whatever, you may already know the kind of technical training you want. This book, *THE PRACTICAL STUDENT,* is about the other practical skills you need: establishing goals, managing time, setting priorities, organizing tasks, listening, reading, thinking, writing, speaking. These are skills that will remain valuable to you life long—in different jobs, positions, and industries and even between for-profit and nonprofit sectors of the economy.

Employers are aggressively seeking employees that combine the best of technical and personal skills. The rest is up to you. This book will help you learn to be the best in school—and thereby learn to be the best in life.

—Omer Waddles
Washington, D.C.

PREFACE TO THE INSTRUCTOR

Q: "What, in a nutshell, is this book about?"

A: "This book is specifically intended for <u>career students</u>. It shows them <u>how they can learn to be the best in school—and thereby learn to be the best in life</u>."

—The Authors

The Audience for This Book

THE PRACTICAL STUDENT: *Career-Oriented Success* is a textbook for first-year students attending career and proprietary schools or career or certificate programs (such as nursing, cosmetology, and electronics) in community colleges and four-year colleges. The text is especially appropriate for the course generally entitled *College Success, Personal Development,* or the like. This course is designed to help students master the important academic skills and some of the personal skills needed to succeed in higher education and the workplace.

The Key Features of This Book

The ***key features*** of THE PRACTICAL STUDENT are as follows.

1. The book is designed for students enrolled in career schools, proprietary schools, and certificate or career programs in community colleges.

2. The focus throughout is that the skills mastered for success in higher education are the same skills needed for success in life and on the job.

3. Essential skills and strategies are presented concisely for busy students.

4. The book features a highly interactive approach to teaching and learning.

We elaborate on these features below.

KEY FEATURE #1: THE BOOK IS INTENDED SPECIFICALLY FOR CAREER STUDENTS. This book is ***designed for students who are enrolled in career schools, proprietary schools, and certificate or career programs in community colleges.*** In other words, they are usually different from the stereotypical picture of a college student who is 18–24 years old, attends school full time, lives in a college residence hall, and participates in extracurricular activities. More specifically, the book is generally for students . . .

who are principally in school to learn occupational or career skills,

who may live off campus, often at home, and commute;

who often must work while attending school;

who may be a single parent (and need child day care);

who may be older than 24;

who may be the first in their families to go on to higher education;

who may struggle to make ends meet;

who may be racially and ethnically diverse;

who may come from outside the country;

who may be continually stressed.

This text features strategies specifically for this student audience.

KEY FEATURE #2: THE FOCUS THROUGHOUT IS THAT THE SKILLS MASTERED FOR SUCCESS IN HIGHER EDUCATION ARE THE SAME SKILLS NEEDED FOR SUCCESS IN LIFE AND ON THE JOB.

This book provides a ***practical philosophy based on action.*** This book is designed to help students be the best—that is, achieve mastery—in two areas:

- ***Be the best in academics:*** We show readers how to master the academic and personal skills needed to succeed in career education—how to manage their time, improve their memory, handle finances, work toward their career goals, and so on.

- ***Be the best in life:*** We show students how the skills one needs for success in higher education are the same skills one needs for success in life—in work, in relationships, in stress management, in finances. We pay great attention to the connection between higher education and achieving one's goals in life.

KEY FEATURE #3: SKILLS AND STRATEGIES ARE PRESENTED CONCISELY FOR BUSY STUDENTS.

Because ***it is concise and presents information in easily mastered units,*** THE PRACTICAL STUDENT is designed to serve the needs of career students, who are more apt to have to combine school and commuting, school and work, and school and family obligations.

THE PRACTICAL STUDENT covers both ***academic success strategies*** and ***personal success strategies*** in 12 short chapters. Specifically:

- ***Academic success strategies:*** We cover making the transition to higher education, goal setting, time management, learning styles and note taking, memorizing and reading techniques, test taking, and researching and presenting written and oral reports in the first seven chapters.

- ***Personal success strategies:*** We cover critical and creative thinking; use of information technology; management of stress, conflict, and money; career and work; and campus and community resources in the last five chapters. Instructors teaching abbreviated courses can skip any of these or teach them in any order.

- ***Special topics:*** Instead of having a full chapter for each special-interest topic, as some other books do, we integrate coverage within the appropriate chapter to provide better context for material.

Values clarification, for instance, is discussed in Chapter 2, "Targeting Success." *Learning styles* are considered in Chapter 4, "Learning & Lectures." *Math confidence* is discussed in Chapter 5, "Recall & Reading." *Multicultural diversity* is covered in Chapter 12, "Resources."

KEY FEATURE #4: THE BOOK FEATURES A HIGHLY INTERACTIVE APPROACH TO TEACHING AND LEARNING. *THE PRACTICAL STUDENT* takes a very focused approach in presenting material—*heavy use of interactive features, techniques to reinforce learning,* and *flexible organization for instructors.* Here's how:

- **Heavy use of interactive features:** Recognizing that most first-year classes are interactive ones, we provide a number of features that ask the student to become actively engaged with the material:

   (1) **Practical Explorations,** or learning exercises, are activities that ask students to examine their feelings and behaviors to help increase recognition and improvement of study habits. (Examples: "How Do You Spend Your Time?" "How Do You Learn Best?") There are **25 such Practical Explorations** in the book, as listed in the Detailed Contents beginning on page xv.

   (2) **Classroom Activities** are collaborative exercises that instructors may elect to assign, in or out of the classroom. (Examples: "How's Your Memory?" "What Kinds of Negative Thoughts Do You Have During Tests?") There are 49 such Classroom Activities in this book, grouped at the end of each chapter.

   (3) **The Examined Life: Student Assignments for Journal Entries** is a regular end-of-chapter feature that asks students to explore their own thoughts on how to apply what they have just read in the chapter.

   (4) **Essentials for Time & Life Management** is a six-step strategy that shows students how to set daily tasks from life goals. It requires answering the six questions: Why am I in school? What are my plans? What are my actions? What is my master timetable? What is my weekly timetable? What is on the To Do list for today?

- **Techniques to reinforce student learning**: To help students in acquiring knowledge and developing critical thinking, we offer the following to provide learning reinforcement:

   (1) **Interesting writing,** studies show, significantly improves students' ability to retain information. We use high-interest strategies—such as the personal anecdote, the colorful fact, the apt direct quote—to make the material as involving and memorable as possible.

   (2) **Brief interviews with 24 students** representing different career fields, ages, and ethnic backgrounds help readers make a meaningful personal connection to the strategies and material.

   (3) **Key terms AND definitions are printed in boldface** in order to help readers avoid any confusion about which terms are important and what they actually mean.

(4) ***Section "previews"*** offer additional reinforcement. These are the "abstracts" presented at the beginning of each section, which helps students preview, and later review, the material that follows.

(5) ***Material is presented in "bite-size" portions.*** Major ideas are presented in bite-size form, with generous use of advance organizers, bulleted lists, and new paragraphing when a new idea is introduced.

(6) ***Sentences are kept short and to the point***—the majority not exceeding 22–25 words in length.

■ ***Flexible organization:*** Chapters may be taught in any sequence, or omitted, at the instructor's discretion. For instance, Chapter 12, "Resources," may be assigned early in the course.

Supplements & Support

Several useful supplements accompany this text. They include the following:

INSTRUCTOR'S RESOURCE MANUAL. This supplement for *THE PRACTICAL STUDENT* helps instructors teach the chapters of this text by making available additional activities and exercises, advice, teaching suggestions, and answers to questions students commonly ask.

THE WADSWORTH COLLEGE SUCCESS INSTRUCTOR'S COURSE GUIDE. A useful resource for instructors and administrators, this guide covers topics such as building campus support for a first-year course, creating and administering the course, and refining it for the future. (ISBN 0-534-22991-3)

CNN COLLEGE SUCCESS TODAY. This exclusive alliance with Cable News Network (CNN) and Wadsworth allows us to offer contemporary video coverage of key topics in college and career success. Plus we offer a new tape each year!

THE WADSWORTH VIDEO SERIES. This series has an extensive selection of videos on improving grades, maximizing mental performance, stress management, healthful eating and nutrition, AIDS, and substance abuse prevention. ***Your ITP representative will be happy to provide a complete video list.***

WORLD OF DIVERSITY VIDEOS. Two-video set by David Matsumoto.

YOUR COLLEGE EXPERIENCE: STRATEGIES FOR SUCCESS VIDEOS. A collection of 12 five- to seven-minute videos produced by the University of South Carolina and SCETV. To order call 803-777-6029.

AT&T WORLDNET SERVICE—FREE INTERNET ACCESS FOR ONE MONTH!
Through our alliance with AT&T WorldNet℠ Service, ITP can now offer purchasers of ITP products one month* of unlimited access to AT&T WorldNet and the Internet. For even greater value to you and your students, ITP has customized AT&T WorldNet to include links to specific college success–related sites.

INFOTRAC COLLEGE EDITION—AN ONLINE LIBRARY OF RESOURCES AT YOUR FINGERTIPS! With this exclusive offer from ITP to adopters, you can give your students InfoTrac's online access to over 600 scholarly and popular publications, with issues dating back four years. This is an incredible opportunity to teach your students the online research and data-research skills they need—for an extremely low price.

COLLEGE EDITION FRANKLIN QUEST PLANNER. This exclusive offer gives your students access to the best professional time management system—at an extremely low price—and it includes an audiotape that trains students on how to use the system! The planner, now available for shrinkwrapping to any Wadsworth College Success text, is perfect for training students to manage their time effectively. Features include specific suggestions and exercises for building and reinforcing time management skills.

COLLEGE SUCCESS GUIDE TO THE INTERNET. Authored by Daniel J. Kurland, *College Success Guide to the Internet* is written especially for students and instructors of college success and freshman orientation courses. This practical guide includes step-by-step instructions and tips for learning to use the Internet to best advantage. As an added bonus, a substantial portion of the book features numerous and helpful Internet sites and activities grouped by key topics discussed in college success courses. (ISBN 0-534-54369-3)

COLLEGE SUCCESS INTERNET-AT-A-GLANCE. Available for shrinkwrapping with any Wadsworth College Success title, this handy little pocket guide—a one-page laminated foldout reference—lists URL sites related to such topics as career choice, money management, and health. (ISBN 0-534-54370-7)

SUCCESS ONLINE. *(http://www.success.wadsworth.com)* Success Online is a service combining instruction and learning that is delivered in a networked environment. Available free to adopters and at a nominal fee to others, this Internet service includes professional resources, opportunities for online discussion, valuable online library offerings and services, and virtual conference center opportunities. Instructors also receive guidance on starting orientation courses, sample syllabi,

---

*Telephone access and other charges, taxes, and other terms and conditions may apply. At the end of the free month, you may choose to continue the service at a low hourly or monthly fee.

online access to Wadsworth/ITP texts, e-mail to authors, and electronic access to *The Keystone Newsletter*.

For students, the site provides interactive exercises and tutorials, links to Web resources, discussion groups, chat rooms, and a virtual community of other students to extend their learning. It also offers students online access to *InfoTrac College Edition*, plus helpful material on study skills and career selection.

NEWSLETTER. *The Keystone Newsletter* of the Wadsworth College Success Series enables instructors to share ideas with colleagues around the country.

CUSTOM PUBLISHING & BUNDLING OPTIONS. Wadsworth makes available several ways of customizing this text to specifically suit instructors' preferences. For instance, instructors wishing to use only the first six or seven chapters may have these produced separately. In addition, instructors may have local materials shrinkwrapped with *THE PRACTICAL STUDENT*. For further information about content, binding options, quantities, and price, contact your local sales representative or Wadsworth's Customer Service Department at 1-800-245-6724.

Acknowledgments

Three names are on the front of this book, but there are a great many other talented people whose efforts helped to strengthen our own.

Foremost among the staff of Wadsworth Publishing Company were Karen Allanson, Susan Badger, Rob Zwettler, Lauren Ward, Chaun Hightower, Godwin Chu, and Ryan Vesely, who did a terrific job of supporting us. We are also very appreciative of the great help given us by Walt Kirby of Delmar Publishers. In addition, we are deeply grateful to Jerry Holloway and others in the production, permissions, and design departments: Pat Brewer, Kathy Head, Bob Kauser, Stephen Rapley, and Susan Walters.

Outside of Wadsworth, we were ably assisted by a community of top-drawer publishing professionals. Directing the production of the entire enterprise, as well as doing the copyediting, was Stacey Sawyer—Brian's wife and an author herself and thus fully equipped to understand authors' travails. Stacey, once again you've pulled a book out under intolerable deadlines, and once again we're in your debt. Thanks for everything!

We also were extremely fortunate to be able to get the services of Seventeenth Street Studios and designer Randall Goodall, who came up with the highly colorful and inviting interior design and cover. Seventeenth Street Studios also handled the composition and art preparation, and we greatly appreciate their efforts. We also wish to thank copyeditor Patterson Lamb, keyboarder Barbara Lewis, and proofreader Martha Ghent.

Carl Wahlstrom would like to acknowledge the support and encouragement of many friends and associates, including and most importantly his best friend and wife, Nancy, for her continued support, patience, and understanding; Don Green for his tremendous support, suggestions, and direct input; Glenn DuBois for his caring about this project and student success; Meredith Altman, Charley Boyd, and Brenda Beal for encouragement and being part of the team; and Stuart Steiner for his continued support. A special thank you goes to Michael Garrett and his assistant, Sarah Cole, for their photographic support, which helps to make this book a student-centered resource. Carl would also like to thank all his friends and associates in the New York College Learning Skills Association. Last, but surely not least, he would like to express his gratitude to his students for providing him with a source of energy and warmth to help facilitate their growth and learning.

Acknowledgment of Reviewers & Survey Respondents

We are grateful to the following reviewers and survey respondents for their consultations and for their comments on recent drafts of the manuscript:

Monica Breidenbach, *DeVry Institute of Technology, Kansas City, MO*
Janice Cline, *Fugazzi College, Nashville, TN*
Edward F. Ellis, *Kentucky College of Business, Danville, KY*
Beppie Harrison, *Dorsey Business Schools, Roseville, MI*
John T. Hohman, *Kentucky College of Business, Louisville, KY*
Fredrick Holmes, *Ogeechee Technical Institute, Statesboro, GA*
Melody L. Hunt, *Indiana Business College, Marion, IN*
Guy E. Ilagan, *Trident Technical College, Charleston, SC*
Sandra Jewell, *Kentucky College of Business, Lexington, KY*
Ted Munday, *Kentucky College of Business, Lexington, KY*
Mark Newton, *Gwinnett Technical Institute, Lawrenceville, GA*
Jimmie Lou Rice, *Kentucky College of Business, Lexington, KY*
Anthony Rose, *Eastern Kentucky University, Irvine, KY*
Karon J. Roza, *Education America, Little Rock, AR*
Maris Roze, *DeVry Institute of Technology, Oakbrook Terrace, IL*
Shaun Stull, *Kentucky College of Business, Richmond, KY*
Jim Thigpen, *Fugazzi College, Nashville, TN*
Carol Walters, *Educational Medical, Inc., Tampa, FL*

We Want to Hear from You!

We welcome your response to this book, for we are truly trying to make it as useful as possible. Write to us in care of Editor, College Success, Wadsworth Publishing Company, 10 Davis Drive, Belmont, CA 94002 (fax: 1-800-522-4923). Or contact us directly at the following:

Carl Wahlstrom
Phone: 716-343-0055
Fax: 716-343-0433
e-mail: Wahlstrom@sgccva.
sunygenesee.cc.ny.us

Brian K. Williams
Phone: 702-832-7336
Fax: 702-832-3026
e-mail: briankw@mindspring.com

Casandra Kelly Dansby
Phone: 813-621-0041
Fax: 813-623-5769
e-mail: kdansby@cci.edu

Detailed Contents

CHAPTER 1. STARTING UP:
Challenges & Rewards for the Practical Student 1

The Practical Student: Who Are You? 2
How Could a Practical Education Make a Difference in Your Life? 3
How Higher Education Can Improve Your Career Skills 5
Seven Challenges for the Practical Student 8
Onward 18
Notes 19
Classroom Activities: Directions to the Instructor 20
The Examined Life: Student Assignments for Journal Entries 21

CHAPTER 2. TARGETING SUCCESS:
Why Are You Here? What Is Your Fear? 23

Why Are You Here? Values & Your Reasons for Pursuing a Practical
  Education 24
  *Practical Exploration #2.1: Your Values About Getting a Practical
  Education* 26
What Is Your Fear? Anxiety as a Positive & Negative Motivator 28
  Practical Exploration #2.2: Higher Education: What Is Your Fear? 29
Survival Skills: What Strengths Do You Bring to Your Education? 30
  Practical Exploration #2.3: Who's in Charge Here? 31
Setting Your Educational Goals from Life Goals 35
  Practical Exploration #2.4: What Are Your Long-Range Goals? 38
  *Practical Exploration #2.5: What Are Your Plans? Intermediate-Range
  Goals* 39
  *Practical Exploration #2.6: What Are Your Actions? Steps to Implement
  Your Plans* 42
Onward 44
Notes 45
Classroom Activities: Directions to the Instructor 46
The Examined Life: Student Assignments for Journal Entries 47

CHAPTER 3. TIME MANAGEMENT:
How to Find Time to Handle Everything 49

Getting Real About Studying 50
Three Steps for Improving Your Time Management 52
  Practical Exploration #3.1: Your Master Timetable for This Term 54
  Practical Exploration #3.2: Your Weekly Timetable for This Term 58
  Practical Exploration #3.3: Your "To Do" List for This Week 61
Battling the Killer Time Wasters 61
  Practical Exploration #3.4: How Do You Spend Your Time? 62
Onward 72
Notes 73
Classroom Activities: Directions to the Instructor 74
The Examined Life: Student Assignments for Journal Entries 75

CHAPTER 4. LEARNING & LECTURES:
Learning Styles & Note Taking   77

The Four Learning Styles: Which Fits You?   78
Practical Exploration #4.1: How Do You Learn Best?   78
Lectures, Learning Styles, & Life   81
Making Lectures Work: What They Didn't Tell You in High School   82
*Practical Exploration #4.2: Listening Questionnaire: How's Your
    Classroom Performance?*   82
The 5R Steps: Record, Rewrite, Recite, Reflect, Review   86
Optimizing the Classroom Game   91
Onward   95
Notes   96
Classroom Activities: Directions to the Instructor   96
The Examined Life: Student Assignments for Journal Entries   97

CHAPTER 5. RECALL & READING:
Better Memorizing, Reading, & Study Techniques   99

The Importance of Managing Long-Term Memory   100
How to Improve Your Memory Power   103
Reading for Pleasure Versus Reading for Learning   109
*Practical Exploration #5.1: What Do You Know About the Reading
    Process?*   109
The Five-Step SQ3R Reading System   117
The Three-Step 3Rs Reading System   120
Dealing with Special Subjects: Math, Science, Languages, & Others   123
Onward   128
Notes   130
Classroom Activities: Directions to the Instructor   131
The Examined Life: Student Assignments for Journal Entries   133

CHAPTER 6. EXAMS:
Taking Tests with Confidence & Integrity   135

Taking Charge of Taking Tests   136
How to Cope with Test Anxiety in the Classroom   141
Practical Exploration #6.1: Negative Thoughts & Positive Thoughts   143
The Six-Step Examination Approach   143
Mastering Objective Questions   146
Mastering Written Examinations: Short & Long Essays   151
The Important Matter of Academic Integrity   159
*Practical Exploration #6.2: How Would You Respond to Challenges
    to Honesty?*   160
Onward   165
Notes   165
Classroom Activities: Directions to the Instructor   166
The Examined Life: Student Assignments for Journal Entries   167

CHAPTER 7. WRITING & SPEAKING
Making Powerful Written & Oral Presentations   169

What Do Instructors Look for in a Term Paper?   171

Writing a Term Paper: Five Phases 173
Phase 1: Picking a Topic 174
Phase 2: Doing Initial Research & Developing an Outline 176
Phase 3: Doing Your Research—Using the Library 179
    Practical Exploration #7.1: Research: Looking Up a Topic in the Library 189
Phase 4: Sorting Your Notes, Revising the Outline, & Writing the First Draft 188
Phase 5: Revising, Finalizing, & Proofreading Your Paper 193
Making an Oral Presentation 196
Onward 203
Notes 203
Classroom Activities: Directions to the Instructor 204
The Examined Life: Student Assignments for Journal Entries 205

CHAPTER 8. THINKING SMART:
Critical, Creative, & Other Kinds of Thinking 207

Different Kinds of Intelligence—Including Emotional Intelligence or "EQ" 208
Critical Thinking: What It Is, How to Use It 210
Creative Thinking 217
    Practical Exploration #8.1: Creativity: How Good Are You at Different
        Types of Sensory Images? 220
Onward 221
Notes 222
Classroom Activities: Directions to the Instructor 223
The Examined Life: Student Assignments for Journal Entries 225

CHAPTER 9. INFORMATION TECHNOLOGY:
Using Computer & Communications Tools 227

Personal Computers 228
Computer Software 234
Communications Tools—Including the Internet & Web 242
Onward 247
Notes 247
Classroom Activities: Directions to the Instructor 248
The Examined Life: Student Assignments for Journal Entries 249

CHAPTER 10. PERSONAL GROWTH:
Managing Stress, Conflict, & Money 251

Stress: Causes & Manifestations 252
    Practical Exploration #10.1: The Student Stress Scale 255
Managing Stress 256
Conflict & Communication: Learning How to Disagree 262
    Practical Exploration #10.2: What Are Your Feelings About Conflict? 263
Assertiveness: Better than Aggressiveness or Nonassertiveness 268
    Practical Exploration #10.3: How Assertive Are You? 269
A Crash Course in Money Handling 270
    Practical Exploration #10.4: The Money Diagnostic Report: Where
        Does It Come From, Where Does It Go? 271
Financial Aid 275
Onward 279

Notes 279
Classroom Activities: Directions to the Instructor 281
The Examined Life: Student Assignments for Journal Entries 283

CHAPTER 11. CAREER & WORK:
Vocational Direction, Job Hunting, Résumés, & Interviewing 285

What Do You Want to Be After You Graduate? 286
Tests to Help Establish Career Interests 289
Practical Exploration #11.1: The "Career Video": What Interests &
Skills Are You Attracted To? 290
Practical Exploration #11.2: What Can You Learn from a Visit to the
Career Counseling & Job Placement Office? 292
The Job of Looking for a Job 293
Practical Exploration #11.3: How Can You Build an Impressive
Résumé? 301
Onward 303
Notes 304
Classroom Activities: Directions to the Instructor 306
The Examined Life: Student Assignments for Journal Entries 307

CHAPTER 12. RESOURCES:
Assistance, Opportunity, & Diversity 309

A Look Around the Campus 310
Practical Exploration #12.1: Learning to Use Your School's Catalog 313
Academic Help 315
Physical & Emotional Help 321
Other Kinds of Assistance 324
Activities & Campus Life 327
The Multicultural "Salad Bowl": Diversity of Genders, Ages, Cultures,
Races, & So On 329
Onward 334
Notes 335
Classroom Activities: Directions to the Instructor 336
The Examined Life: Student Assignments for Journal Entries 337

Sources & Credits 339

Glossary/Index 340

CHAPTER ONE

STARTING UP
Challenges & rewards
for the practical student

IN THIS CHAPTER: This chapter considers some of the rewards to be obtained and challenges you may face as a practical student.

■ ***The practical student—who are you?*** You're probably going to a career school, vocational school, technical school, trade school, or community college career program or certificate program.

■ ***How higher education can improve your career skills:*** The four principal ways of learning in higher education—via lectures, readings, writing, and laboratories—can be used to further your career.

■ ***Seven challenges:*** You need to adjust quickly to the extra responsibilities of higher education, upgrade your skills, get to know others on campus, and so on.

■ **Even in today's radically changing workplace, there are jobs that pay middle-class wages or better and offer a chance for promotion. And they don't require a four-year college degree.**

The catch?

"Such jobs are rarely open to people with just a high-school diploma," points out business reporter Ilana DeBare. "Almost all of them require some education beyond high school."[1]

This kind of specific training, known as *career education* or *vocational-technical education*, may require a year or two to provide the necessary skills (although there are also four-year career programs and even master's degree programs). But it can lead to a rewarding future for people who can't afford or prefer not to follow a longer college program.

"With it," says economics writer Jonathan Marshall, "you have a shot at being a nurse or electronics technician. Without it, you have a shot at McDonald's."[2]

Indeed, you have a shot at a great many careers—from business to commercial art to computers to criminal justice to health care to travel and tourism, and so on—that far exceed the $10,000 yearly pay of a minimum-wage job. Your earnings might be in the comfortable range of $30,000 – $40,000 a year. Or they might be the $80,000 a year being paid to some computer-knowledgeable auto mechanics—or even more, in some top sales and management jobs.[3]

Whatever field you choose, the purpose of this book is to help you learn skills to not just survive but *BE THE BEST* in school—the same skills that, as we will show, will help you be the best in life.

The Practical Student: Who Are You?

PREVIEW A great many career or vocational-technical students don't fit the profile of the mass media's picture of a student in a traditional college or university who lives on campus, is between 17 and 24 years old, goes to school full time, and graduates in four years. Instead, the practical student usually lives off campus, is often older, is often working while going to school, is a parent, and is not inclined or able to spend four years earning a degree.

What is a typical career or vocational-technical student?

Interestingly, for the most part, he or she is NOT someone who lives on campus, is 17–22 years old, takes a full load of courses, doesn't work, and graduates on schedule. Of course, some career or vocational-technical students *do* fit this profile, and this book is for them as well.

You, however, may not fit the description served up on television or in magazines of a typical college student. Instead, you may share some or all of the following characteristics. You may be a student . . .

■ who is in school to learn an occupation or trade

■ who is not after a liberal-arts education

- who may have gone to a substandard high school
- who may live off campus, often at home, and commute
- who often must work while attending school
- who may be a single parent (and need child day care)
- who may be older than 24
- who may be the first in your family to go on to higher education
- who may struggle to meet ends meet
- who may be racially and ethnically diverse from the majority population
- who may come from outside the country
- who may be continually stressed

At various points in the book we will address all these concerns.

Even if only one or two things on this list describe your situation, this book is for you. The fact that you are a *career* or *vocational-technical* student seeking a *practical education* means you may have different needs from those of many other students in higher education.

How Could a Practical Education Make a Difference in Your Life?

PREVIEW Students with a higher education usually make more money, are more knowledgeable and competent, and experience more personal growth than those with a high school education. These factors may contribute to an increase in happiness.

Suppose you were to decide right now NOT to continue on with a career or vocational education. What would you be missing if you didn't finish?

Let's take a look.

INCREASED INCOME. With the widespread competitive and technological changes of the last few years, it has become clear that the rewards go to those with skill and education. "Well-educated and skilled workers are prospering," says Robert Reich, former U.S. secretary of labor, whereas "those without education or skills drift further and further from the economic mainstream."[4]

There is much supporting evidence:

■ ***Link between more education and more income:*** The more education people have, the higher their income, according to studies by Princeton University economists Orley Ashenfelter and Alan Kreuger. From grade school through graduate school, every year spent in school adds 16% to the average person's lifetime earnings. This means that a two-year degree, for instance, can be expected to increase an individual's earnings by about *one-third.*[5]

■ ***Growth in employer demands:*** In the 1990s, jobs requiring degrees in higher education were projected to grow 1.5% per year, according to the head of one economic advisory firm. For high-school diplomas, the demand was expected to grow only 0.6% per year.[6] Seldom do uneducated people advance in their careers as rapidly as those who have learned advanced skills in a higher education setting.

■ ***Growth in good-paying jobs not requiring four-year degree:*** "I've seen statistics that by the year 2000, 80% of new jobs will require less than a [four-year] bachelor's degree, but more than a high-school diploma," says George Cartsonis of Oakland Community College in Michigan.[7]

A study by the nonprofit Michigan Future Inc., of the University of Michigan, found that among 54 job fields with average (median) earnings of at least $33,000 a year, 23 required no four-year college degree. Employed in these occupations were police officers, firefighters, engineering technicians, purchasing agents, automobile sales agents, supervisors of precision production workers, tool and die makers, and repairers of electrical or electronic equipment.[8] Many of the jobs cited in the study require some community-college or technical training.

Although a practical education won't *guarantee* you higher earnings, it certainly provides better odds than just a high school diploma. Moreover, your exposure to higher education will probably help you develop additional "street smarts"—that is, flexibility—so that whatever happens in the job market you'll be better able to land on your feet.

INCREASED PERSONAL DEVELOPMENT. Money, however, is not the only reason for seeking education beyond high school. Higher education can also provide some of the most significant experiences possible in life—those having to do with personal growth and change. The very fact that higher education serves up unfamiliar challenges and pressures can help you develop better adjustment skills, such as those of time management.

Some of the positive changes that studies show to be characteristic of people who have had higher education are these:[9]

- ***Increase in knowledge, competence, and self-esteem:*** The higher education experience increases people's knowledge of content, as you might expect, extending their range of competencies and providing them with a greater range of work skills. It also helps them develop their reasoning abilities. Finally, it increases their self-esteem.

- ***Increase in personal range:*** Higher education helps people to develop their capacity for self-discovery and to widen their view of the world. They become more tolerant, more independent, more appreciative of culture and art, more politically sophisticated, and more future oriented. They adopt better health habits and become better consumers and citizens. They may even become better parents: Children who watch their parent or parents improve their everyday lives through higher education are more likely to seek such education themselves.

INCREASED HAPPINESS. Is there a relationship between educational level and happiness? A lot depends on what is meant by "happiness," which is hard to measure. Still, wealthy people tend to be happier than poor people, points out one psychologist. "Does that mean that money buys happiness," he asks, "or that happy people are likely to succeed at their jobs and become wealthy?"[10]

Whatever the case, better educated people do make more money, as we have shown. They also have the opportunity to explore their personal growth and development in a way that less educated people cannot. This gives them a chance to discover what makes them happy. And most college graduates experience an increase in feelings of self-confidence and pride in themselves.

How Higher Education Can Improve Your Career Skills

PREVIEW The four principal ways of learning in higher education are via lectures, readings, writing, and laboratories. The skills you develop to master these learning activities can be used not only to improve your grades but also to further your career in the work world.

Let's get down to basics: How is knowledge transferred to you in school? Can you apply the methods of learning in career and vocational-technical education courses—whatever the subject—to help you be successful in your career *after* school?

The answer is: Absolutely!

THE FOUR PRINCIPAL WAYS OF INSTRUCTION. Although systems of higher education in other countries operate somewhat differently, in the colleges and technical institutes of the United States and Canada, most first-year students acquire knowledge in four principal ways-—by lectures, reading, writing, and laboratories. Let's consider these:

- **Lectures:** Students attend lectures by instructors and are tested throughout the school term on how much they remember.

  Relevance to your career: When you are out of school and go to work in the business or nonbusiness world, this method of imparting information will be called a "presentation," "meeting," or "company training program." And the "test" constitutes how well you recall and handle the information in order to do your job. (Sometimes there's an actual test, as in government civil service, to see whether you qualify for promotion.)

- **Readings:** Students are given reading assignments in textbooks and other writings and are tested to see how much they recall. Quite often lectures and readings make up the only teaching methods in a course.

  Relevance to your career: In the work world, comparable ways of communicating information are through reports, memos, letters, instruction manuals, newsletters, trade journals, and books. Here, too, the "test" constitutes how well you interpret and use the information to do your work.

- **Writing:** Students are given assignments in which they are asked to research information—using sources ranging from the library to the Internet—and write it into a term paper. Generally, you need not recall this information for a test. However, you must manage your time so that you can produce a good paper, which is often an important part of the course grade.

  Relevance to your career: In the work world, a research paper is called a "report," "memo," "proposal," or "written analysis." Police officers, nurses, salespeople, and managers all write reports. How well you pull together facts and present them can have a tremendous impact on how you influence other people. This factor in turn affects how you are able to do your job.

  Employers consistently report that good writing skills are essential to career success. People with poor writing skills are less likely to advance in the work world. Moreover, many legal or other business records are permanent; thus, poor writing skills can easily cause embarrassment to an employer and supervisors.

- **Laboratories:** Laboratories are practice sessions. You use knowledge gained from readings, and sometimes lectures, to practice using the material, and you are graded on your progress. For example, in computer science or office technology, you may take a lab that gives you hands-on instruction in word processing. In an electronics, auto-mechanics, mould-making, dental-hygiene, or cosmetology course, you also put the lessons learned elsewhere into practice. In studying corrections or police work, you may do interning, field work, cooperative education, or on-the-job training that helps you practice what you've learned.

  Relevance to your career: In the world of work, your job itself is the laboratory. Your promotions and career success depend on how well you pull together and practice everything you've learned to do the job.

There are also other instructional techniques. Instead of lectures, you may have discussion groups, or *seminars*, but you'll likely still be tested on the material presented in them. Instead of readings, you may have to *watch films, slides, or videotapes* or *listen to audiotapes,* on which you may be tested. Instead of term papers or laboratories, you may be assigned *projects.* For example, in drafting, you may be asked to create something. In other subjects, you may be asked to do a field trip and take notes. Still, most of these alternative methods of instruction make use of whatever skills you bring to bear in lectures, reading, writing, and laboratory work.

HOW LEARNING IN HIGHER EDUCATION CAN HELP YOUR CAREER. We have pointed out that each of these instructional methods or situations has counterparts in the world of work. This is a very important matter.

Whenever you begin to think that whatever you're doing in school is irrelevant to real life—and we have no doubt you *will* think this from time to time—remember that the *time-management methods* by which you learn are *necessary skills for success in the work environment.*

If you know how to take efficient notes of lectures, for example, you can do the same for meetings.

If you know how to extract material from a textbook, you can do the same for a report.

If you know how to research a paper, as by using the Internet, you can easily adapt to finding your way around a company's computer network.

Moreover, these and other learning skills will be valuable all your life because they are transferable skills between jobs, between industries, and between the for-profit (business) and nonprofit (education and government) sectors of the economy. They are also valuable in nonwork areas, as in volunteer activities.

In sum: If you master the skills for acquiring knowledge in higher education, these skills will serve you well in helping you live the way you want to live professionally and personally.

The rest of this chapter considers the challenges you face and the strengths you bring to meet those challenges.

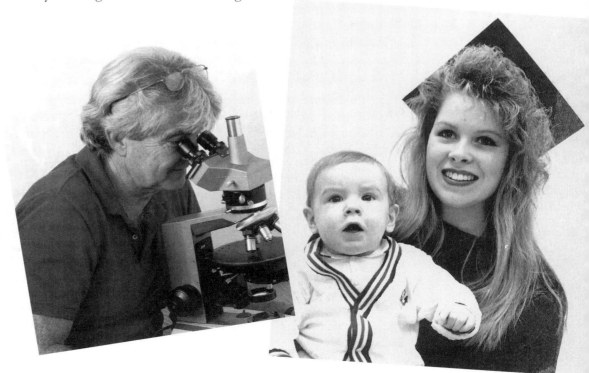

Seven Challenges for the Practical Student

PREVIEW   As a career or vocational-technical student, you have seven challenges: (1) to quickly adjust to the extra responsibilities that higher education imposes compared to high school; (2) to begin upgrading academic skills, if necessary; (3) to get to know others on campus; (4) to learn to balance school, commuting, and work; (5) to help your family adjust to your new responsibilities; (6) to help your old friends understand your new commitments; and (7) to adjust to new personal challenges.

You may be attending a career program or professional program in a community college. Or it may be in a vocational-technical school or proprietary school. Or it may be some sort of career-oriented program in a four-year college. Whatever the institution, your first exposure to higher education may well be "like moving to a foreign country," as Karen Leven Coburn, an associate dean of students, puts it. "There's a new landscape, a new culture, and a new language."[11] No wonder it's been said that the first year is often characterized "by feelings of panic and incompetence."

In this book, we'll do our best to help you try to minimize these feelings of anxiety and inadequacy. To achieve this, you need to meet the following challenges:

1. Quickly adjust to the extra responsibilities that higher education imposes— responsibilities you probably didn't have in high school. This is crucial.

2. Begin upgrading your academic skills, if necessary, so you can be competitive.

3. Get to know other people on campus—students, instructors, and staff— which may take some extra effort.

4. Learn to balance school, commuting, and work.

5. Help your family adjust to your new responsibilities, if you're living at home.

6. Help your old friends—including any boyfriends/girlfriends—understand your new commitments.

7. Adjust to new personal challenges.

Let us consider these.

CHALLENGE #1: ADJUSTING TO THE EXTRA RESPONSIBILITY OF HIGHER EDUCATION COMPARED TO HIGH SCHOOL. Regardless of the kind of institution they're attending, many first-year students in higher education have one overarching difficulty in common. This difficulty is: getting used to the reality that higher education is not high school.

High school is required of all students. Higher education is not.

High schools have homerooms. Higher education does not.

In high school, you have the same daily class schedule. Where you're going now, the schedule can vary every day.

In high school, textbooks are given to you. Now you have to buy your own.

In high school, teachers take class attendance. Now your instructors often do not.

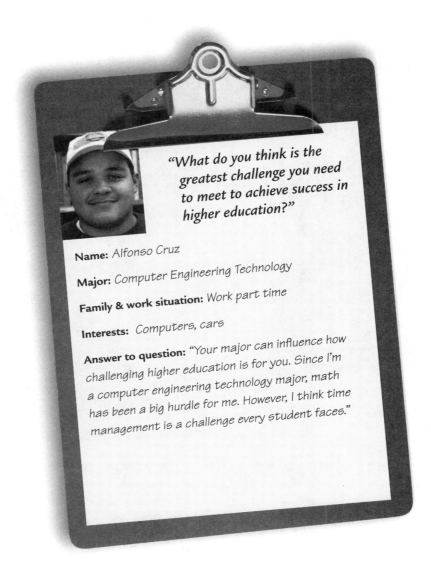

"What do you think is the greatest challenge you need to meet to achieve success in higher education?"

Name: Alfonso Cruz

Major: Computer Engineering Technology

Family & work situation: Work part time

Interests: Computers, cars

Answer to question: "Your major can influence how challenging higher education is for you. Since I'm a computer engineering technology major, math has been a big hurdle for me. However, I think time management is a challenge every student faces."

High schools require a doctor's note saying you were ill if you miss a class. Now you probably won't have to provide one.

High schools emphasize teachers teaching. Higher education emphasizes learners learning.

High schools may not require you to devote a lot of time to homework. Now you have to devote *a lot* of time to studying.

Finally, the biggest difference is: *high school probably didn't require as much PERSISTENCE AND COMMITMENT as will be required of you now.*

In short, in going from high school to higher education, you are going from a system with many rules to one with fewer rules. You are going from an educational structure that often restricts freedom to one that allows a good deal of freedom.

But this new environment has a condition attached to it: You're going from an environment with *some* demands to one with *lots more* demands—and you're expected to take more responsibility for your actions. In particular, this will mean learning to manage your time in a different way.

CHALLENGE #2: UPGRADING YOUR ACADEMIC SKILLS. Are you up for the level of work required of career or vocational-technical students? It's possible you've been out of high school for several years or have never learned certain skills. However, it certainly won't be your instructors' fault if you find it a struggle to keep up in their courses. It's up to you to catch up on the necessary skills.

What kinds of skills are we talking about? Many students find that high school didn't give them the foundation they need in reading, writing, and math. We offer suggestions for reading textbooks and writing papers later in this book. However, your institution may offer special courses—developmental reading, writing, and mathematics classes—that are designed to help students do the work required in higher education. You can discuss with your academic advisor (as we explain in Chapter 3) which classes might be best for you.

Taking developmental classes is not something to feel ashamed or resentful of. Maybe you had the misfortune to have had a substandard high-school education. However, you now have the *good* fortune to be able to do something about it. Indeed, one of the great things about the educational systems of North America is that (unlike those in many other countries) they offer lots of second chances. Developmental classes can be your second chance.

You can also think about developmental education this way: All kinds of people find later in life that they've suddenly developed an interest in an activity—job hunting, public speaking, management, investing, painting, golf, computer operation, a foreign language—for which they've had little previous training. So they do the obvious thing: They go to some sort of school to learn the basics that they missed earlier. That's what you would be doing with developmental courses.

In any case, it's not up to your instructors to reach down and give you an "A" because you have the best of intentions to do well but may have been disadvantaged by a poor academic background. Or because you work nights or must cope with children. It's up to you to reach up and earn that "A" by powering up your academic skills.

CHALLENGE #3: GETTING TO KNOW OTHERS ON CAMPUS. Many career or vocational-technical students commute to school. If you're one of these, you may find yourself surrounded by people you don't know, many of whom are quite different from you. Yet even while in the midst of many people, you may often feel alone.

Making friends is easier for students (especially traditional-age students) who live on residential campuses—those with on-campus dormitories, residence halls, and live-in fraternities and sororities. This is because students continually cross paths when they're not in class, as in dormitory hallways and dining areas. At commuter schools, however, many students—regardless of age—simply leave campus after class. Outside of class, they may be reluctant to speak with fellow students, join clubs, or go to social functions. As a result, in one survey, 76% of college presidents stated that students' lack of participation in campus events was one of the most serious problems affecting student life.[12]

Even if students spend some time in the library or in the cafeteria, they may not find it easy to connect with other students. They may resist reaching out because they worry that others will reject them for being supposedly unattractive, uninteresting, unintelligent, uncool, or just unlike them. Connecting with others requires becoming somewhat assertive. (For example, you might try introducing yourself to someone that you find yourself walking out the door with on leaving a class.)

Maybe you feel you already have sufficient friends outside of school. However, getting to know other students—and instructors and advisors—is important if only for one reason: *They help you stay in school.*

Who are you going to borrow notes from if you miss a class? (Another student.)

Who are you going to talk to for clarification on an assignment? (The instructor.)

Who's going to explain what sequence of courses you need to take? (Your advisor.)

Who's going to offer ideas for handling common problems—dealing with families, outside jobs, day care, getting financial aid, and so on? (Others on campus, such as the financial aid advisor.)

Who's going to boost your spirits and say, "You can do it!"? (Other students like you.)

Making connections is important. *Overcoming isolation makes you feel as though you belong and helps motivate you to do the level of work that higher education requires.*

The proof of this is shown in a 1996 study by the University of California at Los Angeles, which found that although more people are going to college, fewer are graduating. The reason? More students commute to school and work off campus.

"Staying home detracts from your ability to finish," says UCLA education professor Alexander Astin, the principal author of the study. "You get less committed. It's less a change from your high school years."[13]

CHALLENGE #4: BALANCING SCHOOL, COMMUTING, & WORK. Let's assume, for the moment, that you are going to school full time, taking a full load of courses. If that's the case, you should be aware that classes and studying alone can take more time than a full-time job! This is because of the rule of thumb—which does not apply in most high schools but certainly applies in higher education—that YOU SHOULD ALLOW AT LEAST 2 HOURS OF STUDYING FOR EVERY HOUR YOU SPEND IN CLASS.

Thus, if you take a full-time course load of 16 units (credits), which represents 16 hours a week of going to class, you should assume you need to put in an *additional* 32 hours of studying a week—reading textbooks, reviewing lecture notes, writing papers, and so on. The 16 hours of class time and 32 hours of study time, then, would total 48 hours a week—*more* than the standard 40-hour-a-week job.

Perhaps you are going to school part time rather than full time. Many career and vocational-technical students do, as we mentioned. However, even if you're taking just one course (of 5 units, say), class time and study time might add up to 15 hours. This is a big chunk out of the week, if you have other demands on your time.

Regardless of the type of campus—urban, suburban, rural; residential or nonresidential—probably most career and vocational-technical students feel continually starved for time. However, a great many readers of this book must allow time for two activities on top of doing their school work—*commuting* and *working*.

- **Commuting:** How many hours a day will it take you to get from home or work to school and back? (And how about any additional hours for picking up children or doing shopping, if necessary?) Some people may spend 2 *hours or more a day* just riding or driving.

    If you take public transportation, it's possible you can use some of the commuting time for studying—if you don't have to stand up, aren't too tired, and are able to concentrate.

    If you drive, most of your attention necessarily has to be on your driving, unless you're riding with someone else.

    Thus, unless you're willing to be a bit creative (as we'll discuss), commuting can be lost time—gone, useless—except perhaps for allowing you to let your mind wander and relax mentally.

- **Working:** Many career and vocational-technical students have to work while going to school. Some, in fact, work full time or work at more than one job. As we mentioned, working can handicap your ability to get ahead in school. This is not only because it takes time away from the books but also because it drains you of energy you could certainly use later while studying.

    Perhaps you're fortunate enough to have a job (or jobs) in which you can find time to study, if your employer allows it. Being a weekend or night-shift security guard, for example, or the person who hands out towels at a health club may provide long, uninterrupted moments that you can use for yourself.

On the other hand, a job, no matter how energy- and time-demanding, could fit right in with your future plans. Working as a clerk in a television station, for instance, may help illuminate for you exactly what you have to do academically to get the before-the-camera TV career you want. Alternatively, the job you hold may be exactly on the career path you want, and the purpose of school is to give you the courses or degrees that will advance you along this path.

Is there any way you can use commuting or work time for study purposes? Depending on your situation, you can carry 3×5-inch note cards that can help you memorize important terms, formulas, names, dates, and so on. If you have a Walkman-type portable audiotape player or a tape deck in your car, you can listen to tapes on school-related subjects. In Chapter 3, "Time Management," we describe these and other study tips in detail.

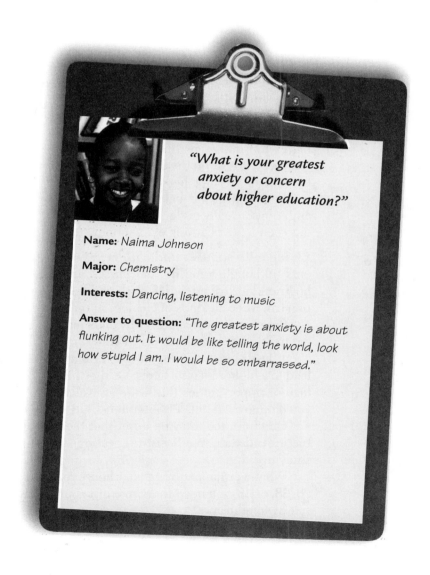

"What is your greatest anxiety or concern about higher education?"

Name: Naima Johnson

Major: Chemistry

Interests: Dancing, listening to music

Answer to question: *"The greatest anxiety is about flunking out. It would be like telling the world, look how stupid I am. I would be so embarrassed."*

**CHALLENGE #5: HELP YOUR FAMILY ADJUST TO YOUR SCHOOL RESPON-
SIBILITIES.** Because many career and vocational-technical students don't
live in campus student housing, where do they tend to live? Some share apartments or houses off campus with others their own age. However, many live with
their families. There are (at least) two variations here:

■ *Living with parents or other older adults:* Many career students of traditional student age—that is, 17 to 24—continue to live with their parents. Or
they live with the same adults—such as grandparents or aunts or uncles—that
they lived with while in high school.

Unlike students who move out to live on campus, students who live at home
experience the same family pressures they always have. Thus, for example, they
may be expected to continue doing housekeeping chores, shopping and cooking, and babysitting of younger brothers and sisters. Some may even be expected to follow curfew rules imposed on them in high school, such as being home
by midnight every night.

In addition, they are exposed to the usual household conflicts and crises,
such as problems about money or a family member's alcohol abuse. On top of
the family demands, of course, they now have the new demands associated with
higher education.

Are the people in your household proud and supportive of your desire to go
on in school? Some families see the student as fulfilling their own dreams for a
better life, although this can put extra pressure on the student to succeed.
However, it is often the case—particularly for students who are the first in their
families to attempt higher education—that other members of the household
will be resentful and jealous. Indeed, they may actively work *against* your school
ambitions, usually under the guise that you're not "pulling your own weight" (by
doing chores or earning extra money).

■ *Living with spouses and children:* Older students may not live with their parents (although some do, of course). Instead, they may live with a spouse or
boyfriend/girlfriend and/or with children. The time demands of higher education can force all kinds of changes in the nature of the relationship.

Spouses or boyfriends/girlfriends may resent the loss of attention or of having to take on extra burdens. If you've cut back on work hours, they may worry
about less money coming in (even though your new career skills will probably
lead to a higher income later). Or they may be jealous that you are taking advantage of opportunities that weren't available to them. They may be afraid that
you'll outgrow them, leave them behind, or become "smarter" than they are.

Children, too, may be upset that the parent is able to spend less time with
them. And they may insist on getting attention during times you need to be
studying.

Whatever the nature of your household and whatever your age, whether 18,
28, 38, or 48, you need to try to enlist your family members as allies in your pursuit of an education.

Make them aware that you'll have to devote more time to school than you've
had to in the past. Post your class schedule and study schedule in a prominent
place at home (such as on the refrigerator door). Tell them that your study time
is sacred. You can indicate this, for example, by hanging a DO NOT DISTURB
sign near your study place when you sit down to hit the books. Tell everyone
that you'll now have to use evenings and weekends for studying rather than for

your former activities. Ask children to help you by, for instance, drawing the DO NOT DISTURB sign or color-coding test-question study cards.

Above all, you need to explain the reasons you're pursuing a practical education in the first place, reasons that we'll help you identify in Chapter 2, "Targeting Success." Members of your household may appreciate what you're doing, for example, if you can show them that the more education you have, the more money you're apt to make.

Finally, the members of your family will feel much better about allowing you to pursue your educational goals if you just *THANK* them. For instance, if someone babysits your children for free, you could take a piece of notebook paper and draw up a little "Certificate of Thanks" for them. People are less likely to feel resentful if you acknowledge their help in advancing your educational career.

CHALLENGE #6: HELP FRIENDS UNDERSTAND YOUR NEW COMMITMENTS.

Whenever we try something new, there are often old friends and acquaintances who are disturbed by the change. If you're promoted to a higher position at work, for instance, your former co-workers may no longer feel able to kid around with you the same way (since you're now their boss).

Similarly, if you're serious about career education, you may encounter the same kind of strain in your relationships with your old friends who are not going on in school. This can happen in two ways:

- *Strains on friendships:* In high school, your studies were probably not so demanding, and it was easy for you simply to hang out with friends, go to parties, or go out every night. Now you won't have this much free time, but your old friends who are not pursuing higher education may not appreciate this. Indeed, if you say "I've got to go home and study," they may even scorn you as pretending to be better than they are. Your friends may feel you're rejecting them, and their natural response is to act resentful.

- *Strains on relationships:* Telling a boyfriend or girlfriend (or a spouse) that you can't spend as much time together can cause similar reactions. However, they may express their concerns in a different way from your other friends. They may say, "So you no longer think I'm good enough for you, now that you're going on in school!" Or they may go a step further and worry that you'll meet "someone better" on campus and start a new relationship.

The opinion of friends, including spouses or boyfriends/girlfriends, may be very important to you. At bottom, though, you need to decide just how important higher education is to you. This comes down to the strength of your *motivation*, a matter we will discuss in Chapter 2.

In dealing with friends and relatives, realize that your educational plans mean that others may actually have to restructure their lives to accommodate yours. Tell them that you hope higher education will help you achieve a fuller life but that you don't want to give up everything that's good about your life so far. Explain what you want to do, then ask for their help and moral support. Follow up by expressing your appreciation, as in writing notes of thanks.

CHALLENGE #7: ADJUST TO NEW PERSONAL CHALLENGES. By now it may be clear that the first year of career or vocational-technical education is not just the "thirteenth grade" of high school. There really are significant differences, but they mainly come down to you—your attitude, your motivation, your determination.

Reality check: What do you think the dropout rate is for first-year college students? That is, what percentage fail to return to the same college the second year?

Answer: More than one in four students (26.9%), according to a report of 2,564 colleges. For community colleges, 44.3% of first-year students did not return the second year.[14]

Now, this doesn't mean that all these dropouts *flunked* out. Some may have simply transferred to another institution. Others may have dropped out because of lack of money. Still, one reason for the great number of dropouts, it is speculated, is that higher-education enrollments have skyrocketed and so there are more people attending "who aren't prepared academically to deal with the work."[15]

Aside from lack of money, people who end up leaving higher education do so for the following reasons:[16]

- ***They are underprepared academically, and this lack leads to frustration and feelings of failure and lowered self-esteem:*** Some students are underprepared—in reading, writing, and math skills, for instance—and find themselves in courses that are too difficult for them. (Then they may be angry and resentful because they think someone has somehow set them up or sold them a bill of goods.) *It's important to know that your institution offers all kinds of academic support services—for example, math tutoring. But it's best not to wait until you're in trouble to find them.*

    If you sense even in the first couple of weeks of your first term that you're slipping, tell the instructor of the class for which you are reading this book. Or go to the student counseling center. Be honest also about telling your academic advisor if you're worried about being in over your head. School officials can't help if they are unaware you need their assistance.

- ***They are overprepared academically, and this leads to boredom:*** Some first-year students complain that their courses repeat work they already covered in high school. This is why good academic advising by a counselor is important.

- ***They perceive higher education as being not useful:*** First-year students who don't think their work in higher education will be useful beyond the classroom are high candidates for dropping out. This perception may be particularly common among first-year students who have not chosen a career direction or major. However, it also happens to those who do have career goals but who consider general-education requirements (a big part of the first year in many institutions) irrelevant.

    It's essential to remember that when you entered your program of study—your degree plan—you automatically agreed to fulfill certain requirements. You may not like every course or professor, but requirements are requirements. Courses weren't included on your degree plan arbitrarily. They were put there after a lot of discussion by academic officials of many levels, including state levels.

    One of the important lessons of this book is that the techniques you learn for success in higher education—regardless of the courses you take—are the same techniques that will help you to success in life. From this point of view, then, higher education *is* useful.

- ***They have unrealistic expectations about higher education:*** Some first-year students don't have realistic expectations about themselves and career education. For example, some come to school expecting great things to happen without much investment on their part. They may expect the instructor in a class, not themselves, to provide most of the educational effort. Thus, they devote little effort in making higher education work for them.

- ***They are uncertain about their career or major:*** It's okay to come to campus undecided about your career or major. Indeed, higher education is a great place to explore these possibilities. Even so, you should be aware that indecision about these important goals is a reason for dropping out.

    This is why taking general education courses early in your college career is particularly important. Should you then decide to switch career fields or majors, you may find that some of the courses will transfer to your new major. If, however, you start out as a computer science major and take computer courses exclusively, then switch to criminal justice as a major, you may find that many computer courses won't transfer for credit in your new major.

- ***They don't have a personal support system:*** Most first-year students have to start from scratch building a personal support system. This means making friends with other students, counselors, and professors or otherwise finding support. No one in your life is quite as likely to understand your struggle as others involved in education.

    Ask a couple of other dedicated students in a class you share to join you in a study group. Exchange phone numbers. Studying together not only helps you become better prepared for exams. It also promotes cohesion and a feeling of mutual support.

    Getting to know people may take more effort on a commuter campus than on a residential campus. Nevertheless, whoever you are, a support system *is* available.

    In general, all these difficulties can be boiled down to three matters:

- *Motivation*

- *Support*

- *Skills achievement*

    These are your major challenges during the coming year. This book gives a lot of attention to these issues.

Onward

PREVIEW   Higher education is about deciding what you want your life to be and how to achieve it.

"Get a life!" everyone says.
But what, exactly, is "a life," anyway? And how do you "get" it?
We pass this way only once. The calendar leaves fall away. And then it's over.
Some things just happen to us, but a lot of things we choose. How many people, though, wake up at the age of 60 or 70 and say: "I missed the boat; there were better things I could have chosen to do"?
Over a lifetime everyone acquires a few regrets. But the things that people regret the most, according to a survey of elderly people by Cornell University researchers, is not what they *have done* so much as what they *haven't done*. And

chief among the regrets are (1) *missed educational opportunities* and (2) *failure to "seize the moment."*[17]

You are at a time and place to seize some splendid opportunities. Career and vocational-technical education allows you to begin examining the choices available to you—about what you want your life to be. We're talking about the main event here, the Big Enchilada—deciding what is *truly* important to you.

■
NOTES

1. DeBare, I. (1997, March 3). Good pay without a B.A. *San Francisco Chronicle,* pp. D1, D3.

2. Marshall, J. (1997, March 3). Education beyond high school is worth the price. *San Francisco Chronicle,* pp. D1, D3.

3. Eldridge, E. (1997, March 3). High-tech skills give auto mechanics more power. *USA Today,* p. 1B.

4. Reich, R. Interviewed in Belton, B. (1994, September 2). Reich: College education a buffer against recession. *USA Today,* p. 3B.

5. Passell, P. (1992, August 19). Twins study shows school is sound investment. *New York Times,* p. A14.

6. Wessel, D. (1994, September 26). For college graduates, a heartening word. *Wall Street Journal,* p. A1.

7. Cartsonis, G. Quoted in Hoover, R. (1997, March 16). No degree? No problem. *San Jose Mercury News,* p. 2PC; reprinted from *Detroit News.*

8. Michigan Future Inc., University of Michigan. Study reported in Hoover, 1997.

9. Katz, J. (Ed.). (1968). *No time for youth: Growth and constraint in college students.* San Francisco: Jossey-Bass.

10. Kalat, J. W. (1990). *Psychology* (2nd ed.). Belmont, CA: Wadsworth, p. 440.

11. Coburn, K. L. Quoted in Kutner, L. (1992, September 3). For college freshmen, the first breath of freedom can hold a difficult and frightening lessen. *New York Times,* p. B4.

12. Boyer, E. L. (1990). *Campus life: In search of community.* Princeton, NJ: Carnegie Foundation for the Advancement of Teaching.

13. Astin, A. W., et al., study at University of California at Los Angeles. Reported in: Henry, T. (1996, October 14). More in college; fewer graduate. *USA Today,* p. 1D.

14. Study of American College Testing, Iowa City, IA, reported in Henry, T. (1996, July 11). College dropout rate hits all-time high. *USA Today,* p. 1A.

15. Saterfiel, T. Quoted in Henry, 1996.

16. Levitz, R., & Noel, L. (1989). Connecting students to institutions: Keys to retention and success. Pp. 65–81 in Upcraft, M. L., & Gardner, J. N., & Associates (Eds.). *The freshman year experience: Helping students survive and succeed in college.* San Francisco: Jossey-Bass.

17. Anonymous. (1995, April). What's your biggest regret in life? *Health,* p. 14.

Classroom Activities: Directions to the Instructor

Some of the most powerful learning occurs during small-group discussion and projects. (A small group consists of about three to six students.) Thus, this book offers frequent suggestions for group activities. Here's the first group.

1. **Going on in school—another "rite of passage."** Have students form into small groups in the classrooom, far enough apart that they won't disturb other groups. Students within each group should take turns introducing themselves and saying a few words about their backgrounds.

    They should then describe some rites of passage they have been through. A *rite of passage* involves physical or emotional changes in one's life, changes in how others view you, new behaviors you take on, and new responsibilities. It is often accompanied by stress. Higher education is clearly a rite of passage. Other examples are changing from a child to an adolescent, joining a particular group of friends or gang, getting married, earning one's first paycheck.

    One person in each group should act as recorder or secretary and make a list of the different rites of passage discussed. He or she should then copy the list onto the classroom blackboard.

    The class at large should consider the lists developed by each group. Questions for discussion: What are the similarities? the differences? Were any possibilities overlooked? What are different ways of dealing with rites of passage (anger, avoidance, feelings of fight-or-flight, and so on). Which of these ways are most appropriate? How do the past rites of passage compare to the first week of career education?

2. **Ice breaker: What kinds of students are in the class?** The goal of this exercise is to have students of roughly similar backgrounds assemble in small groups. This serves as an ice breaker in helping students to get to know each other and to form the bases for mutual-aid study groups.

    If time permits, ask each member of the class to tell one or two ways he or she may differ from the standard media stereotype of a college student. (That stereotype is usually someone who lives on campus, is 17 to 22 years old, takes a full load of courses, doesn't work, and graduates on schedule.) See the list of possible characteristics of practical students at the beginning of this chapter for possibilities.

    Write the characteristics on the blackboard. When everyone has contributed, try to determine five or so categories of commonalities (for example, students who have been out of high school five years or more, students who are parents, students who work, students who are foreign born).

    Ask students with similar dominant characteristics to assemble in different corners of the room. Have them introduce themselves to each other.

    Discuss the benefits of mutual support groups in college. Ask if anyone would object to meeting with others in their group outside of class for purposes of forming a study group.

3. **What do you think you will get out of higher education?** Ask students to make lists of all the things they think higher education could do for them. Then have students meet in small groups and discuss some of these benefits.

The Examined Life:
Student Assignments for Journal Entries

"The unexamined life is not worth living," the great Greek philosopher Socrates believed. If ever there was a time to examine your life, it is now, during the first year of higher education.

As you read this book, you should be considering such basic questions as these:

1. Why did I choose the direction I'm taking?

2. How do I feel about the things I've seen, read, or heard?

3. What do I think of this idea, that person, those beliefs?

4. How can I make use of the experiences I'm experiencing?

The place to express these thoughts and to keep track of the progress you are making is in a *journal*. By writing in a journal, you come to a better understanding of yourself.

At the end of each chapter, we will indicate some suggestions or assignments for journal entries. We also provide lines to write them on. (Your instructor may suggest that entries be handed in so that he or she can help you deal with certain concerns.)

Here is the first group of journal entry suggestions.

JOURNAL ENTRY #1.1: HOW COULD A PRACTICAL EDUCATION MAKE A DIFFERENCE IN YOUR LIFE? List some of the hopes you have for how a career or vocational-technical education could change your life.

_____

_____

_____

_____

_____

_____

JOURNAL ENTRY #1.2: HOW COULD THE SKILLS FOR SUCCESS IN HIGHER EDUCATION BENEFIT YOU IN YOUR CAREER? Based on jobs you've held in the past or a job you hold now, how do you think the skills required for success in higher education—those required for lectures, reading, writing, and laboratories—might benefit you at work?

_____

_____

_____

_____

_____

_____

JOURNAL ENTRY #1.3: WHICH OF THE SEVEN CHALLENGES CONCERN YOU MOST? Which of the seven challenges described in this chapter concern you most? In what way do they worry you?

_____

_____

_____

_____

_____

_____

CHAPTER TWO

TARGETING SUCCESS

Why are you here? What is your fear?

IN THIS CHAPTER: If the first year of higher education is "punctuated by feelings of panic and incompetence," as one observer put it, that's normal. This chapter begins to address these feelings. We consider the following subjects:

■ *The "why" of higher education:* Why are you here? We explore this fundamental question.

■ *The fears of higher education:* What are your fears about higher education? You're not alone. They are probably mostly the same fears everyone has—and they can be lessened.

■ *Your strengths:* You bring certain strengths to higher education that will help you achieve success.

■ *Life goals and educational goals:* We look at steps for translating your life goals into educational goals.

■ "Motivation depends not only on what you want to do," says a Columbia University psychiatry professor, "but what you think you'll have to give up to do it."[1]

As you may already be finding out, pursuing post–high school education means giving up some things. Some recreational activities, for instance. Or pay from a full-time job. Or time with your friends or family.

Is the kind of practical education you're pursuing worth it? The extent to which you can answer "yes" indicates the strength of your motivation.

Motivation is everything. Higher education is not like being in jail. You can walk away from it at any time. And no doubt there will be times when you will *want* to. So what, ultimately, is going to make you determined not only to stay but to do your best while you're there? The answer depends on how you deal with two important questions:

1. Why are you here?

2. What is your fear?

Why Are You Here? Values & Your Reasons for Pursuing a Practical Education

PREVIEW Your reasons for pursuing career or vocational-technical education reflect your values. Values, the truest expression of who you are, are principles by which you lead your life. A value has three characteristics: (1) It is an important attitude. (2) It is a matter on which you take action. (3) It should be consciously chosen.

No doubt you are pursuing a career or vocational-technical education for the most practical of reasons: To get a good job. To make better money. To do what you like to do. To help yourself and your family. The choice you make reflects your values.

WHAT VALUES ARE. Your values are the truest expression of who you are. A value is a principle by which you lead your life. It is an important belief or attitude that you think "ought to be" (or "ought not to be"). Moreover, it is a belief that you feel strongly enough about to take action on and that you have consciously chosen.

There are three important parts here:

1. *A value is an important attitude:* A value is an important attitude or belief that you hold. Examples: "A practical education should help me get a good job." "Fairness means hiring according to ability, not family background." "Murder is wrong except in self-defense." "It's worth trying my hardest to get an 'A.'" ("Chocolate is better than vanilla" is a preference, not a value.)

2. *A value is a matter on which you take action:* You can *think* whatever you want, but if you don't back up your thought with some sort of action, it cannot

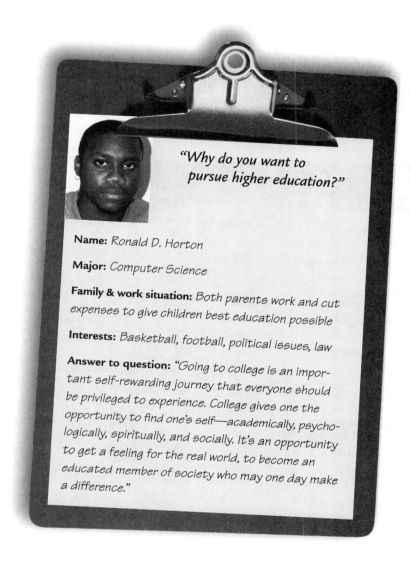

"Why do you want to pursue higher education?"

Name: *Ronald D. Horton*

Major: *Computer Science*

Family & work situation: *Both parents work and cut expenses to give children best education possible*

Interests: *Basketball, football, political issues, law*

Answer to question: *"Going to college is an important self-rewarding journey that everyone should be privileged to experience. College gives one the opportunity to find one's self—academically, psychologically, spiritually, and socially. It's an opportunity to get a feeling for the real world, to become an educated member of society who may one day make a difference."*

be considered a value. If you watch someone cheat on an exam, but you don't do anything about it, your attitude that "cheating is wrong" is, for all practical purposes, not really a value.

3. *A value should be consciously chosen:* Values are not very strong if they are not truly your own. Many first-year students hold ideas or opinions received from their parents or friends—ideas about which they may not have given much thought, such as the belief that the amount of money you make is the main measure of happiness in life. For an idea to be a value rather than just a belief, you have to have thought enough about it to consider accepting or rejecting it. You have to have made it yours. You can't just say "That's the way it is."

YOUR VALUES ABOUT HIGHER EDUCATION. What kinds of values do you hold? This is not a frivolous question, as values have a great bearing on how you view the whole subject of higher education. Being a career or vocational-technical college student is an important value because it means you are taking charge of your destiny—an ambition most people (particularly prospective employers) respect.

To see how your values affected your actions about pursuing a practical education, try Practical Exploration #2.1.[2]

PRACTICAL EXPLORATION #2.1

YOUR VALUES ABOUT GETTING A PRACTICAL EDUCATION

Take at least 10–15 minutes for this activity. The purpose is to see how your values and family background affected your actions in getting a career or vocational-technical education.

■ A. FAMILY MATTERS

1. Higher education is not a tradition in my family. (Family includes not only parents and grandparents or guardians but also uncles, aunts, and brothers and sisters.)

   ____ True ____ False
   ____ Somewhat true

2. My father/guardian completed (check one): ____ grade school ____ high school ____ college ____ graduate or professional school ____ other (identify)
   _____
   _____

3. My father/guardian (check one):
   ____ supports
   ____ does not support
   my decision to go to this school.

4. My mother/guardian completed (check one): ____ grade school ____ high school ____ college ____ graduate or professional school ____ other (identify)
   _____
   _____

5. My mother/guardian (check one):
   ____ supports
   ____ does not support
   my decision to go to this school.

6. My spouse/boyfriend/girlfriend (check one):
   ____ supports
   ____ does not support
   my decision to go to this school.

7. My spouse/boyfriend/girlfriend completed (check one):
   ____ grade school
   ____ high school ____ college
   ____ graduate or professional school ____ other (identify)
   _____
   _____

■ B. HIGHER EDUCATION & FREE CHOICE

1. Regarding the influence of my parents/guardians or others, I'd say my going to college was the following (check one): (a) ____ It was mainly my decision but a little bit others' decision. (b) ____ It was mainly others' decision but a little bit my decision. (c) ____ It was about equally both mine and others' decisions. (d) ____ It was never talked about; it was just assumed I'd go.

2. If I wasn't going on in school, I would do the following instead:
   _____
   _____
   _____
   _____
   _____
   _____
   _____
   _____
   _____
   _____

3. If I had the money and could do anything I wanted to this year, I would rather be doing the following:
   _____
   _____
   _____
   _____
   _____
   _____
   _____
   _____
   _____

4. Looking over my last three responses, I feel that I am going on in school because of the following (check one): (a) ____ I am choosing to go and want to go. (b) ____ I don't really choose to go and don't really want to go, but others want me to. (c) ____ I don't feel I have a choice, but I want to go anyway. (d) ____ I don't know, I'm confused.

(continued on next page)

#2.1 CONTINUED

■ C. PUBLIC REASONS, PERSONAL REASONS

1. When people ask me why I chose this school, I tell them the following. (List three or four reasons.)

   a. _____
   _____

   b. _____
   _____

   c. _____
   _____

   d. _____
   _____

2. When people ask me why I am interested in a particular major or career field (or why I am undecided), I tell them the following. (List three or four reasons.)

   a. _____
   _____

   b. _____
   _____

   c. _____
   _____

   d. _____
   _____

3. The reasons I chose (if I chose) the particular major or career field mentioned in C.2 that I *don't* tell people about are as follows. (Examples: "My parents want me to do it." "I'm afraid I lack the talent or brains to do something else I might like better." "It's a matter of conscience.")

   a. _____
   _____

   b. _____
   _____

■ D. REASONS FOR GOING ON IN SCHOOL

The following is a list of reasons for going on in school. Rank them in order of importance to you, with 1 meaning most important, 2 of secondary importance, 3 of third in importance, and so on.

My reasons for going on in school . . .

a. ___ To please my parents.

b. ___ To have fun.

c. ___ To get a degree.

d. ___ To prepare for a career.

e. ___ To make friends.

f. ___ To better support my family/help my children.

g. ___ To avoid having to work for a while.

h. ___ To find a girlfriend/boyfriend/mate.

i. ___ To raise my economic level/get a better job.

j. ___ To explore new ideas and experiences.

k. ___ To acquire knowledge.

l. ___ To gain maturity.

m. ___ To learn how to solve problems.

n. ___ To learn how to learn.

o. ___ To gain prestige.

p. ___ To become a better citizen.

■ E. IDENTIFYING YOUR VALUES REGARDING HIGHER EDUCATION

Look back over this Personal Exploration. Identify the top three values that influenced your decision to attend the school you are in. Write a brief essay in the following space. In the essay explain how each of the three values led you to a take a particular kind of action in choosing the present institution.

_____
_____
_____
_____
_____
_____
_____
_____
_____
_____
_____
_____
_____
_____
_____
_____
_____
_____
_____
_____
_____
_____
_____
_____
_____
_____
_____

YOUR VALUES ABOUT PERSISTENCE. "It's not what we do once in a while that shapes our lives," writes Anthony Robbins, best-selling author of *Awaken the Giant Within*. "It's what we do consistently."

Watching a basketball game, we may see a player make some great moves. Attending a performance, we may hear a musician do some brilliant riffs. But what we don't see is the hours of practice and preparation that led up to those few moments of glory. We don't see the determination, the perseverance, behind those few seconds that brought us to our feet in wild applause.

Your values about hanging in there—about staying the course, about persevering, about *PERSISTENCE and COMMITMENT*—may be the most important you have. "Nothing takes the place of persistence," President Calvin Coolidge wrote. "Talent will not. Nothing is more common than unsuccessful people with talent. Genius will not. Unrewarded genius is almost a proverb. Education will not. The world is full of educated derelicts. Persistence alone has solved and always will solve the problems of the human race."

Coolidge may not have been one of the greatest American presidents, but the belief he expressed is probably true: *Nothing takes the place of persistence.*

The world does not reward those who wail and bemoan their fate. If you had an underprivileged background, or went to a substandard high school, or have to juggle a job and children along with going to school, that's unfortunate. But others also have those problems and still manage to get through school.

Obtaining an education is not always easy. It requires persistence and commitment.

But having these qualities will pay off all your life.

What Is Your Fear? Anxiety as a Positive & Negative Motivator

PREVIEW Anxiety can motivate you to do well, but too much anxiety can motivate you to withdraw from competition. It's important to identify fears about higher education so they won't become motivators for dropping out. Common fears include fear of flunking out, of the pressure, of loneliness, of not finding one's way around, of running out of money.

As you know from playing video games or sports, a certain amount of anxiety can actually motivate you to accomplish positive results. Anxiety about losing a game (or the will to win) makes you alert, focuses the mind, and induces you to try to do well. Similarly, some fear of losing the game of higher education can motivate you to do your best.

Too much anxiety, however, can motivate you to perform negatively. That is, you may be so overwhelmed by fear that you want to withdraw from the competition. This can and does happen to students in career and vocational-technical education. But it need not happen to you.

IDENTIFYING YOUR FEARS. Concerns and fears about higher education are actually *normal*. However, it's important to identify them so that you can take steps to deal with them. Stop at this point and take a few minutes to try Practical Exploration #2.2. Complete the exercise before you read the next section.

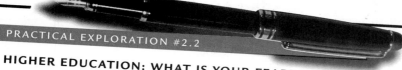

HIGHER EDUCATION: WHAT IS YOUR FEAR?

Identifying your fears about higher education is the first step in fighting them.

■ WHAT TO DO

For each of the following statements, circle the number below corresponding to how much you agree or disagree:

1 = strongly disagree
2 = somewhat disagree
3 = neither disagree nor agree
4 = somewhat agree
5 = strongly agree

I am afraid that . . .

1. Higher education will be too difficult for me.   1 2 3 4 5

2. I will get homesick.   1 2 3 4 5

3. I might flunk out.   1 2 3 4 5

4. I won't be able to handle the amount of school work.   1 2 3 4 5

5. My study habits won't be good enough to succeed.   1 2 3 4 5

6. I'll get lost on campus.   1 2 3 4 5

7. I'll be a disappointment to people important to me, such as my parents, family, or children.   1 2 3 4 5

8. I won't have enough money and will have to drop out.   1 2 3 4 5

9. I won't be able to handle working and/or family responsibilities and school at the same time.   1 2 3 4 5

10. I will get depressed. 1 2 3 4 5

11. I won't be able to manage my time being on my own.   1 2 3 4 5

12. I'll oversleep or otherwise won't be able to get to class on time.   1 2 3 4 5

13. I won't be able to maintain the grade average I want. 1 2 3 4 5

14. The school will find out that I'm basically incompetent and will kick me out.   1 2 3 4 5

15. I won't be able to compete with other students.   1 2 3 4 5

16. I won't make any friends.   1 2 3 4 5

17. I won't be able to overcome my shyness.   1 2 3 4 5

18. I'll have problems with my housemates or family.   1 2 3 4 5

19. I won't be able to handle writing/spelling or math.   1 2 3 4 5

20. My instructors will find out I'm inadequate.   1 2 3 4 5

21. There will be no one to help me.   1 2 3 4 5

22. I'll choose the wrong career field.   1 2 3 4 5

23. I'll have to cheat in order to survive the tough academic environment.   1 2 3 4 5

24. My family or my job will complicate things, and I won't be able to keep up.   1 2 3 4 5

25. Other (write in):

_____
_____
_____
_____
_____
_____

1 2 3 4 5

Add the number of points: _____

■ MEANING OF YOUR SCORE

100–125 *High*
You are very fearful or very concerned about your higher education experience. Although these concerns are not unusual, it would be a good idea to check into some college resources to assist you in dealing with your worries. Such resources include career and personal counseling, the school's learning center, and the financial aid office.

75–99 *Average*
You are somewhat fearful or somewhat concerned about your higher education experience. Welcome! Join the crowd! Your concerns are typical and are shared by the majority of students. To assist you in addressing these issues, you may wish to identify the appropriate resources—counseling center, learning center, financial aid—for assistance.

74 or less *Low*
You have few fears, perhaps are even laid back. Even so, it would be useful to identify support services (such as counseling or learning center) in case you ever need them.

■ INTERPRETATION

We all tend to think that any one worry we have is unique, that it is ours alone, that no one else ever experiences it with the intensity that we do. This is not true! Indeed, the fears and concerns listed above are quite common. So also is the reluctance to seek help, to get support. But seeking support is probably what will help you overcome the fear. Resources such as counseling and financial aid are described elsewhere in the book.

COMMON FEARS OF STUDENTS IN HIGHER EDUCATION. What are common fears of students in higher education—not just practical students but all students?[3,4] They include the following:

- Fear of flunking out—this may be the biggest

- Fear of not being able to manage everything

- Fear of the pressure—of the work and responsibility, of not being able to compete

- Fear of loneliness, of not finding supportive friends

- Fear of not finding one's way around

- Fear of running out of money

Then there are all the specific fears—about being on your own, about not having a good time, even about oversleeping. Many students at career and vocational-technical schools express concerns about not being able to balance their school work and their family and/or job responsibilities.

With the help of this book and this course, however, you can get beyond those fears and make your education the success you want it to be.

Survival Skills:
What Strengths Do You Bring to Your Education?

PREVIEW Four qualities are helpful for achieving success in higher education—and in life: (1) Sense of personal control and responsibility. (2) Optimism. (3) Creativity. (4) Ability to take psychological risks.

People who are successful in higher education—and in other pursuits in life—have the following qualities:

- Sense of personal control and responsibility

- Optimism

- Creativity

- Ability to take psychological risks

SENSE OF PERSONAL CONTROL & RESPONSIBILITY. How much personal control do you feel you have over your destiny? **The term *locus of control* refers to your beliefs about the relationship between your behavior and the occurrence of rewards and punishment.** (*Locus* is pronounced "*loh*-kuss.") People's beliefs may fall on a range, or continuum, from *external* locus of control to *internal* locus of control:

- ***External:*** Do you believe strongly in the influences of chance or fate or the power of others? **People who believe their rewards and punishments are controlled mainly by outside forces or other people are said to have an *external locus of control.***

■ *Internal:* Do you believe that "I am the captain of my fate, the master of my soul"? **People who believe their rewards and punishments are due to their own behavior, character, or efforts are said to have an *internal locus of control.*[5]**

Behind the "locus of control" idea is the notion that *your beliefs influence your actions* (and, conversely, your actions influence your beliefs). Do you believe you have the capacity to alter your habits? Can you make a conscious effort to change? Can you will yourself into new kinds of behavior? If you can, you can probably do what's required to bring about many of the good things that you want to happen.

You may wish to try Practical Exploration #2.3 to see what your locus of control is.

PRACTICAL EXPLORATION #2.3

WHO'S IN CHARGE HERE?

Are you in charge of your fate, or is a great deal of it influenced by outside forces? Answer the following questions to see where you stand.

1. Do you believe that most problems will solve themselves if you just don't fool with them?
   ❏ Yes   ❏ No

2. Do you believe that you can stop yourself from catching a cold?
   ❏ Yes   ❏ No

3. Are some people just born lucky?
   ❏ Yes   ❏ No

4. Most of the time do you feel that getting good grades means a great deal to you?   ❏ Yes   ❏ No

5. Are you often blamed for things that just aren't your fault?
   ❏ Yes   ❏ No

6. Do you believe that if somebody studies hard enough he or she can pass any subject?
   ❏ Yes   ❏ No

7. Do you feel that most of the time it doesn't pay to try hard because things never turn out right anyway?   ❏ Yes   ❏ No

8. Do you feel that if things start out well in the morning, it's going to be a good day no matter what you do?   ❏ Yes   ❏ No

9. Do you feel that most of the time parents listen to what their children have to say?
   ❏ Yes   ❏ No

10. Do you believe that wishing can make good things happen?
    ❏ Yes   ❏ No

11. When you get punished, does it usually seem it's for no good reason at all?   ❏ Yes   ❏ No

12. Most of the time, do you find it hard to change a friend's opinion?
    ❏ Yes   ❏ No

13. Do you think cheering more than luck helps a team win?
    ❏ Yes   ❏ No

14. Did you feel that it was nearly impossible for you to change your parents' minds about anything?
    ❏ Yes   ❏ No

15. Do you believe that parents should allow children to make most of their own decisions?
    ❏ Yes   ❏ No

16. Do you feel that when you do something wrong, there's very little you can do to make it right?
    ❏ Yes   ❏ No

17. Do you believe that most people are just born good at sports?
    ❏ Yes   ❏ No

18. Are most other people your age stronger than you are?
    ❏ Yes   ❏ No

19. Do you feel that one of the best ways to handle most problems is just not to think about them?
    ❏ Yes   ❏ No

20. Do you feel that you have a lot of choice in deciding who your friends are?   ❏ Yes   ❏ No

21. If you find a four-leaf clover, do you believe that it might bring you good luck?   ❏ Yes   ❏ No

22. Did you often feel that whether or not you did your homework had much to do with the kind of grades you got?   ❏ Yes   ❏ No

23. Do you feel that when a person your age is angry with you, there's little you can do to stop him or her?
    ❏ Yes   ❏ No

(continued on next page)

#2.3 CONTINUED

24. Have you ever had a good-luck charm? ❑ Yes ❑ No

25. Do you believe that whether or not people like you depends on how you act? ❑ Yes ❑ No

26. Did your parents usually help you if you asked them to? ❑ Yes ❑ No

27. Have you ever felt that when people were angry with you, it was usually for no reason at all? ❑ Yes ❑ No

28. Most of the time, do you feel that you can change what might happen tomorrow by what you do today? ❑ Yes ❑ No

29. Do you believe that when bad things are going to happen, they are just going to happen no matter what you try and do to stop them? ❑ Yes ❑ No

30. Do you think that people can get their own way if they just keep trying? ❑ Yes ❑ No

31. Most of the time, do you find it useless to try to get your own way at home? ❑ Yes ❑ No

32. Do you feel that when good things happen, they happen because of hard work? ❑ Yes ❑ No

33. Do you feel that when somebody your age wants to be your enemy, there's little you can do to change matters? ❑ Yes ❑ No

34. Do you feel it's easy to get friends to do what you want them to do? ❑ Yes ❑ No

35. Do you usually feel that you have little to say about what you get to eat at home? ❑ Yes ❑ No

36. Do you feel that when someone doesn't like you, there's little you can do about it? ❑ Yes ❑ No

37. Did you usually feel it was almost useless to try in school because most other children were just plain smarter than you were? ❑ Yes ❑ No

38. Are you the kind of person who believes that planning ahead makes things turn out better? ❑ Yes ❑ No

39. Most of the time, do you feel that you have little to say about what your family decides to do? ❑ Yes ❑ No

40. Do you think it's better to be smart than to be lucky? ❑ Yes ❑ No

■ SCORING

Place a check mark to the right of each item in the key when your answer agrees with the answer that is shown. Add the check marks to determine your total score.

1. Yes ❑	2. No ❑	3. Yes ❑
4. No ❑	5. Yes ❑	6. No ❑
7. Yes ❑	8. Yes ❑	9. No ❑
10. Yes ❑	11. Yes ❑	12. Yes ❑
13. No ❑	14. Yes ❑	15. No ❑
16. Yes ❑	17. Yes ❑	18. Yes ❑
19. Yes ❑	20. No ❑	21. Yes ❑
22. No ❑	23. Yes ❑	24. Yes ❑
25. No ❑	26. No ❑	27. Yes ❑
28. No ❑	29. Yes ❑	30. No ❑
31. Yes ❑	32. No ❑	33. Yes ❑
34. No ❑	35. Yes ❑	36. Yes ❑
37. Yes ❑	38. No ❑	39. Yes ❑
40. No ❑		

Total score: _____

■ INTERPRETATION

Low scorers (0–8):
Nearly one student in three receives a score of 0 to 8. These students largely see themselves as responsible for the rewards they obtain or do not obtain in life.

Average scorers (9–16):
Most students receive from 9 to 16 points. These students view themselves as partially in control of their lives. Perhaps they view themselves as in control academically but not socially, or vice versa.

High scorers (17–40):
Nearly 15% of students receive scores of 17 or higher. These students view life largely as a game of chance. They see success as a matter of luck or a product of the kindness of others.

Studies have shown that people who have an internal locus of control—that is, low (not high) scores in the Practical Exploration—are able to achieve more in school.[6] They are also able to delay gratification, are more independent, and are better able to cope with various stresses. This is the quality of *persistence and commitment* we were talking about.[7] Some people may have both an internal and external locus of control, depending on their situation. For instance, they may feel they can control their lives at home but not in the workplace.

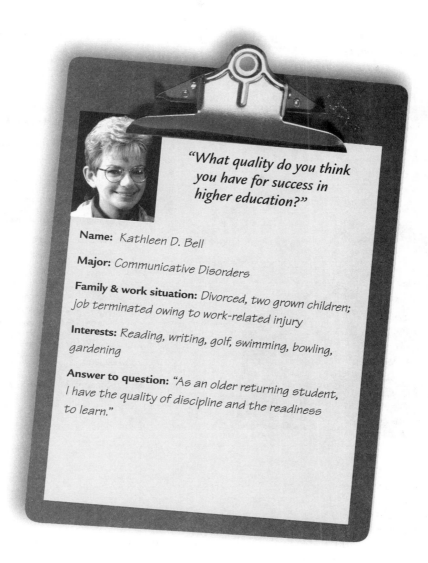

"What quality do you think you have for success in higher education?"

Name: Kathleen D. Bell

Major: Communicative Disorders

Family & work situation: Divorced, two grown children; job terminated owing to work-related injury

Interests: Reading, writing, golf, swimming, bowling, gardening

Answer to question: "As an older returning student, I have the quality of discipline and the readiness to learn."

OPTIMISM. "Mom, where are all the jerks today?" asks the young girl as she and her mother are driving along. "Oh," says the mother, slightly surprised. "They're only on the road when your father drives."

Psychotherapist Alan McGinnis tells this story to make a point: "If you expect the world to be peopled with idiots and jerks, they start popping up."[8]

For commuters, it may be easy to think they are surrounded by jerks, idiots, and worse. Even so, are you an optimist? Or are you what some people like to call a "realist," when they actually mean a pessimist? If you expect things to turn out badly, you are inviting what is known as a "self-fulfilling prophecy."

Perhaps optimism is related to matters of personal control. Pessimists may be overwhelmed by their problems, whereas optimists are challenged by them, according to McGinnis, author of *The Power of Optimism*.[9] Optimists "think of themselves as problem-solvers, as trouble-shooters," he says. This does not mean they see everything through rose-colored glasses. Rather they

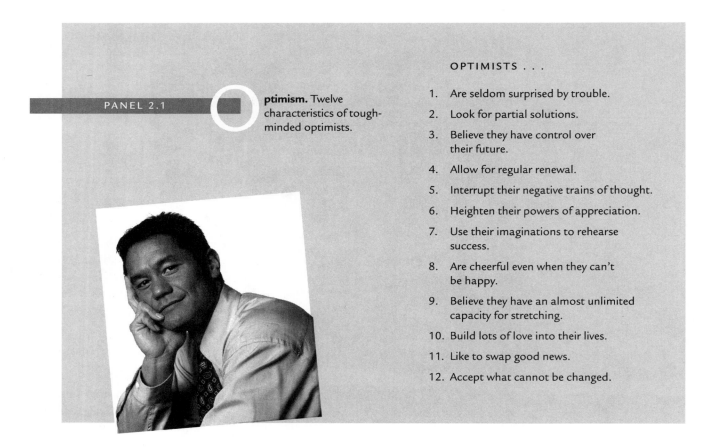

Optimism. Twelve characteristics of tough-minded optimists.

OPTIMISTS . . .

1. Are seldom surprised by trouble.
2. Look for partial solutions.
3. Believe they have control over their future.
4. Allow for regular renewal.
5. Interrupt their negative trains of thought.
6. Heighten their powers of appreciation.
7. Use their imaginations to rehearse success.
8. Are cheerful even when they can't be happy.
9. Believe they have an almost unlimited capacity for stretching.
10. Build lots of love into their lives.
11. Like to swap good news.
12. Accept what cannot be changed.

have several qualities that help them have a positive attitude while still remaining realistic and tough-minded. *(See ■ Panel 2.1.)*

CREATIVITY. The capacity for creativity and spontaneity, said psychologist Abraham Maslow, is an important attribute of the psychologically healthy person. This attribute is not limited to some supposed *artistic* class of people; it is built into all of us. ***Creativity* refers to the human capacity to express ourselves in original or imaginative ways.** It may also be thought of as the process of discovery. As Nobel Prize–winning biochemist Albert Szent-Györgyi expressed it, "Discovery consists of looking at the same thing as everyone else and thinking something different."[10]

Being creative means having to resist pressure to be in step with the world. It also means accepting the inevitability that you will have to deal with the unpredictable. It means looking for several answers, not the "one right answer." As Roger von Oech, founder of a creativity consulting company, puts it: "Life is ambiguous; there are many right answers—all depending on what you are looking for."[11] It means forgetting about reaching a specific goal, because the creative process can't be forced. One should, in von Oech's phrase, think of the mind as "a compost heap, not a computer," and use a notebook to collect ideas.

ABILITY TO TAKE PSYCHOLOGICAL RISKS. What is risk taking? We're not endorsing the kind of risk taking that might jeopardize your health (which you may see people do every day as you watch aggressive drivers zig-zag through stop-and-go traffic, causing near whiplash to themselves and others). We are principally concerned with situations in which what is at risk is mainly your *pride*. That is, the main consequences of failure are personal embarrassment or disappointment. This kind of risk taking—*having the courage to feel the fear and then proceeding anyway*—is a requirement for psychological health.

Consider failure: None of us is immune to it. Some of us are shattered but bounce back quickly. Others of us take longer to recover, especially if the failure has changed our lives in a significant way. But what *is* failure exactly? Carole Hyatt and Linda Gottleib, authors of *When Smart People Fail*, point out that the word has two meanings:

- **Failure can be an event:** First, "failure" is a term for an event, such as failing a test or not getting a job. Plainly, things just don't always work out. This kind of failure—of systems, of procedures, of plans, of expectations—you may not be able to do anything about.

- **Failure can be a judgment about yourself:** Second, "failure" is a *judgment you make about yourself*—"so that 'failure' may also mean not living up to your own expectations."[12]

This kind of failure is something you can do something about. For instance, you can use your own inner voice—your "self-talk"—to put a different interpretation on the event, one that is more favorable to you. (For example, "I didn't get the job because I'm better at dealing with people than at typing.")

One characteristic of many peak performers, according to psychologist Charles Garfield, is that they continually *reinvent* themselves. Doing this requires constantly taking psychological chances. The late jazz musician Miles Davis, for example, was always changing his musical direction in order to stay fresh and vital. Novelist James Michener took himself on a new adventure of travel and research with every book he wrote.[13] These are examples of psychological risk taking that lead toward success.

Setting Your Educational Goals from Life Goals

PREVIEW The six-step strategy called "Essentials for Time & Life Management" describes how to set daily tasks from life goals. The first three steps are described here. Step 1 is to determine your ultimate goals. Step 2 is to identify your plans for achieving them. Step 3 is to identify the actions you need to take to realize your plans.

We make decisions all the time. *Taking* action is making a decision. So is *not taking* action. There's nothing wrong with inaction and aimlessness, if that's what you want to do, but realize that aimlessness is a choice like any other. Most first-year students seeking a practical education, however, find that school works better if they have a program of aims. The following pages tell you how to set up such a program.

PANEL 2.2

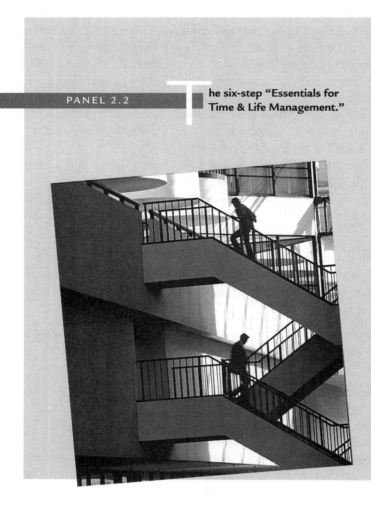

The six-step "Essentials for Time & Life Management."

The steps for transforming your life goals into daily tasks are as follows:

- **Step 1:** The planning process starts when you answer the question "Why am I in school?"—that is, define your life goals or long-range goals.

- **Step 2:** You then proceed to "What are my plans?"—setting your intermediate-range goals.

- **Step 3:** This leads to "What are my actions?"—the steps you will take to achieve your goals.

- **Step 4:** "What is my master timetable?" In this step you set your schedule for the semester or quarter.

- **Step 5:** "What is my weekly timetable?" This is the schedule you follow from week to week.

- **Step 6:** "What is on the To Do list today?" This is the errand list or "things to do" list that is no different from the To Do list that millions of people make every day.

ESSENTIALS FOR TIME & LIFE MANAGEMENT: SETTING DAILY TASKS FROM LIFE GOALS. Essentials for Time & Life Management is a six-step program for translating your life goals into daily tasks. *(See* ■ *Panel 2.2.)* The idea is to make your most important desires and values a *motivational force* for helping you manage your time every day.

In Chapter 3, you will see how you can apply these steps and employ them as strategies for time management. Here let us do Steps 1–3.

STEP 1: WHY AM I PURSUING HIGHER EDUCATION? Why are you here? Even if you haven't picked a career field yet, it's important to at least *think* about your long-range goals, your *life goals*.

These goals should be more than just "I want an education so I can make a lot of money." You need ultimate goals but not goals that are too general. Better to state the goals not in terms of surpassing other people—for there will always be people yet to be surpassed—but rather in terms of fulfilling your own potential. These goals should express *your* most important desires and values—not necessarily what your family wants you to do or what you think society expects of you. Some examples of life goals are shown in the accompanying list. *(See* ■ *Panel 2.3.)*

Examples of life goals.

Heroes: To follow in the footsteps of . . . (name a hero or heroine). (*Example:* an entertainer, political figure, someone you know—a teacher, a successful relative or family friend.)

Sacrifice: What is worth sacrificing for and what the sacrifice is. (*Examples:* giving up making a lot of money in order to help people; giving up close family life in order to travel the world.)

Values: What you hold to be most important and dear to you.

Love: How you would express it and to whom.

Family: What its importance is to you at present and in the future.

Security: What the least security is you would settle for financially, emotionally.

Principles: What you would stand up for and base your life on.

Creativity: What things you would like to create.

Curiosity: What questions you want to satisfy.

Personal challenges: What abilities you need to prove about yourself.

Death: What you hope to accomplish in the face of your own mortality.

As we've mentioned, higher education is not an easy experience. In order to pull yourself through some difficult times, you will need to know *why* you are doing all this. Now is the time to set down your long-range goals. See Practical Exploration #2.4 below.

PRACTICAL EXPLORATION #2.4

WHAT ARE YOUR LONG-RANGE GOALS?

The top five goals I hope school will help me reach are . . .

1. _____
_____
_____
_____
_____
_____
_____

2. _____
_____
_____

3. _____
_____
_____
_____
_____
_____
_____
_____
_____

4. _____
_____
_____

5. _____
_____
_____
_____
_____
_____
_____
_____
_____

STEP 2: WHAT ARE MY PLANS? Maybe you already know what you want to be: accountant, businessperson, computer repairer, corrections officer, dental assistant, electronics technician, firefighter, manager, modelmaker, nurse, paralegal, police officer, salesperson, whatever.

Maybe you don't know what you want to be, but you know that you want to explore areas that express your values: to help people, to make good products, to create, to educate, to exercise your curiosity, to entertain, or whatever.

In any event, now you need a plan, a rough strategy, of how to achieve or figure out your career or life goals.

In making a plan, you need to take your thoughts about your life goals or career goals and then do the following things:

- ***Decide on a career field or major (if only tentatively) and two or more alternatives:*** Looking at the school's course catalog, state what career field will probably help you realize your life goals. Also, state two or more alternative career areas you think you would enjoy pursuing.

- ***Think of obstacles:*** You need to think of the possible problems that may have to be overcome. Not enough money? Job and family responsibilities? Uncertainty about whether you're suited for this path? (Lack of motivation can be a killer.) Deficient math or writing or language or other skills necessary for that field? Lack of confidence that you're "career material"?

- ***Think of reinforcements:*** Think of what you have going for you that will help you accomplish your goals. Burning desire? Sheer determination? Parental support? Personal curiosity? Relevant training in high school? Ability to get along with people? Acquaintance with someone in the field who can help you? It helps to have positive reinforcement over the long haul.

To begin this process, do Practical Exploration #2.5.

PRACTICAL EXPLORATION #2.5

WHAT ARE YOUR PLANS? INTERMEDIATE-RANGE GOALS

The point of this exercise is not to lock in your decisions. You can remain as flexible as you want for the next several months, if you like. The point is to get you thinking about your future and what you're doing in school—even if you're still undecided about your major or career field.

■ **WHAT TO DO: DETERMINING YOUR INTERMEDIATE-RANGE GOALS**

Look at the five goals you expressed in Practical Exploration #2.4. Now determine how these goals can be expressed relating to school.

Example: Suppose your life goals or long-range goals include:

1. "To enter a career field that lets me help people."

2. "To find out how I can become a world traveler."

3. "To explore my interest in health and science."

4. "To meet interesting people."

You might list possible majors in Health, Nursing, and International Relations. In addition, you might list nonacademic activities—for instance, "Join International Club." "Go to a meeting of Nursing Society."

Decide on Three or More Alternative Majors: Determine which major or career fields seem of particular interest to you. You can simply do this out of your head. However, it's better if you look through the school catalog.

Three possible majors or career fields that might help me fulfill my life goals are the following:

1. _____
   _____

2. _____
   _____

3. _____
   _____

Decide on Nonacademic Activities Supporting Your Goals: Determine what kind of extracurricular activities interest you. Again, you can make this up out of your head, or you can consult the catalog or people in the campus community.

(continued on next page)

Five possible areas of extracurricular activities that might help me advance my educational goals are the following:

1. _____

2. _____

3. _____

4. _____

5. _____

Identify Possible Obstacles: List the kinds of possible problems you may have to overcome in your school career.

Examples: Possible money problems. Conflict with job and family responsibilities. Temptation to pursue too active a social life. Uncertainty about a major. Lack of preparation in mathematics.

The five following obstacles could hinder me in pursuing my school career:

1. _____

2. _____

3. _____

4. _____

5. _____

Identify Reinforcements: List the kinds of things you have in your life that will support you in the achievement of your educational goals when the going gets rough.

Examples: Support of your parents, husband/wife, or boyfriend/girlfriend. Personal curiosity. Knowing someone in a career you're considering. History of enjoying similar fields or activities in high school.

The five following facts or ideas could help sustain me in pursuing my school career:

1. _____

2. _____

3. _____

4. _____

5. _____

STEP 3: WHAT ARE MY ACTIONS? Step 2 provides you with the general guidelines for your practical-education path. Step 3 is one of *action*. You have a plan for your education; now you have to act on it (or why bother doing the preceding steps?). As part of taking action, you need to look at what areas need to be improved in order for you to excel. Are your math, reading, or writing skills a bit shaky? Take advantage of the (often free) assistance of your institution and get tutorial help. This is not something to be embarrassed about. Lots of people find they need practice of this sort to upgrade their skills.

In Practical Exploration #2.6, you will need to accomplish the following:

- ***Determine the courses needed to accomplish your goals:*** You need to know what courses you will probably take in which semester or quarter to make progress toward your goal. Generally you can tell the courses you need for a particular major by looking in the school's catalog. (Look for language such as the following: "Students seeking the Associate in Applied Science Degree in

Industrial Modelmaking must complete at least 64 credit hours, including 30 credit hours of General Education requirements and 34 credit hours of Modelmaking courses and technical electives.")

Laying out course sequences will take some time. However, *students who don't do such planning could find themselves out of step on some course requirements. This could require extra semesters or quarters later on,* as a particular course you need may be offered only in the fall quarter or only in the spring quarter. If you have not signed up for the course, you may have to wait an entire year before it is offered again.

- ***Determine what nonacademic activities to pursue:*** If you're working, commuting long distances, or have family responsibilities, you may think "I don't have time for fun and games outside of school!" You may be right—in which case, you should simply skip this part.

  But wait a minute. Suppose some "nonacademic activity" is exactly what could help you survive in college. Suppose you were to take an hour or two a week to meet with other people like yourself for study help, friendship, support, and sharing of experiences. You might be an adult returning student, parent, part-timer, or foreign student; you could be a gay, black, Hispanic, or Asian student. In many institutions offering career or vocational-technical programs, there is likely to be a way for you to connect with groups of students whose experience is similar to yours.

  Alternatively, suppose the "nonacademic activity" could advance your career. You might consider looking into internships, the computer club, law club (for prospective paralegals), or the like. Or suppose you just want to work out at the gym or look into sharing rides, finding new day care, or fulfilling a similar need. Whatever it is, write it down in the Practical Exploration you're about to do.

- ***Determine how to overcome obstacles, if possible:*** Money worries? Family problems? Work conflicts? See if you can identify some solutions or avenues that might lead to solutions (such as checking with the Financial Aid Office).

- ***Get advice about your tentative plans, then revise them:*** Take your plans (including your list of obstacles) to your academic advisor and discuss them with him or her. In addition, we strongly recommend taking them to a counselor in the career counseling center. Because all this advice is free (or included in your student fees or tuition), you might want to take advantage of it. It could help you develop a reality-based plan that might save you from a semester or two of misdirection.

To identify your courses of action, do Practical Exploration #2.6.

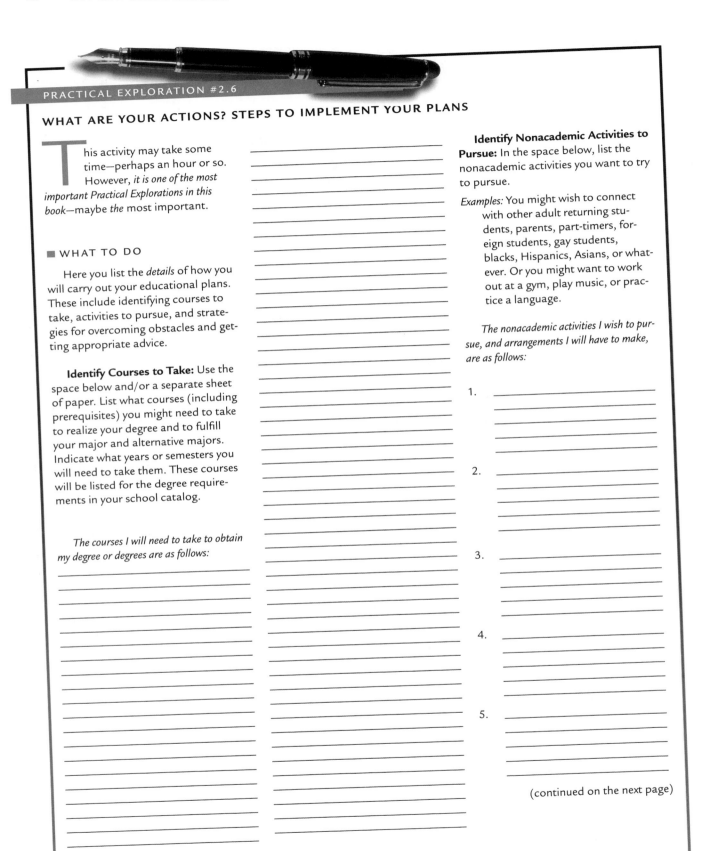

PRACTICAL EXPLORATION #2.6

WHAT ARE YOUR ACTIONS? STEPS TO IMPLEMENT YOUR PLANS

This activity may take some time—perhaps an hour or so. However, *it is one of the most important Practical Explorations in this book*—maybe *the* most important.

■ WHAT TO DO

Here you list the *details* of how you will carry out your educational plans. These include identifying courses to take, activities to pursue, and strategies for overcoming obstacles and getting appropriate advice.

Identify Courses to Take: Use the space below and/or a separate sheet of paper. List what courses (including prerequisites) you might need to take to realize your degree and to fulfill your major and alternative majors. Indicate what years or semesters you will need to take them. These courses will be listed for the degree requirements in your school catalog.

The courses I will need to take to obtain my degree or degrees are as follows:

(Continue on a separate sheet of paper, if necessary.)

Identify Nonacademic Activities to Pursue: In the space below, list the nonacademic activities you want to try to pursue.

Examples: You might wish to connect with other adult returning students, parents, part-timers, foreign students, gay students, blacks, Hispanics, Asians, or whatever. Or you might want to work out at a gym, play music, or practice a language.

The nonacademic activities I wish to pursue, and arrangements I will have to make, are as follows:

1.

2.

3.

4.

5.

(continued on the next page)

#2.6 CONTINUED

Identify Strategies for Overcoming Obstacles: If you're worrying about obstacles, now is the time to begin to deal with them. In the space below, indicate the steps you will take.

Examples: For "Possible money problems," you might state you will look into financial aid. For "Family conflicts," you might look into child-care possibilities.

The possible obstacles I need to overcome, and the steps I will take to begin to overcome them, are as follows:

1. _____
   _____
   _____
   _____
   _____
   _____

2. _____
   _____
   _____
   _____
   _____
   _____

3. _____
   _____
   _____
   _____
   _____
   _____

4. _____
   _____
   _____
   _____
   _____
   _____

5. _____
   _____
   _____
   _____
   _____

Get Advice About Your Plans: This section takes very little time, but it may involve using the telephone and then following up with a personal visit. The point of the activity is to identify and then follow through on courses of action you need to take.

Examples: With your list of prospective majors and course sequences in hand, call your academic advisor. Make an appointment to meet and discuss your concerns. If you're thinking about joining a child-care co-op, call to find out what you have to do. If you're worried that money might be a problem, call the Financial Aid Office to discuss it. (Some kinds of action need not involve a telephone. For example, you could tell your family members that you need to sit down and talk about child-care arrangements and study time.)

Here are the telephone numbers I need to call, or people I need to see and when, about a certain matter. The date following signifies when I took the action.

1. PERSON TO CONTACT (AND PHONE NUMBER) AND MATTER TO BE DISCUSSED
   _____
   _____
   _____
   _____

   ACTION WAS TAKEN ON (DATE)
   _____
   _____

2. PERSON TO CONTACT (AND PHONE NUMBER) AND MATTER TO BE DISCUSSED
   _____
   _____
   _____
   _____

   ACTION WAS TAKEN ON (DATE)
   _____
   _____

3. PERSON TO CONTACT (AND PHONE NUMBER) AND MATTER TO BE DISCUSSED
   _____
   _____
   _____
   _____
   _____

   ACTION WAS TAKEN ON (DATE)
   _____
   _____

4. PERSON TO CONTACT (AND PHONE NUMBER) AND MATTER TO BE DISCUSSED
   _____
   _____
   _____
   _____

   ACTION WAS TAKEN ON (DATE)
   _____
   _____

5. PERSON TO CONTACT (AND PHONE NUMBER) AND MATTER TO BE DISCUSSED
   _____
   _____
   _____
   _____

   ACTION WAS TAKEN ON (DATE)
   _____
   _____

Onward

PREVIEW Besides persistence and commitment, another secret of success in career and vocational-technical education is discipline. The stronger your motivation for pursuing higher education, the more you're apt to develop the discipline that will help you prevail.

We mentioned that *persistence and commitment* are the secret of success in obtaining an education. But there's another secret—*discipline,* using self-control to manage your time and master your tasks.

Discipline means showing up for every class on time. It means taking notes of lectures and frequently reviewing those notes so you understand them. It means doing assigned readings not just once but as often as is required to memorize the material. It means devoting two hours to study for every hour of class. It means taking developmental classes, if necessary, to improve your reading, writing, and math skills. It means dealing with objections of family and friends about your spending time on your studies.

At the heart of discipline is the answer to the question, *Why do you want to pursue higher education?* The clearer your purpose and the higher your resolve, the greater will be your chances for success.

NOTES

1. Person, E. S. Quoted in Anonymous (1990, September). Motivation. *Self,* p. 215.

2. Adapted from Friday, R. A. (1088). *Create your college success: Activities and exercises for students.* Belmont, CA: Wadsworth, pp. 116–19.

3. Carter, C. (1990). *Majoring in the rest of your life: Career secrets for college students.* New York: Noonday Press, pp. 61–62.

4. Rotter, J. B. (1966). Generalized expectancies for internal versus external control of reinforcement. *Psychological Monographs, 80*(Whole No. 603).

5. Rotter, J. B. (1966). Generalized expectancies for internal versus external control of reinforcement. *Psychological Monographs, 80*(Whole No. 603).

6. Findley, M. J., & Cooper, H. M. (1983). Locus of control and academic achievement: A literature review. *Journal of Personality & Social Psychology, 44,* 419–27.

7. Lefcourt, H. M. (1982). *Locus of control: Current trends in theory and research.* Hillsdale, NJ: Erlbaum.

8. McGinnis, A. Quoted in Maushard, M. (1990, October 22). How to get happy: What makes optimists tick. *San Francisco Chronicle,* p. B5. Reprinted from *Baltimore Evening Sun.*

9. McGinnis, A. L. (1990). *The power of optimism.* San Francisco: Harper & Row.

10. Szent-Györgyi, A. Quoted in von Oech, R. (1983). *A whack on the side of the head.* Menlo Park, CA: Creative Think, p. 7.

11. von Oech, 1983, p. 21.

12. Hyatt, C., & Gottlieb, L. (1987). *When smart people fail.* New York: Simon and Schuster, p. 20.

13. Garfield, C. Quoted in: Rozak, M. (1989, August). The mid-life fitness peak. *Psychology Today,* pp. 32–33.

Classroom Activities: Directions to the Instructor

1. *What are your values about higher education?* Have students review their answers to Practical Exploration #2.1, "Your Values About Getting a Practical Education." The purpose of that survey was to see how their values and family background affected their actions about pursuing higher education.

   In a small group (three to five people), students are to discuss some of the answers. Questions for discussion: What role did your family or people close to you have in your decision to pursue career education? What would you do (or rather do, if you had the money) if you weren't going to school? What top three values influenced you to go to school?

2. *Who's in charge?* Ask students to meet with others in a small group and to review their answers to Practical Exploration #2.3, "Who's in Charge Here?"

   Questions for discussion: What is *one area* in which you feel you can influence and control people and events? Discuss this area and the feelings of mastery and power it gives you. Discuss whether you think this control and influence could be applied to your academic work in career education.

3. *Why are you here? Your reasons for seeking career education.* Have students form into small groups (three to five people each). Ask them to discuss some of the reasons for seeking career education. Are there any reasons that students openly profess to people [that they actually feel shaky about?] Are there any reasons they care to bring out that might benefit from group discussion?

4. *What are your fears? Your greatest concerns and anxieties?* Have students take a few minutes to list, on a half sheet of paper or 3 × 5 card, their greatest concerns and anxieties. Some of them may be about higher education, of course, but some may be about other matters (which their pursuit of career education may affect or aggravate). Important: *Students should not* sign their names to the cards.

   Collect the lists and shuffle them. Call on students to come to the front of the class, pick a list at random, and copy the material on the blackboard. One area of the board should be saved; you, the instructor, will write down common themes here.

   Questions for discussion: What are common themes or overlapping issues? What are your reactions to the most common themes? What techniques or resources do you have to cope with these concerns?

5. *What are your long-range goals?* Ask students to form into small groups and to take turns describing their life goals, referring to their answers to Practical Exploration #2.4, "What Are Your Long-Range Goals?"

   Questions for discussion: How do your goals compare to, or differ from, those of others? How will pursuit of career education help you reach these goals?

   Question for classroom-wide discussion: How do the goals in your group compare with those of other small groups in your class?

The Examined Life:
Student Assignments for Journal Entries

JOURNAL ENTRY #2.1: WHY ARE YOU HERE? This is the most important question you can answer about higher education. Write at least 25 words about this matter.

_____
_____
_____
_____
_____
_____
_____
_____

JOURNAL ENTRY #2.2: WHAT IS YOUR FEAR? This is probably the second most important question you can answer about higher education. Write at least 25 words about your two or three principal fears.

_____
_____
_____
_____
_____
_____
_____
_____

JOURNAL ENTRY #2.3: WHAT ARE YOUR STRENGTHS? Write about what you consider your strengths that will help see you through.

_____
_____
_____
_____
_____
_____
_____

JOURNAL ENTRY #2.4: WHAT KINDS OF THINGS MAY CAUSE DIFFICULTY? What kinds of things might cause you difficulty or create problems that may threaten your success as a career or vocational-technical student? How can you deal with them?

_____
_____
_____
_____
_____
_____
_____

JOURNAL ENTRY #2.5: WHAT SUPPORT DO YOU HAVE FOR YOUR EDUCATION? What kinds of support do you have that will help you succeed in your higher education?

_____

_____

_____

_____

_____

_____

_____

TIME MANAGEMENT
How to find time to handle everything

IN THIS CHAPTER: One of the most important skills you can have is the ability to manage your time in order to fulfill your goals. We consider these subjects:

- **Setting priorities:** How to set semester/quarter, weekly, and daily tasks.

- **Beating time wasters:** How to avoid distractions, delaying tactics, and procrastinations and gain The Extra Edge.

▪ If you don't feel you're a terrific student or time manager, just fake it.

Seriously.

Even if you haven't done well in school in the past, pretend now that you're the ultimate student. Act as though you're a scholar. Play at being organized. Simulate being a good time manager.

There's a reason for all this: If you *act* like the person you want to become, you will *become* that person. This is true whether it's being less shy, having a more optimistic outlook, having more self-esteem, or being a better student. After you have gotten used to your new role, the feelings of discomfort that "this isn't natural for me" will subside. *You are more apt to ACT your way into a new way of thinking than to THINK your way into it.*[1]

If you don't believe this works, just consider that people act their way into behavior change all the time. People may not feel as if they can handle the responsibilities of a promotion or a new job beforehand, but they usually do. Being a parent looks pretty awesome when you're holding a newborn baby, but most people in the world get used to it.

"If you want a quality, act as if you already had it," suggested the psychologist William James. "Try the 'as if' technique." In other words: *Fake it till you make it.*

In this chapter, we'll show you how to fake your way into managing your time.

Getting Real About Studying

PREVIEW The universal advice is that students are expected to devote 2 hours of studying for every hour of class.

You may hear a fellow student say offhandedly, "Yeah, I got an A in the course. But I hardly had to study at all."

Don't believe it.

Sure, perhaps there really are some people who can get by this way (or courses that are really that easy). However, most people who talk like that just want to look as though they are brainy enough not to need to study. In general, though, the reality is that either they *are* studying a lot or they are *not* getting top grades.

Here is clearly an area in which you have to be tough-minded: Most of the time, studying *is* hard work. It *does* take time. It *does* take personal commitment. Most students *don't* like to do it. Studying *isn't* usually something to look forward to (although learning and exploring may be fun).

You need not feel upset or guilty about this. Accept that studying is not always something you're going to do because you feel like it. Then you can begin to organize your time so that you can always get enough studying done.

The general universal advice given on all campuses of higher education— vocational-technical school, community college, or whatever—is this:

Students are expected to devote at least 2 hours of study for every hour of class.

By "study," we mean reviewing notes, reading assignments, writing papers—all the activity known as "homework." Some classes may require less than 2 hours, but some might require *more*. Indeed, some might require 3 or 4 hours of study for every hour in class, if you find the subject hard going. (No one said that life is fair—and here again is where you'll have to call on your qualities of *persistence and commitment*.)

Thus, suppose you have 16 hours of class time, a standard full-time course load. If to this you add 32 hours of study time, then *at least* 48 hours a week should be devoted to school work. (This is still short of the workload of some business executives, who work 50, 60, or more hours a week.)

How are you going to handle your classes and studying *on top of* working, commuting, family responsibilities, and so on?

"What's the biggest advantage in managing your time?"

Name: Laqueta Dublin

Major: Electrical Engineering

Family & Work Situation: One of four children; work part time.

Interests: Reading for enjoyment, all types of music

Answer to question: "The biggest advantage to managing your time is a minimum-stress finals week. If you do your work throughout the school term, when it's time to take your finals, all you have to do is review. You will also have more time to relax and hang out."

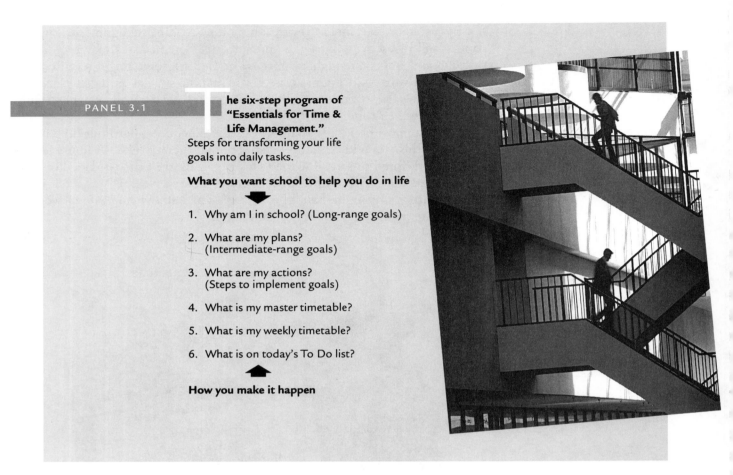

PANEL 3.1

The six-step program of "Essentials for Time & Life Management." Steps for transforming your life goals into daily tasks.

What you want school to help you do in life

▼

1. Why am I in school? (Long-range goals)

2. What are my plans? (Intermediate-range goals)

3. What are my actions? (Steps to implement goals)

4. What is my master timetable?

5. What is my weekly timetable?

6. What is on today's To Do list?

▲

How you make it happen

Three Steps for Improving Your Time Management

PREVIEW This section describes the rest of the six-step "Essentials for Time & Life Management" plan on how to set daily tasks from your life goals. We discuss how to lay out your master timetable for the school term, how to set your weekly timetable, and how to do a daily or weekly To Do list with reminders and priorities.

In Chapter 2, we presented our six-step program for translating life goals into daily tasks. *(See ▪ Panel 3.1.)* The idea, we said, was to make your most important desires and values a *motivational force* for helping you manage your time every day.

In Chapter 2, we explained the first three steps. Now let us explain steps 4–6, which focus your goals on daily tasks:

▪ **"What is my master timetable?"** In this step you set your schedule for the semester or quarter.

▪ **"What is my weekly timetable?"** This is the schedule you follow from week to week.

▪ **"What is on the To Do list today?"** This is the errand list or "things to do" list that is no different from the To Do list that millions of people make every day.

WHAT IS MY MASTER TIMETABLE? Once you've determined your line-up of courses for the next few school terms, you need to block out your master timetable for the term you're now in. The reason for this is so you can establish your *priorities*.

To make a master timetable for the semester or quarter, do the following:

■ *Obtain a month-at-a-glance calendar with lots of writing room:* You should use the blank calendar shown on pages 55–56, Practical Exploration #3.1. (Or buy a month-at-a-glance calendar covering all the weeks in the school term. It should have big squares for all the days of the month, squares large enough to write 5 to 10 words in.) When filled in with due dates and appointments, this will become your master timetable for the semester or quarter. *(See ■ Panel 3.2.)*

■ *Obtain your institution's academic calendar:* The school academic calendar may be printed in the school's catalog. Sometimes it is sold separately in the bookstore. The academic calendar tells you school holidays, registration dates, and deadlines for meeting various academic requirements. It usually also indicates when final exam week takes place.

PANEL 3.2

The master timetable. This illustration shows an example of one month of a student's semester or quarter. Note it shows key events such as deadlines, appointments, and holidays.

Sunday	Monday	Tuesday	Wednesday	Thursday	Friday	Saturday
			1 Parent-Teacher Conf. 3 p.m.	**2**	**3** Crim Just	**4**
5	**6** English essay	**7**	**8** Dentist 3 p.m.	**9**	**10**	**11** Sue's Party 8 p.m.
12	**13**	**14** Math test	**15**	**16**	**17** Crim Just test	**18**
19 Band in Park 3 p.m.	**20** English essay	**21**	**22**	**23**	**24** ← Holidays	**25**
26	**27** Crim Just paper due	**28** Math test	**29**	**30** Thanksgiving		

November

- ***Obtain the course outline for each course:*** **The course outline or course information sheet is known as the *syllabus* ("sil-uh-bus"). The syllabus tells you midterm and final exam dates, quiz dates (if any), and due dates for term papers or projects.** The syllabus is given to you by your instructor, usually on the first day of class.

Now go through the school calendar and all your course outlines. Transfer to your master timetable calendar all class times, important dates, and deadlines. These include pertinent due dates, dates for the beginning and end of the term, and school holidays. Also add other dates and hours you know about. Examples are those for part-time job, medical and dental appointments, concerts, football games, and birthdays. (*See* ■ *Panel 3.2.*) Leave enough space for any given day so you can add other entries later, if necessary. *NOTE:* Consider using a different, highly visible color—flaming red, say—to record critical dates such as test dates.

To begin making up your own master timetable for the present semester or quarter, do Practical Exploration #3.1. After it is completed, you can three-hole-punch it and carry it in your binder or notebook. Or you can post it on the wall above the place where you usually study.

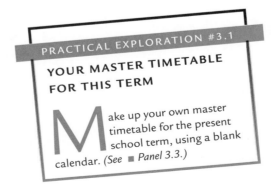

PRACTICAL EXPLORATION #3.1

YOUR MASTER TIMETABLE FOR THIS TERM

Make up your own master timetable for the present school term, using a blank calendar. (*See* ■ *Panel 3.3.*)

B lank calendar for the school term.

Sunday	Monday	Tuesday	Wednesday	Thursday	Friday	Saturday

Sunday	Monday	Tuesday	Wednesday	Thursday	Friday	Saturday

Sunday	Monday	Tuesday	Wednesday	Thursday	Friday	Saturday

Sunday	Monday	Tuesday	Wednesday	Thursday	Friday	Saturday

WHAT IS MY WEEKLY TIMETABLE? Now we get down to the business end of the Essentials for Time & Life Management: making up a weekly timetable. *(See ■ Panel 3.4.) The main point of creating a weekly timetable is to schedule your study time.*

PANEL 3.4

The weekly timetable. This illustration shows an example of the important activities in a student's weekly schedule. The most important purpose of this schedule is to program in study time. Some students, however, may wish to program in other fixed activities. Examples are workouts, church attendance, household responsibilities, and travel time to school.

	Monday	Tuesday	Wednesday	Thursday	Friday	Saturday	Sunday
7 a.m.				Work		Work	
8		Work		Work	English	Work	
9	English	Work	English	Work	Study	Work	
10	Study	Work	Study	Work	Study	Work	
11	Study	Work	Study	Work	Study	Work	
Noon		Commuter Club		Adult Student Group		Work	Study
1 p.m.	Psych	Study	Psych	Study	Psych	Work	Study
2	Study	Math	Study	Math	Study	Work	Study
3	Study	Study	Study	Study	Study	Work	
4							
5							Study
6	Work	Work	Work	Work	Work		Study
7	Work	Work	Work	Work	Work		Study
8	Work	Work	Work	Work	Work		
9	Work	Work	Work	Work	Work		
10							
11							

Some first-year students aren't sure what is meant by "study time." They think of it as something they do a day or two before a test. By *study time* we mean *everything connected to the process of learning*. This means preparing for tests, certainly, but also reading textbook chapters and other required readings, doing library research, writing papers, doing projects, and so on. Studying is *homework*, and it's an ongoing process.

By actually creating a weekly timetable to schedule their study time, students are putting themselves on notice that they take their studying *seriously*. They are telling themselves their study time is as important as their classes, job, family meals, or other activities with fixed times.

They are also alerting others that they are serious, too. Some students post their weekly schedule on their bedroom doors, if they're living at home. (Thus, if someone drops into your room to talk, you can point to the schedule and say, "Unfortunately, I have to study now. Can I talk to you in half an hour?")

If you don't schedule your study time, you may try to study only when nothing else is going on. Or you will study late at night, when your energy level is down. Or you will postpone studying until the night before a test.

The weekly master plan should include those activities that happen at fixed, predictable times. These are your classes, work, regularly scheduled student or family activities—and your regularly scheduled studying times. As mentioned, study time should amount to about 2 hours of studying for every hour of class time, perhaps more.

If you want, you can add meals, exercise, and commuting or transportation times. However, we believe that the fewer things you have on your calendar, the more you'll pay attention to the things that *are* there. Otherwise, you may begin feeling overregulated. You shouldn't schedule break times, for instance; you'll be able to judge for yourself the best times to stop for a breather. (We describe extended study time and breaks later in the chapter.)

To begin making up your own weekly timetable for this semester or quarter, do Practical Exploration #3.2. This, too, may be three-hole-punched and carried in your notebook and/or prominently posted near your principal study place.

PRACTICAL EXPLORATION #3.2

YOUR WEEKLY TIMETABLE FOR THIS TERM

Make up your own timetable that indicates your recurring responsibilities every week in this term. *(See ■ Panel 3.5.)*

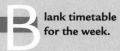

Blank timetable for the week.

	Monday	Tuesday	Wednesday	Thursday	Friday	Saturday	Sunday
7 a.m.							
8							
9							
10							
11							
Noon							
1 p.m.							
2							
3							
4							
5							
6							
7							
8							
9							
10							
11							

PANEL 3.6

Examples of daily & weekly "To Do" lists. An "*" may be placed beside those activities that are most urgent.

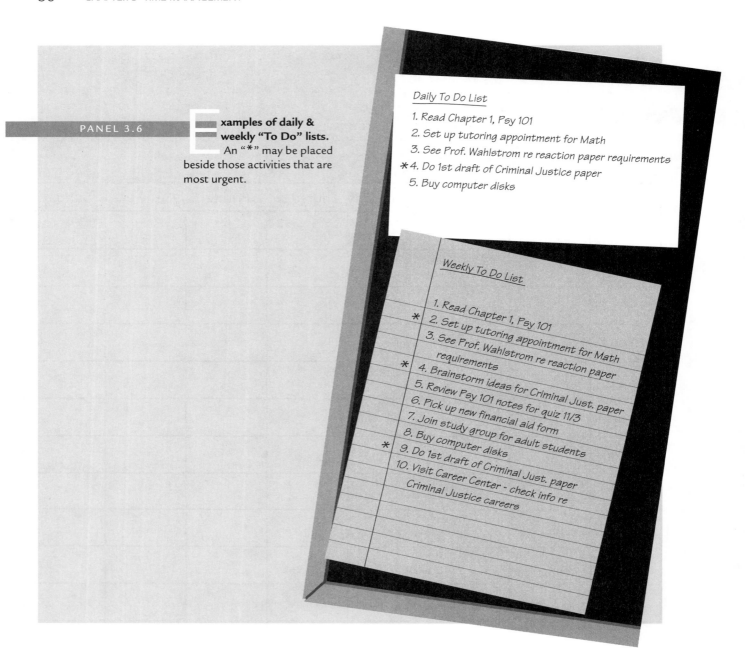

Daily To Do List

1. Read Chapter 1, Psy 101
2. Set up tutoring appointment for Math
3. See Prof. Wahlstrom re reaction paper requirements
*4. Do 1st draft of Criminal Justice paper
5. Buy computer disks

Weekly To Do List

1. Read Chapter 1, Psy 101
* 2. Set up tutoring appointment for Math
3. See Prof. Wahlstrom re reaction paper requirements
* 4. Brainstorm ideas for Criminal Just. paper
5. Review Psy 101 notes for quiz 11/3
6. Pick up new financial aid form
7. Join study group for adult students
8. Buy computer disks
* 9. Do 1st draft of Criminal Just. paper
10. Visit Career Center - check info re Criminal Justice careers

WHAT IS MY DAILY "TO DO" LIST? The final step is just like the informal "To Do" lists that many people have, whether students or nonstudents. *(See ▪ Panel 3.6.)*

The To Do list can be made up every week or every evening, after referring to your master timetable and weekly timetable. The To Do list can be done on a notepad or on a 3 × 5 card. Either way, it should be easy to carry around so that you can cross things off or make additions. You can be as general or as detailed as you want with this piece of paper, but the main purpose of a To Do list is twofold:

▪ ***Reminders:*** Remind yourself to do things you might otherwise forget. Examples are doctor's appointments, things to shop for, and books to return to the library. Don't forget to write down promises you made to people (such as to get them a phone number or a photocopy of your class notes).

■ **Priorities:** Set priorities for what you will do with your day. It may be unnecessary to list your scheduled classes, as you will probably go to them anyway. You might want to list an hour or half hour for exercise, if you're planning on it. (It's good to exercise at least three times a week for 20 minutes or more.) You may wish to list laundry, shopping, and so on.

However, *the most important thing you can do is to set priorities for what you're going to study that day.* Thus, your To Do list should have items such as "For Tues.—Read math chapter 13" and "Wed. p.m.—Start library research for Business Communication paper."

Most managers and administrators find a To Do list essential to avoid being overwhelmed by the information overload of their jobs. Because you, too, are on the verge of drowning in information and deadlines, you'll no doubt find the To Do list a helpful tool. Clearly, the To Do list is another application that you can carry over from your educational experience to the world outside of school.

Now try doing Practical Exploration #3.3.

PRACTICAL EXPLORATION #3.3

YOUR "TO DO" LIST FOR THIS WEEK

On a separate piece of paper make up your own weekly To Do list for the present week.

Battling the Killer Time Wasters

PREVIEW There are four principal strategies you can use to prevent wasting time. (1) Schedule study sessions that actually work. Study during the best times of day, don't schedule overly long sessions, allow short breaks, and reward yourself afterward. (2) Fight procrastination. Concentrate on boring assignments intensively for short periods; study with a friend or in a study group. Break long tasks into smaller ones, tackle difficult tasks first, and meet unsettling tasks head on. (3) Fight distractions. Establish regular study sites, set up a good study environment, combat electronic and telephone distractions, and learn to handle people distractions. (4) Gain The Extra Edge. Use waiting time for studying, use spare time for thinking, listen to tapes of lectures.

Even if you had 25 hours in a day, could you manage the time any more efficiently? What about 26 or 27 hours?

Everyone gets the same ration, a disappointingly small 24 hours a day. Although some people are indeed smarter, usually the ones who excel at school and at work simply *use* their time better. If you try Practical Exploration #3.4— "How Do You Spend Your Time?" (next page)—for a week, you can begin to see where your time goes.

HOW DO YOU SPEND YOUR TIME?

The purpose of this activity is to enable you to see where your time goes. Honesty is important. The idea is to figure out how much time you *do* spend on studying. Then you can determine if you could spend *more* time.

■ KEEPING A LOG OF YOUR TIME

Record how many hours you spend each day on the following activities. (There are 168 hours in a week.)

	MON	TUES	WED	THUR	FRI	SAT	SUN
1. Sleeping							
2. Showering, dressing, and so on							
3. Eating							
4. Communing to and from class, work, and so on							
5. Going to classes							
6. Working							
7. Watching television							
8. Leisure activities (such as movies, dating, parties)							
9. Other scheduled matters— church, tutoring, volunteering							
10. Other (such as "hanging out," "partying," "child care")							
11. Studying							
TOTAL HOURS							

■ YOUR INTERPRETATION

We put "Studying" at the bottom of the list so you can see how other activities in your life impinge on it.

Now consider the following:

1. Do you feel you are in control of your time? _____

2. Are you satisfied with the way you spend your time? _____

3. On what three activities do you spend the most time?

_____

_____

_____

_____

_____

_____

4. Do you feel you're giving enough time to studying? _____

5. If you had to give more time to studying, what two or three activities could you give up or cut down on?

_____

_____

_____

_____

_____

CONSIDERING HOW YOU SPEND YOUR TIME. You have 168 hours in a week (7 days of 24 hours each equals 168 hours). Let's see where the time is apt to go.

- *Sleeping:* Everyone needs between 6 and 9 hours of sleep a night. (If you short yourself on sleep, you may find the "sleep deficit" causes you to fall asleep in class. But it's possible you may be able to make it up by, for example, napping on the bus.)

- *Showering, dressing, grooming:* This might take 30 to 60 minutes a day. It depends on how long you shower, whether you shave, if you put on makeup at home or on the bus, and so on.

- *Eating:* This might take an hour or more a day, perhaps 14 to 21 hours in a week. If you skip breakfast and even lunch, you still probably have at least a snack or two throughout the day. Dinner might be just a quick visit to Burger King or microwaving a prefab dinner pulled from the freezer. Or it might involve shopping for, preparing, cooking, eating, and cleaning up after a full-scale meal for your family. (And making lunches for others for the next day.) In any case, you'd be surprised at the amount of time eating takes out of your week.

- *Commuting, travel time, errands:* Travel time—between home and campus, between campus and job, and so on—might take an hour or more a day, perhaps 10 to 16 hours a week. In 1990, the average commute to work by car was 10.4 miles and 19.7 minutes.[2] In the city, travel time may take much longer.

  When computing travel time, you have to remember to include time waiting at bus or subway stops, hunting for parking places, and walking from bus stop or car to classes. You also have to total all the time involved in getting yourself not only to campus, job, and home but also, for example, in picking up children from day care, shopping, and running errands.

- *Classes and work:* Figuring out the amount of time you spend in class is easy. If you're enrolled in three courses totaling 9 credit hours, you should be spending 9 hours a week in class.

  If you work while going to school, you can probably easily figure out the hours your job requires each week. (Two exceptions are if you're subject to unpredictable overtime hours or if you're working as a temp for a temporary-employment agency.)

  Incidentally, time researchers John P. Robinson and Geoffrey Godbey, authors of *Time for Life*, have found that, despite everyone's notion that they are overworked, the average work week has shrunk since 1965—about 6 hours shorter for working women and about 7 hours for men.

- *Television:* TV, say Robinson and Godbey, is "the 800-pound gorilla of free time."[3]

  Since 1965, these sociologists have asked thousands of people to keep hour-by-hour diary accounts of what they do and for how long, from the time they wake up to the time they go to sleep. In the 32 years since they began their study, they have found that television has gobbled up ever more free time. Today women watch 14.5 hours a week (up from 9.3 in 1965). Men watch 15.8 hours (up from 11.3).

  Television is such an ingrained habit, says Robinson, that "people say they don't have any time because they're watching television. It's like some sort of force, alien force out there, over which they have no control."

"What's the biggest time waster for you?"

Name: Charles Neumeister

Major: Packaging Science

Family & Work Situation: Full-time student

Interests: Crew (rowing), Web surfing, old cars, genealogy

Answer to question: "The biggest time waster for me is probably the Internet."

Paradoxically, although we spend far more time watching television than doing any other leisure-time activity (including reading books or magazines or listening to music), Americans report in surveys that TV is one of the first activities they would give up if they had to. Is this something you feel you could do?

■ *Studying:* As mentioned, on average you should devote 2 hours of studying outside of class for every hour you are sitting in class. With three courses requiring 9 hours a week in the classroom, for example, you should be spending 18 hours a week doing homework.

Add up the hours in these categories for the week, then subtract them from 168. What's left over is the time you have left for *everything else*. This means EVERYTHING: "hanging out," parties, sports, playing with or helping children, doing household chores (if not included above), religious activities, and so on.

Does it seem, then, that you're suddenly going to have to be more efficient about how you manage your time? What follows are some suggestions for battling the killer time wasters.

SCHEDULE STUDY SESSIONS THAT ACTUALLY WORK. Creating a schedule for studying *and sticking with it* are terribly important. Indeed, this is probably the single most valuable piece of advice anyone can give you.

There are, however, certain things to consider when you sit down to block out the master timetable that includes your study time:

- **Make study times during your best time of day:** Are you a "morning person" or a "night person"? That is, are you most alert before breakfast or most able to concentrate in the evening when it's quiet? When possible, schedule some of your study time for the times of day when you do your best work. These are particularly good times for doing difficult assignments, such as writing research papers.

- **Don't schedule overly long sessions:** Imagine how you're going to feel at the start of a day in which you've scheduled 10 hours for studying. You'll probably take your time getting to work and won't do more than 7 to 9 hours of actual studying that day anyway.

  To avoid setting yourself up for failure, we suggest programming *no more than* 8 hours of studying in a day. Also, divide that time block into two 4-hour sessions separated by perhaps a couple of hours of time off. (Actually, many students will find they just can't stand 8 hours of studying in a single day.) And if you do schedule long blocks of study time, mix the subjects you're working on so you'll have some variety. The point, after all, is not how *long* you study but how *effective*ly you study.

  Perhaps an even better strategy, however, is to schedule *several short sessions* rather than a handful of long sessions.

- **Allow for 5- to 10-minute study breaks:** Some people are like long-distance runners and do better by studying for long sessions—for example, 50 minutes followed by a 10-minute break. Others are like sprinters and perform better by studying for 25 minutes followed by a 5-minute break.

  Of course, you don't have to go exactly by the clock, but you should definitely permit yourself frequent, regularly scheduled breaks. Taken at regular intervals, breaks actually produce efficiencies. They enable you to concentrate better while studying, reduce fatigue, motivate you to keep going, and allow material to sink in while you're resting.

  Breaks should be small ways of *pleasuring yourself*—going for a soft drink, taking a walk outside, glancing through a newspaper. We don't recommend getting on the phone, picking up your guitar, or dropping in on a friend, however, unless you can keep it short. You don't want the diversion to be so good that it wrecks your study routine.

- **Reward yourself when you've finished studying:** The end of the course is weeks away, the attainment of a degree months or years. What's going to keep you going in the meantime?

  You need to give yourself as many immediate rewards as you can for studying, things to look forward to when you finish. Examples are a snack, phone talk with a friend, some music or TV time. Parts of your school career will be a grind, but you don't want it to be *just* a grind. Rewards are important.

If, after scheduling in your study time, you find it still isn't enough, you need to see where you can make adjustments. Can you reduce the number of courses? Work fewer hours? Get help with chores from family members? Whatever, the main thing is to make your scheduled study time effective when you're doing it.

FIGHT DISTRACTIONS! A phone call comes in while you're studying, and 20 minutes later you finish the conversation. Are you later going to tell yourself that you actually studied during your scheduled study time? Or are you going to pretend that you'll simply make up the work some other time?

There are many such possible interruptions, but it's important that you not lie to yourself—that you not play games with your study time. The following are some strategies for preventing or handling various common distractions:

- ■ ***Establish a couple of places where all you do is study:*** You see students studying just about everywhere, which is fine. However, it's important that *you establish a couple of places for regular studying* and, if possible, do nothing else there. Unless you can't avoid it, don't routinely study on your bed, where you might fall asleep. Avoid studying at the kitchen table, where you may be inspired to eat. Don't work in the student lounge in front of the TV. If you use your study places only for studying, they will become associated just with that and will reinforce good study behavior.[4]

■ **Establish a good study environment:** For your principal study site, the best arrangement is a separate room, such as a spare room, that you treat as your home office. Otherwise, use a corner of your bedroom. Turn a desk or table to the wall to provide you with as much privacy as possible from others sharing the room.

Make this spot as comfortable and organized as you can. Make sure you have the right temperature, good lighting, and a comfortable chair. The desk should have room on it for a computer or a typewriter, as well as reading/writing space. Books and supplies should be within reach. Having a personalized bulletin board is useful. Post important information, such as calendars, schedules, and announcements, on the wall nearby. (You can also post motivational slogans—EDUCATION: ONE ASSIGNMENT AT A TIME!—and notes nearby.)

Adult returning students in particular may have to be somewhat assertive with others in their household about their need for a quiet space. Sometimes having a "noise machine," such as an air purifier or electronic white-noise machine, can mask distracting noise and help you concentrate better. Some students use earplugs.

If your living area is too distracting, you can do as many students do and make the library your primary study place. Some libraries have small tables tucked away in quiet areas. Moreover, the entire atmosphere of quiet is supportive to studying.

■ **Fight electronic distractions:** Electronic equipment has completely taken over many households and residences. If the noise becomes too overwhelming and you can't get it turned down by common agreement, go somewhere else. Plan to do your studying in the library or other quiet place such as a laundry room.

We realize this is a tricky matter, because so many students think they can study better with television or music as background noise. Indeed, it may be possible to study to certain kinds of music, such as classical music. However, the evidence suggests that the best studying is done when it's quiet.

■ **Fight telephone distractions:** Of course you don't have to make any outgoing calls during your scheduled study times, and you should resist doing so. As for incoming calls, there are four things you can do:

1. Be disciplined and don't answer the phone at all. (What kind of power is it that the telephone has over us? When it rings, do we *have* to pick it up?)

2. Answer the phone, but tell the caller you'll have to call back because "I'm studying for an important course right now " or "I have something important going on here."

3. Tell whoever answers the phone to take a message for you. You can then call back on your 5-minute study break, if you can manage to keep the conversation short. Even better, you can call back after you've finished studying.

4. Let an answering machine or voice-mail system collect your calls, then call back later.

We personally suggest letting another person or a machine take the calls. You're then like business people who have answering machines or secretaries hold their calls while they're doing important work, then return them all at once later.

- *Fight people distractions:* People interruptions can be a real problem, and eventually you have to learn to "Just say no." You shouldn't be complaining or accusatory, but polite and direct. There's a piece of advice that says, *Don't complain, don't explain, just declare.* So when interrupted, you just declare: "Jackie, this is interesting, but I have to study right now. Can we talk later?"

  Early on you need to develop some understanding with your housemates or family members about your study requirements. Show them your study schedule. Tell them when you're at your desk, you're supposed to be doing your schoolwork. Ask them for their assistance in helping you to accomplish this. One writer says that a student he knows always wears a colorful hat when he wants to study. "When his wife and children see the hat, they respect his wish to be left alone."[5]

  What if you're a parent and have nowhere to put a young child (not even in front of a television set or in a room full of toys)? In that case, just plan on doing the kind of studying that is not too demanding, expecting to be interrupted. Or use your study breaks to play with the child. Or take a few minutes to play attentively with the child before you hit the books, then say you have work to do. Or even read your textbook aloud to them, making it sound interesting (a tactic that will probably last as long as the child's attention span). As long as the child feels he or she is getting *some* of your attention, you can still get some things done.

  Of course, you can't control everything. Things will come up that will cut into your study time, as in the electricity going off or the flu wiping you out. That's why it's important to think of your scheduled study sessions as practically sacred. In addition, however, you need to be willing to study at various other, "fill-in" times. Let us explain how this works.

FIGHT DELAYING TACTICS! All of us put off doing things sometimes. Delaying tactics can result when your prospective task is *boring, long,* or *difficult.* You need to look hard to see whether one of these reasons applies, then fight back by applying the appropriate strategies:

- *Fight boring assignments with short concentrations of effort:* If the task is boring, you need to concentrate on seeing how fast you can get a portion of it done. That is, you need to concentrate on the benefits of completing it in a short time rather than on the character of the task itself.

  Thus, you can say to yourself, "I'm going to work on this for 15 minutes without stopping, applying my full concentration. Then I'm going to move along to something else." You can stand anything for 15 minutes, right? And this task may seem more acceptable if it's not seen as several hours of work—especially if you plan a mini-reward for yourself (getting a soft drink, say) at the end of that time.

- *Fight long assignments by breaking them into smaller tasks:* Most people have a difficult time tackling large projects, such as research papers. Indeed, most of us tend to take on simple, routine tasks first, saving the longer ones for later when we'll supposedly "have more time."[6] Thus, we often delay so long in getting started on large assignments that we can't do an effective job when we finally do turn to them.

  The way to avoid this difficulty is to break the large assignments into smaller tasks. You then schedule each of these tasks individually over several days or weeks. (That's how this book got written—in small amounts over several weeks.) For example, when reading a chapter on a difficult subject, read just five or seven pages at a time.

■ ***Fight difficult tasks by tackling them first and by making sure you understand them:*** If you have one particular area of study that's difficult or unpleasant, *do that one first,* when your energy level is higher and you can concentrate best. For instance, if you find math problems or language learning more difficult than reading a psychology text, tackle them first. The easiest tasks, such as list-making and copying-type chores, can be done late in the day, when you're tired.

If a task seems difficult, you may also take it as a warning signal: Maybe there's something about it you don't understand. Are the directions clear? Is the material over your head? If either of these conditions is true, *run, do not walk,* to your instructor. Ask for clarification, if directions are the problem. Be frank with the instructor if you think the material (statistics? grammar? lab experiments?) is hard to comprehend or perform. It may be that what you need is to quickly get yourself the help of a tutor.

We cannot stress enough the importance of taking your own worries seriously if you find that what you're studying is too difficult. However, if you can deal with this before the school term is too far along, you'll probably be all right.

Some students find that it helps to get together with a friend in the same course to study boring or difficult subjects. By exchanging ideas about the subject matter, you may find the time goes faster. Indeed, an extremely valuable aid to learning is the ***study group*, in which a group of classmates get together to share notes and ideas.** In a study group you can clarify lecture notes, quiz each other about ideas, and get different points of view about an instructor's objectives. Being in a group also helps to raise everyone's morale. It makes you realize that you are not alone.

FIGHT PROCRASTINATION & OTHER NEGATIVE REACTIONS! Delaying tactics generally occur unintentionally or only occasionally. ***Procrastination*, on the other hand, is defined as putting off things intentionally and habitually.**

Although it's tempting to think of procrastinators as people who are disorganized or lazy, this is not the case, according to psychologist Linda Sapadin, author of *It's About Time.*[7] There are six styles of procrastinators, Sapadin says—perfectionists, dreamers, worriers, crisis makers, defiers, and overdoers.[8] *(See ■ Panel 3.7.)* Time-management tips, she says, won't help. Rather, what's required is that

PANEL 3.7

Six styles of procrastinators.
Psychologist Linda Sapadin has identified six types of procrastination and methods of coping with them.

■ **Perfectionists:** These types always worry they will fall short of their unrealistically high standards and become so involved in trying to avoid mistakes that they get stuck in details. They need to permit themselves to make accomplishments that will get something done.

   Recommendation: Sapadin suggests changing the self-talk voice in your head to say "I could" instead of "I should"—for example, " I could do this today." In addition, perfectionists need to have specific time limits set in order to complete a task.

■ **Dreamers:** Unable to deal with details, dreamers tend to be vague and unrealistic, thinking in terms of "someday" or "soon."

   Recommendation: Dreamers need to make up short lists with specific tasks to do that day. They need to ask "who, what, how, when" questions when starting a project.

■ **Worriers:** Worriers, always saying "What if . . . ?" lack confidence in their ability to make decisions; they become easily overwhelmed.

   Recommendation: Worriers need to learn it is better to make mistakes and learn from them than to avoid making decisions at all. They need to break up large projects into manageable chunks.

■ **Crisis makers:** Crisis makers have low boredom thresholds and can't get motivated until the last minute. They prefer the adrenaline rush of life on the edge and so postpone projects until the crisis stage.

   Recommendation: Crisis makers need to realize that they need not be fascinated by a project in order to start or finish it. They should find another way to satisfy their need for excitement, such as competitive sports.

■ **Defiers:** Defiers may be (1) people who are aggressive, argumentative, and sulky or (2) promisers who don't deliver (passive-aggressives).

   Recommendation: Both types need to avoid blaming and self-righteous indignation. Argumentative types need to become aware of their overreaction to suggestions or instructions. Promisers who don't deliver need to realize that "yes" constitutes an agreement to produce.

■ **Overdoers:** Overdoers make extra work and don't focus on what really needs to be done. They also have difficulty saying no to requests.

   Recommendation: Overdoers need to learn to set priorities and to say no constructively. They need to delegate tasks when possible.

procrastinators understand the *emotional* problems that are hobbling them, then work to change the thinking behind them. If you don't understand why you delay time after time and always feel recurring regret but aren't confident you can't change—an erroneous presumption—you need to consider this angle.

Procrastination is only one kind of emotional response to task avoidance. There are, however, several other reasons that may cause students to blow an assignment or a course because something about it is emotionally disagreeable or frightening.

Maybe, for instance, it's some aspect of *shyness*, so that you find making an oral presentation nearly unbearable. (Shyness, incidentally, is an extremely common condition, afflicting 4 out of 10 people.)[9] Maybe it's some deep embarrassment about your writing or language skills. Maybe you think "I'm no good at math." Maybe you're queasy about doing biology lab experiments. Maybe there's a former boyfriend/girlfriend in the class whose presence is upsetting you. Maybe the instructor turns you off in some way.

These and most similar situations can be helped, but *you have to reach out and get the help.* If you don't feel you can take the problem up with your instructor, then *immediately* go to the student counseling center. Counseling and tutoring are open to you, normally without any additional charge, as part of the support system available to you as a student. But try not to wait until you're overwhelmed.

GAINING THE EXTRA EDGE. We often read of the superstar athlete who spends many extra hours shooting baskets or sinking putts. Or we hear of the superstar performer who endlessly rehearses a song or an acting part. These people don't have The Extra Edge just because of talent. (There's *lots* of talent around, but few superstars.) They have put in the additional hours because they are in a highly competitive business and they want to perfect their craft. Students are in the same situation.

What do you think when you walk across campus and see students studying on the lawn or in a bookstore line or at the bus stop? Perhaps you could think of them as doing just what the superstar basketball player does when shooting extra hoops. *They are making use of the time-spaces in their day to gain The Extra Edge.*

Here are some techniques that can boost your performance:

- **Always carry some schoolwork and use waiting time:** Your day is made up of intervals that can be used—waiting for class to start, waiting for meals, waiting for the bus, waiting for appointments. These 5- or 10- or 20-minute periods can add up to a lot of time during the day. The temptation is to use this time just to "space out" or to read a newspaper. However, it can also be used to look over class notes, do some course-related reading, or review reading notes.

  If you find yourself at times not carrying books or lecture notes, make a point of carrying 3 × 5 cards. These cards can contain important facts, names, definitions, formulas, and lists that you can pull out and memorize.

  Students learning a foreign language often carry *flash cards*, with foreign words on one side and the English meaning on the other. **Flash cards are cards bearing words, numbers, or pictures that are briefly displayed as a learning aid. One side of the card asks a question; the other side provides the**

answer. Flash cards are also sold in bookstores for other subjects, such as biology, to help you learn definitions. You can make up flash cards of your own for many courses.

The 5-minute mini-study session is far more valuable than might first seem. The way to better memorizing is simply to *practice practice practice,* or *rehearse rehearse rehearse.* Just as the superstars do.

■ *Use your spare time for thinking:* What do you think about when you're jogging, walking to class, standing in a bank line, inching along in traffic? It could be about anything, of course. (Many people think about relationships or sex.) However, there are three ways your mind can be made to be productive:

1. Try to recall points in a lecture that day.

2. Try to recall points in something you've read.

3. Think of ideas to go into a project or paper you're working on.

Again, the point of this use of idle time is to try to involve yourself with your schoolwork. This is equivalent to football players working plays in their heads or singers doing different kinds of phrasing in their minds. The superstars are always working at their jobs.

■ *Make tapes of lectures and listen to them:* This advice is particularly suitable for students with a tape deck in the car or those with a portable tape player who ride the bus. At the end of a long day you might just want to space out to music. But what about at the beginning of the day, when you're fresh?

Making tapes of lectures is no substitute for taking notes. But listening to the tapes can provide you with *additional reinforcement.* This is especially the case if the lecture is densely packed with information, as, for example, a history or biology lecture might be.

SPECIAL NOTE: Be sure to ask your instructors for permission to tape them. Some are uncomfortable having tape recorders in their classes. Some institutions, in fact, *require* that you get the permission of instructors. At other schools, however, students are assumed to have the right to tape any instructor during class.

Onward

PREVIEW Avoiding cramming is important, as it usually only produces stress without the grades to show for it.

Perhaps you have a sneaky suspicion that all this time-management stuff really isn't necessary. After all, maybe in high school you put off a lot of studying, then at the last minute stayed up late *cramming*—studying with great intensity. Indeed, maybe you know that lots of students in higher education seem to use this method.

Unfortunately, as a regular study technique, cramming leaves a lot to be desired. You'll probably find yourself greatly stressed without retaining much

and without the grades to show for it. This is because in career and vocational-technical education there is so much more to learn.

So we come back to one of the most important lessons one can learn about school—the importance of *persistence and commitment*. "It's said that good things come to those who wait," says Wilt Chamberlain, the basketball former superstar. "I believe that good things come to those who work."

NOTES

1. Myers, D. G. (1992). *The pursuit of happiness: Who is happy—and why.* New York: William Morrow, p. 116.

2. Samuelson, R. J. (1996, July 1). The endless road "crisis." *Newsweek*, p. 47.

3. Robinson, J. P., & Godbey, G. (1997). *Time for life.* Quoted in Hirsch, A. (1997, July 26). Author says there's more free time than we think. *San Francisco Chronicle*, p. A21; reprinted from *Baltimore Sun*.

4. Beneke, W. M., & Harris, M. B. (1972). Teaching self-control of study behavior. *Behavior Research & Therapy, 10,* 35–41.

5. Ellis, D. (1991). *Becoming a master student* (6th ed.). Rapid City, SD: College Survival, Inc., p. 53.

6. Lakein, A. (1973). *How to get control of your time and your life.* New York: Peter H. Wyden.

7. Sapadin, L. (1997). *It's about time.* New York: Penguin.

8. Sapadin, L. Reported in Peterson, K. S. (1997, July 22). Helping procrastinators get to it. *USA Today,* p. 7D.

9. Zimbardo, P. G. (1977). *Shyness: What it is, what to do about it.* Reading, MA: Addison-Wesley, p. 14.

CLASSROOM ACTIVITIES: DIRECTIONS TO THE INSTRUCTOR

1. ***What is happiness? Educating yourself for the way you want to live.***
   Students are in career or vocational-technical programs, presumably, in the pursuit of their ultimate happiness—or at least in pursuit of something that will make them happier than they are now. But what, in fact, *is* happiness?

   Ask students to take 5 minutes to write what they think happiness is and what would make them happy. Then have them discuss what happiness is. Discussion questions: What is the way you want to live? How will education help you accomplish it? How does your definition of happiness differ from others' definitions? Could you be happy under others' terms? Could you be happy doing something your family doesn't approve of?

2. ***Getting together a study group.*** Research shows that students who study in groups often get the highest grades. The reasons are many: Students in a group fight isolation by being members of a social circle, give each other support and encouragement, and help each other work through lecture notes and readings and prepare for exams. This activity shows students how to organize and perform in a study group.

   Organize students into groups of three to five (preferably a group that they've not been part of before). Have students introduce themselves to each other, then consider the following questions, which have to do with this chapter. What are the biggest problems you have in studying? What are your principal distractions or time wasters? What time-spaces in your day could you use for mini-studying? What are the principal questions that will be asked about this chapter on the next exam? How do you feel about continuing this study group through the term for this course? What are some of your other, more difficult courses for which a study group would be helpful? Who would you ask to join in forming one?

3. ***What are your killer time wasters?*** Ask students to make lists of their biggest time wasters. Get suggestions from the class and write them on the board. Poll the class to see how many students share each area listed, and write the number down. Ask students to discuss what they might do to make more effective use of their time.

The Examined Life:
Student Assignments for Journal Entries

JOURNAL ENTRY #3.1: HOW DO YOU WASTE TIME? Do you find, after keeping a record of your time usage for two or three days, that you waste time in certain specific ways, such as watching too much TV? Do these time-wasting ways serve some other purposes in your life, such as alleviating stress or furthering friendships? Give some thought to how these needs might be addressed in some other ways so that you can save more time for schoolwork.

_____

_____

_____

_____

_____

_____

_____

JOURNAL ENTRY #3.2: WHAT CAN YOU DO TO MANAGE YOUR TIME BETTER? Just as business and professional people often look for ways to improve their time-management skills, so can students. What kinds of things did you note in this chapter that might help you manage your time better?

_____

_____

_____

_____

_____

_____

_____

JOURNAL ENTRY #3.3: ARE YOU INTO PARTYING? Some students get so deeply into "partying" that they find it has a major impact on their time. Often the kind of escape sought in partying is brought about by the stresses of the constant academic demands of school. Is this a possible area of concern for you?

_____

_____

_____

_____

_____

_____

JOURNAL ENTRY #3.4: WHAT ARE YOUR OTHER RESPONSIBILITIES?

What are some of the other responsibilities you have besides school? Are there some nonessential tasks that could be delegated to others?

_____

_____

_____

_____

_____

_____

_____

CHAPTER FOUR

LEARNING & LECTURES
Learning styles & note taking

IN THIS CHAPTER: You discover something
quite important about yourself—your learning
style—and how understanding it can help your
note-taking abilities. We consider these topics:

- ***Your learning style:*** Which senses you tend to favor
  for learning—sound, sight, touch, or all three.

- ***Making lectures work:*** Whatever you think of lectures, they can be made to work for you.

- ***Memorizing material:*** How to use the "5R steps"
  to memorize information from a lecture.

- ***Optimizing the classroom:*** How to fight boredom
  and fatigue.

■ **Lecturing may be an efficient way for instructors to convey information. Is it a good way for students to receive it?**

Lecturing is certainly an easy way for instructors to transfer knowledge: They talk and students listen. Perhaps this is why the lecture system is one of the mainstays of higher education. Whether it is efficient for any given student, however, depends a lot on his or her preferred learning style.

The Four Learning Styles: Which Fits You?

PREVIEW There are four types of learning styles, corresponding to the principal senses: auditory (hearing), visual (sight), kinesthetic (touch), and mixed modality (all three). You may favor one of these over others.

Educators talk about differences in **learning styles—the ways in which people acquire knowledge.** Some students learn well by listening to lectures. Others learn better through reading, class discussion, hands-on experience, or researching a topic and writing about it. Thus, your particular learning style may make you more comfortable with some kinds of teaching and learning, and even with some kinds of subjects, than with others.

To find out the ways you learn best, try Practical Exploration #4.1.

PRACTICAL EXPLORATION #4.1

HOW DO YOU LEARN BEST?

There are 12 incomplete sentences and three choices for completing each. Circle the answer that best corresponds to your style, as follows:

1 = the choice that is *least* like you.

2 = your second choice.

3 = the choice that is *most* like you.

1. When I want to learn something new, I usually . . .

   a. want someone to explain it to me.   1 2 3

   b. want to read about it in a book or magazine.   1 2 3

   c. want to try it out, take notes, or make a model of it.   1 2 3

2. At a party, most of the time I like to . . .

   a. listen and talk to two or three people at once.   1 2 3

   b. see how everyone looks and watch the people.   1 2 3

   c. dance, play games, or take part in some activities.   1 2 3

3. If I were helping with a musical show, I would most likely . . .

   a. write the music, sing the songs, or play the accompaniment.   1 2 3

   b. design the costumes, paint the scenery, or work the lighting effects.   1 2 3

   c. make the costumes, build the sets, or take an acting role.   1 2 3

4. When I am angry, my first reaction is to . . .

   a. tell people off, laugh, joke, or talk it over with someone.   1 2 3

   b. blame myself or someone else, daydream about taking revenge, or keep it inside   1 2 3

   c. make a fist or tense my muscles, take it out on some thing else, hit or throw things.   1 2 3

5. A happy event I would like to have is . . .

   a. hearing the thunderous applause for my speech or music.   1 2 3

   b. photographing the prize picture of an exciting newspaper story.   1 2 3

   c. achieving the fame of being first in a physical activity such as dancing, acting, surfing, or a sports event.   1 2 3

(continued on next page)

6. I prefer a teacher to . . .

   a. use the lecture method, with informative explanations and discussions.   1 2 3

   b. write on the chalkboard, use visual aids and assigned readings.   1 2 3

   c. require posters, models, or in-service practice, and some activities in class. 1 2 3

7. I know that I talk with . . .

   a. different tones of voice.   1 2 3

   b. my eyes and facial expressions.   1 2 3

   c. my hands and gestures.   1 2 3

8. If I had to remember an event so I could record it later, I would choose to . . .

   a. tell it aloud to someone, or hear an audiotape recording or a song about it.   1 2 3

   b. see pictures of it, or read a description.   1 2 3

   c. replay it in some practice rehearsal, using movements such as dance, play acting, or drill.   1 2 3

9. When I cook something new, I like to . . .

   a. have someone tell me the directions, a friend or TV show.   1 2 3

   b. read the recipe and judge by how it looks.   1 2 3

   c. use many pots and dishes, stir often, and taste-test.   1 2 3

10. My emotions can often be interpreted from my . . .

    a. voice quality.   1 2 3

    b. facial expression.   1 2 3

    c. general body tone.   1 2 3

11. When driving, I . . .

    a. turn on the radio as soon as I enter the car.   1 2 3

    b. like quiet so I can concentrate.   1 2 3

    c. shift my body position frequently to avoid getting tired.   1 2 3

12. In my free time, I like to . . .

    a. listen to the radio, talk on the telephone, or attend a musical event.   1 2 3

    b. go to the movies, watch TV, or read a magazine or book.   1 2 3

    c. get some exercise, go for a walk, play games, or make things.   1 2 3

■ SCORING

Add up the points for all the "a's, then all the "b's," then all the "c's."

Total points for all "a's": _____

Total points for all "b's": _____

Total points for all "c's": _____

■ INTERPRETATION

If "a" has the highest score, that indicates your learning style preference is principally *auditory*.

If "b" has the highest score, your learning style preference is principally *visual*.

If "c" has the highest score, your learning style preference is *kinesthetic*.

If all scores are reasonably equal, that indicates your learning style preference is *mixed*.

See the text for explanations.

People have four ways in which they favor learning new material: *auditory, visual, kinesthetic,* and *mixed.*[1] Let's consider these.

AUDITORY LEARNING STYLE. Auditory has to do with listening and also speaking. ***Auditory learners* use their voices and their ears as the primary means of learning.** They recall what they hear and what they themselves express verbally.

"When something is hard to understand, they want to talk it through," write professors Adele Ducharme and Luck Watford of Valdosta State University in Georgia. "When they're excited and enthusiastic about learning, they want to verbally express their response. . . . These learners love class discussion, they grow by working and talking with others, and they appreciate a teacher taking time to explain something to them."[2]

If you're this type of person, it's important to know that such learners are easily distracted by sounds. Thus, it's a good idea that they *not* listen to the radio while studying, because they attend to all the sounds around them. An effective study technique, however, is to repeat something aloud several times because that helps them memorize it. These types of learners may do well in learning foreign languages, music, and other areas that depend on a strong auditory sense.

VISUAL LEARNING STYLE. Visual, of course, refers to the sense of sight. ***Visual learners* like to see pictures of things described or words written down.** "They will seek out illustrations, diagrams, and charts to help them understand and remember information," say Ducharme and Watford. "They appreciate being able to follow what a teacher is presenting with material written on an overhead transparency or in a handout."

For visual learners, an effective technique for reviewing and studying material is to read over their notes and recopy and reorganize information in outline form.

KINESTHETIC LEARNING STYLE. *Kinesthetic* (pronounced "kin-es-*thet*-ik") has to do with the sense of touch and of physical manipulation. ***Kinesthetic learners* learn best when they touch and are physically involved in what they are studying.** These are the kinds of people who fidget when they have to sit still and who express enthusiasm by jumping up and down.

"These learners want to act out a situation, to make a product, to do a project, and in general to be busy with their learning," say Ducharme and Watford. "They find that when they physically do something, they understand it and they remember it."

MIXED-MODALITY LEARNING STYLE. Modality (pronounced "moh-*dal*-it-y") means style. As you might guess, ***mixed-modality learners* are able to function in all three of these learning styles or "modalities"—auditory, visual, and kinesthetic.** Clearly, these people are at an advantage because they can handle information in whatever way it is presented to them.

LEARNING STYLES, LECTURES, & READING. Lectures would seem to favor auditory learners. Textbooks would seem to favor visual learners. Lectures and readings are two of the principal pipelines by which information is conveyed in career education.

However, suppose one or both of these methods don't suit you? Because you don't usually have a choice about how a subject is taught, it's important to get comfortable with both methods. This means you need to be able to *extract* the most information out of a lecture or textbook—take useful notes, for example—regardless of your learning preference and the instructor's style. We show how to do that in this chapter and the next.

Lectures, Learning Styles, & Life

PREVIEW Because you can't control the way information is conveyed to you, either in school or in your career, it's important to become comfortable with the lecture method. This means discovering how to extract material from the lecture and learn it.

Of the four learning styles described—auditory, visual, kinesthetic, and mixed modality—lectures would seem to favor auditory learners. *Auditory learners,* you'll recall, use their voices and their ears as the primary means of learning.

But suppose you're not an auditory learner. That is, suppose you're a *visual learner* and favor pictures or words written down. Or you're *kinesthetic* and favor touching and physical involvement. (If you're *the mixed-modality type,* you can function in all three learning styles.)

In the work world, too, you don't always have a choice about the method by which information is conveyed to you. You may often have to attend a meeting, presentation, speech, or company training program. There, as we pointed out earlier, the "examination" will consist of how well you recall and handle the information in order to do your job.

It's important, therefore, that you learn to get comfortable with the lecture method of teaching. Thus, you have two tasks:

- **Be able to extract material:** You need to be able to *extract* the most information out of a lecture—that is, take useful notes, regardless of your learning preference and the instructor's style.

- **Be able to learn material:** You need to be able to *learn* the lecture material so that you can do well on tests.

The rest of the chapter shows you how to accomplish this.

Making Lectures Work:
What They Didn't Tell You in High School

PREVIEW Cutting classes has been found to be associated with poor grades. Being in a class, even a boring one, helps you learn what the instructor expects. It also reflects your attitude about your academic performance—whether you want to get through school successfully or merely slide by. Being an active participant means bringing syllabus and textbooks to class and doing the homework and reviewing previous assignments in order to be ready for each new lecture.

How do you approach the whole matter of going to class? You may have picked up many of your classroom habits while you were in high school. Do you sit in the back, find yourself constantly distracted during lectures, have difficulty taking notes? To get an idea of your present performance in the classroom, try Practical Exploration #4.2.

PRACTICAL EXPLORATION #4.2

LISTENING QUESTIONNAIRE: HOW'S YOUR CLASSROOM PERFORMANCE?

Read each statement and decide how the habit reflects your listening. Answer as follows:

"Yes"—if you use the habit over half your listening time.
"No"—if you don't use the habit very much at all.
"Sometimes"—if you use the habit periodically.

1. Do you often doodle while listening?
   - ❏ Yes
   - ❏ No
   - ❏ Sometimes

2. Do you show attending behaviors through your eye contact, posture, and facial expressions?
   - ❏ Yes
   - ❏ No
   - ❏ Sometimes

3. Do you try to write down everything you hear?
   - ❏ Yes
   - ❏ No
   - ❏ Sometimes

4. Do you listen largely for central ideas as opposed to facts and details?
   - ❏ Yes
   - ❏ No
   - ❏ Sometimes

5. Do you often daydream or think about personal concerns while listening?
   - ❏ Yes
   - ❏ No
   - ❏ Sometimes

6. Do you ask clarifying questions about what you do not understand in a lecture?
   - ❏ Yes
   - ❏ No
   - ❏ Sometimes

7. Do you frequently feel tired or sleepy when attending a lecture?
   - ❏ Yes
   - ❏ No
   - ❏ Sometimes

8. Do you mentally review information as you listen to make connections among points?
   - ❏ Yes
   - ❏ No
   - ❏ Sometimes

9. Do you often call a lecture boring?
   - ❏ Yes
   - ❏ No
   - ❏ Sometimes

10. Do you recall what you already know about a subject before the lecture begins?
    - ❏ Yes
    - ❏ No
    - ❏ Sometimes

11. Do you generally avoid listening when difficult information is presented?
    - ❏ Yes
    - ❏ No
    - ❏ Sometimes

(continued on next page)

12. Do you pay attention to the speaker's nonverbal cues?

❑ Yes

❑ No

❑ Sometimes

13. Do you often find yourself thinking up arguments to refute the speaker?

❑ Yes

❑ No

❑ Sometimes

14. Do you generally try to find something of interest in a lecture even if you think it's boring?

❑ Yes

❑ No

❑ Sometimes

15. Do you usually criticize the speaker's delivery, appearance, or mannerisms?

❑ Yes

❑ No

❑ Sometimes

16. Do you do what you can to control distractions around you?

❑ Yes

❑ No

❑ Sometimes

17. Do you often fake attention to the speaker?

❑ Yes

❑ No

❑ Sometimes

18. Do you periodically summarize or recapitulate what the speaker has said during the lecture?

❑ Yes

❑ No

❑ Sometimes

19. Do you often go to class late?

❑ Yes

❑ No

❑ Sometimes

20. Do you review the previous class lecture notes before attending class?

❑ Yes

❑ No

❑ Sometimes

■ SCORING

Count the number of "Yes" answers to *even-numbered* items: _____

Count the number of "Yes" answers to *odd-numbered* items: _____

■ INTERPRETATION: The even-numbered items are considered *effective* listening habits.

The odd-numbered items are considered *ineffective* listening habits.

If you answered an item as "Sometimes," determine how often and under what circumstances you find yourself responding this way. Identify the areas where you have written "Yes" or "Sometimes" to odd-numbered items and write an explanation here:

_____

_____

_____

_____

_____

_____

_____

_____

_____

_____

_____

_____

_____

_____

_____

_____

_____

_____

_____

_____

_____

CLASS ATTENDANCE & GRADES. In high school, you may have been required to attend every class every school day. What a surprise, then, when you find in higher education that in many classes instructors don't even take attendance and that you are free to cut if you choose. Of course, it may be easy to be selective about which classes to go to and which not to attend. In the wintertime, for instance, it isn't hard to choose between staying in a warm bed and getting up for an 8:00 A.M. class—particularly if you think the instructor or the subject is boring.

However, you may not be aware of an important fact: *poor class attendance is associated with poor grades.* According to one study, "unsuccessful" students—those defined as having grades of C– or below—were found to be more commonly absent from class than "successful" students, those with a B average or above.[3] (See ■ *Panel 4.1.*)

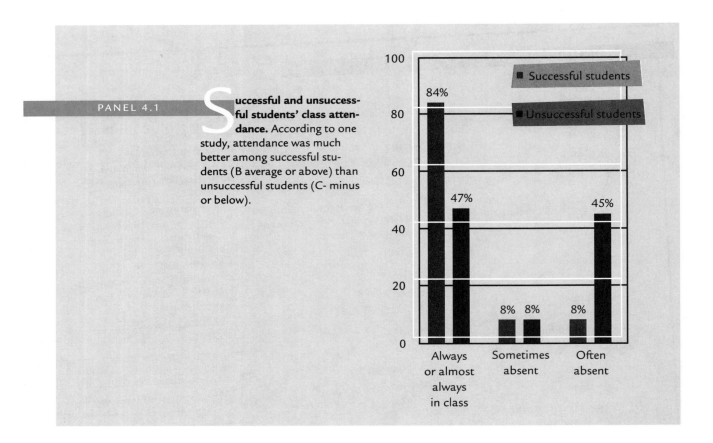

Successful and unsuccessful students' class attendance. According to one study, attendance was much better among successful students (B average or above) than unsuccessful students (C- minus or below).

There are two answers to this—things they don't usually tell you in high school:

- **Being in class helps you learn what the instructor expects—and to anticipate exams:** Even if the instructor is so hard to follow that you learn very little from the lectures, it's still important to go to class. "If nothing else," one team of writers point out, "you'll get a feel for how the instructor thinks. This can help you to anticipate the content of exams and to respond in the manner your professor expects."[4]

- **Going to class goes along with a successful attitude about career education in general:** There are probably two kinds of students: passive students, or those who try to slide by in school, and active students, or those who try to triumph in school.

  Students who try to *slide by* in school are those who look for all the ways to pass their courses with the least amount of effort: they cut class, borrow other students' notes, cram the night before exams, and so on.

  Students who try to *triumph in* school take the attitude that, sure, there are certain shortcuts or efficiencies to making one's way through higher education (this book is full of such tips). However, they realize that always trying to cut corners is not productive in the long run. Thus, among other things, they try to attend every class.

  Which one would an employer want to hire? Here again we have the relevance of your higher education to life outside school: A can-do attitude in higher education is the kind of quality needed for you to prevail in the world of work.

BEING AN ACTIVE PARTICIPANT: PREPARING FOR CLASS. Being an active rather than passive student means becoming involved in the course. Besides attending regularly and being on time for class, try to prepare for your upcoming classes by doing the following:

- ■ *Use the course syllabus as a basic "road map":* The *syllabus* is a *very* important document. **The *syllabus* (pronounced "sill-uh-buss") is a course outline or guide that tells you what readings are required, when assignments are due, and when examinations are scheduled.** This basic road map to the course is a page or more that the instructor hands out on the first class day.

  It's a good idea to three-hole-punch the syllabus and include it in the front of your binder or staple it inside the front of your notebook. That way you will automatically bring it to class and can make any changes to it that the instructor announces (such as a new date for a test).

- ■ *Do the homework before the lecture:* A syllabus will often show that certain readings coincide with certain lectures. It usually works best if you do the readings *before* rather than after the lectures. Like putting your toe in the water, reading first will help you know what to expect. If you do the homework before the lecture, you'll understand the instructor's remarks better.

- ■ *Anticipate the lecture:* Not only will doing the required readings before class prepare you for the lecture, but so will reading over your lecture notes from the last class. Often the next lecture is a continuation of the last one. In addition, you can look at the syllabus to see what's expected.

  When doing the homework, develop questions on the readings. Bring these to class for clarification.

- ■ *Bring the textbook to class:* Some people come to class carrying only a notebook and pen (and some don't even bring those). Are they the "A" and "B" students? If we had to guess, we would say they are not the top grade getters.

  Students who are successful performers in school don't feel they always have to travel light. Besides their notebook, they also carry the principal textbook and other books (or supplies and equipment) relevant to the course. This is because instructors often make special comments about material in the textbook, or they draw on the text for class discussion. Some instructors even follow the text quite closely in their lectures. Thus, if you have the text in the classroom, you can follow along and make marks in the book, writing down possible exam questions or indicating points of emphasis.

The 5R Steps: Record, Rewrite, Recite, Reflect, Review

PREVIEW Because the greatest amount of forgetting happens in the first 24 hours, you need not just a note-taking system but also a note-reviewing system. Five steps for committing lecture notes to long-term memory are Record, Rewrite, Recite, Reflect, and Review.

Many students have the idea that they can simply take notes of a lecture and then review them whenever it's convenient—perhaps the night before a test. And it's easy to think you are doing well when you attend every class and fill page after page of your notebook.

However, simply writing everything down—acting like a human tape recorder—by itself doesn't work. *The name of the game, after all, is to learn the material, not just make a record of it.* Writing things down now but saving all the learning for later is simply not efficient. As we discuss in the next chapter, research shows that the most forgetting takes place within the first 24 hours, then drops off. The trick, then, is to figure out how to reduce the forgetting of that first 24 hours.

Effective learning requires that you be not only a good note *taker* but also a good note *reviewer.* This may mean you need to change the note-taking and note-learning approach you're accustomed to. However, once these new skills are learned, you'll find them invaluable not only in school but also in your career.

One method that is helpful in note taking and note learning consists of five steps known as **the 5R steps, for Record, Rewrite, Recite, Reflect, Review.** They are:

- *Step 1—Record:* Capture the main ideas.

- *Step 2—Rewrite:* Following the lecture, rewrite your notes, developing key terms, questions, and summaries.

- *Step 3—Recite:* Covering up the key terms, questions, and summaries, practice reciting them to yourself.

- *Step 4—Reflect:* To anchor these ideas, make some personal association with them.

- *Step 5—Review:* Two or three times a week, if possible, review your notes to make them more familiar.

"Too much!" we hear students say. "I've got a lot of things to do. I can't be forever rehashing one lecture!"

Actually, the system may not take as much time as it seems to at first. Certainly it need not take much more *effort* than if you try to learn all the information by cramming—absorbing all the material in one sitting.

In any event, studies show that increased practice or rehearsal not only increases retention. It also improves your *understanding* of material, because as you go over it repeatedly, you are able to concentrate on the most important points.[5]

You probably can appreciate this from your own experience in having developed some athletic, musical, or other skill: the more you did it, the better you got. Like an actor, the more you practice or rehearse the material, the better you will be able to overcome stage fright and deliver your best performance on examination day.

Let's consider what these five steps are:

STEP 1: RECORD. You'll see many of your classmates with pens racing to try to capture every word of the lecture. Don't bother. You're not supposed to be like a court reporter or a secretary-stenographer, recording every word. You should be less concerned with taking down everything than in developing a *system* of note taking. Here is how the system works:

- ***Leave blank margins on your note page:*** This is a variation on what is known as the *Cornell format* of note taking. *(See ▪ Panel 4.2.)* Draw a vertical line, top to bottom, 1½ inches from the left edge of the paper, a similar line 1½ inches from the right side, and a horizontal line 1½ inches up from the bottom. As we explain below, you will use these blank margins for review purposes. (Do not write on both sides of the paper. You can use the back side of the sheet in conjunction with your next page of notes.)

- ***Take notes in rough paragraph form:*** At some point you may have been told to take notes in outline form, using the standard "I, A, 1, a," format. If you're good at this, that's fine. However, most instructors don't lecture this way, and you should not have to concentrate on trying to force an outline on the lecture material.

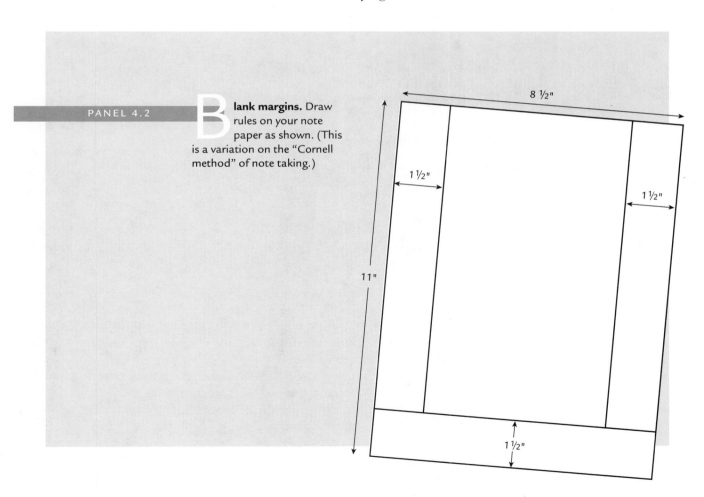

PANEL 4.2

Blank margins. Draw rules on your note paper as shown. (This is a variation on the "Cornell method" of note taking.)

8 ½"

1 ½"

1 ½"

11"

1 ½"

Simply take your notes in rough paragraph form. Put extra space (a line or two) between new ideas and divisions of thought. Don't try to save on the cost of notepaper by cramming notes onto every line of the page.

- **Try to capture the main ideas:** Don't try to take down everything the instructor says. Not only will this create a mass of information that you will have to sort through later, but it will also interfere with your learning. Instead of learning how to pay attention and concentrate on what's important, you become simply a tape recorder. An extremely important part of your note-taking system, then, is to try to capture just the key ideas. More on this below.

- **Develop a system of abbreviations:** Some people take highly readable notes, as though preparing to let other people borrow them. You shouldn't concern yourself primarily with this kind of legibility. The main thing is that *you* be able to take ideas down fast and *you* be able to read them later.

  Thus, make up your own system of abbreviations. For example, "w.r.t." means "with regard to"; "sike" means "psychology"; "para" is borrowing the Spanish word for "in order to." *(See ■ Panel 4.3.)*

  By adopting these practices, you'll be well on your way to retaining more information than you have in the past.

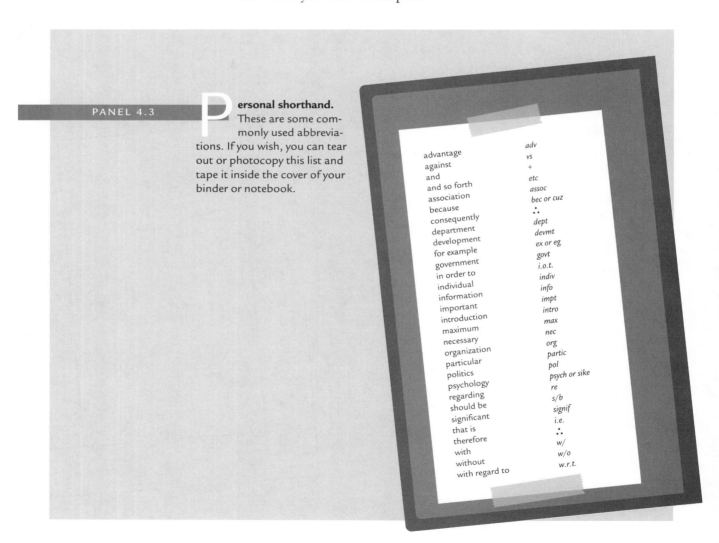

PANEL 4.3

Personal shorthand. These are some commonly used abbreviations. If you wish, you can tear out or photocopy this list and tape it inside the cover of your binder or notebook.

advantage	adv
against	vs
and	+
and so forth	etc
association	assoc
because	bec or cuz
consequently	∴
department	dept
development	devmt
for example	ex or eg
government	govt
in order to	i.o.t.
individual	indiv
information	info
important	impt
introduction	intro
maximum	max
necessary	nec
organization	org
particular	partic
politics	pol
psychology	psych or sike
regarding	re
should be	s/b
significant	signif
that is	i.e.
therefore	∴
with	w/
without	w/o
with regard to	w.r.t.

STEP 2: REWRITE. *This is extremely important.* The point of this step is to counteract the brain's natural tendency to forget 80% of new information in the first 24 hours.

As soon as possible—on the same day you took lecture notes—you should do one of two things:

1. Either recopy/rewrite your notes, or

2. At least go over them to familiarize yourself and to underline key issues and concepts and make notations in the margins.

Of course, it's not *necessary* to recopy your notes. The point we must emphasize, however, is that this very activity will give you the extra familiarization that will help to imprint the information in your mind.

Alternatively, if you don't have time or aren't strongly motivated to rewrite your notes, you should take 5 or 10 minutes to make use of the blank margins you left around your notes. By rewriting and underlining you reinforce the material, moving it from your short-term into your long-term memory.

Here's what to do:

■ ***Read, rewrite, and highlight your notes:*** Read your notes over. If you can, rewrite them—copy them over in a separate notebook or type them up on a word processor—with the same margins at the left, right, and bottom as we described above. Now read the notes again, using highlighter pen or underlining to emphasize key ideas.

■ ***Write key terms in the left margin:*** In the left margins, write the key terms and main concepts. (*See* ■ *Panel 4.4.*) Reviewing these important terms and

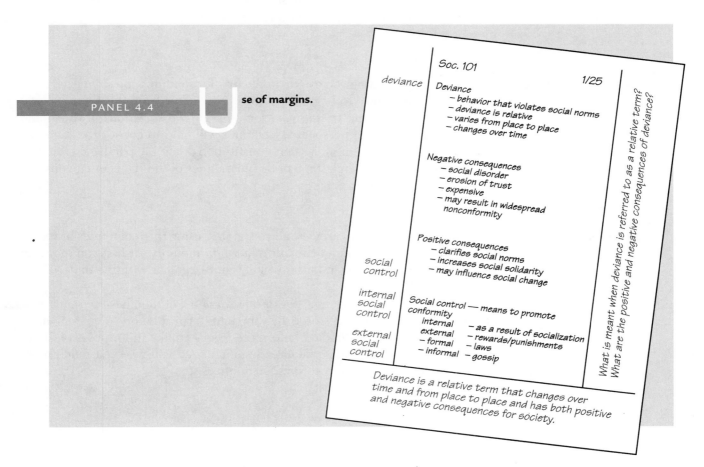

PANEL 4.4   Use of margins.

concepts is a good way of preparing for objective questions on tests, such as true-false or multiple-choice questions.

■ ***Write one or two questions in the right margin:*** On the right side of each page, write two questions about the material on the page. *(See* ■ *Panel 4.4 again.)* Reviewing these questions later will help you prepare for tests featuring essay questions or subjective questions.

■ ***Write a summary on the last page:*** At the bottom of the last page of that day's notes, summarize in a few words the material in the notes. *(See* ■ *Panel 4.4 again.)* Some students write these summaries in red or green ink. With this eye-catching color, they can then flip through their notes and quickly take in all the summary information.

We cannot stress enough how important it is to take time—*absolutely no later than one day after your class*—to go over your notes, rewriting them if you can but certainly writing key terms, questions, and summaries at the end.

STEP 3: RECITE. Another reinforcement technique is *recitation.* This consists of covering up your detailed notes and using the key terms or concepts in the left margin to say out loud (or under your breath to yourself) what you understand your notes to mean. You can also do this with the questions in the right margin and the summary in the bottom margin.

Recitation is an activity you can do at your desk, on the bus, when you're doing homework, or when you have 5 or 10 minutes between classes. It is a particularly effective reinforcing technique because the activity of verbalizing gives your mind time to grasp the ideas and move them from short-term to long-term memory.

STEP 4: REFLECT. Reflecting is something you can do in the first few minutes you sit in class waiting for the next lecture to begin. Look over your notes from the previous class period in the course and try to make some *personal associations* in your mind with the material. Such personal associations will help to anchor the material. For example, if you're in a class on constitutional law for paralegal students, imagine how you might link some of the guarantees of the rights of citizens to a dispute with your landlord.

STEP 5: REVIEW. Two or three times a week, review all your notes, using the techniques of recitation and reflection to commit the information to memory. At first you may find that the review takes longer, but as you get more familiar with the material the review will get easier.

Toward the end of the semester or quarter you will then have perhaps 80% of the lecture information stored in your long-term memory. The remaining 20% can be learned in the days before the exam. Unlike the process of cramming, having this much material already memorized will give you much more confidence about your ability to succeed on the test.

Optimizing the Classroom Game

PREVIEW The best way to fight boredom and fatigue in the classroom is to make attending class a game. Three ways to improve your classroom game are to learn (1) to focus your attention, (2) to participate, and (3) to overcome classroom obstacles.

The way to deal with attending class is to treat it as a game. The point of the game is to struggle against two enemies to get the grade you want. The two enemies are *boredom* and *fatigue*:

- **Boredom:** Boredom is a very real factor. Television may have raised our expectations as to how stimulating education ought to be. However, many instructors—indeed, most people in general—can't be that interesting all the time.

- **Fatigue:** Fatigue can also be a real factor. This is particularly so for students who are struggling with other demands, such as those of work and family, or who short themselves on sleep.

As a student, then, you need to turn yourself into an active listener and active participant in the classroom to get past these two hurdles.

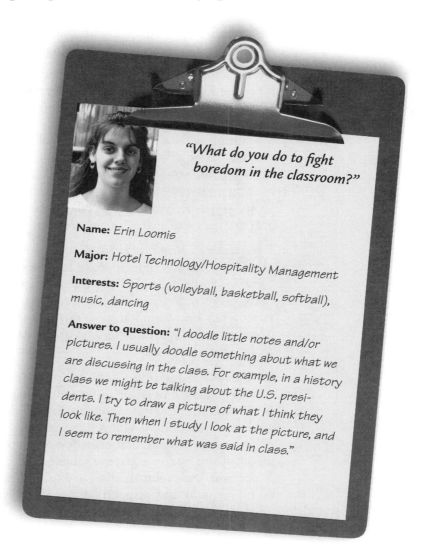

"What do you do to fight boredom in the classroom?"

Name: Erin Loomis

Major: Hotel Technology/Hospitality Management

Interests: Sports (volleyball, basketball, softball), music, dancing

Answer to question: "I doodle little notes and/or pictures. I usually doodle something about what we are discussing in the class. For example, in a history class we might be talking about the U.S. presidents. I try to draw a picture of what I think they look like. Then when I study I look at the picture, and I seem to remember what was said in class."

Let's consider three ways to improve your classroom game:

- Learning to focus your attention
- Learning to participate
- Learning to overcome classroom obstacles

LEARNING TO FOCUS YOUR ATTENTION.　Once you've come to class, what do you do then? You learn to pay attention. Being attentive involves *active listening,* which is different from the kind of passive listening we do when "listening" to television (sucking at the electric bottle, as they say). Active listening is, in one writer's description, "paying attention so that your brain absorbs the meaning of words and sentences."[6]

Being an active listener requires that you do the following:

- **Take listening seriously:**[7] Make up your mind you *will* listen. Everything begins with your attitude—hence this decision. Students can coast through the classroom experience yawning, daydreaming, and spacing out, thereby missing a lot, or they can *decide* to listen.

    Making the commitment to learn and taking an active part in obtaining information also improves your ability to remember the material. If you find your mind wandering, pull your thoughts back to the present and review mentally what the speaker has been saying.

- **Sit up front and center:** For a variety of reasons, some students don't want to sit at the front of the class. However, when you go to a musical event or stage performance, you probably *want* to sit down front—because you're interested and you want to see and hear better.

    Sitting in the front and center rows in the classroom will also help you hear and see better, of course. Moreover, the very act of sitting in that place will actually stimulate your interest. This is because you have taken the physical step of *making a commitment*—of putting yourself in a position to participate more. (Also, you'll be less likely to talk to classmates, write letters, or fall asleep if you're where the instructor can see you.)

- **Use tricks to stay alert:** Some adult students who come directly from work to class use a number of techniques to combat fatigue. First they change into comfortable clothes and shoes before class, or they "dress down," removing ties, belts, jackets, and so on. They go to the rest room and splash water on their faces. They bring a pillow to sit on—especially if they need to ease a backache. They go outside during class breaks to breathe in fresh air and stretch themselves or walk around.

- **Stay positive and pay attention to content, not delivery:** If you *expect* a lecture to be boring or lacking in content, we guarantee you it will be. By contrast, if you suppress negative thoughts, ignore distractions about the speaker's style of delivery or body language, and *encourage the instructor with eye contact, interested expression, and attentive posture,* you will find yourself much more involved and interested in the subject matter.

    If you find yourself disagreeing with something the speaker says, don't argue mentally, but suspend judgment. (Maybe make a note in the margin and

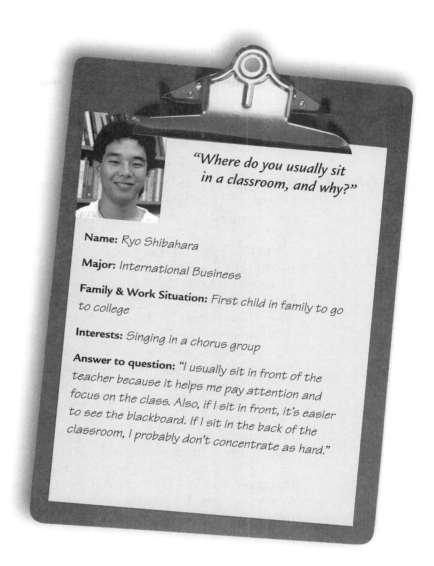

"Where do you usually sit in a classroom, and why?"

Name: Ryo Shibahara

Major: International Business

Family & Work Situation: First child in family to go to college

Interests: Singing in a chorus group

Answer to question: *"I usually sit in front of the teacher because it helps me pay attention and focus on the class. Also, if I sit in front, it's easier to see the blackboard. If I sit in the back of the classroom, I probably don't concentrate as hard."*

bring the matter up later during class discussion.) Assess the instructor's reasoning, then make up your mind.

■ ***Listen for "bell" phrases and cues to determine what is important:*** All lecturers use phrases and gestures that should "ring a bell" and signal importance.

　　A *bell phrase*—also called a *signal word* or *signal phrase*—is an indicator of an important point. Bell phrases are important because they indicate you should note what comes after them and remember them. Examples of bell phrases are "Three major types . . ."; "The most important result is . . ."; "You should remember . . ."; "Because of this . . ."; "First . . . second . . . third . . ."

　　A *bell cue* is an action or gesture that indicates important points. Examples are (1) diagrams or charts; (2) notes on the blackboard; (3) pointing, as to something on the board or a chart; (4) underlining or making a check mark by key words; (5) banging a fist; and (6) holding up fingers.

　　When a class is long or tedious, you can turn it into a game by telling yourself you will try to detect as many bell phrases and cues as possible. Then, every time you pick up one, put a check mark in your notes. You'll find that when you do this you'll become more actively involved. Not only does it fight boredom and fatigue but it also increases the quality of your note taking.

Even if you're somewhat shy and hate to get involved in class participation, the preceding suggestions will sharpen your listening skills, comprehension, and memorization, all of which will help you perform well on tests. If you *really* want to be a peak-performing student, however, you should go to the next step—participation.

LEARNING TO PARTICIPATE. Are you the type of person who prefers to be invisible in the classroom? No doubt you've noticed many students are. They sit in the back row, never ask questions, and can go an entire semester without talking to the instructor.

In doing this, one can probably scrape by. However, life does not reward the passive. If you ever need a reference from an instructor for a job or to transfer to another school, how will you know whom to ask if you've never given the instructor an opportunity to know you? When you're starting on your career, what skills will you be able to draw on to speak up in meetings, give presentations, or persuade authority figures of your point of view? As we've said all along, the skills you practice in the classroom, regardless of subject, really are practice for life outside of or after school.

For many students, shyness and lack of assertiveness are very real, even incapacitating problems. We deal with these elsewhere in the book (in Chapter 10), and if it's an important issue for you, we urge you to skip ahead and read that material soon. Even those who are not shy are often reluctant to "make a fool of myself," to risk being laughed at.

However, there comes a time in life when, *if you can't push beyond these limitations and let go of the fear of "being laughed at," there is a real question as to whether you will be able to get what you want in your career and in your relationships.* Learning to participate in a public dialogue is simply part of the growth process.

Class participation, whether in a lecture or a discussion section, further reinforces memorization because it obliges you to become actively engaged with the material and to organize it in your mind. Here are some suggestions for participation:

- *Do your homework:* There is an understood contract—namely, that you should have kept up with the homework assignments, such as the textbook readings. That way you won't embarrass yourself by asking questions or making remarks about something you are already supposed to have read.

- *Respect the opinions of others:* If the questions or remarks of others seem off-the-wall or biased, don't try to trash them. A spirit of cordiality and absence of intimidation is necessary to keep learning channels open and tempers cool.

- *Follow your curiosity:* We've all had the experience of holding back on asking a question, then hearing someone else raise it and be complimented by the instructor with "That's a very good question!" Follow your instincts. You have a right to ask questions, and the more you do so, the more you will perfect this particular art.

LEARNING TO OVERCOME CLASSROOM OBSTACLES. You now know what to do if the instructor or subject matter is boring. What do you do if the instructor speaks too fast or with an accent? If your shorthand or ear is not good enough to keep up, here are some strategies:

- ***Do your homework before class:*** If you keep up with the reading assignments, doing them before the lecture rather than afterward, you'll often be able to fill in gaps mentally and select key points.

- ***Leave holes in your notes:*** Whenever you miss something important, leave spaces in your notes, with a big question mark in the margin. Then try to fill in the missing material through other methods, as explained below.

- ***Trade notes with classmates:*** If you and others in class take readable notes (even using private shorthand), you can easily make photocopies of your notes and exchange them. Two or three students may find that among them they are able to pick up most of a lecture.

- ***Use a tape recorder:*** The trick here is not to make a tape recorder a *substitute* for note taking. Then you'll merely be taking the same amount of time to listen to the lecture again—and perhaps still be confused. Use the tape recorder as a backup system, one in which you can use the fast-forward and reverse buttons to go over material you had trouble following in class. (Remember to get permission from the instructor to use a tape recorder in his or her class.)

- ***Ask questions—in class or after:*** If the instructor has a question period, you can ask questions to clarify what you missed. Or see the instructor after class or during his or her office hours.

NOTE: Some students are reluctant to talk to instructors during office hours for fear of "bothering" them. But you're not bothering them; that's what they're there for. Instructors are *paid* to be available for your questions.

Onward

PREVIEW You'll be exposed to lectures all your life.

For your entire life, the lecture format will be enacted over and over again in different settings. If it's not an instructor or professor speaking, it could be your boss, or an expert in an area of particular interest to you, or a speaker at a neighborhood meeting, or a political leader on television. Thus, the skills you've learned in this chapter will be of value well beyond your time in school.

Did the skills we discussed in this chapter seem like a lot of work? If so, is that a problem? It looks like we're back to the question of persistence again. "Opportunity is missed by most people because it is dressed in overalls and looks like work," said inventor Thomas Edison.

NOTES

1. Guild & Garger, 1986. Cited in Ducharme, A., & Watford, L., Explanation of assessment areas (handout).

2. Ducharme & Watford.

3. Lindgren, H. C. (1969). *The psychology of college success: A dynamic approach.* New York: Wiley.

4. Weiten, W., Lloyd, M. A., & Lashley, R. L. (1990). *Psychology applied to modern life: Adjustment in the 90s* (3rd ed.). Pacific Grove, CA: Brooks/Cole, p. 22.

5. Bromage, B. K., & Mayer, R. E. (1986). Quantitative and qualitative effects of repetition on learning from technical text. *Journal of Educational Psychology,* 78(4), 271–78.

6. Pauk, W. (1989). *How to study in college.* Boston: Houghton-Mifflin, p. 122.

7. Lucas, S. E. (1989). *The art of public speaking.* New York: Random House.

CLASSROOM ACTIVITIES: DIRECTIONS TO THE INSTRUCTOR

1. ***How well does your learning style suit the lecture method of teaching?*** Have the class, in a small- or large-group situation, look back at Practical Exploration #4.1. Ask each student to determine which learning style—auditory, visual, kinesthetic, or mixed-modality—he or she seems to favor.

   Then ask students to discuss the following questions: What experiences have you had that make you think you like one learning style better than others (if that's the case)? How well does your learning style relate to the lecture method of presenting information? In a work situation, have you had any difficulty with retaining information from presentations and meetings? Because not everything in life is delivered to you in an easy manner, what kinds of strategies would you recommend for getting the most out of the lecture system?

2. ***How's your classroom performance?*** Have students look at the results of their Practical Exploration #4.2, "Listening Questionnaire: How's Your Classroom Performance?"

   In a small group situation, ask students to go through this Personal Exploration and discuss some of the items to which they answered "Yes." Discussion questions: What things are you doing right? What things need changing? Because changing one's behavior is not always easy, what kinds of prompts or reinforcement will you give yourself to help you change negative behavior to positive behavior?

3. ***What are examples of bell phrases and bell cues?*** Ask students to look at their lecture notes from other classes. (Alternatively, have them monitor two of their lectures in other classes this week in preparation for this class discussion.) Questions for discussion: What bell phrases and bell cues do you observe your instructors using? How does putting yourself in a state of alertness to these cues affect your levels of boredom and fatigue?

The Examined Life:
Student Assignments for Journal Entries

JOURNAL ENTRY #4.1: WHAT IS YOUR BEST LEARNING STYLE? Which is your predominant learning style—sight, hearing, or touch? What kind of work can you do to improve your skills with other learning styles?

_____
_____
_____
_____
_____
_____
_____

JOURNAL ENTRY #4.2: SHOULD YOU CHANGE YOUR NOTE-TAKING BEHAVIOR? How should you change your note-taking habits from your accustomed methods?

_____
_____
_____
_____
_____
_____
_____

JOURNAL ENTRY #4.3: WHICH INSTRUCTORS DO YOU HAVE TROUBLE WITH? What kinds of instructors, or what particular instructors, do you have trouble following when they lecture? Why, and what can you do about it?

_____
_____
_____
_____
_____
_____
_____

JOURNAL ENTRY #4.4: ARE YOU TOO SELF-CONSCIOUS ABOUT OTHER STUDENTS? Are you afraid other students will laugh at you for being too obviously engaged in the lecture and learning process? Are you afraid they will consider you some sort of wimp because you're not obviously detached, indifferent, or supposedly cool? Why does this bother you? What does this self-consciousness—this tremendous concern about how people think about you—imply for your future in school or in a career?

_____

_____

_____

_____

_____

_____

_____

JOURNAL ENTRY #4.5: HOW DO YOU RATE YOURSELF AS A STUDENT PERFORMER? For each of the following activities, rate yourself according to the following standard:

A: Excellent   B: Above average   C: Average   D: Below average   F: Poor

1. Listen actively in class	A	B	C	D	F
2. Attend consistently	A	B	C	D	F
3. Participate and ask questions	A	B	C	D	F
4. Participate in study groups	A	B	C	D	F
5. Use bell cues and bell phrases	A	B	C	D	F
6. Do readings prior to class	A	B	C	D	F
7. Effectively and consistently use 5Rs in note taking	A	B	C	D	F

CHAPTER FIVE

RECALL & READING
Better memorizing, reading, & study techniques

IN THIS CHAPTER: You discover one of your most valuable tools—your memory—and how to use it in reading textbooks. We consider:

- **The importance of managing memory:** Cramming, short-term versus long-term memory, the "forgetting curve."

- **How to improve your memory:** Overlearning, studying a little at a time frequently, avoiding interference, making material meaningful, using verbal and visual memory aids.

- **Reading System #1:** *SQ3R Method*—surveying, questioning, reading, reciting, reviewing.

- **Reading System #2:** *3Rs Method*—reading, recording, reciting.

- **Dealing with special subjects:** Reducing anxiety, devoting more time, using special study tools.

■ What would be your greatest wish to help you through higher education?

M aybe it would be for a photographic memory, a mind that could briefly look at something just once and later recall it in detail. Perhaps 5% to 10% of school-age children have this kind of memory, but it seldom lasts into adulthood.[1]

You can see, though, why a photographic memory would be so valuable. *If so much of instruction in higher education consists of testing you on how much you remember, your ability to memorize great quantities of information becomes crucial.*

The Importance of Managing Long-Term Memory

PREVIEW Much of teaching in higher education consists of lectures and reading, which require memorization for testing. "Cramming" for exams—massive memorization at the last minute—is not advisable because there is too much to learn. Memory is principally *immediate, short-term,* or *long-term.* Boosting your long-term memory is better than favoring your short-term memory because of the "forgetting curve," whereby retaining of information drops sharply after 24 hours.

How good is your memory? **Memory is defined as a mental process that entails three main operations: recording, storage, and recall.**

The main strategy at work seems to be *association*—**one idea reminds you of another.**[2] Actually, even though you may worry that you have a weak memory because you immediately forget people's names after being introduced to them at a party, it's probably just fine.

"I CRAM, THEREFORE I AM." Your mind holds a wonderful mishmash of names, addresses, telephone numbers, pictures, familiar routes, words to songs, and thousands and thousands of other facts. How did you learn them—during several hours late one night or repeatedly over a long time? The answer is obvious.

When it comes to higher education, however, many students try to study for exams by doing a great deal of the work of a semester or quarter all in one night or in a couple of days. This is the time-honored memorizing marathon known as *cramming.* **Cramming is defined as preparing hastily for an examination.**

Many students have the notion that facts can be remembered best if they're *fresh.* There is indeed something to that, as we'll discuss. But does cramming work? Certainly it beats the alternative of not studying at all.

Suppose, however, you crammed all night to memorize the lines for a character in a play. And suppose also that the next morning, instead of going to an examination room, you had to get up on a stage and recite the entire part. Could you do it? Probably not. Yet the quarter or semester's worth of material you have tried overnight to jam into your memory banks for a test may be even more comprehensive than all the lines an actor has to memorize for a play.

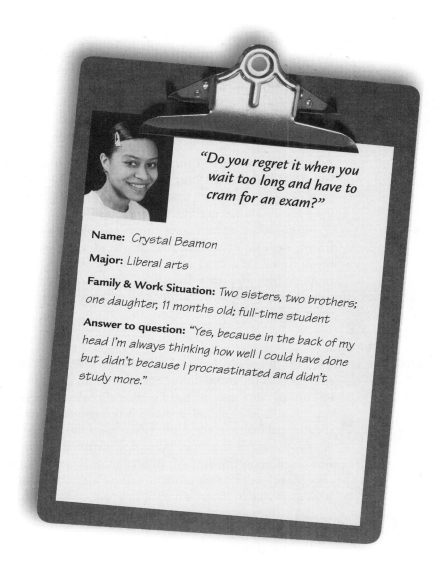

"Do you regret it when you wait too long and have to cram for an exam?"

Name: Crystal Beamon

Major: Liberal arts

Family & Work Situation: Two sisters, two brothers; one daughter, 11 months old; full-time student

Answer to question: "Yes, because in the back of my head I'm always thinking how well I could have done but didn't because I procrastinated and didn't study more."

In sum: Even if you found cramming to be a successful exam-preparation technique in high school, you should begin now to find other techniques for memorizing. In higher education, there is simply too much to learn.

TYPES OF MEMORY: IMMEDIATE, SHORT-TERM, & LONG-TERM. To use your memory truly effectively to advance your career-education goals—and your goals in life—it helps to know how it works. Memory is principally *immediate, short-term,* or *long-term.*

- **Immediate perceptual memory: Immediate perceptual memory is defined as "a reflex memory in which an impression is immediately replaced by a new one."[3]** An example is in typing. As soon as a word is typed it is forgotten.

- **Short-term memory: Short-term memory is defined by psychologists as recording seven elements for a maximum of 30 seconds.** This is about the number of elements and length of time required to look up a telephone number and dial it. Short-term memory has only limited capacity—for instance, about five to nine numbers for most people. To transfer such short-term information into your long-term memory requires reciting or other association techniques, as we'll discuss.

The details of short-term memories fade unless you rehearse them. Or unless some emotionally charged event happens at the same time.

■ **Long-term memory: *Long-term memory* entails remembering something for days, weeks, or years.** Long-term memory often requires that *some kind of change be made in your behavior* so that the information being learned makes a significant enough impression.

Remembering how to perform a musical piece, how to shoot a perfect free-throw, or how to do winning moves in chess requires *repetition*. To achieve these things, you can't just "wing it" by learning something once. You need to practice over and over. Of course, long-term memories also fade, but they do so more slowly.[4] Clearly, you need to practice as a student just as you would practice as an athlete or musician.

THE FORGETTING CURVE: FAST-FADING MEMORIES. To understand why, from the standpoint of learning in higher education, long-term memory is so much more important, consider what psychologists call the *forgetting curve*. In one famous experiment long ago, Hermann Ebbinghaus found that, in memorizing non-sense syllables, *a great deal of information is forgotten just during the first 24 hours*, then it levels out.[5] Although fortunately you need not memorize non-sense syllables, the rate of forgetting also occurs rapidly for prose and poetry. (Poetry is easier to memorize than prose because it has built-in memory cues such as rhymes.) *(See* ■ *Panel 5.1.)*

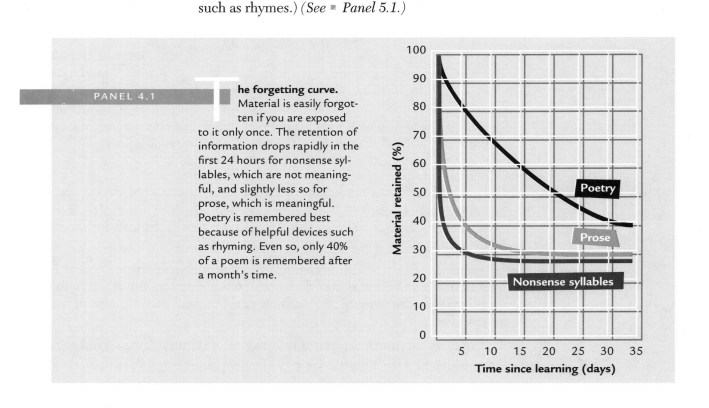

PANEL 4.1

The forgetting curve. Material is easily forgotten if you are exposed to it only once. The retention of information drops rapidly in the first 24 hours for nonsense syllables, which are not meaningful, and slightly less so for prose, which is meaningful. Poetry is remembered best because of helpful devices such as rhyming. Even so, only 40% of a poem is remembered after a month's time.

How good are people at remembering things in the normal course of events?

According to a survey from the National Institute for Development and Administration at the University of Texas, we remember only

10% of what we read

20% of what we hear

30% of what we see

50% of what we see and hear

70% of what we say

90% of what we do and say[6]

One scholar, Walter Pauk, reports a study of people who read a textbook chapter; the results showed that they forgot

46% of what they read after 1 day

79% of what they read after 14 days

81% of what they read after 28 days[7]

As for remembering what one has heard, Pauk describes an experiment in which a group of psychologists who attended a seminar forgot over 91% of what they had heard after 2 weeks.[8]

If you were tested every other day on the lectures you attended and textbooks you read, memorizing wouldn't be much of a problem. But that's not the way it usually works, of course. Ordinarily an instructor will give you an exam halfway or a third of the way into the course. There may be another exam later, followed by a final exam at the end of the course. Each time you will be held accountable for several weeks' worth of lectures and readings. On the last exam, you're usually held responsible for the entire content of the course.

Memory is also important in writing papers. If you start your research or writing and then abandon it for a couple of weeks, it will take you some time to reconnect with your thoughts when you go back to it.

How to Improve Your Memory Power

PREVIEW There are several principal strategies for converting short-term memory to long-term memory: (1) You can practice relaxation. (2) You can practice repeatedly, even overlearn material. (3) You can study a little at a time repeatedly (distributed practice) instead of cramming (massed practice). (4) You can avoid memory interference from studying similar material or being distracted. (5) You can make material personally meaningful to you. (6) You can use verbal memory aids—write out or organize information; use rhymes, phrases, and abbreviations; make up narrative stories. (7) You can use visual memory aids—make up a vivid picture or story of unusual images.

As should be clear by now, *success in career or vocational-technical education principally lies with a strategy in which you convert short-term memories into long-term memories.* Let us suggest a number of techniques for doing this.

1. RELAX & BE ATTENTIVE. You have certainly discovered that you easily recall those things that interest you—things to which you were *attentive*.

"*Attention is conscious, not reflex*," says one memory expert. "It is indispensable to the controlled recording of information."[9]

The goal of improving your memory, then, is to improve your attention, as we explain in this section. The first means for doing this is through relaxation. Anxiety interferes with memorizing, distracting your recall abilities with negative worries. When you are relaxed, your mind captures information more easily.

Thus, when you sit down to read a textbook, write notes for a lecture, or take a test, take a few seconds to *become relaxed*. Close your eyes, take a deep breath, inhale, repeat. Say to yourself, "I plan to remember." If you're still tense, repeat those words a few times.

The rule is this: *Put yourself in a relaxed frame of mind when you're planning to absorb information you will have to remember later.*

2. PRACTICE REPEATEDLY—EVEN OVERLEARN MATERIAL. How well could you play a part in a play or a movie after two readings? five readings? fifteen? Clearly, you can't just speed-read or skim the script. You have to practice actively or rehearse the material. The more you rehearse, the better you retain information. Indeed, it has been found that *overlearning*—continued study even after you think you have learned material—will help you really commit it to memory.[10] **Overlearning is defined as continued rehearsal of material after you have first appeared to have mastered it.**[11]

A good way to learn is to repeatedly test your knowledge in order to rehearse it. Some textbooks come with self-testing study guides to help you do this, but you can also make up the questions yourself or form a study group with friends to trade questions and answers.

The more you rehearse, in fact, the better you may also *understand* the material.[12] This is because, as you review, your mind begins to concentrate on the most important features, thus helping your understanding.

The rule is this: *Study or practice repeatedly to fix material firmly in mind.* You can apply this rule to your social life, too. If you meet someone new at a party, for instance, you can repeat the person's name on being introduced, then say it again to yourself; then wait a minute and say it again.

3. STUDY A LITTLE AT A TIME FREQUENTLY: DISTRIBUTED PRACTICE VERSUS MASSED PRACTICE.

Learning experts distinguish between two kinds of learning or practice techniques: *massed practice* and *distributed practice*.

- ***Massed practice:*** Massed practice is what students do when they are cramming. ***Massed practice* is putting all your studying into one long period of time**—for example, one study session of 8 hours in one day.

- ***Distributed practice:*** Distributed practice takes no more time than cramming. **With *distributed practice* you distribute the same number of hours over several days**—for example, four days of studying 2 hours a day.

Distributed practice has been found to be more effective for retaining information than mass practice, especially if the space between practice periods is reasonably long, such as 24 hours.[13] One reason is that studying something at different times links it to a wider variety of associations.[14]

The rule here is this: *Study or practice a little at a time frequently rather than a lot infrequently.* This rule suggests that you can make use of the time-spaces in your day for studying. You can look over your notes or books or flash cards while on the bus, for example, or waiting for class to start. You can mentally rehearse lists while standing in line. It's like the difference between lifting weights once for 5 hours or five sessions of 1 hour each: the first way won't train you nearly as well as the second way.

4. AVOID INTERFERENCE.

Learning some kinds of information will interfere with your ability to recall other kinds of information, especially if the subjects are similar. **Interference is the competition among related memories.** For example, if you tried to memorize the names of the bones in the human foot and then memorize the names of the bones in the hand, one memory might interfere with the other. And the more information you learn, such as lists of words, the more you may have trouble with new information on successive days, such as new lists of words.[15]

Interference can also come from other things, such as distractions from the people with whom you share your living space, background music, television, and so on. The notion of interference also suggests why you do better at recalling information when it is fresh in mind. In other words, though we don't recommend cramming for exams, we do recommend giving information a thorough last-minute review before you go into the test. A last-minute review puts the "frosting on the cake" of helping you absorb the material, but it's no substitute for studying the material earlier.

The lesson here is this: *When you're trying to memorize material, don't study anything else that is too similar too soon.* This is why it is often a good idea to study before going to sleep: there is less chance of the new information getting competition from other information.[16] It also shows why it's a good idea to study similar material for different courses on different days.[17]

5. MAKE MATERIAL MEANINGFUL TO YOU: DEPTH OF PROCESSING.

Information in memory may be stored at a superficial or at a deep level, depending on how well you understood it and how much you thought about it, according to the *depth-of-processing principle*.[18] **The *depth-of-processing principle* states that how shallowly or deeply you hold a thought depends on how much you think about it and how many associations you form with it.** The deeper the level of "processing" or thinking, the more you remember it.

This means that in memorizing something you shouldn't just mindlessly repeat the material; *you are better able to remember it when you can make it meaningful*.[19] It's important to somehow make the material your own—understand it, organize it, put it in your own words, develop emotional associations with it, link it to information you already know or events you have already experienced. For example, if you are trying to remember that business organizations have departments that perform five functions—*accounting, marketing, production, personnel management,* and *research*—you can look for relationships among them. Which departments do or do not apply to you? Which ones do your relatives work in? Indeed, one way to make material meaningful to you is to *organize* it in some way, which is why outlining your reading can be a useful tool.

To repeat, ***the rule here is this:*** *Make learning personally meaningful to you.* This is also a trick you can use in your social life. If you meet someone new at a party, you can try to remember the new name by associating it with the face of someone else with that name. (When you meet someone named Michael, remember that your uncle is named Michael too, or think of singer Michael Jackson or of basketball player Michael Jordan.)

6. USE VERBAL MEMORY AIDS. One way to make information more meaningful, and so retain it better, is to use memory aids—and the more you are able to personalize them, the more successful they will be. Psychologists call memory aids *mnemonic* ("nee-*mahn*-ik") *devices,* **tactics for making things memorable by making them distinctive.**

Some verbal devices for enhancing memory are as follows:

■ **Write out your information:** This advice may seem obvious. Still, the evidence is that if you write out a shopping list, for example, if you lose the list, you are more apt to remember the items than you would if you hadn't written them out.[20]

Clearly, this is a reason for taking notes during a lecture, quite apart from making a record: The very act of writing helps you retain information.

■ **Organize your information:** People are better able to memorize material when they can organize it. This is one reason that imposing a ranking or hierarchy, such as an outline, on lecture notes or reading notes works so well, especially when the material is difficult.[21]

■ **Use rhymes to remember important ideas:** You may have heard the spelling rule, "I before E except after C" (so that you'll be correct in spelling "receive," not "recieve"). This an example of the use of rhyme as a memory aid. Another is "Thirty days hath September, April, June, and November . . ." to remember which months have 30 rather than 31 days.

Most of the time, of course, you'll have to make up your own rhymes. It doesn't matter how silly they are. Indeed, the sillier they are, the better you may be apt to remember them.

■ **Use phrases whose first letters represent ideas you want to remember:** Probably the first thing music students learn is "Every Good Boy Does Fine" to remember the names of the lines of the treble staff: *E G B D F*. This is an example of using a phrase in which the first letter of each word is a cue to help you recall abstract words beginning with the same letter.

What kind of sentence would you make up to remember that business organizations have departments performing five functions—*A*ccounting, *M*arketing, *P*roduction, *P*ersonnel management, and *R*esearch? (Maybe it would be, "*A*ny *M*an *P*laying *P*oker is *R*ich"—this also plants a picture in your mind that will help your recall.)

■ **Use a word whose first letters represent ideas you want to remember:** To remember the five business functions above, you could switch the words around and have the nonsense word *PRAMP* (to rhyme with "ramp," then think of, say, a wheelchair ramp or a ramp with a pea rolling down it), the letters of which stand for the first letters of the five functions.

A common example of the use of this device is the name "Roy G. Biv," which students use to memorize the order of colors in the light spectrum: *r*ed, *o*range, *y*ellow, *g*reen, *b*lue, *i*ndigo, *v*iolet. Another is "Mark's Very Elegant Mother Just Sent Us Nine Puppies" for the order of the planets in our solar system in relation to the sun: *M*ercury, *V*enus, *E*arth, *M*ars, *J*upiter, *S*aturn, *U*ranus, *N*eptune, *P*luto.

■ **Make up a narrative story that associates words:** In a technique known as the **narrative story method, making up a narrative or story has been shown to help students recall unrelated lists of words by giving them meaning and linking them in a specific order.**[22]

Suppose you need to memorize the words *Rustler, Penthouse, Mountain, Sloth, Tavern, Fuzz, Gland, Antler, Pencil, Vitamin.* This is quite a mixed bag, but if you were taking a French class, you might have to memorize these words (in the foreign language). Here is the story that was constructed to help recall these unrelated words:

"A *Rustler* lived in a *Penthouse* on top of a *Mountain.* His specialty was the three-toed *Sloth.* He would take his captive animals to a *Tavern,* where he would remove *Fuzz* from their *Glands.* Unfortunately, all this exposure to sloth fuzz caused him to grow *Antlers.* So he gave up his profession and went to work in a *Pencil* factory. As a precaution he also took a lot of *Vitamin E.*"[23]

In using verbal memory tricks, then, **the rule is this:** *Make up verbal cues that are meaningful to you to represent or associate ideas.* In social situations, as when you are introduced to several people simultaneously, you can try using some of these devices. For example, "LAP" might represent Larry, Ann, and Paul.

7. USE VISUAL MEMORY AIDS.

Some psychologists think that using visual images creates a second set of cues in addition to verbal cues that can help memorization.[24] In other words, it helps if you can mentally "take photographs" of the material you are trying to retain.

There are two visual memory aids you may find useful—*a single unusual visual image,* or *a series of visual images.*

■ ***Make up a vivid, unusual picture to associate ideas:*** The stranger and more distinctive you can make your image, the more you are apt to be able to remember it.[25]

Thus, to remember the five business functions (research, accounting, marketing, personnel management, production), you might create a picture of a woman with a white laboratory coat (research) looking through a magnifying glass at a man a'counting money (accounting) while sitting in a food-market shopping cart (marketing) that is being pushed by someone wearing a letter sweater that says *Person L* (personnel) who is watching a lavish Hollywood spectacle—a production—on a movie screen (production). (If you wish, you could even draw a little sketch of this while you're trying to memorize it.)

■ ***Make up a story of vivid images to associate ideas:*** A visual trick called the **method of loci (pronounced "*loh*-sigh" and meaning "method of places") is to memorize a series of places and then use a different vivid image to associate each place with an idea or a word you want to remember.**[26]

For example, you might use buildings and objects along the route from your house to the campus, or from the parking lot to a classroom, each one associated with a specific word or idea. Again, the image associated with each location should be as distinctive as you can make it. To remember the information, you imagine yourself proceeding along this route, so that the various locations cue the various ideas. (The locations need not resemble the ideas. For example, you might associate a particular tree with a man in a white laboratory coat in its branches—research.)

In short, when using visual memory tricks, **the rule is this:** *The stranger you make the picture, the more you are apt to remember it.*

Reading for Pleasure Versus Reading for Learning

PREVIEW Reading for pleasure is different from reading for learning. With most pleasure reading you need only remember the information briefly, holding it in your short-term memory. With reading for learning, the information must be stored in your long-term memory so that you can recall it for tests. This means you must read material more than once. Accordingly, you need to treat textbooks seriously. You also need to understand what their basic features are—title page, copyright page, table of contents, preface, glossary, appendix, bibliography, and index. Finally, you need to know what "advance organizers" are for purposes of surveying material.

What are your thoughts about the whole business of reading in higher education? To get an idea, try Practical Exploration #5.1.

PRACTICAL EXPLORATION #5.1

WHAT DO YOU KNOW ABOUT THE READING PROCESS?

Perhaps you regard the reading of textbooks as a reasonably straightforward activity. Or perhaps you find the whole process dreary or mysterious or scary. Answer "Yes" or "No" depending on whether you agree or disagree with the following statements.

1. Reading makes unusual or unique demands on a reader.

    _____ Yes   _____ No

2. Reading is a form of the thinking process. You read with your brain, not your eyes.

    _____ Yes   _____ No

3. Reading is a one-step process.

    _____ Yes   _____ No

4. Effective readers constantly seek to bring meaning to the text.

    _____ Yes   _____ No

5. Many comprehension problems are not just reading problems.

    _____ Yes   _____ No

6. Good readers are sensitive to how the material they are reading is structured or organized.

    _____ Yes   _____ No

7. Speed and comprehension are independent of each other.

    _____ Yes   _____ No

■ ANSWERS

1. *False.* Reading actually does not make unusual demands on a reader. The same mental processes you use to "read" people's faces or grasp the main idea of a situation you observe are used when you read.

2. *True.* Your eyes simply transmit images to the brain. Improving your reading means improving your thinking, not practicing moving your eyes faster or in a different way.

3. *False.* Reading includes three steps: (a) preparing yourself to read (thinking about what you already know about a subject and setting purposes for reading); (b) processing information; and (c) reacting to what you read.

4. *True.* When they are not comprehending, they take steps to correct the situation.

5. *True.* If you fail to understand something you are reading, it could be because it is poorly written. More likely, however, you lack the background information needed to comprehend—you wouldn't understand it even if someone read it aloud to you. Perhaps you need to read an easier book on the same subject first.

6. *True.* Good readers know the subject matter and main idea of each paragraph and understand how each paragraph is organized (for example, sequence, listing, cause and effect, comparison and contrast, definition).

7. *False.* The more quickly you can understand something, the faster you can read it. However, "speed" without comprehension is meaningless. Reading is more than just allowing your eyes to pass over lines of print.

Maybe you already think you read pretty well. After all, you've been doing it for most of your life.

Or maybe you don't feel comfortable about reading. You prefer television to print. Or you think you get information better when someone tells it to you. Or you find English a hard language to follow.

Whatever your skills, *there are techniques to improve your reading abilities so that you can better handle subjects at the level of higher education.* Some of them we'll describe in this chapter. If you don't find what you need here (for example, you feel you need help in reading English as a second language), you can probably get assistance through your school's learning center or reading lab.

TWO TYPES OF READING. Reading is principally of two types—for pleasure and for learning:

- *For pleasure:* You can read action-adventure, romances, sports, and similar material just one time, for amusement. This is the kind of material that appears in many novels, magazines, and newspapers. You don't have to read it carefully, unless you want to.

- *For learning:* Most of the other kind of reading you do is for learning of some sort, because you *have* to understand it and perhaps retain it. For instance, you certainly have to pay close attention when you're reading a cookbook or instructions on how to fix a car.

Reading for learning is something you will have to do all your life, whether it's studying to get a driver's license or finding out how much medicine to give an infant. Indeed, what many managers and administrators are doing all day, when they read reports, letters, and memos, is reading to learn.

But here's the difference between those kinds of reading for learning and reading textbooks:

In higher education, you'll often have to read the same material more than once.

The reason, of course, is that in higher education you have to *understand and memorize* so much of what you read.

READING TO FEED YOUR LONG-TERM MEMORY. "Oh, boy," you may think. "You mean there's no way I can just read stuff once and get it the first time?"

Perhaps you can if you're the sort who can memorize the code to a bicycle or locker combination lock with just one glance. Most people, however, need more practice than that.

This has to do with the notion of short-term memory versus long-term memory. As we discussed, the retention of information drops rapidly in the first 24 hours after you've been exposed to it (the "forgetting curve"). Short-term memory is roughly anything you can't hold in mind for more than 24 hours. Long-term memory refers to information you retain for a good deal longer than 24 hours.

Some students might try to make these facts an argument for cramming— holding off until the last day before a test and then reading everything at once. However, there is no way such postponement can really be effective. Many instructors, for instance, have *cumulative* final exams. They test you not just on the new material you're supposed to have learned since the last exam. Rather, they test you on *all* the material back to the beginning of the course. If you opt for cramming, this puts you in the position of having to cram for the *whole course*. In sum: You need to do the kind of reading that will feed your long-term memory.

TREAT TEXTBOOKS SERIOUSLY. Some students regard their textbooks as troublesome or uninteresting but unfortunately necessary (and expensive) parts of their instruction. Or they think of the books as being perhaps useful but not vital (and so they try to avoid buying them).

There's a likelihood, however, that *half or more of your study time will be devoted to such books.* Thus, when you think about what your career education *is,* half of it is in your books. You need, then, to treat them as the tools of your trade (your trade is being a student)—just as you would an instruction manual if your job requires you, say, to fix motorcycles or lead a tour of Great Britain.

With that in mind, here are a few tips for extracting some benefits from your textbooks:

- *Look the text over before you take the course:* If you have any doubts about a course you're contemplating taking, take a look in the bookstore at the text-book(s) and any other reading materials that will be required for it. This way you can see what the course will cover and whether it is too advanced or too low-level in the light of your previous experience.

- *Buy your books early:* Some first-year students dawdle as long as a week or 10 days before buying some of their books. Not a good idea. The school term flies by awfully fast, and they lose the advantage of a head start. (Also, sometimes when they wait too long the books are sold out.)

- *Look the text over before the first class:* If you are familiar with the principal text before you walk into your first class, you will know what the course is going to cover and know how to use the book to help you. Taking a couple of minutes to go from front to back—from title page to index—will tell you what resources the book offers to help you study better.

BECOME FAMILIAR WITH THE BASIC FEATURES. To get a sense of what a book is like, you need to look for eight particular features in the front and back of the book. (*See ▪ Panel 5.2.*)

- *Title page:* At the front of the book, **the *title page* tells you the title, edition number (if later than the first edition), author, and publisher.** Often the title can give you a sense of the level of difficulty of the book—for example, *Introduction to Business* (introductory level) versus *Intermediate Accounting* (higher level).

- *Copyright page:* **The *copyright page* (on the back of the title page) tells you the date the book was published.** With some of the more rapidly changing fields, such as computer science, you want a book published as recently as possible.

- *Table of contents:* **The *table of contents* lists the principal headings in the book.** Sometimes a "brief contents" will list just parts and chapters, and a "detailed contents" will list other major headings as well.

- *Preface:* **The *preface* tells you the intended audience for the book, the author's purpose and approach, why the book is different from other books in the same field, and perhaps an overview of the organization.** (The preface—which may also be called "Introduction" or "To the Student"—may appear before the table of contents.)

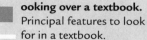

PANEL 5.2 **L**ooking over a textbook.
Principal features to look
for in a textbook.

▼ Title page

POPULATION

An Introduction to Concepts and Issues
Fifth Edition

John R. Weeks
San Diego State University

Wadsworth Publishing Company
Belmont, California
A Division of Wadsworth, Inc.

▼ Copyright page

To Deanna

Editor: Serina Beauparlant
Editorial Assistant: Marla Nowick
Production: Greg Hubit Bookworks
Print Buyer: Randy Hurst
Permissions Editor: Peggy Meehan
Copy Editor: Kathleen McCann
Manuscript Editor: Deanna Weeks
Cover: Henry Breuer
Compositor: Bi-Comp, Incorporated
Printer: Arcata Graphics Fairfield

The cover illustration shows countries in proportion to population. Adapted by the author from United Nations data.

This book is printed on *acid-free paper* that meets Environmental Protection Agency *standards for recycled paper.*

© 1992 by Wadsworth, Inc. All rights reserved. No part of this book may be reproduced, stored in a retrieval system, or transcribed, in any form or by any means, without the prior written permission of the publisher, Wadsworth Publishing Company, Belmont, California 94002.

1 2 3 4 5 6 7 8 9 10—96 95 94 93 92

Library of Congress Cataloging in Publication Data

Weeks, John Robert, 1944–
    Population : an introduction to concepts and issues / John R.
Weeks. — 5th ed.
        p. cm.
    Includes bibliographical references and index.
    ISBN 0-534-17346-2
    1. Population. I. Title.
HB871.W43 1992
304.6—dc20   92-6251
                                                CIP

▼ Table of Contents

DETAILED TABLE OF CONTENTS

PART ONE
A DEMOGRAPHIC PERSPECTIVE 1

CHAPTER 1
INTRODUCTION 3

    ESSAY: *Why Study Demography?* 5

SOURCES OF DEMOGRAPHIC DATA 6
    Population Censuses 7
    The Census of the United States 9
    Registration of Vital Events 18
    Combining the Census and Vital Statistics 21
    Sample Surveys 22
    Historical Sources 22

WHO USES POPULATION DATA? 23

WHERE CAN YOU GO FOR PUBLISHED INFORMATION? 24

SUMMARY AND CONCLUSION 25

MAIN POINTS 26

SUGGESTED READINGS 27

CHAPTER 2
AN OVERVIEW OF THE WORLD'S POPULATION 28

▼ Preface

PREFACE

Population growth in the 1950s and 1960s could have been likened to a runaway train without an engineer, veering perilously close to a collision course with shortages of food and resources. That specter was altered somewhat by the events of the 1970s, especially by a few hopeful signs of a downturn in the birth rates of several large developing nations. In the 1980s and the 1990s the imagery has changed from the collision course to something equally terrifying. We are faced with a situation analogous to an immense locomotive hurtling down the track at a speed faster than the roadbed can tolerate. The engineer is groping for the brakes, but if and when those brakes are fully applied, the train will still cover a huge distance before it comes to a halt. How much havoc will the charging locomotive of population wreak before it stops, and what condition will we be in at that point? These are two of the most important questions that face the world.

Over the years I have found that most people are either blissfully unaware of the enormous impact that population growth and change have on their lives, or else they have heard so many horror stories about impending doom that they are nearly overwhelmed whenever they think of population growth. My purpose in this book is to shake you out of your lethargy (if you are one of those types), without necessarily scaring you in the process. I will introduce you to the basic concepts of population studies and help you develop your own demographic perspective, enabling you to understand some of the most important issues confronting the world. My intention is to sharpen your perception of population growth and change, to increase your awareness of what is happening and why, and to help prepare you to cope with (and help shape) a future that will be shared with billions more people than there are today.

(continued next page)

PANEL 5.2 CONTINUED

▼ Glossary

GLOSSARY

This glossary contains words or terms that appeared in boldface type in the text. I have tried to include terms that are central to an understanding of the study of population. The chapter notation in parentheses refers to the chapter in which the term is first discussed in detail.

abortion   the expulsion of a fetus prematurely; a miscarriage—may be either induced or spontaneous (Chapter 4).

abridged life table   a life table (see definition) in which ages are grouped into categories (usually five-year age groupings) (Appendix).

accidental death   loss of life unrelated to disease of any kind but attributable to the physical, social, or economic environment (Chapter 6).

achieved characteristics   those sociodemographic characteristics such as education, occupation, income, marital status, and labor force participation, over which we do have some degree of control (Chapter 9).

age/sex pyramid   graph of the number of people in a population by age and sex (Chapter 8).

age/sex–specific death rate   the number of people of a given age and sex who died in a given year divided by the total number of people of that age and sex (Chapter 6).

age-specific fertility rate   the number of children born to women of a given age divided by the total number of women that age (Chapter 4).

age stratification   the assignment of social roles and social status on the basis of age (Chapter 11).

age structure   the distribution of people in a population by age (Chapter 8).

Agricultural Revolution   change that took place roughly 10,000 years ago when humans first began to domesticate plants and animals, thereby making it easier to settle in permanent establishments (Chapters 2 and 14).

alien   a person born in, or belonging to, another country who has not acquired citizenship by naturalization—distinguished from citizen (Chapter 7).

Alzheimer's disease   a disease involving a change in the brain's neurons, producing behavioral shifts; a major cause of senility (Chapter 11).

ambivalence   state of being caught between competing pressures and thus being uncertain about how to behave properly (Chapter 5).

amenorrhea   temporary absence or suppression of the menstrual discharge (Chapter 4).

amino acids   building blocks from which proteins are formed (Chapter 14).

anovulatory   pertaining to a menstrual cycle in which no egg is released (Chapter 4).

antinatalist   based on an ideological position that discourages childbearing (Chapter 3).

arable   describes land that is suitable for farming (Chapter 14).

ascribed characteristics   sociodemographic characteristics such as gender and race and ethnicity, with which we are born and over which we have essentially no control (Chapter 9).

average age of a population   one measure of the age distribution of a population—may be calculated as either the mean or the median (Chapter 8).

521

▼ Appendix

APPENDIX
The Life Table, Net Reproduction Rate, and Standardization

THE LIFE TABLE
  Probability of Dying
  Deaths in the Life Table
  Number of Years Lived
  Expectation of Life
  Other Applications of the Life Table

NET REPRODUCTION RATE AND MEAN LENGTH OF GENERATION

STANDARDIZATION   509

▼ Bibliography

BIBLIOGRAPHY

Abelson, P.
14 1975a "The world's disparate food supplies." Science 187: editorial.
14 1975b "Food and nutrition." Science 188 (4188):501.

Adamchak, D., A. Wilson, A. Nyanguru, and J. Hampson
11 1991 "Elderly support and intergenerational transfer in Zimbabwe: an analysis by gender, marital status, and place of residence." The Gerontologist 31:505–13.

Adelman, C.
4 1982 "Saving babies with a signature." Wall Street Journal, 28 July.

Adlakha, A., and D. Kirk
5 1974 "Vital rates in India 1961–71 estimated from 1971 census data." Population Studies 28(3):381–400.

Agassi, J., and I. C. Jarvie
8 1959 Hong Kong. London: Oxford Press.

Ahlburg, D., and M. Schapiro
16 1984 "Socioeconomic ramifications of changing cohort size: an analysis of U.S. postwar suicide rates by age and sex." Demography 21(1):97–105.

Ahonsi, B.
6 1991 "Report on the seminar on anthropological studies relevant to the sexual transmission of HIV, Sonderborg, Denmark, 1990." IUSSP Newsletter 41:79–103.

Akin, J., R. Bilsbarrow, D. Guilkey, B. Popkin, D. Benoit, P. Cantrelle, M. Garenne, and P. Levi
6 1981 "The determinants of breast-feeding in Sri Lanka." Demography 18(3):287–308.

Akpom, C., K. Akpom, and M. Davis
4 1976 "Prior sexual behavior of teenagers attending rap sessions for the first time." Family Planning Perspectives 8:203–6.

Alba, R., and J. Logan
12 1991 "Variations on two themes: racial and ethnic patterns in the attainment of suburban residence." Demography 28:431–53.

Allan, C.
16 1981 "Measuring mature markets." American Demographics 3(3):13–17.

Alonso, W., and P. Starr
1,12 1982 "The political economy of national statistics." Social Science Research Council Items 36(3):29–35.

Alsop, R.
16 1984 "Firms still struggle to devise best approach to black buyers." Wall Street Journal, 25 October.

American Demographics
16 1982 "The demographic future." The Monthly Report of International Demographics (brochure).
16 1983 "Here comes 1984." American Demographics 5(6):11.

Anderson, B., and B. Silver
16 1989 "Patterns of cohort mortality in the Soviet demographic experience." Population and Development Review 15:471–502.

Ankrah, E. M.
6 1991 "AIDS and the social side of health." Social Science and Medicine 32:967–80.

Aries, P.
8 1962 Centuries of Childhood. New York: Vintage Books.

530

▼ Index

INDEX

Abortion
  in Japan, 147
  Malthusian view of, 63
  techniques for, 111
  voluntary, 109, 112–113
Abortion rates, in world, 112
Abridged life table, 510
Abstinence, sexual, 107, 149–150
Accidental deaths, 165, 168
Accidents, 190
Achieved characteristics, 263
Acid rain, 428
Acquired immunodeficiency syndrome (AIDS)
  as cause of death, 188, 190
  as communicable disease, 164
  condom usage and, 105
  demography of, 166–167
Additives, 426
Adults
  older. See Elderly population
  young, migration of, 198–199
Africa, 420
  AIDS in, 188
  growth promoting policies in, 470–471
  growth rates, 48
  high fertility and, 125
African-Americans
  death rates of, 174–175

African-Americans (continued)
  demographic origin and, 500–501, 502
  family income of, 272–273, 281
  life chances and, 280–282
  males, in prison, 277
  residential segregation and, 365–367
  targeting, 484
Age. See also Aging; Elderly population
  differentials in mortality, 177–183
  of elderly population, 334–335
  marital status changes and, 336–338
  migration and, 198–199
  old, definition of, 326–327
  targeting by, 480–482
  unemployment rate and, 270–271
  at entry into sexual union, 94–96
Age at first marriage, 95–96, 276, 313–314
Age at menarche, 94
Age distribution, of older U. S. population, 334–335
Agency for International Development (AID), 443
Age pyramid, of immigrants in United States, 233

Age/sex pyramid, 229
Age/sex-specific death rates (ASDR), 171–172
Age/sex structure
  of city, 235
  definition of, 228, 258–259
  dynamics of, 239–258
  impact of population processes on, 232–238
Age-specific fertility rate (ASFR), 116–117
Age standardization, 116, 518–520
Age stratification, 244–245
Age structure
  crime and, 250–251
  definition of, 82–83
  impact
    on economic development, 395–396
    on population processes, 238–239
  measurement of, 228–231
  social phenomena and, 247–248
  in United States, changes induced by fertility fluctuations and, 248–249
Aging. See also Elderly population
  biological aspects of, 327–328
  future of society and, 343–346
  social aspects of, 328–331

569

- *Glossary:* In the back of the book, **the *glossary* is an alphabetical list of key terms and their definitions,** as found in the text. Quite often the same terms appear within the main body of the text in **boldface** (dark type) or *italics* (slanted type).

- *Appendix:* Also in the back of the book, **the *appendix* contains supplementary material, material of optional or specialized interest.** Examples are tables, charts, and more detailed discussion than is contained in the text. Often there is more than one appendix. Engineering or business students, for instance, will often find time-saving tables contained in appendixes.

- *Bibliography:* Appearing at the back of the book or at the end of each chapter, **the *bibliography*, or "Notes" section, lists sources or references used in writing the text.** This section can be a good resource if you're writing a term paper for the course. Scanning the textbook's bibliography may suggest some valuable places to start your research.

- *Index:* **The *index* is an alphabetically arranged list of names and subjects that appear in the text, with the page numbers on which they appear.** Sometimes there are two indexes—a name index and a subject index. The index is an *extremely* useful tool. If you're not sure a topic is discussed in the book, try looking it up in the index.

UNDERSTAND WHAT "ADVANCE ORGANIZERS" ARE. As we discuss shortly, one concept underlying many reading strategies is that of *surveying*. **A *survey* is an overview.** That is, you take a couple of minutes to look through a chapter to get an overview of it before you start reading it.

Surveying a chapter has three purposes:

1. *It gets you going:* Just beginning to read a densely packed 35-page chapter can be difficult. Surveying the material gets you going, like a slow warm-up lap around the track.

2. *It gives you some familiarity with the material:* Have you ever noticed that when you're reading on a subject with which you're familiar you read more rapidly? For example, you might read slowly about an event reported in the morning paper but read more rapidly a story about that same event in the evening paper or a different newspaper. When you survey a chapter in a textbook, you begin to make it familiar to you. Notice, then, that the survey is not a waste of time. *It enables you to read faster later.*

3. *It gives you "advance organizers" to help you organize information in your mind:* As you do your overview you pick up what are called "advance organizers." ***Advance organizers* are mental landmarks under which facts and ideas may be grouped and organized in your mind.** Thus, when you begin to read the chapter itself, you already have some advance information about it.

Textbooks provide some or all of the following *advance organizers*. It's a good idea to pay attention to these when doing a survey of a chapter.

- *Chapter table of contents:* You can find a breakdown of the headings within the chapter at the front of the book (in the table of contents). Some textbooks repeat this outline of the contents at the beginning of each chapter.

■ ***Learning objectives:*** Not all books have them, but some texts have learning objectives. ***Learning objectives*** **are topics you are expected to learn, which are listed at the beginning of each chapter.** This part usually starts out with a sentence something like this: "After you have read this chapter, you should be able to . . ." The list of objectives then follows.

For example, learning objectives in an introductory computer book might be these: "Explain what desktop publishing is" or "Discuss the principal features of word processing software."

■ ***Chapter summary:*** Many textbooks have a summary at the end of the chapter, describing key concepts of the chapter. *Be sure to read the chapter summary FIRST,* even though you probably won't understand everything in it. It will help you get an overview of the material so it will seem somewhat familiar to you later.

In this book, instead of having a summary at the end of each chapter, we have put a summary (called "PREVIEW") following every main section heading. This section-head summary describes the material you are about to read in the section.

■ ***Review or discussion questions:*** These, too, may appear at the end of the chapter. Sometimes review or discussion questions can be quite important because *they ask some of the questions that will be asked on the test.* Be sure to skim through them.

■ ***List of key terms:*** Key terms may appear in **boldface** type (dark type) or *italics* (slanted type) within the text of the chapter. Sometimes key terms also appear in a list at the end of the chapter.

■ ***Headings, subheadings, and first sentences:*** Read anything that appears as a heading; then read the first sentence following the heading.

Of course, a lot of the advance organizers that you read during the survey step are not going to make complete sense. But some of them will. And most of the material will have a familiar, hence a somewhat comforting, feeling to it when you come back to it on subsequent steps.

In the rest of this chapter, we describe a pair of reading systems devised to help students get the most out of textbooks.

The Five-Step SQ3R Reading System

PREVIEW SQ3R stands for *Survey, Question, Read, Recite, Review.* The advantage of the five-step SQ3R method is that it breaks down reading into manageable segments that require you to understand them before proceeding.

"There's a war on! We must teach them to read faster!"

Maybe that's what psychologist Francis P. Robinson was told in 1941. In any event, Robinson then set about to devise an intensified reading system for World War II military people enrolled in special courses at Ohio State University. Since then, many thousands of students have successfully used his system or some variation of it.

The reason the system is effective is that it *breaks a reading assignment down into manageable portions that require you to understand them before you move on.*

Robinson's reading system is called *the SQ3R method.* **The *SQ3R reading method* stands for five steps: Survey, Question, Read, Recite, Review.**[27] Let's see how you would apply these to the chapter of a textbook you are assigned to read.

STEP 1: S—SURVEY. As we said, a *survey* is an overview. You do a quick 1- or 2-minute overview of the entire chapter before you plunge into it. Look at the advance organizers—the chapter outline or learning objectives, if any; the chapter headings; and the summary, if any, at the end of the chapter. The point of surveying is twofold:

- **You establish relationships between the major segments:** Surveying enables you to see how the chapter segments go together. Understanding how the parts fit in with the whole helps you see how the chapter makes sense.

- **You see where you're going:** If you know where you're going, you can better organize the information as you read. This is just like reading over directions to someone's house before you get there rather than bit by bit while traveling.

Next you apply Steps 2 through 4—Question, Read, Recite—*but only to one section at a time, or to an even smaller segment.* That is, you apply the next three steps section by section, or even paragraph by paragraph, if material is difficult. You apply the last step, Step 5, Review, after you have finished the chapter.

STEP 2: Q—QUESTION. Take a look at the heading of the first section and turn it into a question in your mind. For example, if the heading (in a book about computers) is "Basic Software Tools for Work and Study," ask "What does 'Basic Software Tools' mean?" If the heading is to a subsection, do the same. For example, if the heading is "Word Processing," ask, "How does word processing work?"

Questioning has two important effects:

- **You become personally involved:** By questioning, you get actively involved in your reading. And personal involvement is one of the most fundamental ways to commit information to memory.

- ***You identify the main ideas:*** Giving the heading this kind of attention pin-points the principal ideas you are now going to read about. And it is the main ideas that are important, after all, not the supporting details.

If you are proceeding on a paragraph-by-paragraph basis, because the material is difficult (as in technical courses, such as physics), there may not be any heading that you can convert to a question. In that case, you'll need to put Step 3, Read, before Step 2: You read the paragraph, then create a question about that paragraph.

Incidentally, it's perfectly all right (indeed, even desirable) at this stage to move your lips and ask the question under your breath.

STEP 3: R—READ. *Now* you actually do the reading—but only up to the next section heading (or paragraph). Note, however, that you do not read as though you were reading a popular novel. Rather, *you read with purpose—actively searching to answer the question you posed.* If you don't seem to understand it, reread the section until you can answer the question.

What is the difference between passive and active reading? If you were reading a murder mystery *passively,* you would just run your eyes over the lines and wait, perhaps mildly curious, to see how things came out. If you were reading that mystery novel *actively,* you would constantly be trying to guess the outcome. You would be asking yourself such questions as: Who was the killer? What was that strange phone call about? What motive would she have for the

murder? What was that funny business in his background? And you would be searching for the answers.

You don't need to do that with recreational reading. Reading a textbook, however, should *always* be an active process of asking questions and searching for answers. That's why you have to take study breaks from time to time (perhaps 5 minutes every half hour, or even every 15 minutes, if the material is difficult), because this type of reading is not effortless.

In addition, especially if the segment is somewhat long, you should read (perhaps on a second reading) for another purpose:

- **You should determine whether the section asks any other questions:** The question you formulated based on the section heading may not cover all the material in the segment. Thus, as you read, you may see other questions that should be asked about the material.

- **Ask those questions and answer them:** You probably get the idea: the Question and Read steps are not completely separate steps. Rather, you are continually alternating questions and answers as you read through the segment.

Here are some examples of questions you might frame in your mind as you read a textbook:

What is the main idea of this paragraph?

What is an example that illustrates this principle?

What are the supporting facts?

Who is this person and why is he or she considered important?

What could the instructor ask me about this on the exam?

What is there about this that I don't understand?

If necessary, as you stop and think about key points, you may want to write brief notes to trigger your memory when you get to Step 5, Review.

STEP 4: R—RECITE. When you reach the end of the section, stop and look away from the page. *Recite* the answer you have just discovered for the question you formulated. You should practice this in two ways:

- **Recite the answer aloud:** When we say "aloud," I don't mean so loud that you have other students in the library looking at you. But there's nothing embarrassing about talking *subvocally* to yourself—that is, moving your tongue within your mouth while your lips move imperceptibly. When you move the muscles in your lips and mouth and throat, this vocalizing or subvocalizing helps lay down a memory trace in your mind.

We can't stress enough the importance of reciting aloud or nearly aloud. As Walter Pauk writes, "Reciting promotes concentration, forms a sound basis for understanding the next paragraph or the next chapter, provides time for the memory trace to consolidate, ensures that facts and ideas are remembered accurately, and provides immediate feedback on how you're doing."[28] Pauk also mentions experiments showing that students who read and recite learn much better than students who just read.

■ *Say the answer in your own words:* When you formulate the answer in your own words (perhaps using an example) rather than just repeating a phrase off the page, you are required to *understand* it rather than just memorize it. And when you understand it, you *do* memorize it better.

If you did not take any notes for review earlier, you may wish to at this point. The notes should not be extensive, just brief cues to jog your memory when you move to Step 5, Review.

Don't move on to the next segment until you're sure you understand this one. After all, if you don't get it now, when will you? Once you think you understand the section, move on to the next section (or paragraph) and repeat steps 2, 3, and 4.

STEP 5: R—REVIEW. When you have read all the way through the chapter (or as far as you intend to go in one study session), moving section by section in Question-Read-Recite fashion, you are ready to test how well you have mastered your key ideas. Here's how to do it:

■ **Go back over the book's headings or your notes and ask the questions again:** Repeat the questions and try to answer them without looking at the book or your notes. If you have difficulty, check your answers.

■ *Review other memory aids:* Read the chapter summary and the review questions. Then skim the chapter again, as well as your notes, refreshing your memory.

The Three-Step 3Rs Reading System

PREVIEW 3Rs stands for *Read, Record, Recite*. The three-step 3Rs method has no survey step, but it helps you retain material through reading, rereading, underlining, making questions, and self-testing.

The 3Rs reading system has three steps for mastering textbooks: Read, Record, Recite. This system was described by Walter Pauk, who says it "is perfect for students who like to move quickly into a textbook chapter, or for those who face exams with little time for intensive study."[29] In other words, if (against all advice) you have to resort to cramming, use this method.

STEP 1: READ. There is no surveying or questioning of material first, as in the SQ3R Method. Rather, you just start reading and read a section or several paragraphs. Then do as follows:

■ *Ask what you need to know:* Return to the first paragraph and ask yourself, "What do I need to know in this paragraph?"

■ *Read and reread for answers and say aloud:* Read and reread the paragraph until you can say aloud what you need to know about it.

STEP 2: RECORD. The SQ3R Method, previously discussed, says nothing about making marks or writing in the book, although you can do so if it helps. However, in Step 2 of the 3Rs Method you are *required* to mark up the book. Here's how:

■ **Underline key information:** Once you can say aloud what you need to know, you should underline the key information in the book. It's important that you *underline just the key information—terms, phrases, and sentences—*not line after line of material. This is so that when you come back to review, you will see only the essential material.

■ **Write a brief question in the margin:** After underlining, write a *brief question* in the margin that asks for the information you've underlined. *(See ■ Panel 5.3.)* Forming questions is extremely important to the 3Rs System, so you must be sure to do this.

After you finish this step for these paragraphs, proceed to the next segment or paragraphs and again Read and Record.

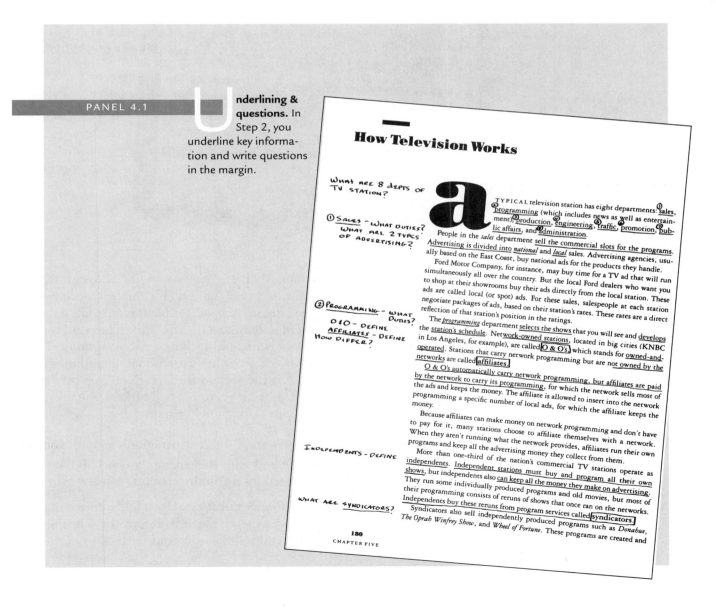

PANEL 4.1 **U**nderlining & questions. In Step 2, you underline key information and write questions in the margin.

How Television Works

WHAT ARE 8 DEPTS OF TV STATION?

A TYPICAL television station has eight departments: sales, programming (which includes news as well as entertainment), production, engineering, traffic, promotion, public affairs, and administration.

① SALES – WHAT DUTIES? WHAT ARE 2 TYPES OF ADVERTISING?

People in the *sales* department sell the commercial slots for the programs. Advertising is divided into *national* and *local* sales. Advertising agencies, usually based on the East Coast, buy national ads for the products they handle. Ford Motor Company, for instance, may buy time for a TV ad that will run simultaneously all over the country. But the local Ford dealers who want you to shop at their showrooms buy their ads directly from the local station. These ads are called local (or spot) ads. For these sales, salespeople at each station negotiate packages of ads, based on their station's rates. These rates are a direct reflection of that station's position in the ratings.

② PROGRAMMING – WHAT DUTIES?
O & O – DEFINE
AFFILIATES – DEFINE
HOW DIFFER?

The *programming* department selects the shows that you will see and develops the station's schedule. Network-owned stations, located in big cities (KNBC in Los Angeles, for example), are called O & O's which stands for *owned-and-operated*. Stations that carry network programming but are not owned by the networks are called affiliates.

O & O's automatically carry network programming, but affiliates are paid by the network to carry its programming, for which the network sells most of the ads and keeps the money. The affiliate is allowed to insert into the network programming a specific number of local ads, for which the affiliate keeps the money.

Because affiliates can make money on network programming and don't have to pay for it, many stations choose to affiliate themselves with a network. When they aren't running what the network provides, affiliates run their own programs and keep all the advertising money they collect from them.

INDEPENDENTS – DEFINE

More than one-third of the nation's commercial TV stations operate as independents. Independent stations must buy and program all their own shows, but independents also can keep all the money they make on advertising. They run some individually produced programs and old movies, but most of their programming consists of reruns of shows that once ran on the networks. Independents buy these reruns from program services called syndicators.

WHAT ARE SYNDICATORS?

Syndicators also sell independently produced programs such as *Donahue*, *The Oprah Winfrey Show*, and *Wheel of Fortune*. These programs are created and

180
CHAPTER FIVE

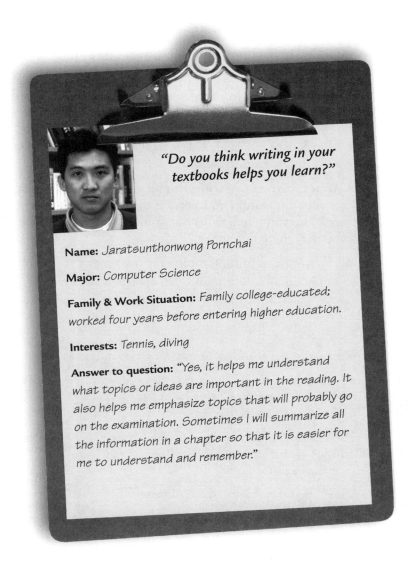

"Do you think writing in your textbooks helps you learn?"

Name: *Jaratsunthonwong Pornchai*

Major: *Computer Science*

Family & Work Situation: *Family college-educated; worked four years before entering higher education.*

Interests: *Tennis, diving*

Answer to question: *"Yes, it helps me understand what topics or ideas are important in the reading. It also helps me emphasize topics that will probably go on the examination. Sometimes I will summarize all the information in a chapter so that it is easier for me to understand and remember."*

Incidentally, a word about underlining: We've sat in libraries and watched students reading a chapter for the first time, underlining the text as they go. At the end, if they are using a green pen, say, the entire chapter looks like a mess of green paint. Obviously, this kind of underlining doesn't work. The point is to use your pen or highlighter to mark only *important* things, not *everything*. This is why it's best to read the chapter (or section) first without underlining, then reread it, doing your underlining on the second reading. (Note: Be sure to use pen or highlighter. If you use felt-tip markers or Magic Markers, the ink will go through the paper—indeed, perhaps through five or more pages.)

STEP 3: RECITE. After you've finished doing Steps 1 and 2 for the chapter, go back to the beginning. Now you will do the Recite step for the entire chapter, as follows:

■ ***Cover the page and ask yourself each question:*** Use a folded piece of paper or your hand to cover the printed page of the text except for the questions you've written in the margins. Ask yourself the questions.

■ ***Recite aloud and check your answers:*** Recite *aloud* the answer to each question. ("Aloud" can mean talking to yourself under your breath.) Then lift the paper and check your answer. If you're not clear on the answer, ask and answer again. Put a check mark in the margin if you need to come back and review again.

Continue the Recite step until you get to the end of the chapter. Then go back and look at the places where you've left a check mark.

Dealing with Special Subjects: Math, Science, Languages, & Others

PREVIEW Mathematics, science, social science, history, foreign languages, and literature may be areas of study that require more study effort than you're accustomed to. The first step is to reduce your anxiety, using positive self-talk. The second step is to devote enough time and practice to the subject. The third step is to avail yourself of such tools as flash cards or index cards; diagrams, charts, and maps; and cassette tapes.

Some students, even though they may be smart in many ways, go into a panic when confronted with a particular subject—technical subjects such as math or chemistry, or detail-oriented subjects such as foreign languages, history, or literature. The specific advice for coping here is this:

■ *Take steps to reduce your anxiety.*

■ *Devote more time and practice to your assignments, and don't fall behind.*

■ *Use special tools for information organizing and study.*

Let's consider these matters.

REDUCING YOUR ANXIETY. "Math anxiety" is very real for a number of people, as is anxiety about the other subjects mentioned. Students may believe that math requires a logical ability or special knack that they don't think they have. With science, they may think there is only one way to solve problems. With history, literature, or foreign languages, they may think they don't have a good enough memory for details.

Here's what to do:

- ***Learn your inner voice:*** The first step is to learn what your inner voice is saying, to pinpoint those inhibiting pronouncements from within. This inner voice is often the *Voice Of Judgment (VOJ)*, the internal broadcast that goes on within all of us.

    As one book describes it, the Voice Of Judgment "condemns, criticizes, attaches blame, makes fun of, puts down, assigns guilt, passes sentence on, punishes, and buries anything that's the least bit unlike a mythical norm."[30]

- ***Pinpoint your negative thoughts:*** Once you've identified the negative thoughts ("I don't think I'm smart enough to get this stuff"), speak them aloud or write them down. Usually, such thoughts come down to two matters:

    (1) *"I don't understand it now, so I never will."* If you think about this, however, you'll realize that there have been many times in the past when you haven't understood something but eventually did. After all, there *was* a time when you couldn't read, ride a bicycle, drive a car, or whatever.

    (2) *"Everybody else is better at this subject than I am."* If you do a reality check— by asking your classmates—you'll find that this just isn't so. Probably a number of people will, if they're honest, say they aren't confident about this subject.

- ***Replace your negative thoughts with positive self-talk:*** Now try to replace the VOJ and use your inner voice as a force for success. You do this by using *positive self-talk,* which can help you control your moods, turn back fear messages, and give you confidence.[31,32] **Positive self-talk consists of giving yourself positive messages.**

    The messages of positive self-talk are not mindless self-delusions. Rather they are messages such as "You can do it. You've done it well before" that correct errors and distortions in your thinking and help you develop a more accurate internal dialog.[33]

■ ***Deal with the stresses:*** The sense of unpleasantness that the anxiety-provok-
ing subject evokes may be felt in a physical way—as clammy hands, constricted
breathing, headache, or other kinds of panicky reactions. Elsewhere in the
book we describe ways to deal with stress, such as techniques of relaxation and
visualization.

For now, however, just try this: Every time you have to deal with a troublesome subject, take a slow, deep breath and slowly exhale; then repeat. Then tell
yourself, "Now I'm ready to deal with this subject calmly and methodically, taking whatever amount of time is necessary." If the anxiety begins to resurface,
repeat the slow, deep breathing twice.

DEVOTE ENOUGH TIME. Once you've dealt with the emotional barriers, then be prepared to
spend more time on the subject. It doesn't matter that it takes you longer to
learn math, physics, French, or whatever than it will some other students;
you're doing this for yourself. (The chances are, however, that a difficult subject
for you is also a difficult subject for many others.)

Spending more time on the subject involves the following:

■ ***Keep up with the assignments:*** Don't fall behind. Subjects such as math and
foreign languages are *cumulative* or *sequential* kinds of knowledge: It's difficult
to understand the later material if you don't understand the earlier material.

Thus, if you feel yourself slipping, *get help right away.* Seek assistance from
a classmate, the instructor, or a tutor. If you're worried about confiding your
anxieties to someone involved with the subject, see your academic advisor. Or
go to the campus counseling center and seek the advice of a counselor.

- **Review the previous assignment before starting the present one:** Precisely because later skills depend on having mastered earlier skills, it's a good idea to review the previous assignment. Being confident you understand yesterday's material will give you the confidence to move on to today's assignment.

- **Apply the SQ3R or 3Rs reading method:** Difficult subjects are precisely the kinds of subjects in which you need to go over things several times, constantly asking questions and marking up the text. The reading methods we described earlier in this chapter will help here.

- **Work practice problems:** Math and foreign languages require that you learn specific skills as well as information. Accordingly, you should work all practice problems that are assigned, whether math problems or language exercises. For example, you should work practice problems at the end of every section within the book and also those at the end of every chapter.

- **Take frequent breaks—and remind yourself of why you're doing this:** Needless to say, studying difficult material is a frustrating business. Go easy on yourself. If you feel you're beating your head against the wall, take frequent breaks. Study some other material for awhile.

    When you come back to your original work, remind yourself why you're studying it—for example, "I need to study chemistry because it's important to my nursing career."

- **Do lab assignments:** Some subjects require use of a laboratory. For biology or chemistry, for example, there is often a lecture portion, in which you take notes about concepts from a lecturer, and a lab portion, in which you do experiments or other hands-on tasks. *The two kinds of classes are not independent of each other:* What's learned in the lab reinforces what's learned in the lecture.

    Many other subjects in career education have labs, precisely because career and vocational-technical education is usually so practical and "hands on": auto repair, commercial art, computer-aided drafting, computer repair, electrical technology, mouldmaking, physical therapy, and so on.

USE SPECIAL TOOLS FOR STUDYING. A whole bag of tools is available for helping to organize information and make special study guides to help you learn difficult subjects. Some of these tools, such as diagrams and charts, may be especially helpful if your learning style tends to be more visual than verbal.

The tools are as follows:

- ***Flash cards or index cards:* A *flash card* is a card bearing words, numbers, or pictures that is briefly displayed as a learning aid.** A flash card may be a 3×5-inch index card that you make up yourself. Or it may be part of a set of cards that you buy in the bookstore to use to study biological terms, foreign language vocabulary, or whatever.

  If you're making up a flash card yourself, on the front write the key term, concept, or problem that you are trying to grasp; write the explanation or answer on the back. Don't forget that you can put *several* terms on one side and their answers on the reverse. For example, for a history course you might list the name of a treaty followed by such questions as "Year?" "Signers?" "Purpose?" "Consequences?" You would list the answers on the back of the card.

  Flash cards can be used for all kinds of subjects. For math or engineering, you can write a term or formula on one side and its definition, meaning, or calculations on the other. In science, you can state the theory or scientist on the front and the important principles or hypothesis associated with it or him or her on the back. For literature classes, you can write the name of a short story or poem on one side and its meaning on the other.

  When you use flash cards, you can sort them into three piles according to how well you've memorized them: (1) cards you know well; (2) cards you know but respond slowly to or are vague about; (3) cards you don't know. You'll find it's pleasing to watch the "I know" pile grow. (And if you must cram for an exam, the second and third piles are the ones to concentrate on.)

  Carry a few flash cards with you wherever you go. Then when you find yourself with a few minutes to spare you can take them out and practice answering the questions on them.

■ **Diagrams, charts, and maps:** Drawing diagrams of concepts helps reinforce learning in two ways: (a) It helps your visual sense, because you can *see* the ideas. (b) It helps your kinesthetic sense, or sense of touch, because you are actually creating something with your hand.

There are all kinds of ways to sketch out concepts and information. What follows are only a few ideas.

(a) **Study diagrams are literal representations of things from real life,** which you have rendered in your own hand. This type of artwork is especially useful in the biological and health sciences: You can draw and label the parts of a cell, the bones in the head, the arteries and veins of the circulatory system. *(See ■ Panel 5.4a.)*

(b) **Process diagrams are useful for representing the steps in a process** and thus are useful in such subjects as biology, geology, or environmental science. For example, you might sketch the process of photosynthesis, the process of global warming, or the geological formation of an ancient lake. *(See ■ Panel 5.4b.)*

(c) **Concept maps are visual diagrams of concepts.** For example, you can make a drawing of psychologist Abraham Maslow's famous hierarchy of needs, the parts of a symphony, or the five departments of a typical business organization. *(See ■ Panel 5.4c.)*

(d) **Time lines are sketches representing a particular historical development.** They are useful in memorizing historical processes, such as the buildup to the Civil War or the growth of computer technology. A time line consists of simply a vertical line with "tick marks" and labels, each indicating the year and its important event. *(See ■ Panel 5.4d.)*

(e) **Comparison charts are useful for studying several concepts and the relationships among them.** Headings are listed across the top of the page and down the left side of the page; the concepts are then briefly described in a grid in the middle of the page. For example, you might compare various religions by listing their names across the top (such as *Christianity, Buddhism, Hinduism*), the principal categories of comparison down the side (*Deity, Holy book, Principal countries*), and then the specifics within the grid. *(See ■ Panel 5.4e.)*

■ **Cassette tapes:** Elsewhere we mentioned that taping lectures can provide a kind of reinforcement, particularly if the lecturer is hard to follow (though taping is no substitute for note taking). Listening to cassette tapes is also valuable for certain specific subjects such as language study. As the core of learning a foreign language is repetition and practice, during spare moments in your day you can use a Sony Walkman, for example, to listen to tapes on which you have recorded new vocabulary terms, verb forms, and idioms.

Onward

PREVIEW   Reading is half your education.

Reading, as we said, may well constitute half your education in school or college—reading textbooks, that is. There is also reading of another sort that you will do—namely, reading your lecture notes. Thus, some of the reading skills you have learned in this chapter will apply to the previous chapter on lectures.

Diagrams, charts, & maps for reinforcement.

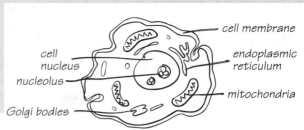

a. Study diagram—example of drawing and labeling a cell.

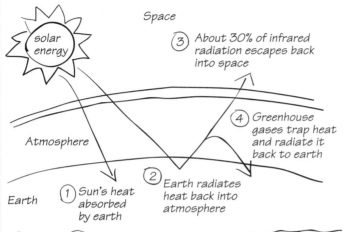

Gases: CFCs from air conditioning; CO_2 from industry, deforestation, & burning of fossil fuels; methane & nitrous oxide from cattle

b. Process diagram—example of representing steps in global warming.

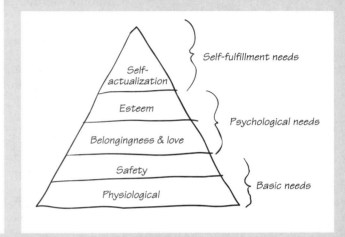

c. Concept map—example of visual diagram of concepts in Maslow's hierarchy of needs.

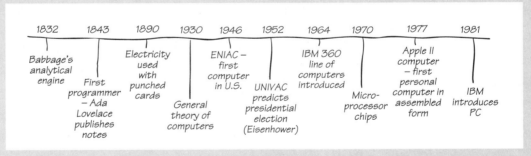

d. Time line—example of historical development of the computer.

	Hinduism	Judaism	Christianity	Islam
Principal geographic locations	India	Israel, Europe, Americas	Especially Europe & Americas; adherents worldwide	Asia, North Africa, Central Africa
Type (number of gods)	Polytheistic	Monotheistic	Monotheistic	Monotheistic
Holy book(s)	Mahabharata, Ramayana	Torah	Bible	Koran

e. Comparison chart—example of concepts of various world religions.

NOTES

1. Haber, R. N. (1979). Twenty years of haunting eidetic imagery: Where's the ghost? *Behavioral & Brain Sciences, 2,* 583–629.

2. Lapp, D. C. (1992, December). (Nearly) total recall. *Stanford Magazine,* pp. 48–51.

3. Lapp, 1992, p. 48.

4. Crovitz, H. F., & Schiffman, H. (1974). Frequency of episodic memories as a function of their age. *Bulletin of the Psychonomic Society, 4,* 517–518.

5. Ebbinghaus, H. (1913). *Memory.* New York: Teachers College. (Original work published 1885.)

6. Survey by National Institute for Development and Administration, University of Texas. Cited in Lapp, 1992.

7. Pauk, W. (1989). *How to study in college* (4th ed.). Boston: Houghton Mifflin, p. 92.

8. Pauk, 1989, p. 92.

9. Lapp, 1992, p. 49.

10. Krueger, W. C. F. (1929). The effect of overlearning on retention. *Journal of Experimental Psychology, 12,* 71–78.

11. Weiten, W., Lloyd, M. A., & Lashley, R. L. (1990). *Psychology applied to modern life: Adjustment in the 90s* (3rd ed.). Pacific Grove, CA: Brooks/Cole.

12. Bromage, B. K., & Mayer, R. E. (1986). Quantitative and qualitative effects of repetition on learning from technical text. *Journal of Educational Psychology, 78*(4), 271–278.

13. Zechmeister, E. B., & Nyberg, S. E. (1982). *Human memory: An introduction to research and theory.* Pacific Grove, CA: Brooks/Cole.

14. Kalat, J. W. (1990). *Introduction to psychology* (2nd ed.). Belmont, CA: Wadsworth, p. 295.

15. Underwood, B. J. (1957). Interference and forgetting. *Psychological Review, 64,* 49–60.

16. Fowler, M. J., Sullivan, M. J., & Ekstrand, B. R. (1973). Sleep and memory. *Science, 179,* 302–304.

17. Thorndyke, P. W., & Hayes-Roth, B. (1979). The use of schemata in the acquisition and transfer of knowledge. *Cognitive Psychology, 11,* 83–106.

18. Craik, F. I. M., & Lockhart, R. S. (1972). Levels of processing: A framework for memory research. *Journal of Verbal Learning & Verbal Behavior, 11,* 671–684.

19. Raugh, M. R., & Atkinson, R. C. (1975). A mnemonic method for learning a second-language vocabulary. *Journal of Educational Psychology, 67,* 1–16.

20. Intons-Peterson, M. J., & Fournier, J. (1986). External and internal memory aids: When and how often do we use them? *Journal of Experimental Psychology: General, 116,* 267–280.

21. Bower, G. H. (1970). Organizational factors in memory. *Cognitive Psychology, 1,* 18–46.

22. Bower, G. H., & Clark, M. C. (1969). Narrative stories as mediators of serial learning. *Psychonomic Science, 14,* 181–182.

23. Weiten, W., Lloyd, M. A., & Lashley, R. L. (1990). *Psychology applied to modern life: Adjustment in the 90s* (3rd ed.). Pacific Grove, CA: Brooks/Cole, p. 24. Adapted from Bower & Clark, 1969.

24. Paivio, A. (1986). *Mental representations: A dual coding approach.* New York: Oxford University Press.

25. McDaniel, M. A., & Einstein, G. O. (1986). Bizarre imagery as an effective memory aid: The importance of distinctiveness. *Journal of Experimental Psychology: Learning, Memory & Cognition, 12,* 54–65.

26. Crovitz, H. F. (1971). The capacity of memory loci in artificial memory. *Psychonomic Science, 24,* 187–188.

27. Robinson, F. P. (1970). *Effective study* (4th ed.). New York: Harper & Row.

28. Pauk, W. (1989). *How to study in college* (4th ed.). Boston: Houghton Mifflin, p. 181.

29. Pauk, 1989, 171.

30. Ray, M., & Myers, R. (1986). *Creativity in business.* Garden City, NY: Doubleday, p. 42.

31. Donahue, P. A. (1989). Helping adolescents with shyness: Applying the Japanese Morita therapy in shyness counseling. *International Journal for the Advancement of Counseling, 12,* 323–332.

32. Zastrow, C. (1988). What really causes psychotherapy change? *Journal of Independent Social Work, 2,* 5–16.

33. Braiker, H. B. (1989, December). The power of self-talk. *Psychology Today,* 24.

Classroom Activities: Directions to the Instructor

1. ***How's your memory?*** Ask each student to make up a list of 14 terms (not people) related to some *one* subject with which he or she is familiar. (Examples: cars, health, the campus.) For the 15th term, have them add the name of a famous person, such as a movie actor.

   Ask students to swap lists face down with someone else in the class. When everyone has someone else's list, ask them to turn the lists over and take 10 seconds (timed by you) to try to memorize the 15 terms. Then tell them to turn the piece of paper over and write as many terms as they can on the back.

   In class discussion, ask students how many terms they were able to remember in 10 seconds. Did everyone recall the name of the movie star or other person on this list? What does this experiment say about people's ability to remember new terms they will need to memorize in a subject they've never studied before?

2. ***Finding examples of the seven memorizing strategies.*** Divide the class into seven small groups with nearly equal numbers of people in each group. Each group should take *one* of the seven memorizing strategies discussed: relaxation, overlearning, distributed practice, avoiding interference, depth of processing, verbal memory aids, visual memory aids.

Have every member of each group generate as many ways as possible to illustrate how to use the particular learning strategy. Later have each group share their best examples with others in the class. Invite discussion or other examples from the class.

3. ***What facts about reading are a surprise to you?*** Have students look at the answers they checked for Practical Exploration #5.1, "What Do You Know About the Reading Process?" In a group-discussion situation, ask them to consider which statements they were surprised to find the opposite of what they thought. Why did they think this? Does anything they've learned change their previous attitudes toward reading?

4. ***What do you think of textbooks?*** If half a student's education is in the textbooks, it's important to determine what his or her attitude is toward them. Ask students to list on a piece of paper three negative things that come to mind about textbooks, then list three positive things.

In class discussion, ask students to describe some of their feelings about textbooks, then consider some of the following questions. If you didn't have textbooks, what would you use instead to get the same information? Would it be more efficient? How much money in a quarter or semester do you spend on recreation and how does that compare to the money spent on books? When you're learning something for work or personal interest, what kinds of sources of information do you use?

5. ***Practicing the SQ3R method.*** This activity may be performed all in class, or partly out of class and partly in class. Divide the class into small groups of four. Then have each group divide into two teams (Team A and Team B) of two people each.

Select two earlier chapters from this book on which the teams are to practice the SQ3R. One team practices the method on one chapter, the other team on the other chapter.

Next, instruct the members of Team A, without looking at the text, to respond to a quiz on the chapter by Team B. Then reverse the roles. Afterward, have the class discuss how well the method worked for them. Ask them what they would do differently.

The Examined Life:
Student Assignments for Journal Entries

JOURNAL ENTRY #5.1: WHAT ARE THE TOUGHEST SUBJECTS TO MEMORIZE? What subjects do you worry you will have the most trouble memorizing? Why is this? What tricks can you use from this chapter to change that?

_____

_____

_____

_____

_____

_____

_____

JOURNAL ENTRY #5.2: WHAT HAVE YOU HAD TO MEMORIZE IN THE PAST? In what areas have you had to do extensive memorizing in the past? Examples might be music, athletic moves or plays, dramatic roles, or skills in conjunction with a job. What motivated you to remember? How did you go about the memorization?

_____

_____

_____

_____

_____

_____

_____

JOURNAL ENTRY #5.3: ARE THERE SOME "SPEED READING" TRICKS YOU DON'T KNOW ABOUT? Be honest: After reading this chapter, do you still think there is some shortcut for absorbing all the volumes of material you'll need to read? Is there some "speed reading" trick that hasn't been mentioned? How do you think this might work? Why don't you do some research to find out what this might be?

_____

_____

_____

_____

_____

_____

_____

JOURNAL ENTRY #5.4: WHAT HAVE YOU LEARNED FROM READING IN THE PAST? No doubt at some point in the past you had to learn a lot of material from reading. (Examples: Material necessary to do your job, religious studies, government paperwork.) What was it? How did you go about absorbing it?

_____

_____

_____

_____

_____

_____

_____

JOURNAL ENTRY #5.5: HOW COULD YOUR PRESENT READING SYSTEM BE IMPROVED? What is your present system for marking up and reviewing textbooks? What mistakes have you made (for example, doing too much underlining or reading only once)? What specific techniques could you use to correct these mistakes?

_____

_____

_____

_____

_____

_____

_____

JOURNAL ENTRY #5.6: HOW DO YOU STUDY ESPECIALLY CHALLENGING MATERIAL? Do you do anything different in studying more challenging material—such as mathematics, foreign language, or history—than you do in studying "regular" subject matter? How is your approach different? What does your Voice Of Judgment tell you about your inadequacies in handling certain types of material (such as math, for example)?

_____

_____

_____

_____

_____

_____

_____

EXAMS

Taking tests with confidence & integrity

IN THIS CHAPTER: Often people assume they have to be really smart to pull A's on tests. Actually, it's not so much a matter of one's basic intelligence as it is other things, which this chapter shows you how to do.

- **Test preparation:** You learn how to become as ready as possible for tests.
- **Anxiety management:** You learn how to cope with anxiety during tests.
- **Test-taking strategy:** You learn a six-step approach to test taking.
- **Coping with various types of tests:** You learn to deal with different types of tests, both objective and subjective.
- **Academic integrity:** You learn the types of academic dishonesty, their consequences, and their alternatives.

■ You are not a victim. You are here by choice. You hope higher education will help you be your best and lead to your ultimate happiness.

Perhaps this is the outlook to have the next time you're facing exams. Remember why you're seeking a career or vocational-technical education in the first place. You are not a prisoner. You're here because you expect school to enhance your life. Exams may not be fun, but they are simply part of the experience of higher education—an experience you have *chosen* to undertake.

Thus, perhaps the attitude to take is "Because I'm here in school voluntarily and want it to enhance my life, I might as well become good at one of the important things school requires—taking tests."

Taking Charge of Taking Tests

PREVIEW Becoming expert at tests means psyching out the instructor, learning how to prepare for specific tests, knowing what to bring to the test, and getting off to the right start in the testing room.

Taking charge of taking tests has four components:

■ Psyching out the instructor

■ Learning how to prepare for specific tests

■ Knowing what to bring to the test

■ Getting started right in the testing room

Let's consider these.

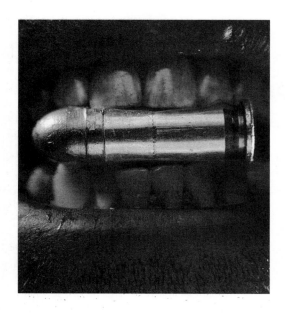

PSYCHING OUT THE INSTRUCTOR. Instructors not only have different ways of teaching but they also have different ways of testing. Some will test mainly on the textbook, some mainly on the lecture material, some on both. It's up to you to be a *detective*—to figure out the instructor's method of operating and to plan accordingly. Actually, this is usually not hard to do. The aim of an instructor, after all, is not to trick you with questions on the test but to find out what you know.

Following are some ways to get a jump on the test by finding out what the instructor will do:

- **Look at the course syllabus:** The syllabus handed out by the instructor on the first class day is often a good guide for test preparation. As mentioned earlier, the *syllabus* ("*sill*-uh-buss") is a course outline or guide that tells you what readings are required, when assignments are due, and when examinations are scheduled.

    This basic road map to the course may tell you a lot about testing. It may tell you what kind of weight testing has in the overall course grade. It may indicate whether low grades may be made up. It may describe what happens if the test is missed. It may indicate whether the lowest grade on a series of tests is dropped when the instructor is determining your average grade for all tests.

- **Look at instructor handouts:** Frequently instructors hand out potential essay questions in advance, or they prepare study guides. Handouts show what the instructor thinks is important. Like an actor learning your lines, you can use such material to practice taking the test. This can not only help prepare you by giving you sample material but it may also help reduce that kind of stage-fright-like condition known as test anxiety.

- **Ask about the specific test:** Particularly before the first test in a class, when you don't know what's coming, make a point to ask the instructor (in class or during office hours) the following:

    1. How long will the test last?

    2. How much will the test results count toward the course grade?

    3. What types of questions will appear on the test? Will they be true-false? multiple-choice? fill-in? essay? all of these? Different questions require different test-taking strategies, as we'll show in a few pages.

        It's also fair to ask the instructor what is most important for you to know. Some instructors may emphasize certain subject areas over others, or they may emphasize the lecture or laboratory material over the textbook.

- **Ask to see copies of old tests:** Some instructors may be willing to provide you with copies of old tests or with the kinds of questions they are inclined to ask. Don't feel it's somehow impolite or incorrect to ask to see old tests. (Sometimes old tests are on file in the library.)

- **Consult students who have taken the course:** If you know others who have already taken the course, ask them about their test experiences. See whether you can get them to share old exams so you can look at the kinds of questions the instructor likes to ask. Indeed, an item from an old test may even reappear on the one you will take, as there are only so many ways to ask a question. (But don't count on it.)

- **In lectures watch for "bell phrases" and "bell cues":** As we mentioned in Chapter 4, all lecturers use phrases and gestures that should "ring a bell" and signal importance.

   A *bell phrase* is a verbal indicator of an important point. Examples of bell phrases are: "Three major types . . . ," "The most important result is . . . ," and "You should remember . . ."

   A *bell cue* is an action or gesture that indicates important points. Examples are pointing, as to something on the board or a chart; underlining or making a check mark by key words; and holding up fingers.

LEARNING HOW TO PREPARE FOR A SPECIFIC TEST.

In addition to the foregoing suggestions, there are strategies to employ when preparing for a specific test.

- **Rehearse study-guide or other practice questions:** Some textbook publishers produce a separate study guide, which you can buy at the campus bookstore. **A *study guide* is a booklet that contains practice questions, along with their answers, covering material in the textbook.** Available for a fairly modest price, the study guide represents an excellent investment because *it gives you a trial run at various types of questions similar to those that are apt to be asked on the test.*

   A variation on the paper-and-print study guide now being seen more frequently is the electronic study guide. **An *electronic study guide* is a floppy disk that students can use on their personal computer (IBM-style or Apple Macintosh) to rehearse practice questions and check their answers.**

   Some textbooks also have practice questions at the ends of the chapters, with answers to some or all of them in the back of the book.

- **Form study groups with other students to generate practice questions:** Forming study groups with some of your classmates is an excellent way to generate possible test questions—especially essay questions—and quiz one another on answers. Moreover, study groups offer reinforcement and inject a bit of social life into your studying.

- **Develop self-study practice sessions:** Besides study guides and study groups, a useful preparation strategy is simply to have your own periodic practice sessions. Every week, set aside time to go through your notes and textbooks and compose practice tests. Specifically, do these:

1. Practice reviewing material that is emphasized. This includes anything your instructor has pointed out as being significant. Practice defining key terms, the terms presented in *italics* or **boldface** in the text. This is an area, incidentally, where you can make excellent use of flash cards. **A *flash card* is a card bearing words, numbers, or pictures that is briefly displayed as a learning aid.**

2. Practice reviewing material that is enumerated, presented in numbered lists (such as the 13 vitamins or warning signs for heart disease). Enumerations often provide the basis for essay and multiple-choice questions.

3. Practice answering questions on material on which there are a good many pages of coverage, either in text or lecture notes. Answer questions you've written in the text margins and in your lecture notes. Formulate essay questions and outline answers.

- ***Study throughout the course:*** The best way to prepare for exams is *not* to play catch-up. Elsewhere (Chapter 5) we mentioned the idea of overlearning. *Overlearning* is continuing to review material repeatedly, even after you appear to have absorbed it. Of course, to overlearn, you must first have learned. This means keeping up with lecture notes and textbooks, rereading them so that you really get to know the material. Space your studying rather than cramming; it is *repetition* that will move information into your long-term memory bank.

- ***Review the evening and morning before the test:*** The night before a test, spend the evening reviewing your notes. Then go to bed without interfering with the material you have absorbed (as by watching television). Get plenty of rest—there will be no need to stay up cramming if you've followed the suggestions of this book. The next morning, get up early and review your notes again.

KNOW WHAT TO BRING TO THE TEST. Asking to borrow a pencil or pen from the instructor on exam day because you forgot to bring one will not get you off to a good start. It makes you feel and look as though you're not exactly in charge. Thus, be sure to bring some sharpened pencils (#2 if the tests are machine scored) or pens (preferably blue or black ink; no red, a color instructors often use for grading).

Besides pencils or pens, other items you should bring are

- ***A watch:*** If the examination room has no clock, you'll need a watch to be able to budget your time during the test.

- ***Blue book or paper and paper clips:*** Some instructors will hand out "blue books" for examinations or require that you bring some along. (They're usually for sale in the campus bookstore.) Otherwise, bring some paper to write on and some paper clips (or small stapler) to attach pages together.

- ***Calculator, dictionary, formulas, or other aids:*** Some instructors allow you to bring items to assist test taking. Be sure to give yourself The Extra Edge by availing yourself of these learning aids if they're permitted!

In math, business, and science courses, you may be allowed to have a calculator.

In foreign language or literature courses, you may be permitted access to a dictionary.

In some math, statistics, business, engineering, and science courses, instructors may allow you to jot down formulas on index cards and bring them to the test.

GETTING STARTED RIGHT IN THE TESTING ROOM. It's important to extend the feeling of "taking charge" to the environment of the testing room. Here's how:

- ***Arrive on time:*** Have you ever been sitting in an exam room and watched some fellow students arrive late, perhaps having overslept? You have to feel sorry for them. They're clearly starting at a great disadvantage, and their faces show it.

   Arrive early. Or if arriving early makes you nervous, because it means listening to other students talk about the test, then arrive on time.

- ***Find a good test-taking spot:*** Find a spot where you won't be distracted. Sitting near the front of the room is good, where you won't see a lot of other people. Or sitting in your normal spot may make you feel comfortable.

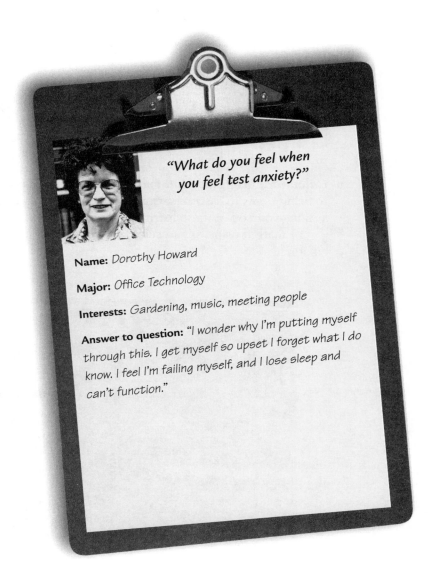

"What do you feel when you feel test anxiety?"

Name: Dorothy Howard

Major: Office Technology

Interests: Gardening, music, meeting people

Answer to question: *"I wonder why I'm putting myself through this. I get myself so upset I forget what I do know. I feel I'm failing myself, and I lose sleep and can't function."*

How to Cope with Test Anxiety in the Classroom

PREVIEW Five short-term strategies exist for coping with test anxiety in the classroom. (1) Press fists against your closed eyes and squint. (2) Drop your head forward and slowly roll it left and right. (3) Alternately tense your muscles, then let go. (4) Concentrate on breathing slowly in and out. (5) Try positive self-talk.

Dry mouth. Rapid breathing. Quickened pulse. Taut muscles. Sweating. Nausea. Headache. These are just some of the *physical* symptoms—which we well recall ourselves—associated with test anxiety.

Then there are the *mental* aspects—panic, mental blocks, foreboding, dread. "You're going to freeze up," the inner Voice Of Judgment says. "You *know* you're going to flunk!"

Test anxiety consists of thoughts and worries (the mental component) and feelings and sensations (the physical component) of stress linked to test taking. Test anxiety has much in common with other kinds of *performance anxiety*—the stresses associated with first dates, public speaking, job interviews, pre-game nervousness, stage fright, and the like.

Anxiety is an indicator of the importance we attach to an event and of our concern that we will not succeed. Thus, anxiety is *normal* under these circumstances. In fact, a certain amount of anxiety can actually be *helpful*. As you've probably noticed in other kinds of challenges (games, for example), some anxiety makes you focus your attention and get yourself "up" to perform. The problem lies in the kind of test anxiety that hinders your performance. What can be done about it?

The best recipe for alleviating feelings of panic is to be prepared. If you've reviewed the material often enough, you can have butterflies in your stomach and still feel confident that you'll pull through. Beyond that, there are various techniques for coping with stress (such as relaxation training and visualization, which we describe in Chapter 10).

Five techniques for handling test anxiety in the classroom are the following.

1. PRESS FISTS AGAINST YOUR CLOSED EYES & SQUINT. This exercise will give you a moment to blank out tensions and distractions. Here's how it works (best not to try this if you wear contact lenses):

Press your fists against your closed eyes.

Squint or tightly close your eyes at the same time.

After a few seconds, take your hands away and open your eyes.

2. DROP YOUR HEAD FORWARD & SLOWLY ROLL IT LEFT & RIGHT. Do the following exercise five times:

Drop your head forward on your chest.

Roll it slowly over to your left shoulder, then slowly over to your right shoulder.

3. ALTERNATELY TENSE YOUR MUSCLES & THEN LET GO. If a particular part of your body, such as your shoulders, is tense, try this tense-and-relax activity. The effect is to make you aware of the relaxed feeling after you have released the tension.

Take a deep breath and hold it.

Make the muscles in the tense place even more tense.

Hold tightly for a few seconds.

Then let out your breath and release the tension.

You can do this for other parts of your body (chest, neck, and so on) or for all parts simultaneously.

4. CONCENTRATE ON BREATHING SLOWLY IN & OUT. This activity will calm some of the physical sensations in your body. Do this for 2 to 5 minutes.

Focus your mind on your breathing.

Breathe slowly through your nose.

Deeply and slowly inhale, filling your lungs.

Then slowly exhale through your mouth.

Avoid taking short breaths.

Once your breathing is calm and regular, you can concentrate on the test.

5. TRY POSITIVE SELF-TALK. When the Voice Of Judgment within you says "You're going to flunk!" make an effort to replace this and other negative thoughts with positive ones. Say to yourself: "Nonsense! I studied enough, so I know I'll be okay." See Practical Exploration #6.1.

PRACTICAL EXPLORATION #6.1

NEGATIVE THOUGHTS & POSITIVE THOUGHTS

What kinds of negative thoughts do you have during tests? Pretend you are sitting in an examination room. Listen to what your inner voice (the Voice Of Judgment) is saying, and write down the thoughts below. *Examples:*

"My mind is a blank; I can't remember anything!"

"I'm going to flunk, and my life will be ruined!"

"Everyone else is leaving early; they're smarter than I am!"

1. _____

   _____

   _____

2. _____

   _____

   _____

3. _____

   _____

   _____

Now try to replace these negative thoughts with positive thoughts, using positive self-talk. Write your responses below. *Examples:*

"Breathe easy, and you'll start to remember some things. If not, come back to the question later."

"Even if you flunk, you'll survive. But don't get distracted. Just concentrate on each step of the test."

"Leaving early doesn't mean they're smarter, maybe the reverse. Just focus on the test, not other students."

1. _____

   _____

   _____

4. _____

   _____

   _____

2. _____

   _____

   _____

   _____

3. _____

   _____

   _____

   _____

4. _____

   _____

   _____

   _____

The Six-Step Examination Approach

PREVIEW The six-step examination approach consists of the following: (1) Unload. (2) Review subjective questions. (3) Do objective questions. (4) Do subjective questions. (5) Do questions left undone. (6) Proofread.

Once you have settled your nerves with some of the exercises described in the previous section, you need to apply a strategy for taking the test itself. The six-step system discussed here has three purposes. First, it is a very efficient method for tackling a test. Second, it helps you stave off panic because it gives you a plan to follow. Third, it helps you build confidence.

Here are the six steps:

1. Unload on the back of the test.

2. Review, but don't answer, the subjective questions.

3. Answer the objective questions.

4. Answer the subjective questions.

5. Answer questions left undone.

6. Proofread the examination.

STEP 1: UNLOAD ON THE BACK OF THE TEST. The first thing you should do after getting the test from your instructor is to *put your name on it.* (You'd be surprised how many students simply forget to sign their examination sheet, baffling the instructor and delaying posting of the final grade.)

After signing it, *without looking at any of the questions,* flip the examination sheet over and simply *unload.* **Unloading means taking 2 to 3 minutes to jot down on the back of the exam sheet any key words, concepts, and ideas that are in your mind.** These are things you think might be on the test. They may also be things you feel a bit shaky about—that is, things you've only recently studied and need to get down on paper while you still have them in mind.

Unloading is important for two reasons:

- *It relieves anxiety:* Just "blowing out" all the information pent up in you at the outset of the test can be extremely useful in helping overcome test anxiety.

- *It helps prevent forgetting:* One term or one idea can be like a string attached to a whole train of ideas that make up an entire essay. Unloading may well produce a key term or idea that leads to a string that you can pull on later in the test.

There is nothing illegal or unethical about unloading. It is not cheating so long as the things you unload are the product of your own brain and not cribbed from somewhere.

STEP 2: REVIEW, BUT DON'T ANSWER, THE SUBJECTIVE QUESTIONS. After unloading, flip the test over. Skip over any objective questions (true-false, multiple-choice) and go to the subjective questions. **Subjective questions are those that generally require long answers,** such as essay-type questions or those requiring lists as answers. Examples of such questions are these:

Describe the principal methods of mouldmaking.

List the four operations of a computer system.

Compare and contrast the main schools of psychology.

You should also take 2 to 3 minutes to do a form of unloading: Write *key words* in the margins next to each question. These key words will serve as a rough outline when you start answering. Don't, however, immediately begin writing answers to the subjective questions (unless these are the only kinds of questions on the exam). Rather, proceed next to the objective questions on the test.

STEP 3: ANSWER THE OBJECTIVE QUESTIONS. *Objective questions* **are those that are true-false, multiple-choice, matching, and fill-in.** There's a good reason for answering these objective questions before answering any subjective questions: *the very process of answering may supply you with extra details for helping you answer your subjective questions.* It may also help you answer a subjective question that you didn't know when you reviewed it in Step 2.

This method of operating shows how you can use the test as a tool. That is, your recognition of the answer to an objective question may help you recall other material that you will use later in the test.

Answer the objective questions as quickly as you can. Don't spend any time on questions you're not sure of. Rather, circle or star them and return to them later.

STEP 4: ANSWER THE SUBJECTIVE QUESTIONS. When grading the test, instructors often assign more importance to some subjective questions than to others. That is, they will judge the answer to one question to be worth, say, 30% of the test grade and another to be worth 10%. Quite often the point values may be mentioned on the examination sheet. If they are not, raise your hand and ask the instructor or test giver. It's your right as a student to know.

To make efficient use of your time, do the following:

- *Read the directions!* This is obvious advice, and it applies to all types of test questions. However, because subjective questions usually have more point values than objective questions do, you want to be sure you don't misunderstand them.

- *EITHER answer the easiest first . . .:* Answer the *easiest* subjective questions first.

- *. . . OR answer the highest-value questions first:* Alternatively, answer the subjective questions with *the greatest point values* first.

■
STEP 5: ANSWER QUESTIONS LEFT UNDONE. By this point you will have answered the easiest questions or the ones that you have most knowledge about. As you get toward the end of the test period, now is your chance to go back and try answering the questions you left undone—those you circled or starred.

A word about guessing: *Unless the directions say otherwise,* often an *unanswered* question will count off just as much as an *incorrectly answered* question, especially on objective questions. Thus, *unless the instructor or test says there's a penalty for guessing,* you might as well take a guess.

■
STEP 6: PROOFREAD THE EXAMINATION. If you get through all your questions before the end of the examination period, it's tempting to hand in your test and walk out early. For one thing, you'll be dying to find relief from the pressure cooker. Second, you may think it somehow looks as if you're smarter if you're one of the first to leave. (However, it's not so. Often it's the ones who don't know, and who have given up, who leave early.)

The best strategy, however, is this: *If you have any time left, use it.* By staying you give yourself The Extra Edge that the early leavers don't. During this remaining time, look over the test and *proofread* it. Correct any misspellings. Reread any questions to make sure you have fully understood them and responded to them correctly; make any changes necessary to your answers.

Mastering Objective Questions

PREVIEW   Different strategies may be employed for the different types of objective questions—for true-false, multiple-choice, matching, or fill-in-the-blank questions.

As mentioned, *objective questions* are true-false, multiple-choice, matching, or fill-in-the blank questions. Objective questions can often be machine scored. Such questions are called "objective" because, for the instructor who is doing the grading, there is no need for interpretation or "judgment calls." By contrast, with "subjective," essay-type questions, the grader has some leeway in how to judge the worth of the answer.

Here are three general strategies to apply to objective questions:[1]

■ ***Guess, unless there's a penalty:*** With objective questions, *never leave an answer blank* unless the instructor or test says there's a penalty for guessing. *Note:* Some instructors have grading systems for objective tests that penalize guessing. (For example, a correct answer may count +1, a nonresponse –1, and a wrong answer –2.) Thus, be sure you know the ground rules before you guess.

■ ***If a penalty exists, guess after eliminating half the choices:*** If the instructor does take points off for guessing, take a guess anyway when you can eliminate half or more of the options—for example, two out of four choices on a multiple-choice test.

■ ***Allow second thoughts, if you've prepared:*** Answer objective questions reasonably quickly, and make a check mark for any answer that you're unsure about. You may decide to change the answer when you do a final survey, based on information suggested to you by later items on the test.

   "Contrary to the popular advice about never changing answers, *it can be to your advantage to change answers,*" say educators Tim Walter and Al Siebert (the emphasis is theirs, not ours). "The research evidence shows that when students have prepared well for an examination, the number of students who gain by changing answers is significantly greater than the number of students who lose by changing answers."[2]

   The key here is "prepared well." If you've studied well for the test, your second thought may be more likely to be correct.

HANDLING TRUE-FALSE QUESTIONS. ***True-false questions* are statements that you must indicate are either "true" or "false."** With such items, you have a 50% chance of getting each one right just by guessing. Thus, instructors may try to put in statements that seem true but on close reading actually are not.

Here are some strategies for handling true-false questions:

■ ***Don't waste a lot of time:*** Go through the true-false items as quickly as you can. Don't spend time agonizing over those you don't know; they usually aren't worth a lot of points compared to other parts of the test. Moreover, later questions may jog your memory in a way that suggests the correct answers.

■ ***Be aware that more answers are apt to be true than false:*** True-false tests generally contain more true answers than false ones. Thus, mark a statement true unless you know for sure it is false.

■ ***Be aware that longer statements tend to be true:*** Statements that are longer and provide a lot of information *tend* to be true, though not always so. Read the statement carefully, however, to be sure no part of it is false.

■ ***Read carefully to see that every part is true:*** For the answer to be true, every part of the statement must be true. That is, a statement is false if *any part of it* is false. (Example: "The original Thirteen Colonies included Massachusetts, Virginia, and Illinois" is a false statement because the last state was not an original colony, though the first two were.)

- **Look for qualifier words:** Qualifier words include the following: *all, none, always, never, everyone, no one, invariably, rarely, often, usually, generally, sometimes, most.* Two suggestions to follow are these:

  1. Statements that use *absolute* qualifier words such as "always" or "never" are usually false. (Example: "It's always dry in Nevada" is false because it does rain there sometimes.)

  2. Statements that use *moderating* qualifier words such as "usually" or "often" tend to be true more often than not. (Example: "It's generally dry in Nevada" is true.)

HANDLING MULTIPLE-CHOICE QUESTIONS. *Multiple-choice questions* **allow you to pick an answer from several options offered,** generally between three and five choices. The question itself is called the *stem*. The choices of answers are called the *options*. Incorrect options are known as *distractors* because their purpose is to distract you from choosing the correct option. Usually only one option is correct, but check the test directions (or ask the instructor) to learn whether more than one answer is allowed.

There are two kinds of strategies to apply to multiple-choice questions—*thinking strategies* and *guessing strategies*. Here are some *thinking strategies*:

- **Answer the question in your head first:** Read the question and try to frame an answer in your mind before looking at the answer options. This will help you avoid being confused by "distractor" options.

- **Eliminate incorrect answers first:** Read *all* the options, as sometimes two may be similar, with only one being correct. (Beware of trick answers that are only partly correct.) Eliminate those options you know are incorrect. Then choose the correct answer from those remaining.

- **Return to questions that are difficult:** Mark those questions that are difficult and return to them later if time permits. Spending time mulling over multiple-choice questions may not pay off in the points the instructor allows per question. Moreover, later questions in the test may trigger a line of thought that may help you with answers when you come back.

- **Try out each option independently with the question:** If you're having trouble sorting out the options, try reading the question and just the first option together. Then try the question and the second option together. And so on. By taking each one at a time, you may be able to make a better determination.

- **Be careful about "All of the above" or "None of the above":** The options "All of the above" or "None of the above" are often the correct choices. However, you have to examine the alternatives carefully. Make sure that *all* of the other options apply before checking "All of the above." Make sure *no one* other option is correct before marking "None of the above."

- **Look for opposite choices:** If two choices are opposite in meaning, one is probably correct. Try to eliminate other choices, then concentrate on which of these two opposite options is correct.

Here are some *guessing strategies* for multiple-choice questions:

- **Guess, if there's no penalty:** Unless the instructor has indicated he or she will take points off for incorrect answers, you might as well guess, if you don't know the answer.

- **Choose between similar-sounding options:** If two options have similar words or similar-sounding words, choose one of them.

- **If options are numbers, pick in the middle:** If the alternative options indicated consist of numbers, high and low numbers tend to be distractors. Thus, you might try guessing at one of the middle numbers.

- **Consider that the first option is often not correct:** Many instructors think you should have to read through at least one incorrect answer before you come to the correct answer. Thus, when you're having to guess, consider that there's a high probability that the first option will be incorrect.

- **Pick a familiar term over an unfamiliar one:** An answer that contains an unfamiliar term is apt to be a distractor, although many students tend to assume otherwise. If you're having to make a guess, try picking an option with a familiar term.

As we said with the true-false questions, when you go back and review your answers, don't be afraid to change your mind, if you realize that you could have made a better choice. The idea that you should always stick with your first choice is simply a myth.

HANDLING MATCHING QUESTIONS. *Matching questions* **require you to associate items from one list with items from a second list.** For example, on a history test you might be asked to associate eight famous political figures listed in Column A with the time period in which each one lived, as listed in Column B.

Strategies for handling matching questions are as follows:

- *Ask if items can be used more than once:* With most matching-questions tests, each item in one column has its unique match in the other column. However, it's possible that items can be used for more than one match. That is, an item in Column B may fit several items in Column A. If you're not sure, ask the instructor.

- *Read all choices before answering, then do the easy matchings first:* Before making your choices, read all options in both columns. Then work the easy items first. Matching the easier items first may help you match the tougher ones later by a process of elimination.

  If you may use an item only once, cross off each item as you use it. (If items can be used more than once, put a check mark next to the ones you have used, rather than crossing them out.)

  Put a question mark next to the matchings you're not sure about. If time permits, you can go back later and take another look at them.

HANDLING FILL-IN-THE-BLANK QUESTIONS. Also known as *sentence-completion questions,* *fill-in-the-blank questions* **require you to fill in an answer from memory or to choose from options offered in a list.** Often the answers are names, definitions, locations, amounts, or short descriptions. Frequently there are clues contained within the incomplete sentence that will help you with your answer.

Strategies for working fill-in-the-blank tests are as follows:

- *Read the question to determine what kind of answer is needed:* Reading the question carefully will tell you what kind of fact is needed: a key term? a date? a name? a definition? By focusing on the question, you may be able to trigger an association from your memory bank.

- *Make sure the answer fits grammatically and logically:* Be sure that subject and verb, plurals, numbers, and so on, are used grammatically and logically. For example, if the statement says "a ____," don't put in "hour" and if it says "an ____," don't put in "minute." "A hour" and "*An* minute" are not grammatical.

  As we've suggested with the other types of objective questions, you should put a star or question mark beside those items you're not sure about. Later material on the test may prompt your memory when you come back to review them.

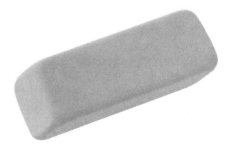

Mastering Written Examinations: Short & Long Essays

PREVIEW Two types of written examinations are short-answer essay and long-answer essay. The strategy for the short-answer essay is to determine the amount of detail needed, depending on time available, point value, and your knowledge. The strategy for the long-answer essay is to meet the standards for relevance, completeness, accuracy, organization, logic, and clarity. This means reading the directions, looking for guiding words; determining choice of essay question; brainstorming ideas and making an outline of your position, supporting details, and summary; writing the three parts of the essay; making sure the essay is clear; and watching your time.

Written examinations generally require you to write essays, either short or long. Both types of essays may be on the same exam.

- *Short-answer essay:* **A** *short-answer essay* **may be a brief one-word or one-sentence answer to a short-answer question, a one- or two-paragraph essay, or a list or diagram.** Usually you are asked to write a response to just one question.

- *Long-answer essay:* **A** *long-answer essay* **generally requires three or more paragraphs to answer.** You may be required to answer one question or several questions, all in the same essay.

Let's consider strategies for both of these.

HANDLING THE SHORT-ANSWER ESSAY. Frequently tests contain questions that require only a short answer—from a single word to two or three paragraphs. Examples:

State the name of a particular theory. *(Might be a one- or two-word answer.)*

Define a certain term. *(Could be done in a sentence.)*

List the basic steps in a process. *(Could be several words or sentences or a list.)*

Describe a particular scientific study. *(Might require a paragraph.)*

Identify and describe three causes of a particular event. *(Might be done in two or three paragraphs.)*

Your strategy here is to provide the instructor with enough information (but not an excessive amount) to show that you understand the answer—whether it's a list, some brief sentences, or a few paragraphs.

How much detail should you provide? This is sometimes difficult to determine. After all, the answer to "Identify and describe three causes of heart disease" could run to several pages. To decide how much detail is appropriate, you need to make a judgment based on three factors:

- *Time available:* How much time do you have for other questions on the exam? You may need to allow for an upcoming long essay question, for example.

- *Point value:* What is the relative weight (number of points) that the instructor assigns to short-answer questions compared with other questions?

- *Your knowledge:* How much do you know about the topic? The instructor might mark you down if you volunteer information that is erroneous.

In general, it's best to write down just the minimum you think necessary. If you're in doubt, write out a response to one short-answer question, then take it up to the instructor and ask if it's long enough.

■ HANDLING THE LONG-ANSWER ESSAY.

The long-answer essay (and to some extent the short-answer essay) is sometimes considered a *subjective* test. This notion would seem to imply there are no "objective" facts and that it's up to the grader to determine how good your answer is. Actually, there usually *are* objective facts, and the instructor looks for them in your answer.

What strategy should you follow on a long-answer question? According to one clinical psychologist and instructor of first-year seminar courses, research shows that instructors award the greatest number of points when an essay answer meets the following six standards:[3]

1. **Relevance:** The answer sticks to the question. That is, the facts and points set down are relevant to the question.

2. **Completeness:** The question is answered completely.

3. **Accuracy:** The information given is factually correct.

4. **Organization:** The answer is organized well.

5. **Logic:** The answer shows that the writer can think and reason effectively.

6. **Clarity:** Thoughts are expressed clearly.

Basically, then, two things are important in answering essay questions: First, *you need to know your facts.* Second, *you need to present them well.*

Let us now proceed to outline a strategy for answering long-answer essay questions.

■ *Read the directions!* This instruction is important for *all* test questions, of course. However, it is especially important here because of the amount of time you're required to invest in responding to long-answer essay questions and the high point values attached to them.

In failing to read the directions carefully, students may answer only one question when three have been asked. Or they may answer three when only one has been asked (thereby depriving themselves of time to respond adequately to later test questions). Or they may go off on a tangent with an answer that earns no credit. We don't know how many times we've written in the margin of a test, "Nice response, but it misses the point. Did you read the directions?"

Reading the directions will help you stay on the topic, thereby helping you to meet Standard #1 above—making the answer *relevant.*

■ *Look for guiding words in the directions:* When you read the directions, look for guiding words—key task words such as *discuss, define,* or *compare*—which may guide your answer. **Guiding words are common words that instruct you in the task you are to accomplish in your essay-question answer.**

Common guiding words are *analyze, compare, contrast, criticize, define, describe, discuss, enumerate, explain, evaluate, illustrate, interpret, outline, prove, relate, state, summarize,* and *trace.* A list of guiding words and their definitions appears in the accompanying box. *(See ■ Panel 6.1.)*

Guiding words. These key words appear in essay-question directions as part of the examination vocabulary. As you read the instructions, circle or underline such words so that you will be sure to focus your answer.

When an examination states . . .	You should . . .
Analyze	Explain the major parts or process of something.
Apply	Show function in a specific context.
Compare	Show similarities.
Contrast	Show differences.
Criticize (Critique) (Evaluate) (Examine)	Present your view (positive or negative) of something, giving supporting evidence for your position.
Define	Give the meaning of a word or expression. (Giving an example often helps.)
Demonstrate	Show function.
Describe	Present major characteristics.
Differentiate	Distinguish between two (or more) things.
Discuss (Review)	Give a general presentation of the question. (Give examples or details to support the main points.)
Enumerate	Present all the items in a series, as on a numbered list or outline.
Experiment	Try different solutions to find the right one.
Explain	Show how and why; clarify something.
Formulate	Devise a rule workable in other situations; put together new parts in several ways.
Identify	Label or explain.
Illustrate	Present examples of something.
Interpret	Explain the meaning of one thing in the context of another.
Justify	Give reasons why; argue in support of a position.
Organize	Put together ideas in an orderly pattern.
Outline	Present main points and essential details.
Perform (Solve) (Calculate)	Work through the steps of a problem.
Propose	Suggest a new idea of your own for consideration.
Restate	Express the original meaning of something in new words.
Revise	Put together items in new order.
Sketch (Diagram)	Outline; draw picture or graph.
Summarize	Present core ideas.
Trace	Present a sequence; start at one point and go backward or forward in order of events.
Translate	Convert from one system to another.

Some examples:

Identify the parts of the cell.	[On a drawing of a cell, label the nucleus, cytoplasm, cell membrane, etc.]
Define seasonal affective disorder.	[Give the meaning of the term—for example, "Condition in which people become seriously depressed in winter and normal or slightly manic in summer."]

As you read the directions, *circle or underline the guiding words* so that you know exactly what is required of you. This will help you achieve Standards #2 and #3—making your answer *complete* and *accurate*.

Often, for instance, an instructor will ask students to "compare and contrast" two ideas. However, some students will show only the similarities ("compare") and not the differences ("contrast"), thus answering only half the question and getting only half the points. Circling guiding words will help you avoid such oversights.

■ ***If you have a choice of essay questions, read them all:*** Some tests will allow you to choose which of, say, two or three essay questions you want to answer. In order to take your best shot, read *all* such questions, circling the guiding words. Then pick the essay question you think you can answer best.

■ ***Brainstorm ideas:*** Now it's time to go to work—by doing some brainstorming and then making an outline. It's best to make your notes on a separate sheet of scratch paper. (If you use a part of the exam-questions sheet or blue book, be sure to cross them out afterward. You don't want to confuse the grader and have your notes figured into your point values—unless you're attaching the outline because you've run out of writing time.)

Here's how to proceed:

1. Do a little brainstorming. **Brainstorming means jotting down all the ideas that come to mind** in response to the directions in the question. Just blow out as many ideas as you can that seem to be pertinent. Do this for a minute or two. It will help ensure that you haven't left anything out—helping you to achieve Standard #2, *completeness*.

2. Next read through your notes and *underline the important ideas.* These will become the basis for your outline and your essay.

■ ***Make an outline of your prospective answer:*** At this point you may feel yourself under extreme pressure to simply begin writing. However, by taking another minute to make an outline you will help achieve Standard #4—your answer will be *organized.*

Many students have found that a certain formula for an outline seems to help them organize their thoughts and touch on the main points of the answer. The outline formula consists of three parts—Your Position, Supporting Details, and Summary. (*See* ■ *Panel 6.2.*)

Part 1, *Your Position*, states your position or viewpoint in response to the question being asked. It says what you are going to write about.

Part 2, *Supporting Details*, lists the supporting evidence for your position. These might be three or more facts. In your outline, jot down key words that represent these facts.

Part 3, *Summary*, restates your position. It may include an additional supporting "mini-fact."

One reason for making an outline is that *if you run out of time and can't finish, you can attach the outline to your test answer and get partial credit.*

■ ***Do Part 1, Your Position, by rewriting or restating the test question, stating your position, and listing the evidence:*** Now begin writing Part 1 of the essay, Your Position. If you follow the formula for the first paragraph that we

PANEL 6.2

PANEL 6.2

Outline of the parts of a long-answer essay. The answer consists of three parts: (1) Your Position, (2) Supporting Details, and (3) Summary. This is the response you might make to a question in a criminal justice course.

The essay question:
CRITICIZE OR DEFEND THE PROPOSITION THAT CAPITAL PUNISHMENT BENEFITS SOCIETY.

Possible outline for answer:

Part 1, Your Position: State your position in response to essay question.

1. Doesn't benefit.

Part 2, Supporting Details: List keywords representing 3 or so facts supporting your position.

2. Why not:
   a. Doesn't deter murders (FBI stats—compare states)
   b. Innocent executed (names)
   c. C.P. applied more to poor than rich (names)

Part 3, Summary: Restate your position; include supporting "mini-fact."

3. C.P. not mark of civilized society. Canada, England, Japan lower murder rate, no C.P.

describe, you will show your instructor that you are achieving Standard #5—your answer is *logical*.

1. In the first sentence, include part of the examination question in your answer (without using the exact same words the instructor used). This will help you overcome inertia or anxiety and get going.

2. Next state the position or point of view you will take.

3. Then list, in sentence form, the facts you will discuss as evidence to support your position, starting with the strongest points in order to make a good impression.

Your first paragraph might read as shown in the accompanying example. (*See* ■ *Panel 6.3.*)

PANEL 6.3

Example of a first paragraph for a **long-answer essay.** The first sentence restates the examination question or direction. The second sentence states the position you will take. The third, fourth, and fifth sentences list the facts you will discuss as evidence to support your position.

The essay question or direction:

CRITICIZE OR DEFEND THE PROPOSITION THAT CAPITAL PUNISHMENT BENEFITS SOCIETY.

The first paragraph of your long-answer essay:

Whether capital punishment actually benefits society has long been a controversial issue in the United States.

[This first sentence somewhat restates the test question.]

I will argue that in the long run it does not.

[This second sentence states your position.]

As evidence, I offer the following supporting facts: First, capital punishment has not been found to deter future murders. Second, some innocent prisoners have been executed by mistake. Third, capital punishment is applied disproportionately to poor people.

[These last three sentences list the supporting facts for your position, which you will develop in subsequent paragraphs.]

Let us consider these three facts . . .

[This is a transition sentence. You will now develop each of the three facts into a full paragraph.]

PANEL 6.4

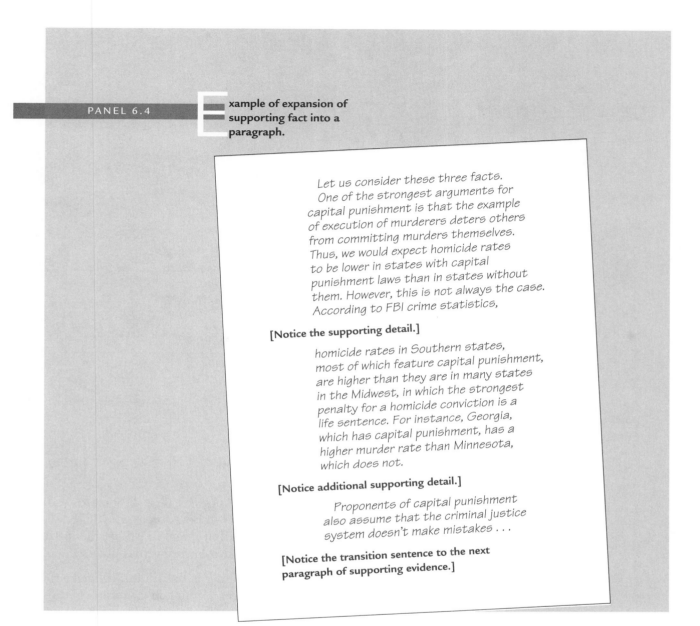

Example of expansion of supporting fact into a paragraph.

Let us consider these three facts.
One of the strongest arguments for capital punishment is that the example of execution of murderers deters others from committing murders themselves. Thus, we would expect homicide rates to be lower in states with capital punishment laws than in states without them. However, this is not always the case. According to FBI crime statistics,

[Notice the supporting detail.]

homicide rates in Southern states, most of which feature capital punishment, are higher than they are in many states in the Midwest, in which the strongest penalty for a homicide conviction is a life sentence. For instance, Georgia, which has capital punishment, has a higher murder rate than Minnesota, which does not.

[Notice additional supporting detail.]

Proponents of capital punishment also assume that the criminal justice system doesn't make mistakes . . .

[Notice the transition sentence to the next paragraph of supporting evidence.]

- **Do Part 2, Supporting Details, by expanding each fact into a paragraph:** Now you take the supporting facts you stated in sentence form in the first paragraph and address them separately. Take each fact and expand it into a full paragraph with supporting details. *(See ▪ Panel 6.4.)* Use transitional sentences to connect the supporting details so that the reader can follow the progress of your discussion.

- **Do Part 3, Summary, by writing a paragraph summarizing your position and adding a supporting mini-fact:** The conclusion is basically a summary paragraph in which you simply restate your position. If you have an additional supporting mini-fact (or a supporting detail you've forgotten until now), this can "punch up" your ending a bit and bring your essay to a dramatic close. *(See ▪ Panel 6.5.)*

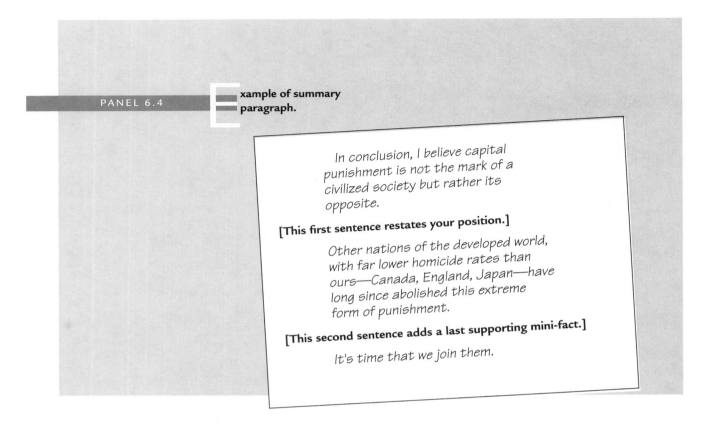

PANEL 6.4 **E**xample of summary paragraph.

> In conclusion, I believe capital punishment is not the mark of a civilized society but rather its opposite.
>
> [This first sentence restates your position.]
>
> Other nations of the developed world, with far lower homicide rates than ours—Canada, England, Japan—have long since abolished this extreme form of punishment.
>
> [This second sentence adds a last supporting mini-fact.]
>
> It's time that we join them.

■ *As you write your essay, make sure it's clear:* Here are some tips to help you achieve Standard #6—*clarity*.

1. *Write legibly,* using a pen rather than a pencil (which is difficult to read) and writing neatly rather than using a frantic scrawl. Because, as we said, grading of essay questions is somewhat subjective, you don't want to irritate the instructor by making your answer hard to read and risking lowering your points.

2. *Write on one side of the paper only.* Writing on both sides will make the ink show through. Writing on one side also leaves you the opposite side of the page as a place to write an insert later in case you've forgotten something.

3. *Leave generous space between paragraphs and in the margin.* Leaving space gives you an opportunity to add material later in such a way that you don't have to cram it in and make it hard to read.

4. *Proofread.* If you have time, go back over your answer and check for grammar, spelling, and legibility so as to boost the clarity of your effort.

■ *Watch your time:* Throughout the test you should keep track of your time, periodically checking to see how much time you have left. Answer the easy questions first, to build confidence, but after that give more time to questions that are worth more points.

As students we used to think test taking was often a matter of luck or having some sort of inherited smarts. However, you can see from the foregoing discussion and examples that it's pretty much a *learned* skill. And there's no question you're capable of learning it.

The Important Matter of Academic Integrity

PREVIEW Academic integrity or honesty is very important. Types of dishonesty include the following: (1) Cheating, or using unauthorized help. (2) Plagiarism, or presenting someone else's ideas as your own. (3) Fakery, or inventing material. (4) Lying, by omission or commission. People will commit such dishonest behaviors for several reasons: (1) They think what they're doing is a "white lie that won't hurt anyone." (2) They are in a crisis and are desperate. (3) They think "everyone does it." You can determine whether behavior is ethical by looking at yourself in the mirror, asking what your parents or friends would say, or asking whether you could defend the behavior in court. Penalties for dishonesty in higher education could be a failing grade, suspension, or expulsion. Alternatives to cheating are (1) being prepared or (2) negotiating with the instructor.

At some point in this book we need to consider the matter of academic integrity or honesty. This is as good a place as any, as one of the areas where problems arise is cheating on tests.

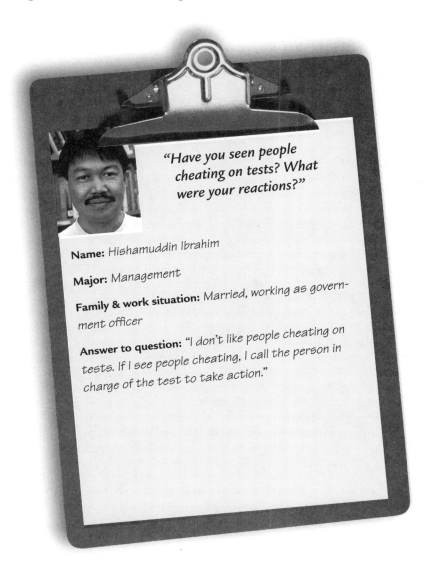

"Have you seen people cheating on tests? What were your reactions?"

Name: Hishamuddin Ibrahim

Major: Management

Family & work situation: Married, working as government officer

Answer to question: "I don't like people cheating on tests. If I see people cheating, I call the person in charge of the test to take action."

There are all kinds of ways to be less than honest in higher education: use crib sheets for tests, exchange signals with other test takers, give instructors false reasons for being late ("I was ill"; "I had car problems"), plagiarize term papers (pass off others' material as your own), buy "canned" term papers already prepared by commercial firms—the devices are endless.

A good place to examine your values is in the area of academic honesty. To get a sense of some of the areas you may encounter, take a look at Practical Exploration #6.2.

PRACTICAL EXPLORATION #6.2

HOW WOULD YOU RESPOND TO CHALLENGES TO HONESTY?

College can throw you into situations that pose basic ethical conflicts. To see how you might fare, answer the following "Yes" or "No":

1. If I were in a classroom taking a final exam and saw two *friends* exchanging secret signals about the answers, I would do the following:

   a. Tell them afterward that I was ticked off because I'd studied hard and they hadn't, and their cheating might affect my grade.

   ❑ Yes ❑ No

   b. Probably say nothing to them.

   ❑ Yes ❑ No

   c. Report them in an unsigned (anonymous) note to the instructor.

   ❑ Yes ❑ No

   d. Complain personally to the instructor.

   ❑ Yes ❑ No

2. If I saw two students who were *unknown* to me exchanging secret signals in a test situation, I would do the following:

   a. Do nothing about it, although I might be contemptuous of them or even upset.

   ❑ Yes ❑ No

   b. Report them in an unsigned (anonymous) note to the instructor, identifying their location in the classroom and what I saw.

   ❑ Yes ❑ No

   c. Complain personally to the instructor.

   ❑ Yes ❑ No

3. I wouldn't cheat on a test myself, but I would not turn in a friend who cheated.

   ❑ Yes ❑ No

4. Lying about why I am late with a paper or missed a class is just a "white lie" that harms no one.

   ❑ Yes ❑ No

5. Higher education (and the world) is so competitive that sometimes you have to bend the rules just to survive.

   ❑ Yes ❑ No

6. So many people cheat. Cheating is wrong only if you get caught.

   ❑ Yes ❑ No

7. If you don't cheat, you're just an honest loser in a world where other people are getting ahead by taking shortcuts.

   ❑ Yes ❑ No

8. I try to be honest most of the time, but sometimes I get in a jam for time and am forced to cheat.

   ❑ Yes ❑ No

9. There's nothing wrong with buying a term paper written by someone else and passing it off as my own.

   ❑ Yes ❑ No

10. If instructors look the other way or don't seem to be concerned about cheating, then I'd be a fool not to take advantage of the system and cheat.

    ❑ Yes ❑ No

■ MEANING OF THE RESULTS

See the discussion in the text.

TYPES OF ACADEMIC DISHONESTY. Academic dishonesty is of several principal types—cheating, plagiarism, fakery, and lying:

- ■ ***Cheating: Cheating* is using unauthorized help to complete a test, practice exercise, or project.** This can mean writing crib notes of critical dates and names for a history test on one's shirt cuff or under the bill of a baseball cap. It can mean arranging a signal with other test takers to exchange answers. It can mean stealing a look at someone else's exam booklet or of a copy of the test before it is given out. It can mean copying someone else's laboratory notes, or field project notes, or computer project.

- ■ ***Plagiarism: Plagiarism* means presenting another person's ideas as your own.** For example, some students, having no opinions of their own about, say, a novel they've been assigned to write a report about in English, may try to pass off the comments of a literary critic as their own ideas. (If you can't come up with any ideas of your own but you simply *agree* with the critic's ideas, that's okay. Only be sure to *cite* the critic.)

- ■ ***Fakery: Fakery* is when a person makes up or fabricates something.** Inventing data for a science experiment, for example, would be fakery.

- ■ ***Lying: Lying* is simply misrepresentation of the facts. Lying may be by omission or commission.**

    In lying by *omission,* crucial facts are simply left out. For example, a student might explain a late paper with "I had computer problems," when what she really means is that the person whose computer she often borrows had to use it.

    In lying by *commission,* facts are simply changed. For example, a student might say his paper was late "because I was sick," when in fact he was just partying.

    The most outrageous—and risky—form of lying is passing off work as your own on which you have expended very little or no effort—for example, a term paper bought from a commercial firm or recycled from a former student in the course.

WHY DO PEOPLE LIE OR CHEAT? According to Sissela Bok, professor of ethics at Brandeis University and author of the book *Lying,* people lie or cheat for one of three principal reasons:[4]

- *Just a little white lie:* People say to themselves they're just telling a little white lie. "It doesn't hurt anybody," they say, "so who cares?" Often, however, the lie *does* hurt somebody. In a course in which students are graded on a curve, for example, the honest term-paper writers who gave up their weekends to meet a course deadline may be hurt by the person who stayed up partying, then lied about being sick when handing in the paper late.

- *Desperation:* People may feel obliged to cheat because of a crisis. To save face with themselves they may say, "I don't usually do this, but here I really have to do it." This is the rationalization of students handing in a phony research paper bought from a term-paper factory because they didn't allow themselves enough time to research and write the paper themselves.

- *"Everyone does it":* This is a very common excuse. As one graduate student at the Massachusetts Institute of Technology said, commenting on a 1991 cheating scandal attributed to extreme academic pressures, students see cheating take place and "they feel they have to. People get used to it, even though they know it's not right."[5]

  People who cheat in higher education, suggests University of Southern California psychology professor Chaytor Mason, are those "who don't think they're smart enough to make it by themselves. One of the greatest threats people feel is being considered unacceptable or stupid."[6]

  Many people who cheat, then, are probably less concerned with looking like a crook than with looking like a schnook. And that certainly shows *their* values. Clearly, this dilemma can be avoided by developing adequate study skills and scheduling enough time for studying.

IMAGINING YOU'RE FOUND OUT. If cheating seems to have been widespread in some places, ethics appear to be making a comeback. According to Michael Josephson, head of the Los Angeles-based Joseph and Edna Josephson Institute for the Advancement of Ethics, studies show that "90% of adults say they want to be considered ethical."[7] According to an executive for The Roper Organization, polls show that students in higher education are deeply concerned with "the moral and ethical standards in our country."[8] Thus, the place for ethics and morality starts with you.

If you have any doubt about the ethical question of something you're doing, you might put yourself through a few paces recommended by a crisis-management expert for business people who are worried about whether they are committing fraud:[9]

- *The Smell Test:* Can you look yourself in the eye and tell yourself that the position you have taken or the act you are about to undertake is okay? Or does the situation have a bad smell to it? If it does, start over.

- *The What-Would-Your-Parents-Say Test:* This is far more demanding. Could you explain to your parents (or family) the basis for the action you are considering? If they are apt to give you a raised eyebrow, abandon the idea. (You might

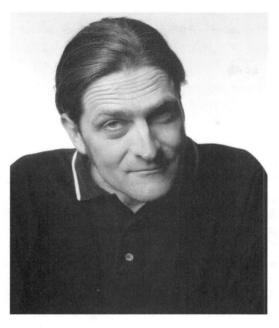

actually have to deal with your parents or family, of course, if you were found to be cheating and were expelled from school.)

- ***The Deposition Test:*** A deposition is testimony taken under oath by lawyers. Could you swear in court that the activity you are doing is right? Or if a future employer or graduate or professional school asked if your grades were satisfactory, could you show them a transcript of your courses containing no Fs—the automatic failing grade given students caught cheating?

THE PENALTIES FOR CHEATING. No matter how much you might be able to rationalize cheating to yourself or to anyone else, ignorance of the consequences is not an excuse. Most schools spell out the rules somewhere against cheating or plagiarizing. These may be embodied in student codes handed out to new students at the beginning of the year. In many courses, instructors frequently give students a handout at the first class that states, "If reasonable evidence exists that indicates you have cheated, you will receive a failing grade."

In general, the penalties for cheating are as follows:

- ***Failing grade:*** You might get a failing grade on the test, the course, or both. This is the slap-on-the-wrist punishment. Actually, it's usually automatic with a cheating or plagiarism offense and is given out *in addition to* other penalties.

    Of course, if you think you might fail the course anyway, you might be inclined to think, "Why not take the chance and cheat?" The reason not to do it is the *additional penalties,* which could vitally affect your future—as well as your feelings about yourself.

- ***Suspension:* Suspension means you are told you cannot return to school for a given period of time,** usually a semester or quarter or a year.

- ***Expulsion: Expulsion* means you are kicked out of school permanently;** you are not allowed to return. This penalty is especially bad because it could make it very difficult to transfer to another school.

ALTERNATIVES TO CHEATING: PREPARATION & NEGOTIATION. Some students cheat routinely, but most do so only once, probably because they are desperate.[10] Here are some suggestions on how to avoid cheating at all:

- *Be prepared:* Some pretty obvious advice is simply: Be prepared. Preparation usually is a matter of developing your time-management and study skills. When you overcome bad habits such as procrastination or spending too much time on nonacademic things, you probably won't even have to think of cheating. Getting the assistance of a tutor may also help.

- *Negotiate with the instructor for more time:* So your instructor is an intimidating figure? You assume he or she won't listen to an explanation of your situation? As instructors ourselves, we understand how it's possible to fall behind and we're always open to a reasonable explanation from our students.

  Note that there may be other times in your life when you'll have to explain nervously to some authority figure why something you were responsible for didn't work out. Explaining to an instructor the reason you need more time to study for a test or to write a paper is simply practice for those other occasions. It's possible you could push back the deadline a couple of days, which may be all you need. Or you might need to take an "Incomplete" in the course, which would allow you to make up the work the following term. (Some schools, however, allow "Incompletes" only for medical reasons.)

  Of course, it's possible the instructor may deny your request, but at least you made the effort. If that's the case, grit your teeth, pull an all-nighter, do the best you can in the short time you have, and make a resolution never to put yourself in this bind again. Learning from experience is the first step toward change.

  But don't cheat. That could really mess up your future. And it certainly reflects poorly on the values you would like to think you hold.

Onward

PREVIEW If you still have high levels of anxiety about testing, you can try other stress-busting techniques.

If, after reading this chapter, you get into a testing situation and find that your anxiety is still much too high, don't give up hope. One way to deal with such tensions is with relaxation training, as we discuss in Chapter 10, using creative visualization and similar methods. Another strategy that is effective in alleviating anxiety-producing situations is systematic desensitization. This consists of replacing your anxiety with relaxation. Visit the counseling department of your school; one of the counselors may be able to show you how to use such techniques.

This was an important chapter because it showed you valuable techniques for being successful on tests. It also asked you to take a hard look at matters of academic honesty and how they relate to your core values.

NOTES

1. Walter, T., & Siebert, A. (1990). *Student success* (5th ed.). Fort Worth, TX: Holt, Rinehart and Winston, pp. 96–97.

2. Walter & Siebert, 1990.

3. Starke, M. C. (1993). *Strategies for college success* (2nd ed.). Englewood Cliffs, NJ: Prentice Hall, p. 82.

4. Bok, S. Cited in Venant, E. (1992, January 7). A nation of cheaters. *San Francisco Chronicle,* p. D3; reprinted from *Los Angeles Times.*

5. Dobrzeniecki, A. Quoted in Butler, D. (1991, March 2). 73 MIT students guilty of cheating. *Boston Globe,* p. 25.

6. Mason, C. Quoted in Venant, 1992, p. D4.

7. Josephson, M. Quoted in: Venant, 1992, p. D3.

8. Himmelfarb, S. (1992, June 1). Graduates feel anxious, not just about jobs [letter]. *New York Times,* p. A14.

9. Woodell, M. L. (1991, November 24). Fraud? Imagine you're in the spotlight. *New York Times,* sec. 3, p. 11.

10. Tetzeli, R. (1991, July 1). Business students cheat most. *Fortune,* pp. 14–15.

Classroom Activities: Directions to the Instructor

1. ***Walking in your instructor's shoes: preparing for an exam.*** This activity requires each student to have a copy of the text plus his or her lecture notes from this course. Divide the class into small groups of three to five people.

   Ask each group to generate four possible long-answer essay questions (those requiring three or more paragraphs, asking for comparison/contrast and the like) that might be asked on the next test. Suggest that students use the kinds of tips described in this chapter to "walk in the instructor's shoes" and psych out what kinds of questions might be asked.

   Ask students in each group to share with the larger class the questions they developed. Have them explain the reasoning behind their choices.

2. ***What kinds of negative thoughts do you have during tests?*** Have students look at their responses to Practical Exploration #6.1, "Negative Thoughts & Positive Thoughts." Or have them, along with others in a small group, write down a list of negative thoughts that they sometimes have during test situations. Ask students also to describe the circumstances that generate such negative thoughts.

   Next ask students to generate a list of positive thoughts to replace the negative thoughts. Have them share their responses and conclusions with the class.

3. ***Applying exam strategies.*** Ask students to take a few minutes to look through Chapter 5 (on memorizing and reading) and write out five examination-style questions. There should be *one example each* of true-false, multiple-choice, matching, fill-in, and subjective (essay) questions.

   Now have students group in teams of five and exchange all their questions (25 in all) with a second team. Each team should work through all the 25 questions it receives, applying the techniques learned in this chapter to solve them.

   Later, students may share their strategies with the rest of the class.

4. ***How would you respond to challenges to honesty?*** Divide the class into small groups. Ask each group to consider a different question from Practical Exploration #6.2, "How Would You Respond to Challenges to Honesty?" After they debate the question, have them share their conclusions and reasoning with the rest of the class.

5. ***Have you ever cheated? What do you think of cheaters?*** This is a classwide discussion activity. The instructor hands out pieces of scratch paper (it's important that all pieces of paper look pretty much alike). Each student is to describe on a piece of paper in 25 words or less one of the following: (a) An incident in which you cheated in school. (b) An incident of cheating you observed in school. (c) An incident of cheating you observed in some other situation.

   Tell students *not* to put their names on the paper. Have them carefully fold up their answers, which are then collected. Have students then take turns coming up to the front of the class, drawing one of the folded comments from a hat or box, then reading it aloud. Ask everyone to discuss the comments. Are there any circumstances under which cheating is excusable? What are the rules of your school's academic integrity standards?

The Examined Life:
Student Assignments for Journal Entries

JOURNAL ENTRY #6.1: **HOW HAVE YOU PREPARED FOR TESTS IN THE PAST?** Consider how you have prepared for tests in the past. How successful has your routine been? Which techniques would you take from this chapter that you would use in the future?

_____
_____
_____
_____
_____
_____
_____

JOURNAL ENTRY #6.2: **HOW AFFECTED ARE YOU BY TEST ANXIETY?** How big a roadblock is test anxiety for you? Which techniques will you try to employ to reduce it next time?

_____
_____
_____
_____
_____
_____
_____

JOURNAL ENTRY #6.3: **WHAT TYPES OF TESTS ARE DIFFICULT FOR YOU?** What kinds of tests do you do the worst on—true-false, multiple-choice, matching, fill-in-the-blank, short-answer essay, or long-answer essay? How will you change your approach in the future?

_____
_____
_____
_____
_____
_____
_____

JOURNAL ENTRY #6.4: **WHAT ABOUT CRAMMING FOR TESTS?** Are you used to cramming for tests? How do you feel about this method? How will you break this habit in the future?

_____

_____

_____

_____

_____

_____

_____

CHAPTER SEVEN

WRITING & SPEAKING

Making powerful written & oral presentations

IN THIS CHAPTER: Does the idea of having to write a paper or give a speech make you ill? Maybe that's because you don't have a formula for doing it. You'll probably have to write a number of papers in school—and in your career (when they're called "reports"). You may also have to give some oral presentations. Now's your chance, then, to develop a strategy for giving both kinds of presentations, written and oral.

This chapter considers the following:

- **How to target your audience:** What instructors look for in a written presentation, such as a research paper.

- **Making a written presentation:** The five phases of conceptualizing, researching, and writing a paper.

- **Making an oral presentation:** Giving a talk or a speech.

▪ Writing papers and giving oral reports is mainly just academic busywork and not required much outside of higher education—right?

That's what we used to think. As students we thought these were just temporary skills we had to learn so instructors would have some basis for grading us.

After we graduated, however, we found out otherwise. The training we had developed in researching, writing, and speaking, we discovered, was *very* important in building a career. If you need to research a business report, make a presentation to clients, or contribute to a newsletter, for instance, you'll be glad you learned how.

Indeed, the new companies in the computer industry consider so-called soft skills—the ability to communicate well with others and to work effectively in teams—essential for all but the most technical jobs. Because of the way today's organizations work, "you can have the smartest [people], but if they can't get along in a group or a team, or if they don't have self-managing capabilities, they'll fail," says Mary Ann Ellis, director of human resources for Raychem Corp. in California.[1]

For now, though, it's a great benefit to learn how to use the library, pull information together, and present your research well. These are vital skills for success in career and vocational-technical education. In this chapter, we'll consider the following:

- What instructors look for in a term paper

- How to write a paper

- How to give an oral presentation

What Do Instructors Look for in a Term Paper?

PREVIEW Instructors grade term papers according to three criteria: (1) Demonstration of originality and effort. (2) Demonstration that learning took place. (3) Neatness, correctness, and appearance of the presentation.

Writing may be something you do for yourself. For instance, you can keep a journal or diary about your feelings, observations, and happenings (as we've urged throughout this book); this is *personal writing.* Or you can write songs or poetry or musings; this is *expressive writing.* Or you can keep private notes about something you're working on, to help you sort out what you think. Here, however, let us consider a kind of writing you do for other people—specifically, term papers for instructors.

Think about the meaning of the word "term" in *term paper.* Doing the paper is supposed to take the greater part of a school *term*—that is, a semester or quarter. Thus, it is supposed to be a paper based on extensive research of a specific subject. When finished it should probably run 10 or more double-spaced pages done on a typewriter or word processor. (This is equivalent to about 20 handwritten pages.) Sometimes you may have to give an oral presentation instead of writing a paper, but much of the work is the same. Because so much effort is required, no wonder instructors often consider the term paper to be worth *50% of the course grade.* This weight suggests the reasons you should give the paper your best shot, rather than knocking it out over a weekend—the equivalent of cramming for a test.

Perhaps the best way to get oriented is to ask, *How do instructors grade term papers?* There are probably three principal standards:[2]

- Demonstration of originality and effort

- Demonstration that learning took place

- Neatness, correctness, and appearance of the presentation

1. DEMONSTRATION OF ORIGINALITY & EFFORT. *Are the ideas in your paper original and does the paper show some effort?* Instructors are constantly on the lookout for papers that do not represent students' own thoughts and efforts. These papers can take three forms, ranging from most serious (and dangerous to the student) to least serious:

- **"Canned" or lifted papers:** Papers known as "canned" papers may be *bought from commercial term-paper-writing services.* Or they may be *rewritten or lifted from old papers,* as from those of other students. Or they may be pulled off the Internet.

    Beware of submitting a paper that is not your own. The instructor might recognize it as the work of a student who was there before you or suspect the style is not yours. If you're found out, you'll not only flunk the course but probably will be put on some form of academic probation. This means you might be suspended or expelled from school.

- **Plagiarized papers:** The ideas and/or expression in a paper may be **plagiarized (pronounced "*play*-jer-ized"); that is, one person presents another**

person's ideas as his or her own. For instance, a student may copy passages from another source without giving credit to the source.

Most instructors have developed a sensitivity to plagiarism. They can tell when the level of thought or expression does not seem appropriate for student writing. Moreover, lifting others' ideas goes against the very nature of why you're supposed to be in higher education to begin with. That is, you're supposed to be here to help yourself learn ways to meet challenges and expand your competence. In any case, plagiarism can also result in an F in the course and possible suspension from school.

- **Unoriginal, no-effort papers:** Quite often students submit papers that *show no thought and effort.* They consist of simply quoting and citing—that is, rehashing—the conflicting ideas of various experts and scholars. There is no evidence that the student has weighed the various views and demonstrated some critical thinking. A 10-page paper that shows original thinking is always better than a 20-page paper with lots of footnotes or text citations but no insights of your own.

This leads us to point 2, about learning.

2. DEMONSTRATION THAT LEARNING TOOK PLACE. Instructors want to see you

demonstrate the very reason you're supposed to be in an institution of higher learning in the first place: *Does the paper show that you've learned something?*

How do you show that you're learning? Our suggestion is this: *Ask a question for which the term paper provides the answer.* Examples of questions are as follows.

"Do men and women view 'date rape' differently?"

"Are alcohol and cigarettes really 'gateway' drugs to illegal drug use?"

"How did the Vietnam War affect the U.S. approach to the war in Bosnia?"

"What's the best way to dispose of radioactive waste?"

Always try, if you can, to make the question one that's important or interesting to you. That way you'll be genuinely motivated to learn something from the answer. At the end of your paper, you'll be able to demonstrate that learning took place. For example, you might conclude "When I first looked into the question of date rape, I wondered whether men and women view the matter differently. As the research in this paper has shown, I have found that . . ."

3. NEATNESS, CORRECTNESS, & APPEARANCE OF PRESENTATION. Like

most readers, instructors prefer neatness over messiness, readability over unreadability. Studies show that instructors give papers a higher grade if they are neat and use correct spelling and grammar. The third standard, then, involves form. *Is your paper typed and proofread and does it follow the correct form for text citations and references?*

Let's consider these points:

- **_Typed versus handwritten:_** All instructors _prefer_—and many _require_—that you hand in a paper that has been produced on a typewriter or word processor rather than handwritten. Even if you're only a hunt-and-peck typist, try to render the final version of your term paper on a typewriter or word processor. (A word processor is easier for people who make lots of typing mistakes.) Or hire someone else to type it.

- **_Correct spelling and grammar:_** As you write, look up words in the dictionary to check their spelling. Proofread the final version to correct any mistakes and bad grammar. (And if you're using a word processor, run the final draft through a spelling-checker program, in addition to proofreading it yourself.)

    You may be sick and tired of your paper when you are finally finished with it. Nevertheless, you would hate to blow your grade at the end by allowing the instructor to mark the paper down because you overlooked the small stuff.

- **_Follow correct academic form:_** Different academic disciplines (English and psychology, for example) have their preferred text-citation and works-cited (bibliography) styles. Be sure to follow any directions your instructor gives for these and any other requirements for the form of the paper.

    Now you know what you're aiming for. Let's see how to achieve it.

Writing a Term Paper: Five Phases

PREVIEW The five phases of producing a term paper are as follows. (1) Pick a topic. (2) Do initial research and develop an outline. (3) Do further research. (4) Sort notes, revise the outline, and write a first draft. (5) Revise, type, and proofread the paper.

The audience for a term paper, we said, is an instructor. Writing for instructors is different from other writing. It's not the same, for example, as an essay accompanying an application for admission to a college. Nor is it the same as an article for a newsletter or a letter of complaint to a landlord or government official. Nor is term-paper writing the same as writing an article for an academic journal; it is less formal than that.

In this section, we'll explain how to prepare a term paper for an instructor. There are five principal phases:

- *Phase 1:* Picking a topic
- *Phase 2:* Doing initial research and developing a preliminary outline
- *Phase 3:* Doing your research—using the library
- *Phase 4:* Sorting your notes, revising the outline, and writing a first draft of the paper
- *Phase 5:* Revising, typing, and proofreading your paper

Be aware that the grade on the term paper will count heavily toward the grade in the course. Thus, you should try to spread these phases over the semester or quarter—not do them all in one week or a few days.

Phase 1: Picking a Topic

PREVIEW The first phase, *picking a topic,* has four parts. (1) Set a deadline for picking a topic. (2) Pick a topic important to the instructor and interesting to you. (3) Refine proposed topics into four questions. (4) Check topics with the instructor.

Phase 1 consists of picking a topic. This has four parts:

- Set a deadline for picking the topic
- Pick a topic important to the instructor and interesting to you
- Refine your proposed topics into three questions
- Check with your instructor

SET A DEADLINE FOR PICKING YOUR TOPIC. Students often delay doing this first step. However, the most important advice we can give you about writing papers is this: START EARLY. By beginning early, you'll be able to find a topic that interests you. Moreover, you'll avoid pitfalls such as picking a subject that is too narrow or too large.

Thus, *as soon as you get your instructor's guidelines for the term paper, set a deadline for picking the topic.* In your lecture notes, on a page by itself, write a big note to yourself:

*** *DEADLINE: PICK TERM PAPER TOPIC BY TUESDAY NOON!* ***

In addition, put this on your To Do list and on your weekly planner.

PICKING A TOPIC: TWO SUGGESTIONS. There are two suggestions for picking a topic. You should pick something that (1) is important to your instructor and (2) is interesting to you.

■ **Topics important to the instructor:** You need to determine what is important to your instructor because he or she is the sole audience for your paper.

How do you find out what the instructor believes is significant? First, if he or she has provided any written guidelines, read them carefully. If the assignment is given verbally, take precise notes. You'll also get a better idea of what's important when you meet with the instructor to discuss your proposed topics, as we describe.

■ **Topics interesting to you:** Motivation is everything. Thus, whenever possible, try to choose a topic that interests you. It also helps if you already know something about it. To determine what might be suitable, look through your lecture notes to see what things pop out at you.

EXPRESSING PROPOSED TOPICS AS THREE QUESTIONS. By the time your self-imposed deadline arrives for choosing your topic, you should have three alternative ideas. Because your purpose is to demonstrate that you're learning, these should be expressed as questions.

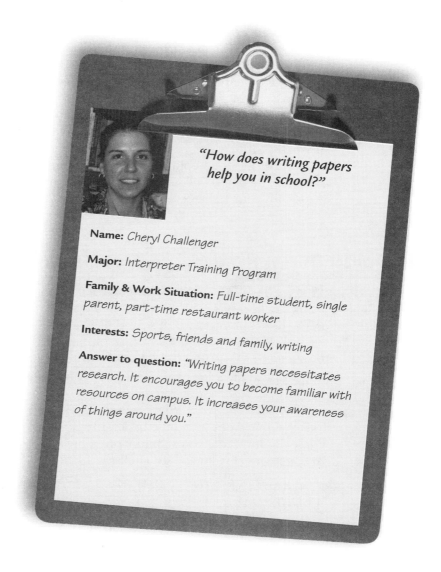

"How does writing papers help you in school?"

Name: Cheryl Challenger

Major: Interpreter Training Program

Family & Work Situation: Full-time student, single parent, part-time restaurant worker

Interests: Sports, friends and family, writing

Answer to question: "Writing papers necessitates research. It encourages you to become familiar with resources on campus. It increases your awareness of things around you."

For example, for an introductory health course, you may decide on the following possible topics.

"What diets are most effective for weight loss?"

"Does meditation prolong life in cancer patients?"

"Does wearing helmets reduce motorcycle injuries?"

Are some of these questions too broad (diets) or too narrow (helmets)? In the next step, you'll find out.

CHECKING TOPIC IDEAS WITH YOUR INSTRUCTOR. It's now a good idea to take your topic questions and show them to your instructor (after class or during office hours). Questions to ask are the following:

■ **Is it important enough?** Ask "Do you think any of these topics are important enough to be worth exploring in a term paper?" The answer will indicate whether you are meeting the first criterion in selecting a topic—does the instructor think it's significant?

■ **Is the scope about right?** Ask "Do you think the topic is too broad or too narrow in scope?" The instructor may suggest ways to limit or vary the topic so you won't waste time on unnecessary research. He or she can also prevent you from tackling a topic that's too advanced. Equally important, the instructor may be able to suggest some books or other resources that will help you in your research.

What if you're in a large class and have difficulty getting access to your instructor (or teaching assistant)? In that case, go to the library and ask a reference librarian for an opinion on the topic's importance and scope. In addition, of course, he or she will be able to steer you toward some good sources of information for your research.

Phase 2: Doing Initial Research & Developing an Outline

PREVIEW The beginning of Phase 2, doing *initial research*, consists of using the library's card or online catalog and guide to periodicals to determine the scope of research material. The second part of Phase 2, *developing an outline,* means doing a tentative outline suggesting the paper's beginning (introduction), middle (body), and end (conclusion). The beginning and middle pose questions you hope your research will answer.

Phase 2 consists of doing initial research and developing an outline. If it took you one week to decide on a topic, it should take you another week to do Phase 2. Here, too, you should write a big note to yourself (and also put it on your weekly calendar and To Do list):

*** *DEADLINE: CHECK OUT RESEARCH FOR TERM PAPER BY WEDNESDAY 5 P.M.!* ***

The idea here is to satisfy yourself about two things:

■ **Research material:** Is enough material available for you to research your paper adequately?

■ **Rough outline:** Do you have a rough idea of the direction your paper will take?

INVESTIGATING RESEARCH MATERIAL. This step need not take long—perhaps a half hour in the library. The idea is to look in a handful of places to get a sense of the research material accessible to you. In particular, two places are the following:

■ **Library catalog:** Look under the subject listing in the library's catalog (online catalog or card catalog) to see what books exist on your topic. Don't assume, however, that just because the books are listed that they are easily available. (They may be checked out, on reserve, or in another campus library. An online catalog may tell you if they're checked out.) Look up some call letters for relevant titles, then visit the shelves and see what books you can find.

■ **Guide to periodicals:** Magazines and journals are apt to be more up to date than books. Check the *Reader's Guide to Periodical Literature* to see what articles are available in your topic area. Jot down the names of the periodicals, then check with the reference librarian to see whether they are available to you.

Further information about the library, including use of the library catalog and guide to periodicals, is given in Phase 3, Research. This preliminary investigation, however, gives you an overview of the subject.

DEVELOPING A WORKING OUTLINE. While you're in the library doing your first research you should also do a preliminary outline or working outline.

Many people resist doing an outline because they think "I don't know where I'm going until I've been there." That is, they think they won't know their direction until they've done all the research and thought about the material. Or they think an outline is somehow going to lock them in to an approach that might not work out.

The purpose of doing a preliminary outline now is twofold. First, it saves you time later. Second, it will provide you with a general road map. You can always change the outline later, but if you set out without one, you may waste time wandering around before you get a sense of direction.

Take a sheet of paper and write *OUTLINE #1* across the top. Then fill in the following three parts—*I. Beginning, II. Middle,* and *III. End.*[3]

I. *BEGINNING—the introduction*
The beginning or introduction describes the *one or two main questions your paper will try to answer.* In the final paper, the beginning will be one or two paragraphs.
Example: "How smart are college athletes?" "Are college athletics dominated by 'dumb jocks'?"

II. *MIDDLE—the body*

The middle or body of the outline describes *some specific questions your paper will try to answer.* These are detailed questions that will help you answer the main questions.

Examples: "What's the grade-point average (GPA) of college football, baseball, and basketball players?" "What's the GPA of competitive swimmers, gymnasts, and tennis players?" "What percentage of athletes graduate compared to most students?" "What percentage drop out?" "What proportion of athletes in pro sports are college graduates?" "Are top athletes usually top scholars, such as Phi Beta Kappa, magna cum laude, Rhodes Scholars?" And so on.

III. *END—the conclusion*

You won't know the end or conclusion, of course, until you've done the research and answered your questions. For now, *just state that you will write a conclusion based on your answers.*

Here are some techniques for developing your outline:

■ *Write questions on index cards:* Get a stack of 3×5 index cards or cut sheets of notepaper into quarters. On each card or quarter-page, write a question you want to answer about your topic. *Write as many questions as you can think of, both general and detailed.*

This kind of activity is known as **brainstorming—you jot down all the ideas that come to mind about a particular matter,** no matter how awful. The key thing is not to be judgmental; that is, no matter how bad an idea is, no scoffing or criticism is allowed. Just write as many questions as you can. This will help you overcome outline fears and anxieties.

■ *Organize index cards into categories:* Now sort your 3×5 cards into stacks. The stacks represent whatever categories come to mind. One stack might contain a few general questions that will make up your introduction. The others will make up specific categories for the body of the outline.

What kinds of categories might you have? Some might be stacks of similar kinds of questions. Some might be advantages and disadvantages, or cause and effect, or compare and contrast. Do whatever kind of grouping seems sensible to you.

■ *Write out your outline:* Copy out the categories and questions into the outline form shown above. You now have a road map to follow to begin your research.

NOTE: If you are used to a computer, you may find an *outlining program* useful rather than 3×5 cards. This kind of software allows you to brainstorm and sort out ideas onscreen.

After developing it, show your outline to your instructor. He or she will be able to determine at a glance whether you seem to be headed in the right direction.

Phase 3: Doing Your Research—Using the Library

PREVIEW Phase 3, *doing research,* usually means using the library. This step requires learning the parts of the library; discovering how to get help from librarians and how to use the library catalog; knowing how to locate books, periodicals and journals, and reference materials; and finding out how to use other libraries. Low-tech ways of collecting information involve use of 3 × 5 cards. High-tech ways involve the use of photocopiers and computers.

Phase 3 consists of doing your research, which usually means making use of the library. In this section, let us consider these aspects:

- Parts of the library

- Using librarians and the library catalog

- Locating books

- Finding periodicals and journals

- Finding reference materials

- Using other libraries

- Low-tech ways to collect information: 3 × 5 cards

- High-tech ways to collect information: photocopiers and personal computers

FINDING YOUR WAY AROUND THE LIBRARY. Particularly at a large institution, you may find that the library is a lot larger than those you're accustomed to. Indeed, there may be more than one library on campus, plus access to libraries elsewhere. The most important one for first-year students is the *central library*, the principal library on campus.

The central library has several parts:

- ***Main section:*** The main section includes six parts:

    1. The desk where you check books out

    2. The library catalog (card or computerized) listing books

    3. A reference section, with dictionaries, encyclopedias, and directories

    4. A periodicals section displaying current newspapers, magazines, and journals

    5. A section (perhaps called the "stacks") housing books

    6. A section housing back issues of periodicals

- ***Other sections:*** In addition, the central library usually has some special sections:

    1. A media center, or section containing audiotapes and videotapes

    2. A section for reserve books, which have been set aside by instructors for certain courses

    3. A vertical file containing pamphlets on special topics

    4. A government documents section

- ***Other services—study areas and machines:*** Most campus libraries also provide study areas. Indeed, because the whole purpose of the library is to enable students to do serious work, there are relatively few distractions there.

  Finally, there may be several kinds of machines available for your use. Examples are machines for reading microfilm and microfiche (materials on film), computer terminals for accessing electronic databases and indexes, and machines for making photocopies. Some libraries provide typewriters or word processors. Some also have machines providing access to audio tapes, CDs, videotapes, slides, films, filmstrips, videodiscs, computer floppy disks, and/or CD-ROM disks.

If you have not had a formal orientation to the library, whether videotaped presentation or actual tour, now is the time. If possible, do it *before* you're under a tight deadline for a research paper, so you won't have to do your research under panic conditions. Some schools offer a credit course in how to use the library—something we would recommend to anyone.

The principal resource, the trained navigators, are the *reference librarians.* Don't hesitate to ask for their help. That's what they're there for. They can tell you whether the library has what you need and show you how to get started. Reference librarians are also the people to go to when you have exhausted other resources. They may refer you to special sources within the library or to different libraries on or off campus.

HOW TO FIND WHAT YOU WANT IN BOOKS. Books may be found on open shelves in the main section of the library. In some places, they may also be back in the "stacks," requiring a library page or runner to go get them. Or they may be in special libraries located elsewhere on campus. Or they may be available by means of **interlibrary loan, a service that enables you to borrow books from other libraries.** Allow extra time—several days or even weeks—and perhaps a small fee, when you're obtaining a book through interlibrary loan.

To find a book, you may use a *card catalog, CD-ROM computerized catalog,* or *online computerized catalog:*

- ***The card catalog:* A library *card catalog* contains information about each book typed on a 3 × 5-inch card, stored in wooden file drawers.** This is the system that has been used by libraries for decades, though it is now being phased out in many places. (If your school doesn't have this, skip this section.)

  Libraries have three kinds of card catalog listings for books: *title, author,* and *subject.* Thus, you can find *The Right and the Power: The Prosecution of Watergate* by Leon Jaworski in three ways. The first is by *title*—under "R." (Words such as "The," "A," and "An" are omitted if they are the first word in a title.) The second is by author's last name—under "J." The third is by subject—under "United States, petitioner"; "Nixon, Richard Milhous,"; or "Watergate Affair." (*See* ▪*Panel 7.1.*)

  When doing research papers, you'll probably often use the subject catalog. Standardized subject headings are listed in the reference work *Library of Congress Subject Headings,* which the reference librarian can help you find.

- ***CD-ROM computerized catalog:* *CD-ROM catalogs* look like music compact disks (CDs), except that they are used to store text and images. CD-ROM stands for Compact Disk—Read Only Memory.** To use a CD-

Three kinds of card catalog listings: title, author, subject. The same book may be found on cards in the three separate catalogs. Note the subject headings at the bottom of the card. These offer more categories that could produce other books pertinent to your area of research.

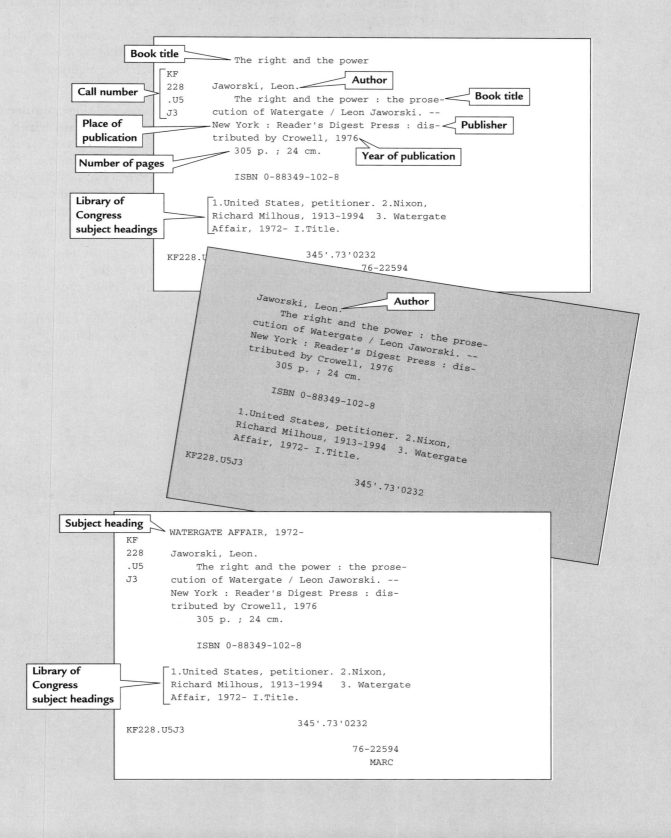

Book title
The right and the power

Call number
KF
228
.U5
J3

Author
Jaworski, Leon.

Book title
The right and the power : the prosecution of Watergate / Leon Jaworski. --

Place of publication
Publisher
New York : Reader's Digest Press : dis-
tributed by Crowell, 1976

Year of publication
Number of pages
305 p. ; 24 cm.

ISBN 0-88349-102-8

Library of Congress subject headings
1.United States, petitioner. 2.Nixon,
Richard Milhous, 1913-1994   3. Watergate
Affair, 1972- I.Title.

KF228.U   345'.73'0232
                           76-22594

Author
Jaworski, Leon.
The right and the power : the prosecution of Watergate / Leon Jaworski. --
New York : Reader's Digest Press : distributed by Crowell, 1976
305 p. ; 24 cm.

ISBN 0-88349-102-8

1.United States, petitioner. 2.Nixon,
Richard Milhous, 1913-1994   3. Watergate
Affair, 1972- I.Title.

KF228.U5J3

345'.73'0232

Subject heading
WATERGATE AFFAIR, 1972-
KF
228   Jaworski, Leon.
.U5   The right and the power : the prose-
J3   cution of Watergate / Leon Jaworski. --
        New York : Reader's Digest Press : dis-
        tributed by Crowell, 1976
            305 p. ; 24 cm.

        ISBN 0-88349-102-8

Library of Congress subject headings
1.United States, petitioner. 2.Nixon,
Richard Milhous, 1913-1994   3. Watergate
Affair, 1972- I.Title.

                           345'.73'0232
KF228.U5J3

                           76-22594
                           MARC

ROM, you put the disk into the microcomputer's CD-ROM drive, then follow directions (perhaps on Help screens) for searching by title, author, or subject.

An advantage of CD-ROMs is that you can use keywords to search for material. **Keywords are any words you use to find specific information.** For example, you could use the keywords "National Socialism" to look for books about Hitler and the Nazi Party.

A drawback of CD-ROMs, however, is that a disk cannot be updated. Instead a new disk must be produced, which your library may do every month or so. Thus, any CD-ROM catalog you consult may lag slightly behind the library's acquisitions.

■ *Online computerized catalog: Online computerized catalogs* **require that you use a computer terminal or microcomputer that has a wired connection to a database.** Online catalogs have all the advantages of CD-ROMs, including the ability to do keyword searches. However, they are more quickly updated. Moreover, they may contain additional information, such as whether a book has been checked out. The instructions for using online catalogs appear on the computer keyboard and/or on the display screen (in Help screens). *(See ■ Panel 7.2.)*

NOTE: *Books in Print* is an annual reference work—organized by title, author, and subject—that lists most books currently in print in the United States. By using the subject category you can also find books in your area of research, although they won't necessarily be in your school's library.

Most school libraries use the Library of Congress system of call numbers and letters. Get the call numbers from the card or computerized listing, then use a map of the library to find the appropriate shelves. Once you've found your book, look at other books in the general vicinity to see whether they could be useful.

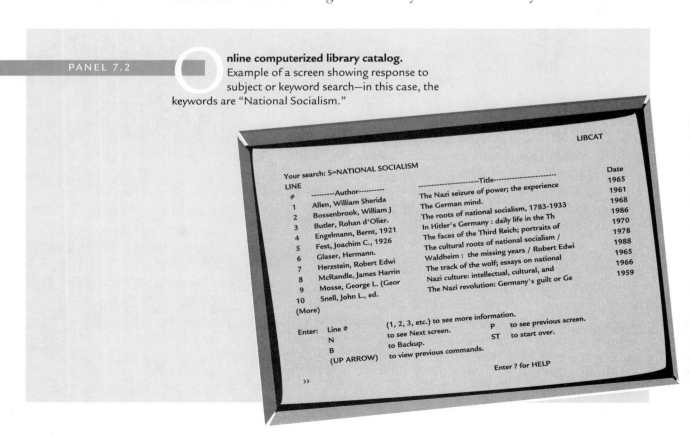

PANEL 7.2

Online computerized library catalog.
Example of a screen showing response to
subject or keyword search—in this case, the
keywords are "National Socialism."

LIBCAT

Your search: S=NATIONAL SOCIALISM

LINE #	----------Author----------	-----------------Title-----------------	Date
1	Allen, William Sherida	The Nazi seizure of power; the experience	1965
2	Bossenbrook, William J	The German mind.	1961
3	Butler, Rohan d'Olier.	The roots of national socialism, 1783-1933	1968
4	Engelmann, Bernt, 1921	In Hitler's Germany : daily life in the Th	1986
5	Fest, Joachim C., 1926	The faces of the Third Reich; portraits of	1970
6	Glaser, Hermann.	The cultural roots of national socialism /	1978
7	Herzstein, Robert Edwi	Waldheim : the missing years / Robert Edwi	1988
8	McRandle, James Harrin	The track of the wolf; essays on national	1965
9	Mosse, George L. (Geor	Nazi culture: intellectual, cultural, and	1966
10	Snell, John L., ed.	The Nazi revolution: Germany's guilt or Ge	1959

(More)

Enter:　Line #　　(1, 2, 3, etc.) to see more information.　　P　to see previous screen.
　　　　　N　　　to see Next screen.　　　　　　　　　　ST　to start over.
　　　　　B　　　to Backup.
　　　　　(UP ARROW)　to view previous commands.

Enter ? for HELP

>>

If you can't find a book on the shelves and decide you really need it, ask a librarian for help. It may be in the reference section or on reserve for a class. If it has been checked out, ask the library to put a hold on it for you when it's returned. Or ask for help getting another copy through interlibrary loan.

HOW TO FIND WHAT YOU WANT IN NEWSPAPERS, MAGAZINES, & JOURNALS.

You can see what general newspapers, magazines, and journals are available by looking at the open shelves in the periodicals reading room. A list of the library's holdings in periodicals should also be available at the main desk.

Here are some avenues for finding articles in the research area you're interested in. *(See ▪ Panel 7.3.)*

PANEL 7.3   Sources for research

Newspaper indexes: Examples of newspapers printing indexes about articles appearing in their pages are *The New York Times Index* and *The Wall Street Journal Index.* Look also for *Newspaper Abstracts* and *Editorials on File.*

Examples of computerized databases providing information about newspaper articles are *Data Times, Dialog, CompuServe, America Online, Prodigy,* and *Nexis.*

Magazine indexes: The *Readers' Guide to Periodical Literature* lists articles appearing in well-known American magazines.

Other indexes, available in printed, microfilm, or CD-ROM form, are *Magazine Index, Newsbank, InfoTrac, Business Index,* and *Medline.*

Journal indexes and abstracts: Examples of indexes and databases for specialized journals are *Accountants' Index, Applied Science and Technology Index, Art Index, Business Periodicals Index, Computer Data Bases, Education Index, Engineering Index Monthly, General Science Index, Humanities Index, Medline,* and *Social Science Index.*

Examples of indexes called abstracts are *Biological Abstracts, Chemical Abstracts, Historical Abstracts, Psychological Abstracts,* and *Sociological Abstracts.*

Some computerized online indexes to journals are available, such as *PsycLit,* a bibliographic database to *Psychological Abstracts.*

Specialized dictionaries: Examples of specialized dictionaries for technical subjects are *Dictionary of Biological Sciences, Dictionary of Film Terms, Dictionary of Quotations, Dorland's Illustrated Medical Dictionary, Grove's Dictionary of Music and Musicians, Mathematical Dictionary,* and *Webster's New World Dictionary of Computer Terms.*

Encyclopedias, almanacs, and handbooks: Examples of encyclopedias on specialized subjects are *Cyclopedia of World Authors, Encyclopedia of Associations, Encyclopedia of Banking and Finance, Encyclopedia of Bioethics, Encyclopedia of Religion and Ethics, Encyclopedia of Sports, Encyclopedia of World Art, Thomas Register of American Manufacturers,* and *The Wellness Encyclopedia.*

Examples of specialized almanacs, handbooks, and other reference sources are *The Business Writer's Handbook, Comparisons, The Computer Glossary, Facts on File, The Guinness Book of World Records, Keesing's Record of World Events, Literary Market Place, The Pacific Rim Almanac,* and *The Secret Guide to Computers.*

Government literature: Publications published by the U.S. Government are listed in *The Monthly Catalog* and *PAIS (Public Affairs Information Service).*

Computer networks: Examples of guides to computerized information networks are *Directory of Online Databases, Encyclopedia of Information Systems and Services,* and *Guide to the Use of Libraries and Information Services.*

■ ***Newspaper indexes:*** In the United States, the newspapers available nationally and in many campus libraries are the *New York Times,* the *Wall Street Journal,* and *USA Today.* Some schools may also subscribe to other respected newspapers such as the *Washington Post* or the *Los Angeles Times.* Some newspapers print indexes that list information about the articles appearing in their pages. Examples are the *New York Times Index* and the *Wall Street Journal Index.* Look also for *Newspaper Abstracts* and *Editorials on File.*

In addition, your library may subscribe to computerized databases providing bibliographical information about articles appearing in hundreds of magazines and newspapers. Ask the librarian how you can use *Data Times, Dialog,* or the reference services of *CompuServe, America Online, Prodigy,* or *Nexis.*

■ ***Magazine indexes:*** The index for the 100 or so most general magazines, many probably available in your library, is the *Readers' Guide to Periodical Literature.* This lists articles appearing in such well-known magazines as *Time, Newsweek, Reader's Digest, Psychology Today,* and *Business Week.*

Other indexes, available in printed, microfilm, or CD-ROM form, are *Magazine Index, Newsbank, InfoTrac, Business Index,* and *Medline.*

■ ***Journal indexes and abstracts:*** Journals are specialized magazines, and their articles are listed in specialized indexes and databases. Examples range from *Applied Science and Technology Index* to *Social Science Index.*

In addition, there are indexes called ***abstracts, which present paragraphs summarizing articles along with bibliographical information about them.*** Examples range from *Biological Abstracts* to *Sociological Abstracts.*

Some journal indexes are accessed by going online through a computer. For example, *PsycLit* is a bibliographic database to *Psychological Abstracts.*

HOW TO FIND OTHER REFERENCE MATERIALS. All kinds of wonderful other reference materials are also available to you. Here's a short list:

- *Dictionaries, thesauruses, style books:* Need to look up specialized terms for your paper? The reference section of the library has not only standard dictionaries but also specialized dictionaries for technical subjects. Examples range from *Dictionary of Biological Sciences* to *Webster's New World Dictionary of Computer Terms.*

  In addition, you may find a thesaurus helpful in your writing. **A thesaurus lists synonyms, or words with similar meanings.** This is a great resource when you can't think of the exact word you want when writing.

  Finally, there are various style books for helping you do text citations and works cited, such as *The Chicago Manual of Style.*

- *Encyclopedias, almanacs, handbooks:* No doubt the library has various kinds of standard encyclopedias, in printed and CD-ROM form. As with dictionaries, there are also encyclopedias on specialized subjects. Examples range from *Cyclopedia of World Authors* to the *Wellness Encyclopedia.*

  There are also all kinds of specialized almanacs, handbooks, and other reference sources. Examples range from *The Business Writer's Handbook* to *The Secret Guide to Computers.*

- *Government literature:* A section of the library is probably reserved for information from both the federal government and state and local governments. The most prolific publisher in the world is the United States Government. To find out publications pertinent to your subject, look in *The Monthly Catalog* and *PAIS (Public Affairs Information Service).*

- *Computer networks:* This is a vast subject in itself. Now many libraries subscribe to computerized information networks, such as DIALOG, ERIC, ORBIT, and BSR. Directories and guides exist to help you learn to use these services. Examples are *Directory of Online Databases, Encyclopedia of Information Systems and Services,* or *Guide to the Use of Libraries and Information Services.*

  In addition, there are many online information services: America Online, CompuServe, Microsoft Network, and Prodigy. Many schools also provide access to the Internet, the so-called network of networks, which unifies over 36,000 individual computer networks.

HOW TO USE OTHER LIBRARIES. In large institutions, various departments and schools often have their own libraries. Thus, the libraries of, say, the business school or nursing school will have material that the main library does not. In addition, you may find it worthwhile to visit local city or county libraries or the libraries of nearby colleges. Although you probably won't be allowed to check out materials, you can certainly use the materials available to the general public.

LOW-TECH WAYS TO COLLECT INFORMATION: 3 × 5 CARDS. Some materials (principally books) you'll be able to check out and have access to at your usual writing desk or study place. However, most libraries won't let you take out magazines, encyclopedias, and general reference materials. Thus, you'll need to be able to take notes in the library.

Traditional 3 × 5 index cards are useful because you can write one idea on each card, then later sort the cards as you please. Index cards should be used in three ways—as *source cards, information cards,* and *idea cards. (See ■ Panel 7.4.)*

■ **Source cards:** Use *source cards* to keep track of works-cited (bibliographical) information. At the time you're looking up your sources, you can jot down the call letters on these cards. Specifically:

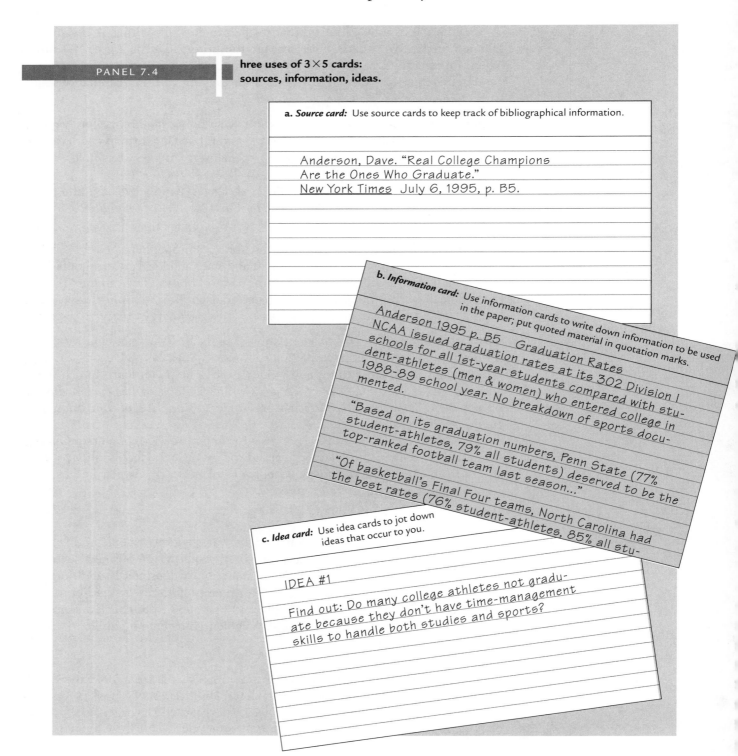

PANEL 7.4

Three uses of 3 × 5 cards: sources, information, ideas.

a. *Source card:* Use source cards to keep track of bibliographical information.

Anderson, Dave. "Real College Champions
Are the Ones Who Graduate."
New York Times July 6, 1995, p. B5.

b. *Information card:* Use information cards to write down information to be used in the paper; put quoted material in quotation marks.

Anderson 1995 p. B5   Graduation Rates
NCAA issued graduation rates at its 302 Division I
schools for all 1st-year students compared with student-athletes (men & women) who entered college in
1988-89 school year. No breakdown of sports docu-
mented.

"Based on its graduation numbers, Penn State (77%
student-athletes, 79% all students) deserved to be the
top-ranked football team last season..."

"Of basketball's Final Four teams, North Carolina had
the best rates (76% student-athletes, 85% all stu-

c. *Idea card:* Use idea cards to jot down ideas that occur to you.

IDEA #1

Find out: Do many college athletes not graduate because they don't have time-management
skills to handle both studies and sports?

1. For each *journal article:* Write down the author's last and first name (for example, "Wahlstrom, Carl"), title of article, title of journal, month and year, volume and issue number, and page numbers.

2. For each *book:* Write down the author's (or editor's) name, book title, edition, city and state of publication, name of publisher, year of publication (listed on the copyright page), and pages you referred to, if necessary.

   Later, when you type your references, you'll be able to arrange these source cards in alphabetical order by authors' last names.

- **Information cards:** Use *information cards* to copy down information and quotations. This is the actual research material you will use. The card will have three areas:

1. *Source abbreviation:* At the top of each card, put an abbreviated version of the source, including the page number. (Example: "Wahlstrom 1998, p. 23." If you have two 1998 Wahlstrom references, label them *a* and *b*.) If you use more than one card for a single source, number the cards.

2. *Information:* In the lower part of the card, write the information. If it's a direct quote, enclose it in quotation marks.

3. *Keyword zone:* Reserve the top right corner of the card as a "keyword zone." In this area put one or two keywords that will tie the card to a place on your outline. (Example: "Graduation rates.") The keyword can also tie the card to a new subject, if it is not on the outline.

- **Idea cards:** Use *idea cards* to jot down ideas that occur to you. To make sure you don't mix them up with information cards, write "IDEA #1," "IDEA #2," and so on, at the top.

   To keep the cards organized, keep them in three separate stacks each wrapped with a rubber band.

HIGH-TECH WAYS TO COLLECT INFORMATION: PHOTOCOPIERS & PORTABLE COMPUTERS. Using 3×5 cards is a traditional though low-tech way of collecting information. They can also be somewhat time-consuming, as they require that you write out everything by hand.

   Two high-tech ways to collect information in the library are the use of photocopiers and portable computers.

- **Photocopiers:** When you find an article from which you'd like to quote extensively, it may make sense to simply use the library's photocopying machines to copy most or all of the article. Sometimes this means feeding the machine a lot of dimes, but the time saving may still be worth it. Some libraries allow students to open charge accounts for use of these machines.

   For organizing purposes, you can then take scissors and cut up the photocopied material. Then write the source abbreviation and page number in one margin and the "keywords" in the other.

- **Portable computers:** Having a portable computer with a word processing program can be a godsend in collecting library information. (If your library has desktop word processors installed on the premises, you might also be able to use them.)

Even if you're not very fast on the keyboard, it may still be faster than writing out your information by hand. Follow the same format as you would for 3 × 5 cards.

Practical Exploration #7.1 lets you try your hand at researching a topic or author.

Phase 4: Sorting Your Notes, Revising the Outline, & Writing the First Draft

PREVIEW In Phase 4, you first determine your writing place, then sort your notes, revise your outline, and write a thesis statement and working title. You next write your first draft—middle first, then beginning, then end. In writing, you should make your point and give support, quoting experts, avoiding irrelevancies, and giving sources.

Phase 4 consists of sorting your notes, revising your outline, and writing a first draft of the paper. The research phase may have taken a lot of work, but now it's time to put it all together.

ESTABLISHING YOUR WRITING PLACE. Find the kind of writing environment that suits you best. The main thing is that it *help you avoid distractions.* You may also need room to spread out, even be able to put 3 × 5 cards and sources on the floor. If you write in longhand, a table in the library may do. If you write on a typewriter or word processor, you may need to use the desk in your room.

Some other tips:

- **Allow time:** Give yourself plenty of time. A first draft of a major paper should take more than one day.

- **Reread instructions:** Just before you start to write, reread the instructor's directions regarding the paper. You would hate to find out afterward that you took the wrong approach because you overlooked something.

Ready? Begin.

SORTING YOUR NOTES & REVISING YOUR OUTLINE. In gathering your information, you may have been following the questions that appeared on your preliminary outline. However, the very process of doing research may turn up some new questions and areas that you hadn't thought of. Thus, your 3 × 5 cards or source materials may contain information that suggests some changes to the outline.

Here's what to do:

- **Sort your information cards:** Keeping your eye on the key words in the upper right corner of your 3 × 5 cards (or other source material), sort the information material into piles. *Each pile should gather together information relating to a similar question or topic.*

   Now move the piles into the order or sequence in which you will discuss the material, according to your preliminary outline.

RESEARCH: LOOKING UP A TOPIC IN THE LIBRARY

Think of a topic that you are required to research for another class or just for your own interest. Then use three methods to locate three different sources of information about it.

■ A. YOUR TOPIC

The topic for which I am doing research is _____
_____
_____

■ B. FINDING SUBJECT HEADINGS

Check the *Library of Congress Subject Headings* for two subject headings that will lead to information about your topic. Write them down here:

1. _____
   _____
   _____

2. _____
   _____
   _____

■ C. FINDING BOOKS

Look in the subject section of the library's card catalog or electronic catalog. Write down information for three books on your subject. Information should include authors' names, book titles, city and name of publisher, year of publication (look on copyright page), call number.

1. Book #1:
   _____
   _____
   _____

2. Book #2:
   _____
   _____
   _____
   _____

3. Book #3:
   _____
   _____
   _____
   _____

■ D. FINDING MAGAZINE, JOURNAL, AND NEWSPAPER ARTICLES

Use three sources to find three different articles. One should be from a magazine, one from a journal, and one from a newspaper.

1. **Article from a Magazine:** Use the *Reader's Guide to Periodical Literature* to find an article on your topic. Write down the author's name, article title, name and date of magazine, volume number, article page numbers, and call number. Find the article and write down the first and last sentence in it.

   _____
   _____
   _____
   _____
   _____
   _____

2. **Article from a Journal:** Use another periodical index to find another article on your subject, this time from an academic journal. (An example is *Applied Science and Technology Index*; see other examples in Panel 7.3.) Write down the periodical index used, the authors'

names, article title, name and date of journal, volume and issue number, article page numbers, and call number. Find the article and write down the first and last sentence in it.

   _____
   _____
   _____
   _____
   _____

3. **Article from a Newspaper:** Use a newspaper index to find an article on your topic. (Examples are the *New York Times Index* and the *Wall Street Journal Index*.) Write down the newspaper index used, the author's name, article title, name and date of newspaper, section and page numbers, and call number. Find the article and write down the first and last sentence in it.

   _____
   _____
   _____
   _____
   _____

■ E. FINDING OTHER SOURCES

Use other sources to find more information—for example, government literature, encyclopedias, or computer networks.

1. _____
   _____
   _____

2. _____
   _____
   _____

■ ***Revise your outline:*** The piles may suggest some changes in the order of your outline. Thus, you should now take a fresh sheet of paper, write *OUTLINE #2* at the top, and redo the questions or categories.

By now you will be able to write answers to some or all of your questions. *As you rework the outline, write answers to the questions you have listed.* Refer to the sources of your information as you write. For example, suppose you have the question "What percentage of basketball players graduate compared to most students?" You might write "National Collegiate Athletic Association (NCAA) 1997 study: For fifth consecutive year, athletes at major colleges have done better than nonathletes—58% of athletes who entered college in 1990 graduated within 6 years, compared to 56% for all students in same class (Litsky 1997, p. C19)."

Resequence the topics so that they logically seem to follow, with one building on another.

■ ***Write a thesis statement and working title:*** When you have finished reworking and answering questions in *II. Middle* of your outline, go back up to *I. Beginning.* Revise the main question or questions into a thesis statement. **A *thesis statement* is a concise sentence that defines the purpose of your paper.** For example, your original main questions were "How smart are college athletes?" and "Are college athletics dominated by 'dumb jocks'?" These might now become your thesis statement:

"Though graduation rates of college athletes are lower than those for other students, some individual athletes are among the best students."

The thesis statement will in turn suggest a working title. **A *working title* is a tentative title for your paper.** Thus, you might put down on your outline: *Working title: "How Smart Are College Athletes?"*

WRITING YOUR FIRST DRAFT. It's important to realize that writing is a *several-step process,* not a one-time event. The first step is the first draft.

The first draft has one major purpose: *to get your ideas down on paper.* This is not the stage to worry about doing a clever introduction or choosing the right words or making transitions between ideas. Nor should you concern yourself about correct grammar, punctuation, and spelling. Simply write as though you were telling your findings to a friend. *It's important not to be too judgmental about your writing at this point.* Your main task is to get from a blank page to a page with *something* on it that you can refine later.

Proceed as follows:

■ ***Write the middle:*** Skip the beginning, letting your thesis statement be the introduction for now. Instead, follow Outline #2 for *II. Middle* to write the body of your paper, using your information cards to flesh it out. Set down your answers/ideas one after the other, without worrying too much about logical transitions between them. Use your own voice, not some imagined "scholarly" tone.

Follow some of the writing suggestions mentioned in the next section, "Some Writing Tips."

■ **Write the beginning:** When you have finished setting down the answers to all the questions in the middle, go back and do *I. Beginning.* By starting with the middle, you'll avoid the hang-up of trying to get your paper off the ground or of writing an elegant lead. Also, having done the middle, you'll have a solid idea, of course, of what your paper is about. You'll know, for instance, which questions and answers are the most important. These may be different from the questions you asked before you did your research.

Now, then, you'll be able to write the introduction with some confidence. Here's an example:

"A common image many people have of college athletes is that they are 'dumb jocks.' That is, they may be good on the playing field but not in the classroom. Is this true? The facts vary for different sports, colleges, class levels, and other factors. This paper examines these differences."

■ **Write the end:** Finally, you write *III. End.* The end is the conclusion. It does not include any new facts or examples. It provides just the general answer or answers to the main question or questions raised in the beginning. This is the answer you've arrived at by exploring the questions in the middle section. It's possible, of course, that your conclusion will be incomplete or tentative. It's all right to state that further research is needed.

An example of the end of a paper might be as follows:

"As we have seen, although the dropout rate is higher for players in some sports and in some schools, it is not in others. Moreover, college athletes often graduate with honors, and some go on not only to professional sports but also to Rhodes scholarships, Fullbright and Wilson fellowships, and graduate and professional schools. Today the 'strong-back, weak-brain' athlete of the past is largely a myth."

SOME WRITING TIPS. In writing the first draft of the middle, or body, of the paper, you should try to get something down that you can revise and polish later. Thus, don't worry too much if this initial version seems choppy; that's why a first draft is called a "rough" draft.

As you write, try to follow these guidelines:

■ **Make your point and give support:** The "point" you want to make is the answer to each question. (For example, your question might be "Does football require more intelligence than other major sports?") In your writing, this answer will become a statement. Example:

"It's possible that football requires greater intelligence than other major sports do."

Then support the statement with evidence, data, statistics, examples, and quotations. Example:

"Memorizing and executing scores or hundreds of different plays, for instance, takes a lot of intelligence. When scouts for pro football teams look over college players, one question they ask is, 'How is he at learning the playbook?'" (Then give a citation for the source.)

- *Quote experts:* Your statements or arguments are much more convincing when you can buttress them with brief quotes from experts. Quoting authorities also can make your paper much more interesting and readable to the instructor. One caution, however: Don't overdo the quotations. Keep them brief.

- *Avoid irrelevancies:* Don't think you have to use all your research. That is, don't feel you have to try to impress your instructor by showing how much work you've done in your investigation. Just say what you need to say. Avoid piling on lots of irrelevant information, which will only distract and irritate your reader.

- *Give the source of your data and examples:* Your instructor will want to know where you got your supporting information. Thus, be sure to provide sources. These can be expressed with precision on the final draft, following the particular text citation and works cited (bibliographic) style you've decided on. For now put some sort of shorthand for your sources in the first draft.

  For instance, at the end of the sentence above about the football playbook, you could provide the author, year, and page for the source in parentheses. Example: ". . . learning the playbook?' (Wahlstrom 1998, p. 23)."

- *Jot down ideas:* As you proceed through the first draft, jot down any ideas that come to you that don't immediately seem to fit anywhere. You may find a place for them later.

- *Take breaks:* Professional writers find that physical activity gives the mind a rest and triggers new ideas. The brain needs to disengage. Take short breaks to relax. Go get a soda, stroll down the corridor, take a walk outside, or otherwise move your body a bit. Take pen and paper and jot down thoughts.

LETTING THE DRAFT SIT.   Many students write papers right up against their deadlines. It's far, far better, however, if you can get the first draft done early and let it sit in a drawer for a day or so. This will allow you to come back and revise it with a fresh perspective.

Phase 5: Revising, Finalizing, & Proofreading Your Paper

PREVIEW Ideally the fifth phase should take as much time as the first four. This final phase consists of seven parts. (1) Read the paper aloud or have someone else read it. (2) Delete irrelevant material. (3) Write transitions and reorganize. (4) Do fine-tuning and polishing. (5) Type the paper. (6) Proofread the paper. (7) Make a copy.

The last phase, Phase 5, consists of revising, finalizing, and proofreading your paper. How much time should revising take? One suggestion is this: Phases 1–4 should take half your time, and Phase 5 should take the other half of your time. This rule shows the importance of revision.

The steps to take in revision are as follows:

- Read the paper aloud or get someone else to read it

- Delete irrelevant material

- Write transitions and do any reorganizing

- Do fine-tuning and polishing

- Type the paper

- Proofread the paper

- Make a copy

READ ALOUD OR HAVE SOMEONE ELSE READ DRAFTS OF YOUR PAPER.
It's hard for us to spot our own mistakes, particularly during a silent reading. To better catch these, try the following:

- ***Read your draft aloud to yourself:*** If you read aloud what you've written, whether first draft or revised draft, you'll be able to spot missing words, awkward usage, and missing details.

- ***Get feedback from another person:*** By having a friend, family member, or the instructor read any of your drafts, you can get the help of an "editor." (You can offer to read friends' papers in exchange.) Any additional feedback can be valuable.

  SPECIAL NOTE: *Don't take the criticism personally.* If your readers say your paper is "illogical" or "vague," they are not implying you're stupid. When people criticize your draft, they are not criticizing you as a human being. Moreover, remember you don't *have* to do what they say. You're looking for suggestions, not commandments.

DELETE IRRELEVANT MATERIAL.
The best way to start the revision is to take a pencil and start crossing out words. Like a film maker cutting scenes so a movie won't run too long (and bore the audience), you should cut your paper to its essentials.

This is what editors call "blue penciling." Strive for conciseness and brevity. As a mental guideline, imagine someone writing "Repetitious!" or "Redundant!" or "Wordy!" in the margin. Be ruthless. First cut unnecessary sections, pages, and paragraphs. Then cut unnecessary sentences, phrases, and words. Cut even your best ideas and phrases—those gems you're proud of—if they don't move the essay along and advance your case.

WRITE TRANSITIONS & REORGANZE. You may have written the first draft fairly rapidly and not given much thought to making transitions—logical connections— between thoughts. You may also have deleted such connections when you blue-penciled material above. Now's the time to make sure the reader is able to move logically from one of your ideas to another.

You may well discover while doing this that your paper needs to be reorganized, that your outline isn't working right. There are two ways to handle this:

- **Low-tech reorganizing—scissors and glue:** You can use scissors to cut up your paper, then move the cut-up sections around. Use glue (paste) or transparent tape to attach the sections to blank pieces of paper. This activity is known as "cutting and pasting."

- **High-tech reorganizing—word processing:** The same kind of resequencing can be done electronically with a word processing program by using the "cut and paste" function. You use the "cut" command to mark the beginning and end of a section. Then you go to another location in the document and use the "move" command to transfer ("paste") that marked-off section to it.

DO FINE-TUNING & POLISHING. Now you need to take a pencil and do a final editing to make sure everything reads well.

Some suggestions:

- **Have a thesis statement:** Make sure the introduction to the paper has a thesis statement that says what the main point of your paper is.

- **Guide the reader:** Tell the reader what you're going to do. Introduce each change in topic. Connect topics by writing transitions.

- **Present supporting data:** Make sure you have enough examples, quotations, and data to support your assertions.

- **Don't be wordy:** Don't be infatuated with the exuberance and prolixity of your own verbosity. (Loose translation: Don't use big words when short ones will do.) Delete unnecessary words.

- **Check grammar and spelling:** Check your paper for grammatical mistakes. Also check for spelling. Look up words you're not sure about.

- **Follow correct style for documentation:** Follow the instructor's directions, if any, for documenting your sources. The humanities, for example, follow the style developed by the Modern Language Association. The social sciences follow the style developed by the American Psychological Association. Guidebooks are available in the campus bookstore or at the library.

A popular style nowadays is to identify the author's last name and the page reference within parentheses and within the text. For example:

"As one New York Times reporter summarized the NCAA study, white male athletes and nonathletes graduated at the same rate. But athletes had a better

PANEL 7.5

Documentation. One preferred style of documentation is to identify the author's last name with the page reference within parentheses in the text. The complete source is then presented at the end of the paper in a "Works Cited" section.

Example of citation in text:
As one New York Times reporter summarized the NCAA study, white male athletes and nonathletes graduated at the same rate. But athletes had a better graduation rate than nonathletes among black women, black men, and white women (Litsky C19).

Example of "Works Cited" section:

WORKS CITED
Litsky, Frank. "Athletes' Graduation Rate Surpasses Nonathletes'." New York Times 27 June 1997, C19.
Rice, Philip L. Stress and health. 2nd ed. Pacific Grove, CA: Brooks/Cole, 1992.
Thurow, Roger. "Duh . . . NFL Players Really Aren't So Dumb." Wall Street Journal 19 April 1996, B11.

graduation rate than nonathletes among black women, black men, and white women (Litsky C19)."

You then present a complete description of each source in an alphabetical listing at the end of the paper entitled "Works Cited." (*See* ■ *Panel 7.5.*)

THE PRESENTATION: TYPE YOUR PAPER. Presentation is important. Some instructors accept handwritten papers, but they'd rather not, because handwriting is hard to read. In a job interview situation, you have to sell yourself not only by your experience but also by the way you dress and present yourself. Similarly, you have to sell your paper not only by its ideas but by its presentation.

Thus, it's best to type your paper or have it typed. You need not be expert; using two fingers instead of ten just means typing will take a little longer. If you have access to a personal computer, you'll find typing is even less of a chore because correcting mistakes is easier than on a typewriter. You can type (keyboard) on the machine, print out a draft, and make corrections on the draft with a pencil. Then you can type in the corrections and print out a clean draft.

PROOFREADING. In the past, have you had papers come back from the instructor with red ink circling spelling and grammatical mistakes? Those red circles probably negatively affected your final grade, marking you down from, say, an A− to a B+.

With your paper in beautiful final-typed form (and the hand-in deadline perhaps only hours away), it may be tempting not to proofread it. You may not only be supremely tired of the whole thing but not want to "mess it up" by making handwritten corrections. Do it anyway. The instructor won't have any excuse then to give you red circles for small mistakes. (If you're using a word processor, providing a completely clean final draft is very easy.)

MAKE A COPY. Papers do get lost or stolen after they've been handed in (or on a student's way to handing it in). If you typed your paper on a word processor, make sure you save a copy on a floppy disk. If you typed it on a typewriter or handwrote it, use a photocopying machine at the library or an instant-printing shop to make a copy.

Making an Oral Presentation

PREVIEW An oral presentation can involve the same kind of research and writing that is required for a written presentation (term paper). Beyond that, an oral presentation has the following aspects. (1) You need to prepare readable speaker's notes, either full text or notes only. (2) You need to prepare a beginning that goes right to the point, a middle that expands on that, and an ending that repeats the middle points. (3) You need to understand the attention cycle of the audience. (4) You need to know how to reduce your nervousness through rehearsal and preparation, breathing, and mind control. (5) You need to make the delivery while coping with your nervous energy, focusing on the audience, and pacing yourself.

The material you've gathered and organized for a written paper can also be used for an oral presentation. If you're one of the millions of people who are anxious—indeed, panicked—about speaking on your feet before several other people, take heart. Some of us authors used to be that way ourselves, but we've since found some ways to make it easier—and to reduce the panicky feelings.

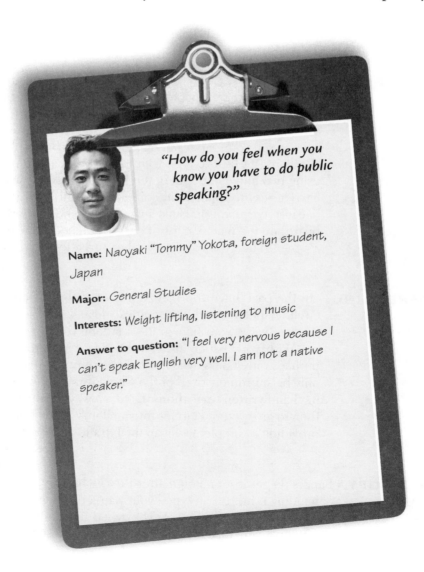

"How do you feel when you know you have to do public speaking?"

Name: Naoyaki "Tommy" Yokota, foreign student, Japan

Major: General Studies

Interests: Weight lifting, listening to music

Answer to question: "I feel very nervous because I can't speak English very well. I am not a native speaker."

It's possible to go all the way through school and not have to make an oral presentation. Some instructors, however, may require it. More important, outside school, the ability to speak to a room full of people is one of the greatest skills you can have. This is supported by a study conducted by AT&T and Stanford University. It found that the top predictor of success and professional upward mobility is how much you enjoy public speaking and how effective you are at it.[4] No doubt you'll need to draw on this skill at some point. Maybe it will only be to make a toast at a wedding. But maybe it will be to present ideas to clients or supervisors on a matter that could profoundly affect your future.

PREPARING YOUR NOTES: TWO METHODS. Obviously, your notes have to be readable. If you have to squint or bend over to read them, you'll be undermining the effect of your presentation. Thus, unless you'll be sitting down when you deliver your speech, assume you'll be reading your notes from about 2 feet away.

Whether your speech takes 10 minutes or an hour, there are two ways to prepare your notes:

- **On 4 × 6 cards:** You can prepare your final text or your notes on 4 × 6 note cards (better than the smaller 3 × 5 cards). Number the cards so that you can put them back in order if they are dropped. Move the cards from front to back of the stack as you go through them.

  If you'll be standing up (or if your vision is not perfect) while you speak, print your notes in large block letters. If you'll be sitting down, type them in all-capital letters.

- **Outlined on paper:** You can also prepare your text or notes on standard size (8½ × 11) paper. The advantage of this method is that you won't distract your audience by shuffling cards.

  When you type your text, type all capital letters, triple-spaced, and allow generous margins to the left and right. One public-speaking expert, Ed Wohlmuth, recommends using standard proofreader's marks in red for emphasis. Put "a triple underline under the first letter of each sentence and circle around each period," he says. "This will help you find the location of each complete sentence very quickly."[5]

  If you use a word processor for typing, some programs will allow you to enlarge the type. Thus, to enhance readability, you can produce notes in a type size two or three times as large as normal typewriter type.

FULL TEXT OR NOTES ONLY? Should you type out the full text of the speech or should you just do notes? Wohlmuth recommends that you write out the entire speech, even if later you convert to notes only. The reason is that doing a word-for-word text will help you ingrain the speech in your memory.[6]

A full text is particularly recommended if you are doing a stand-up speech to an audience of 30 people or more. If you're talking to a small group, whether you're standing up or sitting down, a full-text delivery is probably inappropriate. You want to *interact with* the people in the audience, not talk to them.

THE BEGINNING, MIDDLE, & END. Speech writer Phil Theibert says a speech has just three simple rules:[7]

1. Tell them what you're going to say.

2. Say it.

3. Tell them what you said.

These correspond to the three parts of a paper—beginning, middle, and end (or introduction, body, and conclusion).

■ **Beginning:** The introduction should take 5% to 15% of your speaking time, and it should prepare the audience for the rest of the speech.

Should you begin with a joke? Probably not. If it bombs, your audience will be uncomfortable (and will wonder if more mediocre material is to come) and so will you. Unless you're David Letterman or Jay Leno—whose jokes fail surprisingly often, you'll notice—it's best to simply "tell them what you're going to say."

Also we suggest avoiding phrases such as "I'm honored to be with you here today . . ." Because *everything* in your speech should be relevant, try to go right to the point. For example:

"Good afternoon. The subject of computer security may seem far removed from the concerns of most of us. But I intend to describe how our supposedly private computerized records are routinely violated, who's doing it, and how you can protect yourself."

If you wish, you might tell a *true* story (not a joke) as a way of hooking your audience.[8] For example:

"My topic this morning is computer security. In a few seconds I'm going to explain how our supposedly private computerized records are routinely violated, who's doing it, and how you can protect yourself. First, however, I'd like to tell you a true story about a student, his father, and a personal computer. . . ."

■ **Middle:** In the main body of the speech, the longest part, which takes 75% to 90% of your time, you "say what you said you were going to say."

The most important thing to realize is this: Your audience won't remember more than a few points anyway. Thus, you need to decide *what three or four points must be remembered.*[9] Then cover them as succinctly as possible.

The middle part generally follows the same rules as were explained for the middle part of a term paper. Use examples, quotations, and statistics (don't overdo it on the statistics) to support your assertions and hold your listeners' attention.

Be particularly attentive to transitions. Listening differs from reading in that the listener has only one chance to get your meaning. He or she cannot go back and reread. Thus, be sure you constantly provide your audience with guidelines and transitional phrases so they can see where you're going. Example:

"There are four ways the security of computer files can be compromised. The first way is . . ."

■ **End:** The end might take 5% to 10% of your time. Don't drop the ball here. You need a wrap-up that's strong, succinct, and persuasive. Indeed, many professional speakers consider the conclusion to be as important as the introduction.

The conclusion should "tell them what you told them." You need some sort of signal phrase that cues the audience you are heading into your wind-up.

Examples:

"Let's review the main points we've covered. . . ."

"In conclusion, what CAN you do to protect against unauthorized invasion of all those computerized files with your name on them? I pointed out three main steps. One . . ."

Give some thought to the last thing you're going to say. It should be strongly upbeat, a call to action, a thought for the day, a quotation, a little story. In short, you need a solid finish of some sort. Examples:

"I want to leave you with one last thought . . ."

"Finally, let me close by sharing something that happened to me. . . ."

"As Albert Einstein said, 'Imagination is more important than knowledge.'"

Then say "Thank you" and stop talking.

UNDERSTANDING THE AUDIENCE. As you know yourself, your attention can wander when you're a member of an audience. Thus, you have to understand the basics of the attention cycle and tailor your speech accordingly—particularly the middle part. As Tony Alessandra and Phil Hunsaker, authors of *Communicating at Work*, point out:

Studies have shown that material at the beginning and end of a presentation will be remembered more than the material in the middle. Our attention span lasts only for a short time and then it tapers off. When we sense the end of a message, we pull back in time to catch the last material. Fluctuation of the attention cycle is one of the main reasons we put such emphasis on the introduction and conclusion.[10]

So how do you hold people's attention during the middle of your speech? Alessandra and Hunsaker recommend putting in a lot of mini-cycles with beginnings, middles, and ends, changing the pace every 10 to 15 minutes. You can do this by including appropriate humor, stories, analogies, examples, comparisons, personal testimony, and variation in tone of voice. You can even have activities and exercises that ask for the audience's involvement.

HOW TO REDUCE YOUR NERVOUSNESS: REHEARSAL & PREPARATION. It may be true that the number one fear of most adults—even more than death—is speaking in public.[11] You can't do anything about death, of course, but you can about your fear of public speaking.

Professional speaker Lilly Walters suggests that 75% of your fear can be reduced by rehearsal and preparation. The remaining 25%, she says, can be reduced by breathing and mind control.[12] Stage fright is *normal.* Every professional speaker, actor, musician, and performer gets that feeling of weak knees, sweaty palms, and butterflies in the stomach. The best way to reduce this nervousness is through rehearsal and preparation—in other words, practice practice practice.

Here are some tips for rehearsing the speech:

■ *Read silently:* Read the speech over several times silently. Edit the manuscript as you go to smooth out awkward passages.

■ *Read aloud:* Read the speech several times aloud. Use a loud voice (unless you'll be using a microphone when you speak). Your voice sounds different to you when you talk loudly; you want to be used to this when you give your address. Time yourself so you won't run too long.

■ **Memorize the opening:** Memorize the opening *word for word*. This is essential.

■ **Practice on a spot:** Practice your speech while staring at a spot on the wall. This is particularly good advice for the opening. You are most nervous during the first few minutes. Thus, one professional speaker suggests, you should memorize a dynamite opening and practice it while staring at a spot on the wall. As a result, he says, "you develop such fantastic confidence that it carries you through the rest of the speech."[13]

■ **Practice in a mirror:** Practice delivering the speech while standing in front of a mirror. Observe your gestures, expressions, and posture. Don't worry too much about gestures: the main thing is to do whatever comes naturally.

■ **Practice on audiotape, videotape, or in front of friends:** Any other rehearsal activities can't help but help. Read your speech into an audiotape recorder and listen to the results. Or do the same thing with a videotape recorder, which may be available at the school's media center. Notice voice inflections and mannerisms (such as *you knows*, *umms*, *ahs*). Be sure your voice doesn't trail off at the ends of sentences or phrases.

Try out your address in front of friends or family members. It's possible they will be heavy on the positive ("I think your speech is quite good"). However, you should solicit and listen to any criticism ("Do you know you rock from side to side a lot?").

HOW TO REDUCE YOUR NERVOUSNESS: BREATHING & MIND CONTROL.
When we're nervous, we forget to breathe normally, and this makes us more nervous. To control your breathing, Lilly Walters suggests the following 5-second exercise:

Think, "Deep breath and hold, 1, 2, 3, 4, 5." (Add a "Mississippi" onto the end of each number—it's pretty tough to figure out how long a second is when your adrenaline is racing.) Tell yourself, "Slow release, and inhale 1, 2, etc."[14]

Mind control consists of self-talk. Your inner Voice Of Judgment may be saying a lot of negative things. ("They're going to *hate* me." "I'm going to look like a *fool*." "I'll look *fat*.") You can take comfort, then, from what Walters says:

Have you ever gone to a presentation and really wanted the presenter to be terrible? Most of the time you'd much rather have a good time than a bad time. The same is true for your audience. Most listeners are sitting there, ready and willing to make allowances for your mistakes. In fact, a few mistakes make you human and just that much more lovable.[15]

Instead of letting negative thoughts take over, try positive affirmations that are important to you: "I know what I know." "I'm glad I'm here." "I can do it!" Using self-talk, let your thoughts direct you to success!

DELIVERING THE ORAL PRESENTATION. On the day of the big speech, there are a few things to concentrate on:

■ **Dress appropriately:** Dress to look your best—or at least appropriate to the occasion. Even if you're just doing a report in a classroom, audiences like it when you look a little special (though not out of place).

- **Deal with your nervous energy:** Almost every speaker, even a professional, experiences stage fright. These symptoms actually tell you your body is preparing for a big event; in fact, you need the edge to be your best. The trick is to manage your nervous energy—foot tapping, fiddling with eyeglasses, swaying back and forth—which can be annoying to an audience.

  Ed Wohlmuth suggests buying a kid's rubber ball that's large enough to cover most of your palm. During your waking hours before the speech, squeeze it frequently in each hand. From then on, when you feel nervous energy start to mount, think of the rubber ball.[16]

  Whatever you do, don't use tranquilizers or alcohol. Eat in moderation before your talk. Drink some water (but not gallons) before the speech to ease the dryness in your mouth.

- **Try out the speaker's position:** Get to the classroom or hall early, or go a day or two before. Step behind the podium or wherever the speaker's position is. If the room is empty, speak your introduction aloud, aiming it at the last seat in the room. You might even deliver the entire speech.

  If you plan on using audiovisual aids, flip charts, or a microphone, it's especially recommended that you do a dry run. (Do this with the help of others managing the equipment.)

- **Focus on the audience:** When your speech is under way, *focus on the audience.* Maintain eye contact, shifting your attention among a few friendly faces in the room. When you look at people, the audience becomes less intimidating. If you see people talking among themselves, talk directly to them; this may impel them to stop.

- **Pace yourself and watch your time:** Try to stick to the timetable you set during your rehearsals. You can lay a watch face up on the podium. Or you can position it on the inside of your wrist, where you can glance at it easily without calling attention to what you are doing.

  Pace yourself. Your instinct may be to rush through the speech and get it over with. However, your listeners will appreciate a pause from time to time.

  Remember that it's better to end early than to run long. Because the conclusion is so important, you don't want to have to be rushed at the end because you're squeezed for time.

Possibly you won't have to do many stand-up oral presentations, but learning to speak in public is important, anyway. By learning to speak up in class, for example, you'll become comfortable with asking questions that come to your mind during lectures. Through your involvement and interaction, you'll increase your learning ability—and probably your grades.

Onward

PREVIEW   Education is more than memorizing subjects.

Learning to conceive, research, and write papers and speeches is learning how to think. American education has been criticized because students are required to memorize subjects rather than to understand and analyze them. However, as Wisconsin student James Robinson points out, future survival lies in knowing how to solve problems. "If we do not know how to analyze a problem," he says, "how are we ever going to compete in the real world? The problems we are going to face are not all going to be written down in a textbook with the answers in the back. . . . As students, we must realize that we need to come up with our own solutions."[17]

Robinson is right. And the final payoff is this: It has been found that students who learn how to think do better not only in school but in life.[18] We explore thinking in more detail in the next chapter.

NOTES

1. Ellis, M. E. Quoted in Mitchell, J. J. (1997, March 16). "Soft skills" prized by tech firms. *San Jose Mercury News,* pp. 1E, 3E.

2. Walter, T., & Siebert, A. (1990). *Student success: How to succeed in college and still have time for your friends.* Fort Worth, TX: Holt, Rinehart and Winston, pp. 108–109.

3. Walter & Siebert, 1990, p. 103.

4. Alessandra, T., & Hunsaker, P. (1993). *Communicating at work.* New York: Fireside, p. 169.

5. Wohlmuth, E. (1983). *The overnight guide to public speaking.* Philadelphia: Running Press, p. 119.

6. Wohlmuth, 1983, p. 118.

7. Theibert, P. (1993, August 2). Speechwriters of the world, get lost! *Wall Street Journal,* p. A16.

8. Wohlmuth, 1983, p. 31.

9. Walters, L. (1993). *Secrets of successful speakers: How you can motivate, captivate, and persuade.* New York: McGraw-Hill, p. 203.

10. Alessandra & Hunsaker, 1993, p. 179.

11. Alessandra & Hunsaker, 1993, p. 169.

12. Walters, 1993, p. 32.

13. Malouf, D., cited in Walters, 1993, p. 33.

14. Walters, 1993, p. 36.

15. Walters, 1993, p. 37.

16. Wohlmuth, 1983, p. 133.

17. Robinson, J. R. (1991, November 6). [Letter to editor.] U.S. students memorize, but don't understand. *New York Times,* p. A14.

18. Elder, J. (1991, January 6). A learned response. *New York Times,* sec. 4A, p. 23.

Classroom Activities: Directions to the Instructor

1. ***Getting going on a research paper.*** Have students form into small groups (four to six students each). Then ask them to select one of the following topics: *horse racing, magnetic resonance imaging, information literacy, population control, urban crime, long-distance running, retirement planning, résumé writing.* (Or ask students to consult with you about another topic.)

    Each group is to develop a number of questions on the topic. They are then to use the questions to produce an outline. Group members should write their names at the top of the outline and turn it in to the instructor.

2. ***Looking up a topic in the library.*** This activity involves out-of-class time because it requires a visit to the library. Students are to follow the instructions of Practical Exploration #7.1, "Research: Looking Up a Topic in the Library." They may develop the topic agreed on in Classroom Activity #1 above or may develop a topic required for a paper in another class. They should research the sources requested in the Practical Exploration, either by themselves or in a team with three to five other students.

    Later, have students discuss the following questions in class. What types of information were the easiest to locate and why? Which the most difficult? Is your approach to locating sources low-tech or high-tech and how? How could searching for information be enhanced? What did you learn about the library?

3. ***How do you handle text citations and references?*** Finding the correct form for text citations and/or references may seem somewhat daunting to many students. With a little bit of out-of-class time for research and a bit of in-class time for discussion, however, they may learn to feel more comfortable with this important part of writing papers.

    Instruct students to find correct references for three kinds of source material: (1) books, (2) articles from periodicals, and (3) other sources (such as encyclopedias and government publications). Point out that different academic disciplines have their own preferred reference and footnoting styles.

    In the library, students are to find and copy out text citation and reference styles for books, articles, and other sources that will appear in (a) papers they will submit in most of their courses, and (b) papers they will submit in courses in their major or prospective major.

    Later, selected examples can be posted on the board. Ask the class to discuss the differences among the various forms.

The Examined Life:
Student Assignments for Journal Entries

JOURNAL ENTRY #7.1: WRITING ABOUT SOMETHING IMPORTANT TO YOU Write a few words about something that is very important to you, such as a particular person or event that profoundly affected you. (Use a separate sheet of paper, if you wish.) Describe how writing helps you understand it.

_____
_____
_____
_____
_____
_____
_____
_____

JOURNAL ENTRY #7.2: WHAT MORE DO YOU NEED TO FIND OUT ABOUT THE LIBRARY? How comfortable are you with using the school's library? For each of the following library resources, rate yourself on your confidence in using that resource for research. Use the following system:

A = Very comfortable
B = Comfortable
C = Somewhat uncertain
D = Very uncertain
F = Totally unfamiliar

1. Online card catalog	A	B	C	D	F
2. Microfiche	A	B	C	D	F
3. Interlibrary loan	A	B	C	D	F
4. Newspaper, magazine, and journal indexes	A	B	C	D	F
5. Specialized dictionaries	A	B	C	D	F
6. Internet and/or other computerized networks	A	B	C	D	F

Look at those you rated C, D, or F. What specific steps could you take to become more comfortable with them?

_____
_____
_____
_____
_____
_____
_____

JOURNAL ENTRY #7.3: **WHAT DO YOU NEED TO FIND OUT ABOUT TEXT CITATIONS AND WORKS-CITED (BIBLIOGRAPHY) STYLES?**
One subject that might have been discussed in more detail in this chapter was the proper form for text citations and bibliographies. Is this an area in which you need further help? Who can give you the assistance you need?

_____

_____

_____

_____

_____

_____

_____

_____

JOURNAL ENTRY #7.4: **WHAT ARE YOUR WORRIES ABOUT PUBLIC SPEAKING?** What worries do you have about public speaking? Besides the techniques described in this chapter, what other means are available to help you do better at giving stand-up speeches? For instance, the counseling services may offer assistance, or you could join the group known as Toastmasters, which helps amateur speakers achieve proficiency.

CHAPTER EIGHT

_____

_____

_____

_____

_____

_____

_____

_____

THINKING SMART
Critical, creative, & other kinds of thinking

IN THIS CHAPTER: How smart do you have to be to get through higher education? Or to get through life? A high IQ may help, but there's more to being smart than IQ. In this chapter, we consider different kinds of intelligence and ways to "think smart"—ways of thinking that you can learn to do. We consider:

■ *Different kinds of intelligence:* You learn that there are perhaps seven kinds of intelligence, and one of the most important is "emotional intelligence."

■ *Critical thinking:* You learn critical thinking, or clear or active thinking; its four-step approach; and several types of incorrect reasoning to avoid.

■ *Creative thinking:* You learn creative thinking, which is sparked by being receptive to messiness, avoiding conceptual blocks such as stereotypes, not being afraid to make mistakes, and other techniques.

▪ "Genius" may be one of the most overused words in the English language.

Painter Vincent Van Gogh, composer George Gershwin, and discoverer of the law of gravity Sir Isaac Newton have all been called geniuses. But so also have comedian Bill Cosby, boxer Muhammad Ali, country-rock singer Jerry Lee Lewis, and Wal-Mart founder Sam Walton. Indeed, a computer search of major U.S. publications by *Newsweek* magazine yielded 1,038 uses of "genius" in just one month![1]

Still, maybe this seemingly careless throwing around of the word is more or less appropriate. Geniuses are able to *think smart*, certainly, but their smartness reveals itself in far deeper and wider ways than can be summarized by the kind of analytical thinking reflected by a single number of IQ, or "intelligence quotient," as measured on traditional general-intelligence tests (such as the Stanford-Binet or Wechsler tests). Indeed, scientists now believe there are *several* different kinds of human intelligence.

Different Kinds of Intelligence— Including Emotional Intelligence or "EQ"

PREVIEW There are perhaps seven types of intelligence, which might be summarized as word smart, logic smart, picture smart, body smart, music smart, people smart, and self smart. Perhaps even more important than having a high IQ is having high "EQ," or "emotional intelligence"—the ability to cope, empathize with others, and be self-motivated.

"How much does IQ buy you after you get out of school?" asks Yale University psychologist Robert Sternberg. "Not much," he concludes. "A high IQ doesn't make a better salesperson or a more creative artist or scientist, and it won't enable a doctor to work better with patients. Even college professors will fail if they don't know how to teach or get along with administrators."[2]

SEVEN KINDS OF INTELLIGENCE. In his book *Frames of Mind,* Harvard psychologist Howard Gardner theorized that there are seven types of intelligence. They might be summarized as:

word smart

logic smart

picture smart

body smart

music smart

people smart

self smart[3]

Do you think of yourself as being "smarter" in some of these areas than in others? Are you better at athletics ("body smart"), for example, than at writing ("word smart")? Or at reading your own emotions ("self smart") than at conceiving drawings ("picture smart")? Gardner suggests that you think of yourself as having multiple computers in your mind that process information. "We can all compute the information," Gardner says, "but some of us have better computers in one area than another."[4]

Maybe, then, you're not a genius at the kind of analytical, language, and memorizing skills best measured by IQ tests. But you might have exceptional musical, spatial, or social intelligence. Or perhaps you have qualities such as creativity, sense of humor, leadership, or (very important) *persistence* that, as one writer suggests, "today may propel a person with an undistinguished IQ . . . to extraordinary success and happiness."[5]

EMOTIONAL INTELLIGENCE, OR "EQ" One kind of intelligence that may be even more important than IQ is what has been called "EQ"—emotional intelligence. A term popularized by *New York Times* psychology and health journalist Daniel Goleman in his book by the same name, ***emotional intelligence ("EQ") is the ability to cope, empathize with others, and be self-motivated.***[6] High emotional intelligence, then, would seem to include being "people smart" and "self smart."

According to Goleman, EQ encompasses such traits as empathy (the ability to imagine and relate to other people's feelings), self-awareness, optimism, impulse control, and capacity to manage anxiety and anger. If you haven't begun to develop these traits, explains Goleman, you're not only apt to not be very popular—which can affect your "people skills" and thus hinder your success in the workplace—but you may also have difficulty learning. "Our emotional state has a direct impact on our capacity to take in and act on information," he says.[7] Thus, if you're always angry, anxious, or frustrated, you can't think well, and this mental state can affect your academic performance.

We describe how to manage stress and conflict, which affect your EQ, in Chapter 10, "Personal Growth." In the rest of this chapter, we consider two important kinds of thinking needed for academic success: (1) critical thinking and (2) creative thinking.

Critical Thinking: What It Is, How to Use It

PREVIEW Critical thinking is clear, skeptical, or active thinking. It takes the approach that there is "no shame, no blame" in making and reducing errors. Four steps in critical thinking are (1) getting an understanding of the problem, (2) gathering information and interpreting it, (3) developing a solution plan and carrying it out, and (4) evaluating the plan's effectiveness. Critical thinking uses the tools of reasoning, as in determining when arguments are deductive or inductive. There are several types of incorrect reasoning, or fallacies. They include *jumping to conclusions, false cause, appeal to authority, circular reasoning, irrelevant attack on opponent, straw man argument, slippery slope, appeal to pity,* and *use of questionable statistics.*

Critical thinking means clear thinking, skeptical thinking, active thinking. It involves actively seeking to understand, analyze, and evaluate information in order to solve specific problems. You need to exercise critical thinking, for example, when you're trying to analyze the correctness of someone's point of view—or of your own point of view when you're trying to solve an academic problem or personal problem.

Unlike passive thinking, in which you unquestioningly accept the information given you, critical thinking means you constantly question everything. You're curious to know more. You look further for answers. As a result, you experience what learning really is.

UNCRITICAL THINKING: THE MIND-SET AS ENEMY. The opposite of critical thinking is, of course, uncritical thinking. Uncritical thinking is all around us. People run their lives on the basis of horoscopes, numerology, and similar nonsense. They believe in "crystal healing" and "color therapy." They think cranks and quacks can cure cancer with apricot-pit extract or alleviate arthritis with copper bracelets. Otherwise intelligent people believe that mind power alone can be used to bend spoons.

These are not just bits of harmless goofiness, like wearing your "lucky" shirt to your final exam. James Randi, a debunker of claims made by supporters of the paranormal, suggests just why such uncritical thinking is dangerous.

"We live in a society that is enlarging the boundaries of knowledge at an unprecedented rate," he says, "and we cannot keep up with more than a small portion of what is made available to us. To mix our data input with childish notions of magic and fantasy is to cripple our perception of the world around us. We must reach for the truth, not for the ghosts of dead absurdities."[8]

The enemy of clear thinking is our *mind-sets.* By the time we are grown, our minds have become "set" in patterns of thinking that affect how we respond to new ideas. These mind-sets are the result of our personal experiences and the various social environments in which we grew up. Such mind-sets determine what ideas we think are important and, conversely, what ideas we ignore. As one book on clear thinking points out, we can't pay attention to all the events that occur around us. Consequently, "our minds filter out some observations and facts and let others through to our conscious awareness."[9] Herein lies the danger: "As a result we see and hear what we subconsciously want to and pay little attention to facts or observations that have already been rejected as unimportant."

Having mind-sets makes life comfortable. However, as the foregoing writers point out, "Familiar relationships and events become so commonplace that we expect them to continue forever. Then we find ourselves completely unprepared to accept changes that are necessary, even when they stare us in the face."[10]

REDUCING ERRORS: "NO SHAME, NO BLAME." One way to overcome mind-sets is to take a "no-shame, no blame" approach to admitting errors. Says Gerard Nierenberg, whose book *Do It Right the First Time* advocates this approach to reducing errors in the workplace and in personal life, "30% to 40% of all workers' and executives' time is spent anticipating, correcting, and handling errors." By taking a "no-shame, no-blame" attitude toward our mistakes, he says, we can learn to make fewer of them.

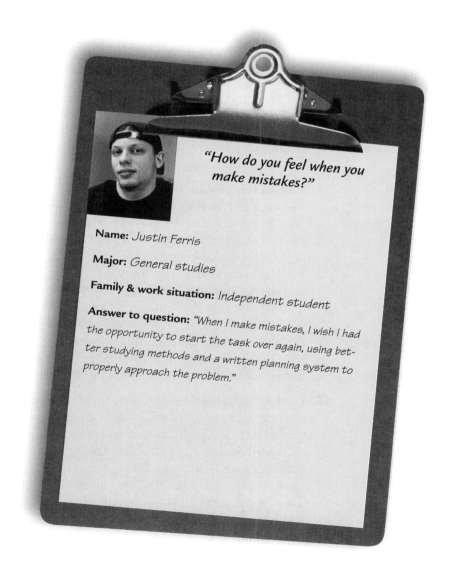

"How do you feel when you make mistakes?"

Name: Justin Ferris

Major: General studies

Family & work situation: Independent student

Answer to question: "When I make mistakes, I wish I had the opportunity to start the task over again, using better studying methods and a written planning system to properly approach the problem."

How does one do this? "First you must determine exactly what is wrong, what the problem is," says Nierenberg. "Next, you determine how extensive the damage is. Then you look at what caused the problem . . . [and] determine the best way to remedy it and how a reoccurrence can be best avoided."[11]

The most important factor in all this is *attitude:* You should learn to acknowledge an error as soon as it's discovered and not feel ashamed of having made it. Then you need to take responsibility openly and honestly, accepting criticism and advice from others without hiding behind self-justification or lies.

THE STEPS IN CRITICAL THINKING. Fortunately, critical thinking can be learned just as you can learn, say, how to play the guitar, install a dishwasher, or explore the Internet.

The four steps in critical thinking are these:

1. Get an understanding of the problem.

2. Gather information and interpret it.

3. Develop a solution plan and carry it out.

4. Evaluate the plan's effectiveness.

Do these four steps seem rather obvious? (You'll notice some resemblance to Nierenberg's recipe for handling errors, discussed above.) Perhaps so, but it's amazing how often we try to "solve" or "fix" something by simply stumbling around, hoping everything will work out.

Let's run through these four steps.

1. ***Get an understanding of the problem:*** How many times have you been told, as for a test, to *read the directions*? How often, when looking at a manual on how to operate a new appliance or assemble a child's toy, have you found yourself *rereading the instructions*? In both cases, you're taking the necessary first step: making sure you understand the problem. This is basic.

If you *don't* take the trouble to make sure you comprehend the problem, you can waste a great deal of time trying to solve it and never do so. Getting an understanding may require you to read over the problem two or more times (as in math), ask someone for clarification (as an instructor), or seek alternative explanations (as in looking at a city road map instead of a state road map).

Often you can get a better understanding of a problem just by talking about it, as in a discussion in a study group with other students.

2. ***Gather information and interpret it:*** Sometimes just by making sure you understand a problem you can see a solution to it. At other times, however, you may need to get additional information and interpret it.

For instance, if the problem you're working on is what courses to take next quarter or semester, you'll need the school's catalog and perhaps a curriculum worksheet to see what courses you need to take in your career field or major. Then you'll need a class schedule that describes the courses that are offered and when.

As another example, if your problem is that you're required to write a paper on serial killers for a criminal justice course, you'll need to get books and other sources about the subject from the library. Then you'll need to interpret the

information to make sure you know the difference between serial killers and mass killers, for instance.

3. *Develop a solution plan and carry it out:* Developing a plan is sometimes the most difficult step. The reason: You may have to choose between several alternatives.

For example, you may have to choose among several courses you could take next term. And whatever course you *don't* take then, you'll have to take later—and hope that course will be offered sometime at a day and hour that works out for you. Or, in writing about serial killers, you'll have to decide between several possible outlines and draw on several possible examples.

Finally, you'll need to carry out the plan—which may or may not turn out to be workable. Maybe one course you sign up for turns out to require far more homework than you bargained for and you can't handle it along with your other commitments. Maybe the direction of your paper can't be supported by the research you did.

4. *Evaluate the plan's effectiveness:* So you completed the semester of courses you planned or handed in your paper on serial killers. Maybe your experience was a disaster, in which case you'll want to know how to do it right next time. (Remember Nierenberg on reducing errors: You should look at what caused a problem for you and determine the best way to remedy it and how a recurrence can be avoided in the future.) Maybe your plan worked out okay, but there were things you might have handled better.

Drawing lessons from your experience is part and parcel of critical thinking, and it's a step that should not be neglected. If the experience was successful, can it be applied to other, similar problems? If only partly successful, can you see ways to change the information-gathering step or the solution-planning step to make it work better? If the experience was a disaster, is there a slogan you can draw from it that you can post over your desk? (Example: NEVER TAKE MORE THAN ONE SCIENCE CLASS IN A SEMESTER. Or, LOOK FOR *RECENT* ARTICLES WHEN RESEARCHING CRIMINAL JUSTICE PAPERS.)

THE REASONING TOOL: DEDUCTIVE & INDUCTIVE ARGUMENTS. The tool for breaking through the closed habits of thought called mind-sets is reasoning. ***Reasoning—giving reasons in favor of this or that assertion—*** is essential to thinking critically and solving life's problems. Reasoning is put in the form of what philosophers call *arguments*. **Arguments consist of one or more *premises*, or reasons, logically supporting a result or outcome called a *conclusion*.**

An example of an argument is as follows:

Premise 1: All instructors must grade students.

Premise 2: I am an instructor.

Conclusion: Therefore, I must grade students.

Note the tip-off word "Therefore," which signals that a conclusion is coming. In real life, such as arguments on TV or in newspapers, the premises and conclusions are not so neatly labeled. Still, there are clues: The words *because* and *for* usually signal premises. The words *therefore, hence,* and *so* signal conclusions. Not all groups of sentences form arguments. Often they may form anecdotes or other types of exposition or explanation.[12]

The two main kinds of correct or valid arguments are inductive and deductive.

■ ***Deductive argument:*** **A *deductive argument* is defined as follows: If its premises are true, then its conclusions are true also.** In other words, if the premises are true, the conclusions cannot be false.

■ ***Inductive argument:*** **An *inductive argument* is defined as follows: If the premises are true, the conclusions are PROBABLY true, but the truth is not guaranteed.** An inductive argument is sometimes known as a "probability argument."

An example of a *deductive argument* is as follows:[13]

Premise 1: All students experience stress in their lives.

Premise 2: Reuben is a student.

Conclusion: Therefore, Reuben experiences stress in his life.

This argument is deductive—the conclusion is *definitely* true if the premises are *definitely* true.

An example of an *inductive argument* is as follows:[14]

Premise 1: Stress can cause illness.

Premise 2: Reuben experiences stress in his life.

Premise 3: Reuben is ill.

Conclusion: Therefore, stress may be the cause of Reuben's illness.

Note the word "may" in the conclusion. This argument is inductive. The conclusion is not stated with absolute certainty; rather, it only suggests that stress *may* be the cause. The link between premises and conclusion is not definite because there may be other reasons for Reuben's illness (such as a virus).

SOME TYPES OF INCORRECT REASONING.

Patterns of incorrect reasoning are known as *fallacies*. Learning to identify fallacious arguments will help you avoid patterns of faulty thinking in your own writing and thinking. It will also help you identify them in others' thinking.

Some principal types of incorrect reasoning are these:

■ ***Jumping to conclusions:*** Also known as *hasty generalization,* the fallacy called ***jumping to conclusions* means that a conclusion has been reached when not all the facts are available.**

Example: Cab drivers may (illegally) refuse to take certain passengers to what they regard as dangerous neighborhoods merely on the basis of the passengers' skin color or looks, jumping to the conclusion that they are dangerous people. But what if that person turns out to be a city councilman, as happened in Boston a few years ago?

■ ***False cause or irrelevant reason:*** The faulty reasoning known as *non sequitur* (Latin for "it does not follow"), which might be better called ***false cause* or *irrelevant reason,* means that the conclusion does not follow logically from the supposed reasons stated earlier.** There is no *causal* relationship.

Example: You receive an A on a test. However, because you felt you hadn't been well prepared, you attribute your success to your friendliness with the instructor. Or to your horoscope. Neither of these "reasons" has anything to do with the result.

■ ***Appeal to authority:*** Known in Latin as *argumentum ad verecundiam,* **the *appeal to authority* argument uses an authority in one area to pretend to validate claims in another area in which the person is not an expert.**

Example: You see the appeal-to-authority argument used all the time in advertising. But what *does* a champion golfer really know about real-estate developments?

■ *Circular reasoning:* **The *circular reasoning* argument rephrases the statement to be proven true. It then uses the new, similar statement as supposed proof that the original statement is in fact true.**

Examples: You declare that you can drive safely at high speeds with only inches separating you from the car ahead. After all, you have driven this way for years without an accident. Or you say that paying student-body fees is for the common good because in the long run paying student-body fees benefits everyone.

■ *Irrelevant attack on opponent:* Known as an *ad hominem* argument (Latin for "to the person"), **the *irrelevant attack on an opponent* attacks a person's reputation or beliefs rather than his or her argument.**

Example: Politicians will frequently try to attack an adversary's reputation. Someone running for student-body president may attack an opponent's "character" or intelligence rather than the opponent's stand on the issues.

■ *Straw man argument:* **The *straw man argument* is when you misrepresent your opponent's position to make it easier to attack, or when you attack a weaker position while ignoring a stronger one.** In other words, you sidetrack the argument from the main discussion.

Example: A politician might attack an opponent as a "socialist" for supporting aid to mothers with dependent children but not for supporting aid to tobacco growers. (This is because the first politician also favors supporting tobacco growers.)

■ *Slippery slope:* **The *slippery slope* is a failure to see that the first step in a possible series of steps does not lead inevitably to the rest.**

Example: The "Domino theory," under which the United States waged wars against Communism, was a slippery slope argument. It assumed that if Communism triumphed in Nicaragua, say, it would inevitably spread to the rest of Central America and finally to the United States.

■ *Appeal to pity:* **The *appeal to pity* argument appeals to mercy rather than arguing on the merits of the case itself.**

Examples: Begging the dean not to expel you for cheating because your impoverished parents made sacrifices for your education exemplifies this fallacy.

■ *Questionable statistics:* Statistics can be misused in many ways as supporting evidence. The statistics may be unknowable, drawn from an unrepresentative sample, or otherwise suspect.

Examples: Stating that people were less happy 10,000 years ago than today is an example of unknowable or undefined use of statistics. Stating how much money is lost to taxes because of illegal drug transactions is speculation because such transactions are hidden or underground.

Fallacies such as these are used every day in promotional pitches, legal arguments, news analyses, and appeals for money. Clearly, being aware of them will serve you well all your life.

Creative Thinking

PREVIEW Creative thinking consists of being receptive to messiness, avoiding conceptual blocks such as stereotypes, not being afraid of making mistakes, and other techniques.

***Creative thinking* consists of imaginative ways of looking at known ideas.** Creative thinking enables you to solve problems for which traditional problem-solving methods don't work.

Creative thinking doesn't just help you think up topics for research papers in school. In the workplace, employees burning with bright ideas are an employer's greatest competitive resource. "Creativity precedes innovation, which is its physical expression," says *Fortune* magazine writer Alan Farnham. "It's the source of all intellectual property."[15]

The popular notion of creative people is that they are oddballs, showboats, or people who wear funny clothes. However, in reality anyone can be creative,

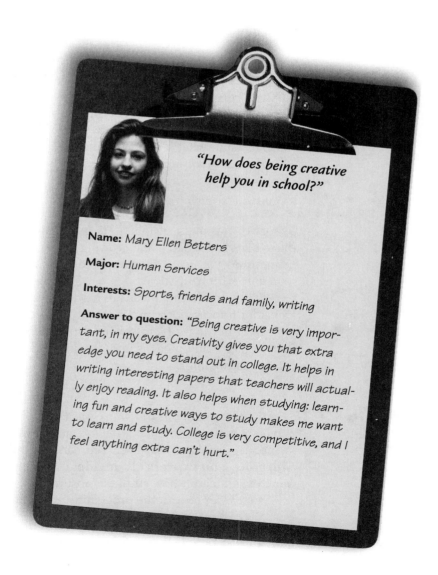

"How does being creative help you in school?"

Name: Mary Ellen Betters

Major: Human Services

Interests: Sports, friends and family, writing

Answer to question: "Being creative is very important, in my eyes. Creativity gives you that extra edge you need to stand out in college. It helps in writing interesting papers that teachers will actually enjoy reading. It also helps when studying: learning fun and creative ways to study makes me want to learn and study. College is very competitive, and I feel anything extra can't hurt."

whether wearing a beret or wearing a suit. And, contrary to the idea that people are born creative, creativity *can* be taught. For instance, creativity expert Edward de Bono, author of *Six Thinking Hats,* suggested the following exercise during one forum for executives. Five people were given a word, *party,* and challenged to use it to generate ideas for a new type of computer keyboard. After a moment, they began tossing out associations: Keyboards that connect through a party line. Keyboards that can be used only by people "invited" (that is, authorized) to use them. Keyboards with "surprise" (preprogrammed) keys. Clearly, then, creativity can be induced in people who might not seem to have it.[16]

You don't have to have a high IQ or be well educated to think creatively. Rather, says Farnham, creative people "are self-motivated, love risk, thrive on ambiguity, and delight in novelty, twists, and reversals."

So how do you begin to learn to think creatively? Here are some suggestions.

BE RECEPTIVE TO DISORDER & MESSINESS. Creativity is a messy process. There are people with an excessive fondness for order who cannot tolerate misleading and ill-fitting data and opinions. However, by allowing yourself to be receptive to such untidiness, you give yourself the chance for a new kind of order.

WATCH OUT FOR CONCEPTUAL BLOCKS. Conceptual blocks, or "mental walls" on creativity, keep you from correctly perceiving a problem or conceiving of its solution. One such block is ***stereotyping*, or selective perception.** This is when you see only what you *expect* to see. (When you see someone wearing a grey business suit, what kind of person do you expect? What about someone with a diamond in his or her nose?)

DON'T BE AFRAID OF MISTAKES. As we hinted earlier in the chapter, the fear of making errors or mistakes, of failing, is quite common. It occurs because most of us have been rewarded while growing up for producing "right" answers. However, sometimes you *want* to permit yourself mistakes because that allows you to come up with fresh ideas.

By saying that no ideas are too risky or embarrassing, you allow yourself to consider information you'd normally ignore. Judgment and criticism are necessary later in the problem-solving process. However, if they occur too early, you may reject many ideas, some of which are fragile and imperfect but may be made mature later.

TRY BRAINSTORMING. The word *brainstorming* was coined by advertising man Alex Osborn for a type of group problem solving in which several people work simultaneously on a specific problem. However, you can use this method by yourself. **In *brainstorming*, you express all the ideas that come to mind about a particular matter,** no matter how stupid or absurd they may seem.

Four rules govern the procedure, according to Osborn:

- ***No judgments allowed:*** No evaluations or judgments are permitted, as they might cause people to defend rather than generate ideas.

- **Be wild:** Think of the wildest ideas possible, in order to decrease individual judgment among individual members.

- **Go for quantity:** The more ideas the better. Quantity is more important than quality and, in fact, quantity *leads to* quality.

- **Build on others' ideas:** Build on and modify the ideas of others whenever possible; this will often lead to ideas superior to the original ones.[17]

TRY MIND MAPPING: BRAINSTORMING WITH PENCIL & PAPER. *Mind mapping* **is brainstorming by yourself with the help of pencil and paper.** To begin a mind-mapping session, suggests James M. Higgins, author of *101 Creative Problem Solving Techniques,* you write the name of the object or problem in the center of a piece of paper and draw a circle around it. Then you brainstorm each major aspect of the object or problem, drawing lines outward from the circle "like roads leaving a city."

As you brainstorm in more detail, you can draw branches from these "roads." "You can brainstorm all the main lines at once and then the branches for each," says Higgins, "or brainstorm a line and its branches, or jump from place to place as thoughts occur."[18]

SURRENDER TO YOUR UNCONSCIOUS. The unconscious mind can be a terrific problem solver, according to Michael Ray and Rochelle Myers, authors of *Creativity in Business.* They suggest that when you're trying to solve something (such as picking a term-paper topic), you should let go of anxious striving. Instead, ask a clear question about the key issue, then turn the problem over to your unconscious, as in your sleep.[19] Relaxation allows the mind to wander over "silly" ideas that may prove to deliver the "Aha!" you are looking for.

ASK DUMB QUESTIONS. Ask questions the way a child would: "What's behind a rainbow?" "What color is the inside of my brain?" "Why are my toes in front of my feet?"[20] Such "dumb" questions have no expectations, assumptions, or illusions. Once you begin, questions will lead to more questions.

BE RECEPTIVE TO ALL YOUR SENSES. Some people are resistant to using *all* their senses— smell, taste, and touch, as well as the more favored sight and sound. Some think verbally rather than visually, or vice versa. It's important to have access to all areas of imagination—to be able to smell and hear a ball park as well as visualize it. In addition, one must be able to manipulate and recombine ideas in the imagination—imagining a volcano in a ball park, for instance.

To see how creative you are in this respect, try Practical Exploration #8.1.

PRACTICAL EXPLORATION #8.1
CREATIVITY: HOW GOOD ARE YOU AT DIFFERENT TYPES OF SENSORY IMAGES?

Rate the following to find out how good you are at different types of sensory images.

c = Clear

v = Vague

n = Nothing

This activity may help you develop your sensory imagery ability, if used extensively. Sight tends to be the predominant sense. However, it should not be allowed to overpower other modes—smell, sound, taste, and touch—which can increase the clarity of one's imagery.

■ IMAGINE:

1.   The laugh of a friend.   c   v   n
2.   The sound of thunder.   c   v   n
3.   The sound of a horse walking on a road.   c   v   n
4.   The sound of a racing car.   c   v   n
5.   The feel of wet grass.   c   v   n
6.   The feel of your wife's/husband's/ girlfriend's/boyfriend's/pet's hair.   c   v   n
7.   The feel of diving into a cold swimming pool.   c   v   n
8.   The feel of a runny nose.   c   v   n
9.   The smell of bread toasting.   c   v   n
10.   The smell of fish.   c   v   n
11.   The smell of gasoline.   c   v   n
12.   The smell of leaves burning.   c   v   n
13.   The taste of a pineapple.   c   v   n
14.   The taste of Tabasco sauce.   c   v   n
15.   The taste of toothpaste.   c   v   n
16.   The muscular sensation of pulling on a rope.   c   v   n
17.   The muscular sensation of throwing a rock.   c   v   n
18.   The muscular sensation of running.   c   v   n
19.   The muscular sensation of squatting.   c   v   n
20.   The sensation of being uncomfortably cold.   c   v   n
21.   The sensation of having eaten too much.   c   v   n
22.   The sensation of extreme happiness.   c   v   n
23.   The sensation of a long attack of hiccups.   c   v   n

STUFF YOUR BRAIN, KEEP IDEA NOTES, & CULTIVATE LUCKY ACCIDENTS.

Stuff your brain with all kinds of words, pictures, and sounds, regardless of whether they seem useful at the time. When you're in the library or before a magazine rack, pick up a magazine or journal you're not familiar with and scan it. Do anything that feeds the mind.

Keep a clipping file of articles and pictures that just strike your fancy. Carry a notepad or 3 × 5 cards and jot down ideas. Write down anything that interests you: insights, jokes, poems, quotes, songs, book titles, possible money-making ideas, and so on. Put in sketches, too, and cartoons.

The point of all this is to create a lot of lucky accidents, an event known as serendipity. *Serendipity,* according to the dictionary, is "the faculty of finding valuable or agreeable things not sought for." If you review your notes and idea files now and then, you'll be surprised how many turn out to be useful.

Onward

PREVIEW   Learn to "incubate" to solve problems and generate ideas.

No doubt you've had the experience of sweating over a problem for hours only to have the answer pop into your head at some other time, when your mind was on something else. What happened is known as *incubation.* When you take a break from something you're working on, your mind keeps on working subconsciously, unknown to you.

As we discussed above in the section on surrendering to your unconscious, you can actually learn to turn on the incubation process and use it to help solve problems subconsciously. Here's how.

First, assemble all the facts and information available concerning the problem. "Then sit down and give them a good going over," says Eugene Raudsepp, president of Princeton Creative Research.[21] That is, familiarize yourself with the information, but don't try to solve the problem yet.

Second, file it away and go do something else, such as take a walk. Raudsepp suggests that you make the activity unrelated to the project you're concerned with. "When you come back," he says, "there's a good chance some things have fallen into place, and you're well on your way to solving your problem."

Writer Mark Golin suggests that you can use the incubation technique at the start of the week—for example, by picking a problem on Monday that needs to be solved by Friday. Look at the problem for an hour or so, then put it aside. On Wednesday afternoon, take out the problem again and look at it. "What might have taken you days to solve before may only take hours now that you've done some of the work in your subconscious."[22]

Incubation is, of course, a form of *persistence.* You continue to work on a problem even past the point where once you might have given up. Once again, we observe the lesson that persistence pays off.

NOTES

1. Defining greatness. (1993, June 28). *Newsweek*, pp. 48–50.

2. Sternberg, R. Quoted in Chollar, S. (1996, April). Rethinking intelligence. *American Health*, pp. 80–83.

3. Gardner, H. (1983). *Frames of mind: The theory of multiple intelligences*. New York: Basic Books.

4. Gardner, H. Quoted in Crossen, C. (1997, June 5). Think you're smart? Then just try to sell a new kind of IQ test. *Wall Street Journal*, pp. A1, A13.

5. Crossen, 1997.

6. Goleman, D. (1995). *Emotional intelligence*. New York: Bantam.

7. Goleman, D. Quoted in Derrow, P. (1996, April). Thinking from the heart. *American Health*, pp. 82–83.

8. Randi, J. (1992, April 13). Help stamp out absurd beliefs. *Time*, p. 80.

9. Ruchlis, H., & Oddo, S. (1990). *Clear thinking: A practical introduction*. Buffalo, NY: Prometheus, p. 109.

10. Ruchlis & Oddo, 1990, p. 110.

11. Gerard, N. Quoted in Powers, L. (1996, November 25). A crusade against error: First, admit they happen. *USA Today*, p. 13B.

12. Kahane, H. (1988). *Logic and contemporary rhetoric: The use of reason in everyday life* (5th ed.). Belmont, CA: Wadsworth.

13. Rasool, J., Banks, C., & McCarthy, M.-J. (1993). *Critical thinking: Reading and writing in a diverse world*. Belmont, CA: Wadsworth, p. 132.

14. Rasool, Banks, & McCarthy, 1993, p. 132.

15. Farnham, A. (1994, January 10). How to nurture creative sparks. *Fortune*, pp. 94–100.

16. Farnham, A. (1994, January 10). Teaching creativity tricks to buttoned-down executives. *Fortune*, p. 98.

17. Osborn, A. (1953). *Applied imagination*. New York: Scribner's.

18. Higgins, J. M. (1995, September–October). Mind mapping: Brainstorming by oneself. *The Futurist*, p. 46; from Higgins, J. M. *101 creative problem solving techniques*.

19. Ray, M., & Myers, R. (1986). *Creativity in business*. Garden City, NY: Doubleday, p. 42.

20. Ray & Myers, 1986, p. 92.

21. Raudsepp, E. Quoted in Golin, M. (1992, April). Subconscious smarts. *Psychology Today*, p. 47; from Raudsepp, E. *Secrets of executive success*.

22. Golin, 1992.

Classroom Activities: Directions to the Instructor

1. ***Using the "no shame, no blame" approach to mistakes.*** Gerard Nierenberg's "no shame, no blame" approach to mistakes is this: "First you must determine exactly what is wrong, what the problem is. Next, you determine how extensive the damage is. Then you look at what caused the problem . . . [and] determine the best way to remedy it and how a reoccurrence can be best avoided."

   Ask students to gather in small groups of three to five participants. Each student is to identify one or more incidents in which he or she encountered academic difficulties (such as doing poorly on a paper or a test or in a course). Individual students are to use the "no shame, no blame" approach to assess how they can prevent a recurrence of the problem, and other students may then comment.

2. ***Applying critical thinking to print media.*** This activity involves applying the principles of critical thinking to print media. Ask students to gather several articles on the same subject or news incident and read them. They should then form small groups to apply critical thinking to the articles.

   Questions for discussion: Does the coverage of the incident vary from source to source? How can you explain the differences (or similarities)? To what extent do the articles use facts to support their conclusions? How do you know the information presented as fact is true? To what extent do the articles use opinions to support their conclusions? Which article do you believe to be the most truthful and why?

3. ***Using mind mapping to solve problems.*** Mind mapping is useful for outlining all the issues and subissues related to a problem, as well as identifying the solutions to a problem and their pros and cons. It also works well for outlining papers and presentations.

   Ask students to take out a sheet of paper and in the center of it write down a problem they want to solve. It can be an idea for a paper, a question about future plans, or a problem in personal relationships. Have them draw a circle around the problem, then take 5 minutes to brainstorm aspects of the problem, drawing "highways" and then smaller "roads" from the circle. After 5 minutes, ask students to discuss how well mind mapping seems to work for them.

   Questions for discussion: Do you find mind mapping useful? Or uncomfortable to use? (About half the people who learn it don't like it.) Do you find the lack of structure bothersome? Do you find it difficult to be spontaneous? What kinds of problems do you think mind mapping might be applied to successfully?

The Examined Life:
Student Assignments for Journal Entries

JOURNAL ENTRY #8.1: HOW HAS YOUR MIND-SET INFLUENCED YOU?
Mind-set is everything. Identify a situation in your life to which your mind-set led you to respond negatively.

_____
_____
_____
_____
_____
_____
_____
_____

JOURNAL ENTRY #8.2: APPLYING CRITICAL THINKING TO YOUR LIFE.
The four steps in critical thinking are (1) getting an understanding of the problem, (2) gathering information and interpreting it, (3) developing a solution plan and carrying it out, and (4) evaluating the plan's effectiveness. Apply these steps to some problem in your life.

_____
_____
_____
_____
_____
_____
_____
_____

JOURNAL ENTRY #8.3: HOW CAN YOU EMPLOY CREATIVE THINKING? In what ways can you employ the techniques of creative thinking besides thinking up subjects for term papers?

_____
_____
_____
_____
_____
_____
_____
_____

CHAPTER NINE

INFORMATION TECHNOLOGY
Using computer & communications tools

IN THIS CHAPTER: Information technology offers tools that are key to your future:

■ *Personal computers:* Most students find they benefit by having access to a personal computer (PC), either IBM-style or Macintosh, desktop or laptop.

■ *Computer software:* With a PC, you can use the following kinds of software to help you in your education and career: word processing, desktop accessories and personal information managers, spreadsheets, database management systems, graphics, communications, integrated programs and suites, and groupware.

■ *Communications tools:* Communications technology offers fax messaging, voice mail, e-mail, online information services, and access to the Internet and the World Wide Web.

▪ Early in the 1990s, a monumental watershed occurred: the Industrial Age gave way to the Information Age.

n 1991 companies for the first time spent more on computing and communications gear," says one report, "than on industrial, mining, farm, and construction machines. Info tech is now as vital . . . as the air we breathe."[1]

"Info tech"—information technology—has brought new kinds of productivity tools into the workplace: computers, fax machines, cellular phones, e-mail, the Internet, the World Wide Web, Web-TV. Learning to use these tools can increase your productivity as a student at the same time it gives you skills that will help you advance your career.

This chapter considers the following:

- Personal computers
- Computer software
- Communications tools

Personal Computers

PREVIEW Most students find they benefit by having access to a personal computer (PC), either IBM-style or Macintosh, desktop or laptop. Buying a PC often requires making a trade-off between power (software that is flexible, hardware that is fast and has great data capacity) and expense. Decisions to make are whether upgradability is important and whether you want a modem to communicate with other computers. PCs are available both used and new.

Students who have a ***personal computer (PC)—a desktop or portable computer that can run easy-to-use, personal-assistance software such as a word processing program***—are certainly ahead of the game. However, if you don't have one or are unable to borrow one, many campuses make computers available to students, either at minimal cost or essentially free as part of the regular student fees. For instance, computers may be available at the library or campus computer lab. Often these computers allow students to communicate via e-mail (electronic mail) to people in other locations or to find things on the Internet.

NOTE: If the system cannot accommodate a large number of students, all the computers may be in high demand at term-paper time. Clearly, having access to your own computer offers you convenience and a competitive advantage.

GETTING YOUR OWN PERSONAL COMPUTER: IBM-STYLE OR MACINTOSH?

In general, personal computers are of two types—*IBM-style* and *Macintosh-style.*

- ***IBM-style:*** The IBM-style (IBM-compatible) is the most popular personal computer in the world. Besides being sold by IBM, so-called clones (or copies) are made by Acer, AST, Compaq, DEC, Dell, Gateway 2000, Hewlett-Packard,

"In what way do you find a personal computer useful?"

Name: Anna Pruski

Major: Accounting

Family & work situation: Married; full-time student; work part time

Answer to question: "I find the word-processing programs the most useful. These programs help me edit and revise my college papers without having to retype them all over again. I also have the convenience of being able to use the computer at home at any time."

NCR, Packard-Bell NEC, Toshiba, and Zenith, to name some of the most reputable manufacturers.

■ *Macintosh-style:* Macintoshes aren't as widespread, but they are generally easier to use than IBM or IBM-compatible PCs. Macintoshes are made by Apple Computer; in the past, clones were made by companies such as Power Computing.

If all you need from a computer is word processing capability—such as for writing term papers—nearly any kind of machine, new or used, will do. Indeed, it's possible you may not even need a printer. Some schools offer "express stations" or "drive-up windows." These allow students to use a floppy disk or connect a computer to a student-use printer to print out their papers. Or, if a friend has a compatible computer, you can ask to borrow it and the printer for a short time to print your work.

What kind of system, IBM or Macintosh, is best for you? That may depend on your career field or major. Students in accounting, business, criminal justice,

nursing, recreation, and travel probably don't need a fancy computer system. For them an inexpensive IBM-style system may be just fine. Some engineering, graphic arts, and computer-drafting students, on the other hand, may need to acquire or have access to Macintosh or high-powered IBM-type systems, which may be pricier. For instance, a drafting student doing computer-aided design (CAD) projects or a graphic artist doing desktop publishing may need reasonably powerful Mac systems.

If your career field does not require a special computer system, a microcomputer can be acquired for relatively little. In fact, new PCs priced at $999 or less now represent nearly one-third of retail sales, according to the market research firm Computer Intelligence of La Jolla, California.[2] (For many of these, the monitor or screen must be bought separately—an additional cost of $200–$300.)

DESKTOP OR LAPTOP PC? Most students who buy computers get **desktop PCs, the personal computers that generally remain stationary on the top of a desk** (although some "tower" units sit on the floor, leaving the keyboard and monitor or screen on the surface of the desk), because they are usually cheaper. However, many like **laptop PCs because they are portable.** That is, you can easily carry one around and work on it whenever this is convenient, as in the campus library. (WARNING: Laptop computers are as easily stolen as any purse or backpack. Thus, if you're out on the street a lot, you might want to leave your laptop at home most of the time.)

There are two categories of laptops:

1. *Notebooks*—4 to 7.5 pounds

2. *Subnotebooks*—2.5 to 4 pounds

Look for a computer that fits your work style. For instance, you may want a portable if you spend a lot of time at the library or are able to study at work. If you do most of your work at home or in your room, you may find it more comfortable to have a desktop PC.

THE TRADE-OFF: MORE POWER OR LESS EXPENSE? Buying a personal computer, like buying a car, often requires making a trade-off between *power* and *expense*.

The word *power* has different meanings when describing software and hardware:

- **Powerful software:** Applied to software, "powerful" means that the program is *flexible*. That is, it can do many different things. For example, a word processing program that can print in different type styles (fonts) is more powerful than one that prints in only one style.

  Although it may sound backward, you should select the software before the hardware. This is because you want to choose software that will perform the kind of work you want to do. First, find the kind of programs you want—word processing, spreadsheets, communications, graphics, Web browser, or whatever. Check out the hardware requirements for those programs. Then make sure you get a PC system that will run them.

- **Powerful hardware:** Applied to hardware, "powerful" means that the equipment (1) is *fast* and (2) has *great capacity*.

  A fast computer will process data more quickly than a slow one. With an older computer, for example, it may take a few seconds to save (store on a floppy or hard disk) a 30-page term paper. On a newer machine, it might take less than a second.

  A computer with great capacity can run complex software and process voluminous files. *This is an especially important consideration if you want to be able to run newer forms of software, which tend to have extensive graphics.* Graphics require a lot of memory, hard-disk storage, and screen display area.

  Translation of technobabble: **Memory is the internal memory, often called "RAM," for Random Access Memory, that the computer uses for temporary storage in order to do quicker, more seamless processing. *Hard-disk storage*, or "hard-drive" storage, is your computer's filing cabinet, which allows you to permanently store all your data, as well as your software.**

  Will computer use make up an essential part of your career field, as it might if you are going into engineering, business, or graphic arts? If so, you may want to try to acquire powerful hardware and software.

CHECKLIST. Besides determining whether you want a desktop or a portable and what software you will need to be able to run, there are two other decisions to make before buying a computer:

- **Is upgradability important?** The newest software being released is so powerful (meaning flexible) that it requires increasingly more powerful (faster, higher capacity) hardware. If you buy an older used computer, you probably will not be able to upgrade it. **Upgrade means that you are able to buy internal parts, such as additional memory, that can run newer software.**

  This limitation is probably fine if you expect to be able to afford an all-new system in a couple of years (or to be working for an employer who will buy you one). If, however, you are buying new equipment right now, be sure to ask the salesperson how the hardware can be upgraded.

■ ***Do I want a modem?* A *modem* is a hardware device needed to send messages from one computer to another via a phone line.** About 40% of personal computers these days have a modem. The speed at which a modem can transmit data is measured in Kbps (kilobits per second) rates. The faster the modem speed, the better. Try not to buy one lower than 28.8 Kbps.

What's the *minimum* hardware system you should get? Some technical details: Probably an IBM-compatible or Macintosh with 640 kilobytes of memory and two floppy-disk drives or one floppy-disk and one hard-disk drive. However, 12 megabytes of memory is preferable if you're going to run many of today's programs. Dot-matrix printers are in widespread use on all campuses (24-pin printers are preferable to 9-pin). To be sure, the more expensive laser printers produce a better image. However, you can always use the dot-matrix for drafts and print out the final version on a campus student-use printer.

Some issues to consider in buying a portable computer are addressed in the accompanying checklist. *(See ■ Panel 9.1.)*

WHERE TO BUY USED. You can probably buy a used or "refurbished" (meaning reconditioned) computer, with software thrown in, for $500–$750 and a printer for under $200. Indeed, a computer that is a year or two old will do almost as much as a new machine. However, any PC that is more than five years old "is virtually useless,"

PANEL 9.1	**G**oing mobile: a buyer's checklist.
	Questions to consider when buying
	a notebook or subnotebook.

1. Is the device lightweight enough so that you won't be tempted to leave it behind when you travel?

   ❏ Yes   ❏ No

2. Does it work with lightweight nickel-hydride batteries instead of heavier nickel-cadmium batteries?

   ❏ Yes   ❏ No

3. Is the battery life sufficient for you to finish the jobs you need to do, and is a hibernation mode available to conserve power?

   ❏ Yes   ❏ No

4. Can you type comfortably on the keyboard for a long stretch?

   ❏ Yes   ❏ No

5. Is the screen crisp, sharp, and readable in different levels of light?

   ❏ Yes   ❏ No

6. Does the system have enough storage for all your software and data?

   ❏ Yes   ❏ No

7. Can the system's hard disk and memory be upgraded to meet your needs?

   ❏ Yes   ❏ No

8. Does the system provide solid communications options, including a fast modem, so you can send files, retrieve data, and plug into a local area network?

   ❏ Yes   ❏ No

9. Can you get service and support on the road?

   ❏ Yes   ❏ No

says one expert; "it won't run much if any of today's software and won't be capable of connecting to the Internet."[3]

The most important thing is to buy *recognizable* brand names, examples being Apple and IBM or well-known IBM-compatibles: Acer, AST, Compaq, Dell, Gateway 2000, Hewlett-Packard, NCR, NEC, Packard Bell, Toshiba, and Zenith. Obscure or discontinued brands may not be repairable.

Among the sources for used computers are the following:

- **Retail sources:** A look in the telephone book Yellow Pages under "Computers, Used" will produce several leads. Authorized dealers (of IBM, Apple, Compaq, and so on) may shave prices on demonstration (demo) or training equipment. Also, colleges and universities may sell off their old equipment when it is being replaced.

- **Used-computer brokers:** There are a number of used-computer brokers, such as American Computer Exchange, Boston Computer Exchange, Damark, and National Computer Exchange. Computer Renaissance is a national chain selling used computers. Refurbished PCs are also available through Internet-based retailers, such as Universal Listing Network of Palo Alto, California (*http://www.uln.com*). Finally, your school may also sell used computers.

- **Individuals:** Classified ads in local newspapers, shopper throwaways, and (in some localities) free computer newspapers/magazines provide listings of used computer equipment.

One problem with buying from individuals is that they may not feel obligated to take the equipment back if something goes wrong. Thus, you should inspect the equipment carefully. *(See ■ Panel 9.2.)* For a small fee, a computer-repair shop can check out the hardware for damage.

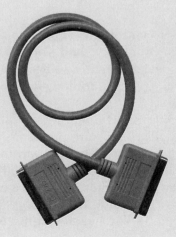

PANEL 9.2

Tips for buying used computers. Buying from an individual means you have little recourse if something goes wrong. The following tips should help you to buy carefully.

- If possible, take someone who knows computers with you.

- Turn the computer on and off a few times to make sure there are no problems on startup.

- Use the computer and, if possible, try the software you want to use. Listen for strange sounds in the hard drive or the floppies.

- Turn the computer off and look for screen burn-in, a ghost image on the screen after the machine has been turned off. It can be a sign of misuse.

- Ask about the warranty. Some companies, including Apple and IBM, permit warranties to be transferred to new owners (effective from the date of the original purchase). A new owner can usually have the warranty extended by paying a fee.

WHERE TO BUY NEW. Fierce price wars among microcomputer manufacturers and retailers have made hardware more affordable. One reason that IBM-compatibles have become so widespread is that non-IBM manufacturers early on were able to copy, or "clone," IBM machines and offer them at cut-rate prices. For a long time, Apple Macintoshes were considerably more expensive; in recent years the company allowed other computer makers to clone its machines, resulting in lower prices, but it has discontinued this practice.

There are several sources for inexpensive new computers:

- *Student discount:* With a school ID card, you're probably entitled to student discounts (usually 10%–20%) through your school's bookstore or campus computer resellers. In addition, during the first few weeks of the term, many campuses offer special sales on computer equipment. Campus resellers also provide on-campus service and support and, says one expert, can help students meet the prevailing campus standards while satisfying their personal needs.[4]

- *Computer superstores:* Big chains such as Computer City, CompUSA, and Microage sell only computers. Computers are also sold at department stores, warehouse stores (such as Costco and Price Club), Wal-Mart, Circuit City, Radio Shack, and similar outlets.

- *Mail-order houses:* Companies like Dell Computer Corp. and Gateway 2000 found they could sell computers inexpensively by mail order while offering customer support over the phone. Their success inspired IBM, Compaq, and others to plunge into the mail-order business.

  The price advantage of mail-order companies has eroded with the rise of computer superstores. Moreover, the lack of local repair and service support can be a major disadvantage. Still, if you're interested in this route, look for a copy of the phone-book-size magazine *Computer Shopper*, which carries ads from most mail-order vendors.

When buying hardware, look to see whether software, such as word processing or spreadsheet programs, comes "bundled" with it. *Bundled* means that software is included in the selling price of the hardware. This arrangement can be a real advantage, saving you several hundred dollars.

Computer Software

PREVIEW Personal computers provide the following kinds of software to help you with educational and work tasks: word processing, desktop accessories and personal information managers, spreadsheets, database management systems, graphics, communications, integrated programs and suites, and groupware.

There are thousands of software programs, available on floppy disks, that will run on computer hardware. The best way to consider the kind of software that might be useful to you is to visualize yourself sitting at a desk in an old-fashioned office: You have a typewriter. You have a calendar, clock, and name-and-address file. You have a calculator. You have desk drawers full of files. You have a telephone. You have an In-box and an Out-box to which someone delivers and

from which someone takes your interoffice and outside mail. Many of these items could also be found on a student's desk. How would a computer and software improve on this arrangement?

This section describes the following kinds of software:

- Word processing

- Desktop accessories and personal information managers

- Spreadsheets

- Database management systems

- Graphics

- Communications

- Integrated programs and suites

- Groupware

WORD PROCESSING. The typewriter, that long-lived machine, has gone to its reward. Today the usual alternative is a personal computer with word processing software and a printer.

***Word processing software* allows you to use computers to create, edit, revise, store, and print text material.** Most current programs provide a number of ***menus,* or lists of choices, for manipulating aspects of your document.** Three common programs for IBM-style Windows computers are Microsoft Word, WordPerfect, and Ami Pro; for Macintoshes they are Word and MacWrite.

Word processing software allows you to use your computer to maneuver through a document with a cursor (a blinking symbol that shows where you are in the text) and *delete, insert,* and *replace* text, the principal correction activities.

There are also additional features, such as Search, Cut, Copy, Paste commands; spell checking; and thesaurus. *(See ■ Panel 9.3.)*

Opting for a personal computer for word processing means you have to make three decisions:

■ **Expense:** You have to be prepared to spend more than you probably would for a typewriter. Used personal computers start at $500. Some inexpensive new ones are available for under $1,000. A fancy new state-of-the-art system that includes software and printer could cost more than $3,000.

■ **Software:** You have to determine what word processing software you want to use. For students, the easiest choice is to select the program used by most other students in their school, especially those in the same career field or major. That way you can easily borrow someone else's system if yours breaks down.

■ **Portability:** You have to make some decisions about portability and printers. A desktop machine is often cheaper than a laptop, but a laptop is more easily carried around. Printers are a problem because (with rare exceptions) they are not built into the computer; indeed, they are often bigger than the computer itself. Transporting both a microcomputer and a printer can be cumbersome, although most people find they don't need to move a printer around. Some small, portable printers (about the size of a cigarette carton) are available, but they are slow to operate.

DESKTOP ACCESSORIES & PERSONAL INFORMATION MANAGERS. Is there any need to have an electronic version of the traditional appointment calendar, clock, and file of phone numbers and addresses? A lot of people with computers still use old-fashioned paper-and-pencil calendars and To Do lists. However, others find ready uses for the kind of software called *desktop accessories* or *personal information managers (PIMs)*.

■ **Desktop accessories: A *desktop accessory,* or *desktop organizer,* is a software package that provides an electronic version of tools or objects commonly found on a desktop: calendar, clock, card file, calculator, and notepad.** Some desktop-accessory programs come as standard equipment with some systems software (such as on Microsoft's Windows). Others, such as Borland's SideKick or Lotus Agenda, are available as separate programs to run in your computer at the same time you are running other software. Some are principally *scheduling and calendaring programs;* their main purpose is to enable you to do time and event scheduling.

Suppose, for example, you are working on a word processing document and someone calls to schedule a job interview next week. You can simply type a command that "pops up" your appointment calendar, type in the appointment, save the information, and then return to your interrupted work. Other features, such as a calculator keypad, a "scratch pad" for typing in notes to yourself, and a Rolodex-type address and phone directory (some with automatic telephone dialer), can be displayed on the screen when needed.

■ **Personal information managers:** A more sophisticated program is the ***personal information manager (PIM),* a combination word processor, database, and desktop accessory program that organizes a variety of**

Features of a word processing program. Word processing software offers features such as the Search, Replace, and Block Move commands; spell checking; and thesaurus.

With a word processor, unlike with a typewriter, you can maneuver through a document and do the principal correction activities—*delete, insert,* and *replace*—with ease. In addition, word processing software offers these other features:

Search and replace: The *Search command* allows you to find any word or number that you know exists in your document. The *Replace command* allows you to automatically replace it with something else.

"Cut and paste" (block and move): Typewriter users were accustomed to using scissors and glue to "cut and paste" to move a paragraph or block of text from one place to another in a manuscript. With word processing, you can exercise the *Block command* to indicate the beginning and end of the portion of text you want to move. Then you can use the *Move command* to move it to another location in the document. (You can also use the *Copy command* to copy the block of text to a new location while also leaving the original block where it is.)

Report format: The *report format* is the layout of the printed page, including print columns, line spacing, justification, and headers or footers. It is easy to have one, two, or three columns of type on the page; to make the lines single-, double-, or triple-spaced (or all three within a document); or to have the text justified or unjustified.

Justify means to align text evenly between left and right margins, as, for example, is done with most newspaper columns. *Unjustify* means to not align the text evenly, as is done with the right side of many business letters ("ragged right").

A *header* is a small piece of text (such as a date) that is printed at the top of every page. A *footer* is the same thing printed at the bottom of every page.

You can also make format changes within a document, such as by centering or indenting headings or by emphasizing text with **boldface,** *italics,* or <u>underlining</u>.

Spelling and grammar checking, thesaurus, outlining, mail-merge: The principal word processing packages have some separate programs or functions that can really reduce your work.

Many writers automatically run their completed documents through a *spelling checker,* which tests for incorrectly spelled words. Another program is a *grammar checker,* which flags poor grammar, wordiness, incomplete sentences, and awkward phrases.

If you find yourself stuck for the right word while you're writing, you can call up an on-screen *thesaurus,* which will present you with the appropriate word or alternative words.

If you need assistance with organizing your thoughts, you might use an outline processor. An *outline processor* allows you to type in thoughts and then tag the topics with numbers and letters and organize them in outline form, with Roman numerals, letters, and numbers.

If you want to send out the same letter to different people, you can use the *mail-merge program* to print customized form letters, with different names, addresses, and salutations for each letter.

information. Examples of PIMs are Ascend, CA-UpToDate, DayMaker Organizer, DateBook Pro, Dynodex, Instant Recall, Lotus Organizer, OnTime for Windows, and Personal Reminder System.

SPREADSHEET SOFTWARE. What is a spreadsheet? Traditionally, it was simply a grid of rows and columns, printed on special green paper, that was used by accountants and other financial types to produce financial projections and reports. A person making up a spreadsheet often spent long days and weekends at the office penciling tiny numbers into countless tiny rectangles. When one figure changed, all the rest of the numbers on the spreadsheet had to be recomputed—and ultimately there might be wastebaskets full of old worksheets.

In the late 1970s, someone got the idea of computerizing all this. **The *electronic spreadsheet* allows users to create tables and financial schedules by entering data into rows and columns arranged as a grid on a display screen.** The electronic spreadsheet quickly became the most popular small-business program. Today the principal spreadsheets are Excel, Lotus 1-2-3, and Quattro Pro. (*See* ■ *Panel 9.4.*)

PANEL 9.4

Characteristics of a spreadsheet program. Spreadsheets can be used to display data in graphic form, such as in pie charts or bar charts, which are easier to read than columns of numbers.

Columns, rows, and labels: *Column headings* appear across the top; *row headings* appear down the left side. Column and row headings are called *labels*. The label is usually any descriptive text, such as APRIL, PHONE, or GROSS SALES.

Cells, cell addresses, values, and spreadsheet cursor: The place where rows and columns intersect is called a *cell*, and its position is called a *cell address*. For example, "A1" is the cell address for the top left cell, where column A and row 1 intersect.

A number entered in a cell is called a *value*. The values are the actual numbers used in the spreadsheet—dollars, percentages, grade points, temperatures, or whatever. A *cell pointer* or *spreadsheet cursor* indicates where data is to be entered. The cell pointer can be moved around like a cursor in a word processing program.

Formulas and recalculation: Now we come to the reason the electronic spreadsheet has taken business organizations offices by storm. *Formulas* are instructions for calculations. For example, a formula might be SUM CELLS A5 TO A15, meaning "Sum (add) all the numbers in the cells with cell addresses A5 through A15."

After the values have been plugged into the spreadsheet, the formulas can be used to calculate outcomes. What is revolutionary, however, is the way the spreadsheet can easily do recalculation. *Recalculation* is the process of recomputing values *automatically,* either as an ongoing process as data is being entered or afterward, with the press of a key.

The "what-if?" world: The recalculation feature has opened up whole new possibilities for decision making. As a user, you can create a plan, put in formulas and numbers, and then ask yourself "What would happen if we change that detail?"—and immediately see the effect on the bottom line.

Spreadsheets can be used to display data in graphic form, such as in pie charts or bar charts, which are easier to read than columns of numbers. In addition, spreadsheets allow a user to change one number in a calculation and see how all other numbers are affected.

DATABASE MANAGEMENT SYSTEMS. In its most general sense, a database is any electronically stored collection of data in a computer system. In its more specific sense, **a *database* is a collection of interrelated files in a computer system. These computer-based files are organized so that those parts that have a common element can be retrieved easily.** The software for maintaining a database is a *database manager* or *database management system (DBMS),* **a program that controls the structure of a database and access to the data.** *(See* ■ *Panel 9.5.)*

PANEL 9.5

Characteristics of a database management system.

Organization of a database: A database is organized—from smallest to largest items—into *fields, records,* and *files.*

A *field* is a unit of data consisting of one or more characters. Examples of a field are your name, your address, or your driver's license number.

A *record* is a collection of related fields. An example of a record would be your name *and* address *and* driver's license number.

A *file* is a collection of related records. An example of a file could be one in your state's Department of Motor Vehicles. The file would include everyone who received a driver's license on the same day, including their names, addresses, and driver's license numbers.

Select and display: The beauty of database management programs is that you can locate records in the file quickly. For example, your college may maintain several records about you—one at the registrar's, one in financial aid, one in the housing department, and so on. Any of these records can be called up on a computer display screen for viewing and updating. Thus, if you move, your address field will need to be changed in all records. The database is quickly corrected by finding your name field. Once the record is displayed, the address field can be changed.

Sort: With a database management system you can easily change the order of records in a file. Normally, records are entered into a database in the order they occur, such as by the date a person registered to attend college. However, all these records can be sorted in different ways. For example, they can be rearranged by state, by age, or by Social Security number.

Calculate and format: Many database management programs contain built-in mathematical formulas. This feature can be used, for example, to find the grade-point averages for students in different majors or in different classes. Such information can then be organized into different formats and printed out.

Today the principal database manager for computers running under Microsoft Windows are Access and Paradox, followed by Filemaker Pro for Windows, FoxPro for Windows, Q&A for Windows, and Approach for Windows. A multimedia program called Instant Database allows users to attach sound, motion, and graphics to forms.

Databases have gotten easier to use, but they still can be difficult to set up. Even so, the trend is toward making such programs easier for both database creators and database users.

GRAPHICS SOFTWARE. Computer graphics can be highly complicated, such as those used in special effects for movies. Here we are concerned with microcomputer applications useful for work and study—namely, *analytical graphics* and *presentation graphics.*

- ***Analytical graphics: Analytical graphics* are graphical forms that make numeric data easier to analyze than when it is in the form of rows and columns of numbers,** as in electronic spreadsheets. The principal examples are bar charts, line charts, and pie charts.

  Most analytical graphics are features of spreadsheet programs, such as Excel. Whether viewed on a monitor or printed out, analytical graphics help make sales figures, economic trends, and the like easier to comprehend and analyze.

- ***Presentation graphics: Presentation graphics* are graphics used to communicate or make a presentation of data to others,** such as clients or supervisors. Presentations may make use of analytical graphics, but they look much more sophisticated. They use different texturing patterns (speckled, solid, cross-hatched), color, and three-dimensionality. Examples of well-known graphics packages are PowerPoint, Curtain Call, Freelance Plus, Harvard Graphics, Hollywood, Persuasion, and Presentation Graphics.

  Some presentation graphics packages provide artwork ("clip art") that can be electronically cut and pasted into the graphics. These programs also allow you to use electronic painting and drawing tools for creating lines, rectangles, and just about any other shape. Depending on the system's capabilities, you can add text, animated sequences, and sound. With special equipment you can do graphic presentations on slides, transparencies, and videotape. With all these options the main problem may be simply restraining yourself.

COMMUNICATIONS SOFTWARE. Many personal computer users feel they have all the productivity they need without ever having to hook up their machines to a telephone. However, having communications capabilities provides you with a great leap forward that vastly extends your range.

Communications software **manages the transmission of data between computers.** For most PC users, this sending and receiving of data is by way of a modem and a telephone line. As mentioned, a *modem* is an electronic device that allows computers to communicate with each other over telephone lines. When you buy a modem, you often get communications software with it. Popular communications programs for personal computers are Smartcom, Crosstalk, ProComm, PC-Dial, Blast, and PC Talk.

With communications software and a modem in your computer, you can connect with friends by e-mail (electronic mail) and make use of the research possibilities of information services (America Online, CompuServe, Prodigy, Microsoft Network) and the Internet and Worldwide Web, as we describe in a few pages.

INTEGRATED PROGRAMS & SUITES. What if you want to take data from one program and use it in another—say, call up data from a database and use it in a spreadsheet? You can try using separate software packages, but one may not be designed to accept data from the other. *Integrated packages* **combine the features of several applications programs into one software package. Usually these capabilities are the ones we have described: electronic spreadsheets, word processing, database management, graphics, and communications.** Thus, if you were a sales manager, you could use a database to get various sales figures for different parts of the country. Then you could compare them using a spreadsheet and graphics program, write a memo about them using a word processing program, and send your memo to the sales representatives using communications software.

Examples of integrated packages are ClarisWorks, Eight-in-One, Lotus Works, Microsoft Works, PFS:First Choice, and WordPerfect Works. In general, integrated packages are less powerful than separate programs used alone, such as a word processing or spreadsheet program used by itself. Moreover, systems software such as Windows makes integrated programs unnecessary, as the user can easily shift between applications programs that are *completely different*. Finally, integrated programs are largely being replaced by *software suites*.

Suites **are applications—like spreadsheets, word processing, graphics, and communications—that are bundled together and sold for a fraction of what the programs would cost if bought individually.** Examples of suites are Microsoft Office 97, Smart Suite, and Perfect Office.

Although cost is what makes suites attractive to many corporate customers, they have other benefits as well. Manufacturers have taken pains to integrate the "look and feel" of the separate programs within the suites to make them easier to use.

Communications Tools

P R E V I E W Communications technology offers fax messaging, voice mail, e-mail, and online information services. It also offers the Internet, which provides access to e-mail, research sources, discussion and news groups, and the World Wide Web, with its directories and search engines.

The first wave of computing, 30 years ago, was driven by the huge computers known as mainframes. Twenty years later came the second wave, which produced the desktop personal computer. Now we are into the third wave, which is being driven by communications networks among computers. Communications technology, then, is vital to your future. The options include the following.

TELEPHONE-RELATED COMMUNICATIONS SERVICES. Services available through telephone connections, whether the conventional wired kind or the wireless cellular-phone type, include these:

- **_Fax messages:_** Asking "What is your fax number?" is about as common a question in the work world today as asking for someone's telephone number. **_Fax stands for "facsimile transmission" or reproduction._** A fax may be sent by dedicated fax machine or by fax modem.

  Dedicated fax machines are specialized devices that do nothing except send and receive documents over transmission lines from and to other fax machines. These are the stand-alone machines nowadays found everywhere, from offices to airports to instant-printing shops.

  A _fax modem_, which is installed as a circuit board inside a computer's cabinet, is a modem with fax capability. It enables you to send signals directly from your computer to someone else's fax machine or fax modem.

- **_Voice mail:_** Like a sophisticated telephone answering machine, **_voice mail_ digitizes incoming voice messages and stores them in the recipient's "voice mailbox" in digitized form. It then converts the digitized versions back to voice messages when they are retrieved.**

  Unlike conventional answering machines, voice-mail systems allow callers to direct their calls within an office by pressing numbers on their touch-tone phone. They also allow callers to deliver the same message to many people within an organization. They can forward calls to the recipient's home or hotel.

  The main benefit is that voice mail helps eliminate "telephone tag." That is, two callers can continue to exchange messages even when they can't reach each other directly.

- **_E-mail: E-mail_, or _electronic mail_, links computers by wired or wireless connections and allows users, through their keyboards, to post messages and to read responses on their display screens.** E-mail allows "callers," or users, to send messages to a single recipient's "mailbox," which is simply a file stored on the computer system. Also, they can send the same message to multiple users on the same system.

  As with voice mail, e-mail helps users avoid playing "telephone tag." It also offers confidentiality. Recipients cannot get into their "mailboxes" to pick up messages unless they enter a _password_, a secret word or numbers that limit access.

E-mail has jumped in use, especially in large organizations, where it helps to speed the exchange of memos and scheduling of appointments. Often a company will use its own specialized computer network. However, the Internet or outside online information services (described next) are also used. E-mail not only speeds communications, but can also reduce telephone, postage, and secretarial costs.

ONLINE INFORMATION SERVICES. An *online information service* provides access to all kinds of databases and electronic meeting places to subscribers equipped with telephone-linked personal computers. Says one writer:

Online services are those interactive news and information retrieval sources that can make your computer behave more like a telephone; or a TV set; or a newspaper; or a video arcade, a stock brokerage firm, a bank, a travel agency, a weather bureau, a department store, a grocery store, a florist, a set of encyclopedias, a library, a bulletin board and more.[5]

There are scores of online services, but perhaps the most prominent are those listed below. *(See ▪ Panel 9.6.)* To use these services, you need a personal computer with hard disk, printer, and modem connected to a telephone line, plus communications software. Communications software is often sold with (is bundled with) modems. Popular information services such as America Online, CompuServe, Prodigy, and Microsoft Network provide subscribers with their own software programs for going online.

Before you can use an online information service, you need to open an account with it, using a credit card. Billing policies resemble those used by cable-TV and telephone companies. As with cable TV, you may be charged a fee for basic service, with additional fees for specialized services. In addition, the online service may charge you for the time spent while on the line. Finally, you will also be charged by your telephone company for your time on the line, just as when making a regular phone call. However, most information services offer local access numbers. Thus, unless you live in a rural area, you will not be paying long-distance phone charges. All told, the typical user may pay $10–$20 a month to use an online service, although it's possible to run up a bill of $100 or more. To

PANEL 4.1   **O**nline services. These are the principal mainstream online services.

America Online (800-827-6364). Easy-to-use interface; ideal for hobbyists and families wanting low-cost access to online features.

CompuServe (800-848-8199). Easy-to-use interface; ideal for people wanting to combine academic or business with hobbyist and family-type activities.

Microsoft Network (MSN) (800-386-5550) Access is built in to the Windows 95 operating system, allowing users to connect with an easy mouse click; splashy graphics; still expanding offerings

Prodigy (800-776-3449). The simplest online service, easy for beginners; rivaled only by CompuServe in number and variety of services.

keep costs down, many users go online only during off-hours (evenings and weekends) when the charges intended for business users are reduced.

As one of the hundreds of thousands of subscribers connected to an online service, you can have access to *e-mail, computer games* (both single-player and multi-player), *research, travel services,* and *shopping services.* The only restriction on the amount of research you can do online is the limit on whatever credit card you are charging your time to. Depending on the online service, you can avail yourself of several encyclopedias. Many online services store unabridged text from newspapers and magazines. CompuServe's Magazine Database Plus, for example, carries full-text articles from more than 90 general-interest publications (business, science, sports, and so on). Other features are book and movie/video news, contests, health reports, parenting advice, car-rental information, microwave cooking instructions, and on and on.

Online services also offer *chat rooms* or *electronic bulletin board services (BBSs)* through which you may "chat with" and share files with like-minded users. Using your computer's communications software, you dial up a bulletin board by pressing the numbers on your keyboard. You are then usually greeted by a welcome screen from the BBS that tells you what to do—what rules to follow and how to get help, if you need it.

As you move around the BBS, you will probably find a library of materials, such as computer games, that you can copy for your own use. You will also find places where other users have posted messages or where you can "chat" (type your messages and read theirs) with people who have similar interests. There seem to be no limits to the topics of electronic talk forums; participants range from bird watchers to socialists to Francophiles to Trekkies.

THE INTERNET & WORLD WIDE WEB. The computer, modem, and telephone line that explore online services and BBSs can also be used to connect with the global network of computers known as the Internet. **The *Internet* is an international network connecting approximately 140,000 smaller networks.**

Some principal services of the Internet are as follows:

- **E-mail:** Internet electronic mail is essentially like the e-mail in an office except that you can exchange messages all over the world. E-mail messages on the Internet can be transmitted from one user to another usually in a matter of seconds.

  Although Internet addresses may seem strange at first, they are not complicated. The Internet address for the President of the United States, for example, is *president@whitehouse.gov.* The first part is the user's name—in this case, *president.* (Yours might be your nickname, initials and last name, or some combination.) The second part is the computer network you use, which follows the @ sign—in this case, *@whitehouse.* The third part, following a period, is the network's "domain"—in this case, *gov* for "government." Some other domains are *com* (commercial organizations), *edu* (education), *mil* (military), *net* (network resources), and *org* (private organizations). A user of the online service America Online (AOL) would have an Internet e-mail address of *user@aol.com.*

- **Information gathering:** "Try as you may," says one writer, "you cannot imagine how much data is available on the Internet."[6] Besides hundreds of online data-

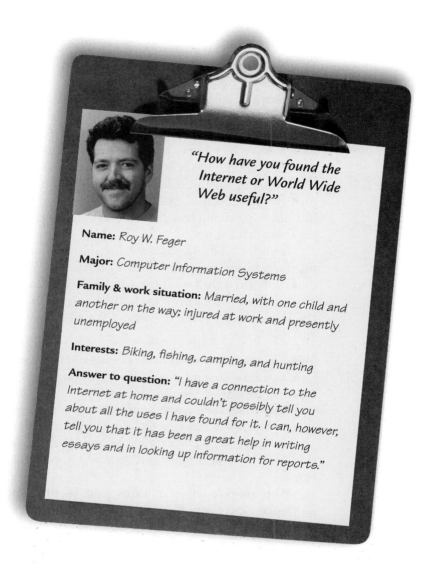

"How have you found the Internet or World Wide Web useful?"

Name: *Roy W. Feger*

Major: *Computer Information Systems*

Family & work situation: *Married, with one child and another on the way; injured at work and presently unemployed*

Interests: *Biking, fishing, camping, and hunting*

Answer to question: *"I have a connection to the Internet at home and couldn't possibly tell you about all the uses I have found for it. I can, however, tell you that it has been a great help in writing essays and in looking up information for reports."*

bases from various universities and other research institutions and online library catalogs, here is a sampling:

The Library of Congress card catalog. The daily White House press releases. Weather maps and forecasts. Schedules of professional sports teams. Weekly Nielsen television ratings. Recipe archives. The Central Intelligence Agency world map. A ZIP Code guide. The National Family Database. Project Gutenberg (offering the complete text of many works of literature). The Alcoholism Research Data Base. Guitar chords. U.S. government addresses and phone (and fax) numbers. The Simpsons archive.[7]

- **Discussion and news groups:** One of the Internet's most interesting features are the news groups, or bulletin board discussion groups. For example, *Usenet* is a loose confederation of 5,000 *newsgroups* or discussion groups on every conceivable subject. Users can post messages for others to read, then check back later to see what responses have appeared.

Examples of topics offered by Usenet news groups are *misc.jobs.offered, rec.arts.startrek.info,* and *soc.culture.african.american.* The category called *alt* news groups offers more free-form topics, such as *alt.rock-n-roll.metal* or *alt.internet.services.*

■ **World Wide Web:** The *World Wide Web* **(WWW, or simply *"the Web"*) is the Internet's most graphical and usable service. It resembles a huge encyclopedia filled with thousands of topics or sites (called "pages"), which have been created by computer users and businesses around the world.** Each site has cross-reference links to other sites.

Sites may theoretically be in *multimedia* form—meaning they can appear in text, graphical, sound, animation, or video form—although at present there are lots of pictures and text but little live, moving content. However, this is in the process of changing.

In order to find your way through the dense data fields of the Web, you need a software program called a browser. **A *Web browser,* or simply *browser,* is software that enables you to "browse through" and view Web sites.** You can move from page to page by using a mouse to click-and-jump through the various sites. Two important Web browsers are Netscape Navigator and Internet Explorer.

■ **Web directories and search engines:** Once you're on your browser, you need to know how to find what you're looking for. Search tools are of two basic types—directories and search engines.

Web directories are search tools classified by topic. One of the foremost examples is Yahoo, which provides you with an opening screen offering 14 general categories. Directories are good tools for *browsing,* as when you want to find Web sites pertinent to a general topic you're interested in, such as heart disease.

Web search engines allow you to find specific documents through keyword searches. Examples of useful search engines are AltaVista, Excite, HotBot, Infoseek, Lycos, and Web Crawler. Search engines are best when you're trying to find very specific information, such as a recipe for home-made beer.

There are three principal ways of getting connected to the Internet:

■ **School or work:** The people with the easiest access to Internet are those involved with institutions of higher education, government agencies, and some businesses. Students in higher education often get a free account through their institution.

■ **Commercial online services:** The large commercial online information services—such as America Online, CompuServe, Prodigy, and Microsoft Network—offer access to the Internet.

■ **Internet service providers:** The commercial online services may be the easiest path to the Internet, but they may charge more than Internet service providers. **Internet service providers (ISPs) are companies that will provide public access to the Internet for a fee.** The cheapest kind of access is the dial-up connection. Here the ISP charges a monthly fee for dialing into an intermediary source that then connects to the Internet.

A network information center called InterNIC has been set up to serve as a clearinghouse for Internet information. To find out more, call (800) 444-4345, or e-mail *info@internic.net.* For public access sites, ask about the PDIAL list.

Onward

PREVIEW   Computers and communications are changing conventional meanings of time and space.

"Computers and communications: These are the parents of the Information Age," says one writer. "When they meet, the fireworks begin."[8]

What kind of fireworks are we talking about? Maybe it is that portable computing and communications technologies are changing conventional meanings of time and space. As one expert pointed out (during a round-table discussion on an online network), "the physical locations we traditionally associate with work, leisure, and similar pursuits are rapidly becoming meaningless."[9]

Through communications technologies, computers, telephones, and wireless devices, we are being linked to invisible networks everywhere. Thus, understanding how information technology works is crucial to your future.

NOTES

1. Stewart, T. A. (1994, April 4). The information age in charts. *Fortune*, pp. 75–79.

2. Computer Intelligence, cited in Langberg, M. (1997, August 10). Bargain basement PCs. *San Jose Mercury News*, pp. 1E, 3E.

3. Langberg, 1997.

4. McGee, C., cited in Meers, T. (1993, September). College computing 101, *PC Novice*, pp. 18–22.

5. Branigan, M. (1992, January). The cost of using an online service. *PC Novice*, pp. 65–71.

6. Tetzeli, R. (1994, March 7). The Internet and your business. *Fortune*, pp. 86–96.

7. Landis, D. (1993, October 7). Exploring the online universe. *USA Today*, p. 4D.

8. Stewart, 1994.

9. Mandel, T., quoted in Talking about portables (1992, November 16). *Wall Street Journal*, p. R18.

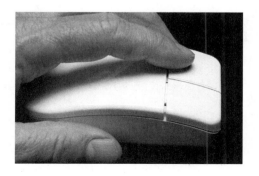

Classroom Activities: Directions to the Instructor

1. ***What are your fears about computers?*** Have students take a few minutes to list, on a half sheet of paper or 3 × 5 card, their concerns, frustrations, and anxieties about information technology—computers and communications devices. Are they worried about being unable to learn certain kinds of software? Are they frustrated by computers "crashing"? Important: Students should *not* sign their names to the cards.

    Collect the lists and shuffle them. Call on students to come to the front of the class, pick a list at random, and copy the material on the board. One area of the board should be saved; you, the instructor, will write down common themes here.

    Questions for discussion: What are common themes? What are your reactions to the most common themes? What techniques or resources do you have to cope with these concerns? What are some horror stories about using computers?

2. ***What is the best way to gain access to a personal computer in your school?*** In class discussion, ask students to share their knowledge about access to computers on campus.

    Questions for discussion: Are computers available in the library? What about student-use printers for printing out research papers? Does the bookstore sell personal computers? Is there a student discount? Where could one buy a used computer? Is there a system on campus for accessing the Internet and World Wide Web?

3. ***Finding help with computing.*** In class discussion, ask students to share various ways to find help with problems related to computers.

    Questions for discussion: What kind of assistance does the school offer in learning about computers? Is there a computer support center? A call-in number? A user support service? Are there some people who could serve as mentors? Is there an online place with FAQs—"Frequently Asked Questions"? Are there some helpful books?

4. ***What are some uses for the Internet and World Wide Web?*** Some students in your class may already have had great exposure to the Internet and the World Wide Web. In class discussion, they may provide some interesting insights in how to use these resources.

    Questions for discussion: How do you gain access to the Net and the Web? Are there terminals or workstations on campus that all students may use? Where are they located? Are there rules for their use? Is there a way a student can connect his or her own modem-equipped personal computer for Internet access? What browsers are best? What search tools (directories and search engines) are most useful? Can the Internet and the Web be used for research for term papers? How?

The Examined Life:
Student Assignments for Journal Entries

JOURNAL ENTRY #9.1: WHAT COMPUTER SKILLS WILL YOU NEED IN YOUR CAREER FIELD? Nearly every career field now uses information technology. What computer skills will be required in your career field? For example, what kinds of software should you become comfortable with? (If you don't know, find out from an instructor or your academic advisor.) At what point in your education will you begin learning these skills?

_____

_____

_____

_____

_____

_____

_____

JOURNAL ENTRY #9.2: HOW GOOD ARE YOU AT KEYBOARDING—AND WHAT CAN YOU DO TO IMPROVE? Can you type using more than two fingers? Until you can type on a keyboard using all ten of your fingers, you won't be completely comfortable using a computer, as keyboarding is the skill most essential to this technology. If you need to upgrade your keyboarding skills, look into inexpensive "typing tutor" software. (Look in the campus bookstore or go to the library and research some computer-magazine articles and ads.) Write what you plan to do to become a better keyboarder.

_____

_____

_____

_____

_____

_____

_____

JOURNAL ENTRY #9.3: WHAT ARE SOME SOURCES OF ASSISTANCE IN USING COMPUTERS? What are some departments, offices, phone numbers, and online sites that offer support services in computing? Who are some people you could turn to for help?

_____

_____

_____

_____

_____

_____

_____

CHAPTER TEN

PERSONAL GROWTH
Managing stress, conflict, & money

IN THIS CHAPTER: Stress is not just a part of higher education but a part of life—and it's often related to personal conflicts and money matters. This chapter considers the following topics:

- *Causes and manifestations of stress:* How to identify and manage the stresses of higher education.
- *Managing stress:* Five strategies for handling stress.
- *Relationships and communication:* The nature of relationships and how to handle conflict.
- *Assertiveness:* Assertiveness versus aggressiveness and nonassertiveness.
- *Money handling:* A crash course in strategies.
- *Financial aid:* How to get financial help for career and vocational-technical education.

■ A great deal of the higher education experience, unfortunately, consists of stress.

This is particularly true for many students in career and vocational-technical education, who are often balancing other demands—work, family, money—besides those of school.

However, stress won't end with graduation, so learning how to cope with it is important. Indeed, there's even a *good* kind of stress, one that propels you to accomplish the things you want to do.

Stress: Causes & Manifestations

PREVIEW Three principal worries of students in higher education are (1) anxiety over wasting time, (2) anxiety over meeting high standards, and (3) feelings of being lonely. *Stress* is the body's reaction; *stressors* are the source of stress. Stressors may be small irritating hassles, short-duration crises, or long-duration strong stressors. A source of stress may be negative and cause "distress" or positive and cause "eustress." Stress may produce certain physical reactions: skin problems, headaches, gastrointestinal problems, and high blood pressure. Stress may also produce emotional reactions such as nervousness and anxiety, and burnout.

Stress or burnout is one of the most common reasons that students leave school without graduating.[1] We say that not to alarm you but simply so you'll know that any feelings of anxiety or tension you have are *commonplace* for students in career and vocational-technical education.

THE WORRIES OF STUDENTS. Students in higher education, says one psychologist, are most hassled by three things:[2]

- ■ *Anxiety over wasting time:* To be in school is to feel as though you should always be studying—particularly if you haven't yet set up a time-management system. Students who don't draw up a schedule of their study times and *stick to it* are particularly apt to suffer constant anxiety over wasting time.

- ■ *Meeting high standards:* Another worry for students is whether they can meet the high standards of career and vocational-technical education. They may worry that they won't do well enough to get good grades or even passing grades.

- ■ *Being lonely:* Many students feel lonely from time to time. They may be lonely because they presently have no friends with common interests, no one with whom to share their worries, or no current love relationship.

TYPES OF STRESSORS: THE CAUSES OF STRESS. To understand how to fight stress, you need to understand the difference between *stress* and *stressors*. **Stress is the reaction of our bodies to an event. The source of stress is called a**

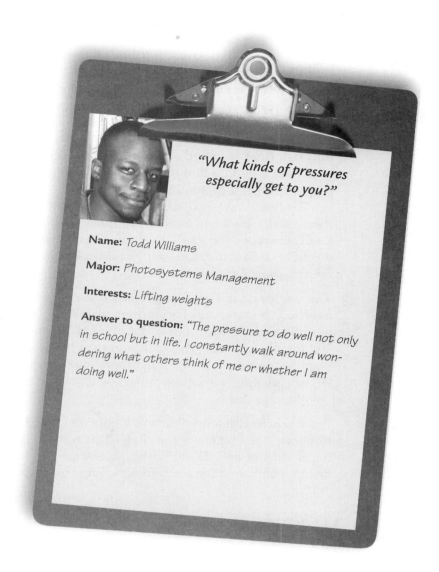

"What kinds of pressures especially get to you?"

Name: Todd Williams

Major: Photosystems Management

Interests: Lifting weights

Answer to question: "The pressure to do well not only in school but in life. I constantly walk around wondering what others think of me or whether I am doing well."

stressor. Stressors may be specific and may range from small to large. That is, they may cover everything from a question you don't understand on a test all the way up to a death in your family.

Some characteristics of stressors are as follows:

- *Three types:* There are three types of stressors—*hassles, crises,* and *strong stressors.* **A *hassle* is simply a frustrating irritant,** such as a term-paper deadline. **A *crisis* is an especially strong source of stress,** such as a horrible auto accident. Though it may be sudden and not last long, it may produce long-lasting psychological (and perhaps physical) effects. **A *strong stressor* is a powerful, ongoing source of extreme mental or physical discomfort,** such as a back injury that keeps a person in constant pain. It can dramatically strain a person's ability to adapt.

    When you consider what these terms represent, it would appear that the stressors of higher education aren't so bad compared to other things that can happen. That is, your main experience is one of *hassles* rather than crises or strong stressors.

■ ***Distressors or eustressors:*** One famous expert on stress, Canadian researcher Hans Selye, points out that stressors can be either negative or positive.[3]

When the source of stress is a negative event, it is called a *distressor* and its effect is called *distress*. An example of a distressor is flunking an exam or being rejected in love. Although distress can be helpful when one is facing a physical threat, too much of it may result in depression and illness.

When the source of stress is a positive event, it is called a *eustressor* and its effect is called *eustress* (pronounced "*you*-stress"). An example of a eustressor is getting an A on an exam or falling in love. Eustress can stimulate a person to greater coping and adaptation.

We can't always prevent distressors. However, we can learn to recognize them, understand our reactions to them, and develop ways of managing both the stressors and the stress. Eustressors, on the other hand, are what impel us to do our best. Examples are the pressure to win games, to try out a new activity, to ask out someone new for a date.

■ ***The number, kind, and magnitude of stressors in your life can affect your health:*** When stressors become cumulative they can lead to depression and illness. Several years ago, physicians Thomas Holmes and Richard Rahe devised a "future illness" scale.[4] The scale, known as the Holmes-Rahe Life Events Scale, identifies certain stressors (life events), both positive and negative. These are stressors that the physicians found could be used to predict future physical and emotional problems.

You may wish to try Practical Exploration #10.1, which contains a version of this scale, the Student Stress Scale. This was designed for people of the traditional student age, 18–24 (although anyone can take it). Note that the scale includes both negative and positive sources of stress.

TYPES OF STRESS: YOUR PHYSICAL & PSYCHOLOGICAL REACTIONS TO THE STRESSORS. Stress—your internal reactions to the stressor—has both physical and emotional sides. Physically, according to researcher Selye, stress is "the nonspecific response of the body to any demand made upon it."[5] Emotionally, stress is the feeling of being overwhelmed. According to one authority, it is "the perception that events or circumstances have challenged, or exceeded, a person's ability to cope."[6]

Specifically, the stress reactions, for you and for most other students, could take the following forms:

■ ***Physical reactions:*** All diseases are to some extent disorders of adaptation.[7] Often, however, an adaptation to stress appears in a particular part of the body—what doctors call a person's *stress site*.

One common stress site, for instance, is the neck or back; tension is often felt as a knot in the muscles there. Some people grind their teeth. Others develop nervous tics and or perspire excessively.

Do you have a "stress site"? Some physical reactions to stress are *skin problems, headaches, gastrointestinal problems, susceptibility to colds and flus,* and *high blood pressure.*[8–11]

■ ***Psychological reactions:*** Individual emotional reactions to stress cover a wide range. Among them are *nervousness and anxiety,* expressed as irritability, diffi-

PRACTICAL EXPLORATION #10.1

THE STUDENT STRESS SCALE

In the Student Stress Scale, each event, such as beginning or ending school, is given a score that represents the amount of adjustment a person has to make in life as a result of the change. In some studies, people with serious illnesses have been found to have high scores on similar scales.

■ DIRECTIONS

Check off the events you have experienced in the past 12 months.

POINTS

1. Death of a close family member ❏ 100
2. Death of a close friend ❏ 73
3. Divorce of parents ❏ 65
4. Jail term ❏ 63
5. Major personal injury or illness ❏ 63
6. Marriage ❏ 58
7. Firing from a job ❏ 50
8. Failure of an important course ❏ 47
9. Change in health of a family member ❏ 45
10. Pregnancy ❏ 45
11. Sex problems ❏ 44
12. Serious argument with close friend ❏ 40
13. Change in financial status ❏ 39
14. Change of scholastic major ❏ 39

15. Trouble with parents ❏ 37
16. New girl- or boyfriend ❏ 37
17. Increase in workload at school ❏ 36
18. Outstanding personal achievement ❏ 36
19. First quarter/semester in school ❏ 31
20. Change in living conditions ❏ 30
21. Serious argument with an instructor ❏ 30
22. Lower grades than expected ❏ 29
23. Change in sleeping habits ❏ 29
24. Change in social activities ❏ 29
25. Change in eating habits ❏ 28
26. Chronic car trouble ❏ 26
27. Change in the number of family get-togethers ❏ 26
28. Too many missed classes ❏ 25
29. Change of college ❏ 24
30. Dropping of more than one class ❏ 23
31. Minor traffic violations ❏ 20

Total points: _____

■ SCORING

To determine your stress score, add up the number of points corresponding to the events you checked.

■ INTERPRETATION

If your score is 300 or higher, you are at high risk for developing a health problem.

If your score is between 150 and 300, you have a 50-50 chance of experiencing a serious health change within two years.

If your score is below 150, you have a 1-in-3 chance of a serious health change.

The following can help you reduce your risk:

■ Watch for early signs of stress, such as stomachaches or compulsive overeating.

■ Avoid negative thinking.

■ Arm your body against stress by eating nutritiously and exercising regularly.

■ Practice a relaxation technique regularly.

■ Turn to friends and relatives for support when you need it.

culty concentrating, and sleep disturbances. Nervousness and anxiety also are expressed in feelings of dread, overuse of alcohol and other drugs, and mistakes and accidents. Another emotional reaction is *burnout*, a state of physical, emotional, and mental exhaustion.[12,13]

Managing Stress

PREVIEW You can adapt to or cope with stress. Adaptation is not changing the stressor or stress. Some ways of adapting are use of drugs and other escapes such as television watching, junk-food eating, or sleeping. Coping is changing the stressor or your reaction to it. There are five strategies for coping: (1) Reduce the stressors. (2) Manage your emotional response. (3) Develop a support system. (4) Take care of your body. (5) Develop relaxation techniques.

Regardless of your age, you have already found ways to deal with stress in your life. The question is: Are these ways really the best? For instance, on some campuses, students drink a lot of alcohol—and we mean *A LOT*. Why? "Stress!" seems to be the answer. In reality, however, heavy alcohol use only leads to *more stress.*[14]

DO YOU CONTROL STRESS OR DOES STRESS CONTROL YOU? Unfortunately, we can't always control the stressors in our lives, and so we will experience stress no matter what we do. Thus, which is more important—what happens to you, or how you handle it? Clearly, learning how to *manage* stress—minimize it or recover from it—is more important.

There are two principal methods of dealing with stress—adaptation and coping:

■ *Adaptation:* **With *adaptation,* you *do not* change the stressor or the stress.** An example is getting drunk. Adaptation is the *bad* way of handling stress.

■ *Coping:* **With *coping*, you *do* change the stressor or change your reaction to it.** For example, if you're feeling stressed about handing in a paper late, you go talk to the instructor about it. This is the *good* way of handling stress.

ADAPTATION: THE NONPRODUCTIVE WAYS OF HANDLING STRESS. Some of the less effective ways in which people adapt to stress are as follows:

■ *Drugs, legal and illegal:* Coffee, cigarettes, and alcohol are all legal drugs. However, too much coffee can make you tense, "wired." Cigarettes also speed up the heart rate and may make it difficult for you to get going in the morning. Moreover, they put you under the stress of always having to reach for another cigarette.

Alcohol is perceived as being a way of easing the strain of life temporarily, which is why it is so popular with so many people. The down side, however, is what heavy drinking makes you feel like the next morning—jittery, exhausted, depressed, all conditions that *increase* stress.

Other legal drugs, such as tranquilizers, and illegal drugs, such as marijuana and cocaine, may seem to provide relaxation in the short run. However, ultimately they complicate your ability to make realistic decisions about the pressures in your life.

■ *Food:* Overeating and junk-food snacking are favorite diversions of many people. The act of putting food in our mouths reminds us of what eased one of the most fundamental tensions of infanthood: hunger.

■ *Sleep and social withdrawal:* Sleep, too, is often a form of escape from exhaustion and depression, and some individuals will spend more than the usual 7–9 hours required in bed. Withdrawal from the company of others is also usually an unhealthy form of adaptation.

How do you adapt to stress now? Consider the kinds of responses you habitually make to the tensions in your life.

COPING: THE PRODUCTIVE WAYS OF HANDLING STRESS—FIVE STRATEGIES.
Now let us turn from negative adaptations to stress to positive coping mechanisms. There are five strategies for coping with stress, as follows:

1. Reduce the stressors.

2. Manage your emotional response.

3. Develop a support system.

4. Take care of your body.

5. Develop relaxation techniques.

STRATEGY NO. 1: REDUCE THE STRESSORS. *Reducing the source of stress is better than avoidance or procrastination.*
"Reducing the stressors" seems like obvious advice. However, it's surprising how long we can let something go on being a source of stress—usually because

dealing with it is so uncomfortable. Examples: Falling behind in your work and having to explain your problem to your instructor. Having misunderstandings with your family, your spouse or boyfriend/girlfriend, or people sharing your living space. Running up debts on a credit card. It may not be easy, but all these problems are matters you can do something about. Getting the advice of a counselor may help. Avoidance and procrastination only make things worse.

STRATEGY NO. 2: MANAGE YOUR EMOTIONAL RESPONSE. *You can't always manage the stressor, but you can manage your reactions. Techniques include understanding and expressing your feelings, acting positively, and keeping your sense of humor and having hope.*

Learning how to manage your emotional response is crucial. Quite often you can't do anything about a stressor (being stuck having to read a dull assignment, for example). However, you can do something about your *reaction* to it. (You can tell yourself that resentment gets you nowhere, or choose to see a particular stressor as a challenge rather than a threat.)

Here are some techniques for managing your emotional response:

- **Understand and express your feelings:** Understanding pent-up feelings is imperative. This advice is supported by a study of students at Southern Methodist University. It was found that those who kept a journal recounting traumatic events and their emotional responses to them had fewer colds and reported fewer medical visits.[15]

  Are you one who believes it's not appropriate to cry? Actually, crying helps. In one study, 85% of women and 73% of men reported that crying made them feel better.[16]

- **Act positively:** To keep their spirits up, some people put up signs of positive affirmation on their bathroom mirrors or over their desks. For example:

  DON'T SWEAT THE SMALL STUFF.
  ONE DAY AT A TIME.
  "NEVER GIVE UP"—Winston Churchill.

  Can you actually *will* yourself to feel and act positively and affirmatively? There is some evidence that you can. Some studies have found that putting a smile on your face will produce the feelings that the expression represents— facial action leads to changes in mood.[17–19]

  You can also make your "inner voice" a force for success. Positive "self-talk" can help you control your moods, turn back fear messages, and give you confidence.[20,21] Positive self-talk is not the same as mindless positive thinking or self-delusion.[22] Rather, it consists of telling yourself positive messages—such as "You can do it. You've done it well before"—that correct errors and distortions in your thinking and help you develop a more accurate internal dialogue.

- **Keep your sense of humor and have hope:** There has been a growing body of literature that *seems* to show that humor, optimism, and hope can help people conquer disease or promote their bodies' natural healing processes.[23–26] There is some disagreement as to how much effect laughter and hope have on healing. Still, so many accounts have been written of the positive results of these two qualities that they cannot be ignored.

STRATEGY NO. 3: DEVELOP A SUPPORT SYSTEM. *Finding social support is vital for resisting stress. Sources of support are friends—in the true sense—counselors, and self-help and other support groups.*

Doing things by yourself can be tough, so it's important to grasp a lesson that many people never learn: *You are not alone. No matter what troubles you, emotional support is available—but you have to reach out for it.*

Some forms of support are these:

■ ***Talk to and do things with friends:*** True friends are not just people you know. They are people you can trust, talk to honestly, and draw emotional sustenance from. (Some people you know quite well may actually not be very good friends in this sense. That is, the way they interact with you makes you feel competitive, anxious, or inferior.) Friends are simply those people you feel comfortable with, regardless of age or social grouping.

It's vital to fight the temptation to isolate yourself. Studies show that the more students participate in activities with other students, the less they suffer from depression and the more they have feelings of health.[27]

- ***Talk to counselors:*** You can get emotional support from counselors. Paid counselors may be psychotherapists, ranging from social workers to psychiatrists. Unpaid counselors may be clergy or perhaps members of the school's student services.

  Sources of free counseling that everyone should be aware of are telephone "hot lines." Here, for the price of a phone call, callers can find a sympathetic ear and various kinds of help. (Hot lines are listed under the heading of CRISIS INTERVENTION SERVICE in the telephone-book Yellow Pages. Other forms of stress counseling are listed under the heading STRESS MANAGEMENT AND PREVENTION.)

- ***Join a support group:*** This week, an estimated 15 million Americans will attend one of about 500,000 meetings offered by some form of support group.[28] Self-help organizations cover all kinds of areas of concern. There are many on various types of drug addiction and offering help to adult children of alcoholics. Others range from single parenting to spouse abuse to compulsive shopping to "women who love too much" to various forms of bereavement. Some of these groups may exist on or near your campus.

  In the true self-help group, membership is limited to peers. There is no professional moderator, only some temporarily designated leader who makes announcements and calls on people to share their experiences. This is in contrast with group-therapy groups, in which a psychologist or other therapist is in charge.

STRATEGY NO. 4: TAKE CARE OF YOUR BODY. *Taking care of the body helps alleviate stress in the mind. Techniques include eating, exercising, and sleeping right and avoiding drugs.*

The interaction between mind and body becomes particularly evident when you're stressed. If you're not eating right (are eating a lot of high-fat and high-sugar foods) and exercising well, or are short on sleep, or are using drugs, these mistreatments of the body will only make the mind feel worse.

STRATEGY NO. 5: DEVELOP RELAXATION TECHNIQUES. *There are three relaxation techniques for de-stressing yourself. One is progressive muscular relaxation, which consists of tightening and relaxing muscle groups. A second is mental imagery, which consists of visualizing a change. A third is meditation, which consists of focusing on removing mental distractions.*

There is an entire body of extremely effective stress reducers that most people in North America have never tried at all.[29] They include the following:

- ***Progressive muscular relaxation:*** The technique of **progressive muscular relaxation consists of reducing stress by tightening and relaxing major muscle groups throughout your body.** If you like, take 10 minutes to try the following.

1. *Get comfortable and quiet.* Sit down or lie in a comfortable setting where you won't be disturbed. Close your eyes.

2. *Become aware of your breathing.* Breathe slowly in through your nose. Exhale slowly through your nose.

3. *Clench and release your muscles.* Tense and relax each part of your body two or more times. Clench while inhaling. Release while exhaling.

4. *Proceed through muscles or muscle groups.* Tense and relax various muscles, from fist to face to stomach to toes. (A good progression is right fist, right biceps. Left fist, left biceps. Right shoulder, left shoulder. Neck, jaw, eyes, forehead, scalp. Chest, stomach, buttocks, genitals, down through each leg to the toes.)

■ **Mental imagery: Mental imagery** is also known as *guided imagery* and *visualization.* **It is a procedure in which you essentially daydream an image or desired change, anticipating that your body will respond as if the image were real.** The accompanying box shows how to do mental imagery. *(See ■ Panel 10.1.)*

PANEL 10.2

Mental imagery. It's recommended that you devote 10 minutes or so to this procedure.

Get comfortable and quiet: Remove your shoes, loosen your clothes, and sit down or lie in a comfortable setting, with the lights dimmed. Close your eyes.

Breathe deeply and concentrate on a phrase: Breathe deeply, filling your chest, and slowly let the air out. With each breath, concentrate on a simple word or phrase (such as "One," or "Good," or a prayer). Focus your mind on this phrase to get rid of distracting thoughts. Repeat.

Clench and release your muscles: Tense and relax each part of your body, proceeding from fist to face to stomach to toes.

Visualize a vivid image: Create a tranquil, pleasant image in your mind—lying beside a mountain stream, floating on a raft in a pool, stretched out on a beach. Try to involve all five senses, from sight to taste.

Visualize a desired change: If you're trying to improve some aspect of your performance, such as improving a tennis serve, visualize the act in detail: the fuzz and seam on the ball, the exact motion of the serve, the path of the ball, all in slow detail.

PANEL 10.2

Meditation. Meditation includes the repetition of a word, sound, phrase, or prayer. Whenever everyday thoughts occur, they should be disregarded, and you should return to the repetition. The exercise should be continued for 10 minutes or so.

Herbert Benson, M.D., author of *The Relaxation Response* and *Your Maximum Mind*, offers the following simple instructions for meditation:

- Pick a focus word or short phrase that is firmly rooted in your personal belief system. For example, a Christian person might choose the opening words of Psalm 23, "The Lord is my shepherd"; a Jewish person, "Shalom"; a nonreligious individual, a neutral word like "One" or "Peace."

- Sit quietly in a comfortable position.

- Close your eyes.

- Relax your muscles.

- Breathe slowly and naturally, and as you do, repeat your focus word or phrase as you exhale.

- Assume a passive attitude. Don't worry about how well you're doing. When other thoughts come to mind, simply say to yourself, "Oh, well," and gently return to the repetition.

- ***Meditation: Meditation* is concerned with directing a person's attention to a single, unchanging, or repetitive stimulus. It is a way of quelling the "mind chatter"**—the chorus of voices that goes on in everyone's head. An age-old technique, meditation is simply a way to eliminate mental distractions and relax the body. The accompanying box shows one method.[30] *(See ■ Panel 10.2.)*

Conflict & Communication: Learning How to Disagree

PREVIEW Communication consists of ways of learning to disagree. In bad communication, you become argumentative and defensive and deny your own feelings. In good communication, you acknowledge the other person's feelings and express your own openly. Expert listening consists of tuning in to your partner's channel. It means giving listening signals, not interrupting, asking questions skillfully, and using diplomacy and tact. Most important, it means looking for some truth in what the other person says. To express yourself, use "I feel" language, give praise, and keep criticism specific.

Why can't people get along better? Must there always be conflict in close relationships, as between family members, boyfriends/girlfriends, roommates, or housemates? To see what your usual approach to conflict is, try Practical Exploration #10.2.

PRACTICAL EXPLORATION #10.2

WHAT ARE YOUR FEELINGS ABOUT CONFLICT?

Check which *one* of the following statements best describes your feelings when you approach a conflict with someone close to you.

1. ❑ I hate conflict. If I can find a way to avoid it, I will.

2. ❑ Conflict is such a hassle. I'd just as soon let the other person have his or her way so as to keep the peace.

3. ❑ You can't just let people walk over you. You've got to fight to establish your point of view.

4. ❑ I'm willing to negotiate to see if the other person and I can meet halfway.

5. ❑ I'm willing to explore the similarities and differences with the other person to see if we can solve the problem to both our satisfaction.

■ INTERPRETATION

Whichever one you checked corresponds to a particular style of dealing with conflict. They are: (1) avoidance, (2) accommodation, (3) domination, (4) compromise, (5) integration. For an explanation, read on.

Researchers have identified five styles of dealing with conflict, one of which is probably closest to yours.

1. ***Avoidance: "Maybe It Will Go Away."*** People who adopt this style find dealing with conflict unpleasant and uncomfortable. They hope that by ignoring the conflict or by avoiding confrontation, the circumstances will change and the problem will magically disappear. Unfortunately, avoiding or delaying a confrontation with the conflict usually means it will have to be dealt with later rather than sooner, at which point the situation may have worsened.

2. ***Accommodation: "Oh, Have It Your Way!"*** Accommodation does not mean compromise; it means simply giving in, although it does not really resolve the matter under dispute. People who adopt a style of easily surrendering are, like avoiders, uncomfortable with conflict and hate disagreements. They are also inclined to be "people pleasers," worried about the approval of others. However, giving in does not really solve the conflict. If anything, it may aggravate the situation over the long term because accommodators may be deeply resentful that the other person did not listen to their point of view. Indeed, the resentment may even develop into a role of martyrdom, which will only irritate the person's partner.

3. ***Domination: "Only Winning Matters."*** The person holding the winning-is-everything, domination style should not be surprised if he or she some day finds an "I'm gone!" note from the partner. The dominator will go to any lengths to emerge triumphant in a disagreement, even if it means being aggressive and manipulative. However, winning isn't what intimate human relationships are supposed to be about; that approach to conflict produces only hostility and resentment.

4. **Compromise: "I'll Meet You Halfway."** Compromise seems like a civilized way of dealing with conflict, and it is definitely an improvement over the preceding styles. People striving for compromise recognize that both partners have different needs and try to negotiate to reach agreement. Even so, they may still employ some gamesmanship, such as manipulation and misrepresentation, in an attempt to further their own ends. Thus, compromise is not as effective in resolving conflict as integration.

5. **Integration: "Let's Honestly Try to Satisfy Both of Us."** In compromise, the solution to the conflict is a matter of each party meeting the other halfway. The integration style, on the other hand, attempts to find a solution that will achieve satisfaction for both partners.

   Integration has several parts:

- **Openness for mutual problem solving:** The conflict is seen not as a game to be won or negotiated but as a problem to be solved to each other's mutual benefit. Consequently, manipulation and misrepresentation have no place; honesty and openness are a necessary part of reaching the solution. This attitude also has the benefit of building trust that will carry over to the resolution of other conflicts.

- **Disagreement with the ideas, not the person:** There is an important part of integration, which we expand on below. This concept is that partners must be able to criticize each other's ideas or specific acts rather than each other generally as persons. It is one thing, for instance, to say "You drink too much!" It is another to say "I feel you drank too much last night." The first is a generality that insults the other's character. The second way states that you are unhappy about a particular incident.

- **Emphasis on similarities, not differences:** Integration requires more work than other styles of dealing with conflict (although the payoffs are better). The reason is that partners must put a good deal of effort into stating and clarifying their positions. To maintain the spirit of trust and problem solving, the two should also emphasize the similarities in their positions rather than the differences.

AREAS OF CONFLICT. The number of subjects over which two people can disagree is awesome. One area about which couples must make adjustments are unrealistic expectations, such as who should do which household chores. Other matters have to do with work and career, finances, in-laws, sex, and commitment/jealousy.[31]

COMMUNICATION: THERE ARE WAYS TO LEARN HOW TO DISAGREE. Even though conflict is practically always present in an ongoing relationship, this does not mean that it should be suppressed. When handled constructively, conflict may bring problems out into the open, where they can be solved. Handling conflict may also put an end to chronic sources of discontent in a relationship. Finally, airing disagreements may lead to new insights through the clashing of divergent views.[32] The key to success in relationships is the ability to handle conflict successfully, which means the ability to communicate well.

BAD COMMUNICATION. Most of us *think* communication is easy, points out psychiatrist David Burns, because we've been talking since we were children.[33] And communication *is* easy when we're happy and feeling close to someone. It's when we have a conflict that we find out how well we really communicate—whether it's good or bad.

Bad communication, says Burns, author of *The Feeling Good Handbook*, has two characteristics:

- **You become argumentative and defensive:** The natural tendency of most of us when we are upset is to argue with and contradict others. The habit of contradicting others, however, is self-defeating, for it creates distance between you and them and prevents intimacy. Moreover, when you are in this stance you show you are not interested in listening to the other person or understanding his or her feelings.

- **You deny your own feelings and act them out indirectly:** You may become sarcastic, or pout, or storm out of the room, slamming doors. This kind of reaction is known as *passive aggression.* However, it can sometimes be as destructive as *active aggression,* in which you make threats or tell the other person off.

There are a number of other characteristics of bad communication. One is *martyrdom,* in which you insist you're an innocent victim. A second is *hopelessness,* in which you give up and insist there's no point in trying to resolve your difficulties. A third is *self-blame,* in which you act as if you're a terrible, awful person (instead of dealing with the problem). A fourth is *"helping,"* in which instead of listening you attempt to take over and "solve" the other person's problem. A fifth is *diversion,* in which you list grievances about past "injustices" instead of dealing with how you both feel right now.

GOOD COMMUNICATION. "Most people want to be understood and accepted more than anything else in the world," says Burns.[34] Knowing that is taking a giant first step toward good communication.

Good communication, according to Burns, has two attributes:

- **You listen to and acknowledge the other person's feelings:** You may be tempted just to broadcast your feelings and insist that the other agree with you. It's better, however, if you encourage the other to express his or her emotions. Try to listen to and understand what the other person is thinking and feeling. (We expand on listening skills below.)

- **You express your own feelings openly and directly:** If you only listen to the other person's feelings and don't express your own, you will end up feeling

shortchanged, angry, and resentful. When you deny your feelings, you end up acting them out indirectly. The trick, then, is to express your feelings in a way that will not alienate the other person.

BECOMING EXPERT AT LISTENING. If communication is listening, how is that done? Some ideas are offered by Aaron Beck, director of the Center for Cognitive Therapy at the University of Pennsylvania. In his book *Love Is Never Enough,* he suggests the following listening guidelines:[35]

■ ***Tune in to your partner's channel:*** Imagining how the other person might be feeling—putting yourself in the other's shoes—is known as *empathy,* trying to experience the other's thoughts and feelings. The means for learning what the other's thoughts and feelings are can be determined through the other steps.

■ ***Give listening signals:*** Use facial expressions, subtle gestures, and sounds such as "uh-huh" and "yeah" to show your partner you are really listening. Beck particularly urges this advice on men, as studies show that women are more inclined to send responsive signals. Talking to someone without getting feedback is like talking to a wall.

■ ***Don't interrupt:*** Although interruptions may seem natural to you, they can make the other person feel cut off. Men, says Beck, tend to interrupt more than women do (although they interrupt other men as often as they do women). They would do better to not express their ideas until after the partner has finished talking.

■ ***Ask questions skillfully:*** Asking questions can help you determine what the other person is thinking and keep the discussion going—provided the question is not a *conversation stopper.* "Why" questions can be conversation stoppers. ("Why were you home late?") So can questions that can have only a yes-or-no answer.

Questions that ask the other's opinion can be *conversation starters.* (Example: "What do you think about always having dinner at the same time?")

Questions that reflect the other's statements help convey your empathy. (Example: "Can you tell me more about why you feel that way?") The important thing is to ask questions *gently*, never accusingly. You want to explore what the other person is thinking and feeling and to show that you are listening.

- **Use diplomacy and tact:** All of us have sensitive areas—about our appearance or how we speak, for example. This is true of people in intimate relationships as much as people in other relationships. *Problems in relationships invariably involve feelings.* Using diplomacy and tact in your listening responses will help build trust to talk about difficulties.

   An especially wise piece of advice about listening comes from David Burns: *Find SOME truth in what the other person is saying and agree with it.* Do this even if you feel that what he or she is saying is totally wrong, unreasonable, irrational, or unfair. This technique, known as *disarming*, works especially well if you're feeling criticized and attacked.

   If, instead of arguing, you agree with the other person, it takes the wind out of his or her sails. Indeed, it can have a calming effect. The other person will then be more open to your point of view. Adds Burns: "When you use the disarming technique, you must be genuine in what you say or it will backfire. You can always find some valid way to agree, no matter how illogical the person's accusations might seem to you. If you agree with them in a sincere way, they will generally soften and will be far more willing to listen to you."[36]

BECOMING EXPERT AT EXPRESSING YOURSELF. It is often tempting to use the tools of war—attacking and defending, withdrawing and sulking, going for the jugular. However, these actions will never take you as far in resolving conflicts in intimate relationships as will kinder and gentler techniques.

In expressing yourself, there are two principal points to keep in mind:

- **Use "I feel" language:** It's always tempting to use accusatory language during the heat of conflict. (Examples: "You make me so mad!" or "You never listen to what I say!") However, this is sure to send the other person stomping out of the room.

   A better method is simply to say "I feel" followed by the word expressing your feelings—"frustrated"; "ignored"; "attacked"; "nervous"; "unloved." This way you don't sound blaming and critical. (Compare this to saying "You make me . . ." or "You never . . .") By expressing how you feel, rather than defending the "truth" of your position, you can communicate your feelings without attacking the other.

- **Express praise and keep criticism specific:** Most of us respond better to compliments than to criticism, and most of us seek appreciation and fear rejection. In any conflict, we may disagree with a person's *specific act or behavior.* However, we need not reject the other as a person.

   For example, you might want to say, "When we go to parties, you always leave me alone and go talk to other people." It's better, however, to combine criticism with praise. For example: "I'm proud to be with you when we go to parties, and I hope you are of me. However, I think we could have even more fun if we stay in touch with each other when we're at a party. Does this seem like a reasonable request?"[37]

Assertiveness: Better than Aggressiveness or Nonassertiveness

PREVIEW Aggressiveness is expressing yourself in a way that hurts others. Nonassertiveness is not expressing yourself, giving in to others and hurting yourself. Assertiveness is expressing yourself without hurting either others or yourself. Both men and women have assertiveness problems, women sometimes being too passive and men too aggressive, although the reverse is also true. Developing assertiveness means observing your own behavior in conflict situations, visualizing a model for assertiveness, and practicing assertive behavior.

It's important to learn to express your disappointments, resentments, and wishes without denying yourself. Yet you also don't want to put other people down or make them angry. This means learning to be *assertive*.

Assertiveness doesn't mean being pushy or selfish but rather being forthright enough to communicate your needs while respecting the needs of others. Being assertive is important in intimate relationships, of course. However, it's also important in many other social interactions in which speaking out, standing up for yourself, or talking back is necessary.

AGGRESSIVE, NONASSERTIVE, & ASSERTIVE BEHAVIOR. Let us consider three types of behavior: aggressiveness, nonassertiveness, and assertiveness. (Distinctions among these behaviors have been put forth in two interesting, readable books by psychologists Robert Alberti and Michael Emmons. They are *Your Perfect Right* and *Stand Up, Speak Out, Talk Back!*[38,39]) The definitions are as follows:

- *Aggressiveness—expressing yourself and hurting others:* **Aggressive behavior means you vehemently expound your opinions, accuse or blame others, and hurt others before hurting yourself.**

- *Nonassertiveness—giving in to others and hurting yourself:* **Nonassertive behavior—also called *submissive* or *passive behavior*—means consistently giving in to others on points of difference. It means agreeing with others regardless of your own feelings, not expressing your opinions, hurting yourself to avoid hurting others.** Nonassertive people have difficulty making requests for themselves or expressing their differences with others. In a word, they are *timid*.

- *Assertiveness—expressing yourself without hurting others or yourself:* **Assertiveness is defined as acting in your own best interests by expressing your thoughts and feelings directly and honestly. It means standing up for yourself and openly expressing your personal feelings and opinions, yet not hurting either yourself or others.** Assertiveness is important in enabling you to express or defend your rights.

To get an idea of your assertiveness, try Practical Exploration #10.3.

PRACTICAL EXPLORATION #10.3

HOW ASSERTIVE ARE YOU?

Answer "Yes" or "No" to each of the following statements.

1. When a person is blatantly unfair, do you usually fail to say something about it to him or her?

   ❑ Yes   ❑ No

2. Are you always very careful to avoid all trouble with other people?

   ❑ Yes   ❑ No

3. Do you often avoid social contacts for fear of doing or saying the wrong thing?

   ❑ Yes   ❑ No

4. If a friend betrays your confidence, do you tell him or her how you really feel?

   ❑ Yes   ❑ No

5. Would you insist that a roommate do his or her fair share of cleaning?

   ❑ Yes   ❑ No

6. When a clerk in a store waits on someone who has come in after you, do you call his or her attention to the matter?

   ❑ Yes   ❑ No

7. Do you find that there are very few people with whom you can be relaxed and have a good time?

   ❑ Yes   ❑ No

8. Would you be hesitant about asking a good friend to lend you a few dollars?

   ❑ Yes   ❑ No

9. If someone who has borrowed $5 from you seems to have forgotten about it, would you remind this person?

   ❑ Yes   ❑ No

10. If a person keeps on teasing you, do you have difficulty expressing your annoyance or displeasure?

    ❑ Yes   ❑ No

11. Would you remain standing at the rear of a crowded auditorium rather than look for a seat up front?

    ❑ Yes   ❑ No

12. If someone kept kicking the back of your chair in a movie, would you ask him or her to stop?

    ❑ Yes   ❑ No

13. If a friend keeps calling you very late each evening, would you ask him or her not to call after a certain time?

    ❑ Yes   ❑ No

14. If someone starts talking to someone else right in the middle of your conversation, do you express your irritation?

    ❑ Yes   ❑ No

15. In a plush restaurant, if you order a medium steak and find it too rare, would you ask the waiter to have it recooked?

    ❑ Yes   ❑ No

16. If a landlord of your apartment fails to make certain necessary repairs after promising to do so, would you insist on it?

    ❑ Yes   ❑ No

17. Would you return a faulty garment you purchased a few days ago?

    ❑ Yes   ❑ No

18. If someone you respect expresses opinions you strongly disagree with, would you venture to state your own point of view?

    ❑ Yes   ❑ No

19. Are you usually able to say no when people make unreasonable requests?

    ❑ Yes   ❑ No

20. Do you think that people should stand up for their rights?

    ❑ Yes   ❑ No

■ INTERPRETATION

There is no scoring system. You can figure out what the answers *should* be. Now it becomes a matter of rehearsing the response so you'll be able to act assertively the next time it's required. What will you do the next time the landlord fails to make repairs? Or the people in your household don't do their fair share of cleaning? Or you need to ask the waiter to have your steak cooked some more?

It's important to learn to *ask for what you want in a civilized way, without hurting the feelings of the other person.* This is what assertive behavior is all about. Consider what happens if you try aggressive or nonassertive behavior. Aggressive behavior probably won't help you get what you want because your pushiness or anger creates disharmony and alienates other people. It may also make you feel guilty about how you treated others. Nonassertive behavior also may not help you get what you want. Though it may be an attempt to please others by not offending them, it may actually make them contemptuous of you.[40]

You need to know, however, that assertive behavior will *not* always get you what you want. Probably no one form of behavior will. Still, if performed correctly, it may improve your chances. The reason is that assertive behavior is not offensive to other people. It makes them more willing to listen to you.

DEVELOPING ASSERTIVENESS. There are different programs for developing assertiveness, but most consist of four steps:[41]

- *Learn what assertive behavior is:* First, you need to learn what assertive behavior is, so that you know what it is supposed to be like. You need to learn how to consider both yours *and* others' rights.

- *Observe your own behavior in conflict situations:* You then need to monitor your own assertive (or unassertive) behavior. You need to see what circumstances, people, situations, or topics make you behave aggressively or nonassertively. You may find you are able to take care of yourself (behave assertively) in some situations, but not in others.

- *Visualize a model for assertiveness:* If possible, you should try to find someone to serve as a model for assertiveness in the specific situations that trouble you and observe that person's behavior. Role models are important in other parts of life, and this area is no exception. If possible, note how rewarding such behavior is; seeing the rewards will reinforce your assertive tendencies.

- *Practice assertive behavior:* Of course, the only way to consistently behave assertively is to practice the behavior. You can do this as a rehearsal, carrying on an imaginary dialog in private with yourself. Or you can actually role-play the behavior, practicing the assertive behavior with a good friend, counselor, or therapist.

A Crash Course in Money Handling

PREVIEW Controlling spending starts with managing big-ticket purchases, such as housing and transportation, which are often trade-offs. You can also find ways to get inexpensive furniture and computers. Tactics exist for controlling telephone charges and food and clothing purchases. Students need to investigate good banking and ATM sources. They need to know how to manage charge cards and credit cards. They also need to make arrangements to be covered by such protection as health, tenants, and automobile insurance.

For many of us, money has a way of just dribbling through our fingers, and we're not really sure where it goes. That's why credit counselors, who help people in debt, have clients keep detailed records of all expenses, even for candy bars and newspapers. Even if you don't have money troubles, before you can *plan* how to manage your money, you need to *observe* your present money patterns. To do this, we suggest doing Practical Exploration #10.4. for a week.

THE MONEY DIAGNOSTIC REPORT: WHERE DOES IT COME FROM, WHERE DOES IT GO?

Tear out or photocopy this page and carry it around with you in an accessible place for a week.

Every time you receive a check or cash (*Money in*), write down its source and the amount. (Example: "Loan from Susie, $10.") Every time you spend money—whether cash, check, or credit card (*Money out*)—write down the expenditure and the amount. (Example: "Movie, food: $12.")

■ **MONEY IN:** Examples of sources of funds: job, parents, grant, savings, loan, friend, tax refund.

MONEY IN FROM	SUNDAY	MONDAY	TUESDAY	WEDNESDAY	THURSDAY	FRIDAY	SATURDAY

Total received for week: _____

■ **MONEY OUT:** Examples of expenditures: books, meals, bus fare, snacks, phone, rent, entertainment, clothes, laundry.

MONEY OUT FOR	SUNDAY	MONDAY	TUESDAY	WEDNESDAY	THURSDAY	FRIDAY	SATURDAY

Total spent for week:

It's almost impossible to grow up in this society and not want to spend more than one's income. The television and print ads just never let us forget life's endless possibilities for parting with our money. Maybe you can't increase your income, but you can almost always find ways to cut spending.

CONTROLLING YOUR SPENDING. Here are some money-saving tips, ranging from big-ticket items to everyday small expenditures:

- *Housing and transportation:* Many career and vocational-technical students live at home and take bus, streetcar, or subway to campus. Or, particularly in the South and West, they may live at home and drive a car to school.

  Housing and transportation sometimes present a trade-off. Living at home may be cheaper than living in your own apartment, so you can afford to maintain a car. Living in an apartment close to campus may cost more, but you can get around on foot, bicycle, or public transportation.

  When comparing prospective rents, be sure to determine whether the rent does or doesn't include utilities, such as electricity, water, and garbage collection. Try to take care of your rental unit by fixing things yourself when possible and making sure to keep up the yard. This will help you get back any security deposits when you move out. It will also help you get a favorable reference from the landlord that will assist you in lining up the next rental.

  Cars can be expensive. The purchase price of a car is only the beginning. Compared with paying for gas, oil, tires, repairs, insurance, and parking, a bus or a bicycle may turn out to be a real bargain.

- *Computers, furniture, refrigerators:* If you have your own apartment or room, remember that the things that cost the most are also those on which you can cut costs. You don't need to go first class on such big-ticket items as computers and furniture. Do you need a television set, CD player, radio, heater, or fan? Check with your housemates, who may have these. Do you need a bed, a desk lamp, a dresser? All of these may be bought used.

  You don't need *both* a typewriter and a computer, but you're well advised to have one or the other. (You might be able to borrow someone else's machine. But what if he or she needs it when you're up against a tight deadline to get a paper done?) Computers may be bought used, especially if all you need them for is typewriter-like purposes, such as writing papers.

  Some students like to have a refrigerator in their rooms, either the 2.8 cubic-foot size or the smaller 1.6 cubic-foot size. These may be rented from local organizations (for perhaps $50–$75) or bought outright for $100–$150 from local discount appliance stores.[42] When these costs are shared with housemates, they become manageable.

- *The telephone:* Probably there's not much hazard in making a lot of local calls—unless you're tying up your family or housemates' phone, too. However, cross-country love affairs and talks with friends at other schools can produce massive long-distance charges.

  If you're the one originating the calls, you may find a telephone timer will help you hold calls to 10 or 15 minutes instead of 2 hours. Also, don't feel you have to answer every incoming call, especially if you're studying. Ask others in your living unit to take a message for you, then call back later.

■ *Food and clothing:* Food can be a great hidden magnet for cash. Consider what the minimum wage is in this country (around $5 an hour before deductions). Then consider how *little* that will buy in the way of soft drinks, potato chips, and other packaged snacks. Even meals at fast-food places can rapidly drain your money.

Clearly, learning how to cook will save you money, even if what you prepare is just spaghetti. So will learning how to shop. Shop from a list; doing this helps keep you disciplined. Don't shop when you're hungry; hunger makes you reach for convenience foods and snacks. Shop for fresh fruits, vegetables, grains, and other foods that are not processed; they are less expensive. Use clip-out coupons from newspapers if they will really save you money. (Don't use them to buy expensive processed foods you would not otherwise buy.)

Some people are hyper-conscious about the way they dress, which is fine as long as they aren't hooked into following every fashion. There are ways to buy clothes cheaply: at the end of the season, other sale times, or at used-clothing stores. If you build your wardrobe around one or two colors, you can do a lot of mixing and matching.

BANKS. One student who, with friends, wrote a guide to college survival, suggests keeping two things in mind when choosing a bank.[43] First, find a bank that has automated teller machines (ATMs) that are handy for you. Second, consider all possible hidden costs of the bank in question.

There are many kinds of checking and savings accounts. On standard checking accounts, some banks charge you a monthly fee, some a fee for every check you write, some both. Some checking accounts pay interest if you maintain a high balance, but often the fees will eat up the interest. If you don't write a lot of checks, you might do better with a savings account, which pays interest. Finally, some banks offer a basic banking account, geared to low-income or retired customers. This allows you to write six or so checks per month without additional charge.

CHARGE CARDS, CREDIT CARDS, & DEBIT CARDS. Studies have shown banks and credit-card companies that students are as responsible with credit as most adults. Consequently, campuses have been deluged with ads and applications, trying to entice thousands of students into The Way of Plastic. Indeed, credit-card companies often waive credit histories and income requirements.[44] As a result, 82% of students in higher education have at least one credit card.[45]

Charge cards that require the bill to be paid off every month. Examples are charge cards given out by American Express and many oil companies.

Credit cards allow the charges to be paid off in installments plus interest, provided you make a minimum payment every month. Examples are cards given out by Mastercard, Visa, and Discover.

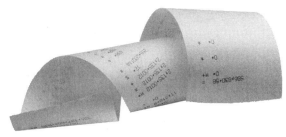

A third kind of card is the debit card, which can be used at certain stores such as some grocery chains. **The *debit card* enables you to pay for purchases electronically by withdrawing funds directly from your savings or checking account.** That is, the debit card acts in place of a paper check.

The advantage of all three types of cards is convenience: you don't have to carry cash. Such cards also allow you to rent cars, buy plane tickets, and book hotel rooms, transactions difficult to do with cash or check. Credit cards can also give you a loan when you need it.

There are, however, some disadvantages:

- *It's easy to forget you're spending money:* "We'll just put it on plastic," students say. Somehow it's easy to spend $80 on that great coat in the store window when you only have to sign a charge slip. It's a lot more difficult when you have to hand over four Andrew Jacksons. With plastic, you get what you want now without the pain of feeling as if you're paying for it.

- *Debts can pile up:* With debit cards, the money is gone from your checking account as soon as you use it. With American Express and other charge cards, you have to pay the bill every month, just like the phone bill. With Visa, Discover, MasterCard, and other credit cards, however, debts can be carried over to the next month. Credit limits for students typically start at $500. Many students find this line of credit too much of a good thing.

    A survey of students at three Michigan universities found that 10% had outstanding credit card bills of more than $700. A handful had bills as high as $5,000 or $6,000.[46]

- *Interest rates can be high:* Credit-card interest rates can be much higher than the rates banks charge for other kinds of loans, such as car loans. (And that's all a credit card is—a loan.) Many cards charge 18%–20% a year. And every month, interest is added to the interest.

    NOTE: If you carry a $6,297 credit-card balance and make only the minimum $200 payment every month, you'll be paying off that debt for—the next 23 years and 10 months! (And that cost could include over $9,570 in interest.)[47]

If you have trouble restraining yourself from charging on your credit cards, there's only one solution: Take scissors and cut them up.

INSURANCE. For a student, there are two or three important kinds of insurance:

- *Health insurance:* This is absolutely essential. The United States is not a country where it's wise to be without health insurance. If something goes wrong, a hospital somewhere (maybe not a good one) will probably take you into the emergency room. However, without health insurance you might not get the level of care you need. Moreover, the hospital's business office will bill you anyway.

    Parents' employer health plans can often be extended to cover college-age children up until the age of around 24. In addition, many schools offer student health plans, and you should check to see what their benefits cover. Are lab tests, surgery, hospital stays, long-term care included? If necessary, pay for supplemental health insurance to cover care not provided on campus.

- *Tenant's insurance:* You should make sure your possessions are covered by insurance against fire and theft. Students who are still dependents of their parents may be covered by their parents' insurance. This is so even if the students live in a campus dormitory or off-campus apartment. It assumes, however, that they still live at home during the summer, are registered to vote there, or carry a driver's license with their parents' address. Your coverage usually amounts to 10% of your parents' coverage, minus the deductible. Thus, if your parents' plan covers $150,000 and has a $250 deductible, you are covered up to $15,000. Check with your insurance company to make sure you're covered as you should be. If not, you should be able to get a special policy for additional premiums.

If you're self-supporting or emancipated or older than about 23, you'll need to get your own tenant's policy.

■ **Car insurance:** If you have a car and are under age 25 (especially if you're an unmarried male), perhaps you've already found that car insurance is one of the most expensive things you can buy. Indeed, it and all other car expenses should seriously make you think about whether you really need a car at school.

If you have an older car, as so many students do, carrying collision insurance may not be worth the expense. This is the kind of insurance that covers any repairs (usually with a deductible) your car might need should anyone run into you. However, you'll want to carry as much comprehensive insurance as you can in case you run into another car, bicyclist, or pedestrian. You should also be covered for hospitalization for any passengers riding in your car.

Before buying car insurance, you should get on the phone with the telephone-book Yellow Pages and do some comparison shopping. Be sure to ask whether you can get a discount on your premiums for maintaining good grades. Some companies offer this feature.

Financial Aid

PREVIEW Financial aid may consist of gifts, such as grants and scholarships. Or it may consist of self-help assistance, such as loans, part-time work, and work-study. Most financial aid is considered "need-based"; to qualify for this, you show economic need. However, some aid is "merit-based," such as academic, music, or sports scholarships. To demonstrate financial need, you or your family must fill out a needs analysis document. Aid is available for parents of students, self-supporting students under 24, and older students.

Student need for financial aid has shot up in recent years. This is partly because institutions of higher education have raised their tuition rates but also partly because of changes in the kinds of students going on in school. For instance, over the past decade, three-quarters of institutions in higher education have reported admitting more students over 25 years of age. Because most of them are part time, they are not eligible for federal financial aid, so they have turned to the schools themselves to cover their aid requirements.[48]

The purpose of this section is to show you the different sources of financial aid available to you. One caution: Allow *lots* of time for the application and approval process. No agency will give you any money if you didn't follow their rules and apply within the deadlines posted. Applying for money is just like applying to get into many schools themselves: These things do not happen instantaneously. You (or your parents) will need time to fill in the forms if you are to meet a filing deadline far in advance of the first day of the school term. Then, if you qualify, school officials will take time to approve the paperwork before they can send you a check. (Help in obtaining financial assistance is offered through a couple of toll-free numbers. Call the Federal Student Aid Information Center at 800-4-FEDAID or the Federal Student Aid Advisory Center at 800-648-3248.)

GIFTS & SELF-HELP, NEED-BASED & MERIT-BASED. The term *financial aid* **refers to any kind of financial help you get to enable you to pay for higher education.** There are two ways to distinguish financial aid:

- *Gifts versus self-help assistance: Gift assistance* **is financial aid you do not have to pay back.** It includes *grants* and *scholarships*.

  Self-help assistance **is financial aid that requires something in return.** *Loans,* which must be repaid, are one example. *Part-time work* and *work-study* is another.

- *Need-based versus merit-based aid:* Most financial aid is need-based. **With need-based financial aid, you or your parents fill out forms stating your resources. The school then determines how much aid needs to be made up from somewhere else** for you to meet your education expenses.

  Merit-based financial aid **is based on some sort of superior academic, music, sports, or other abilities.**

CAN YOU SHOW YOU NEED IT? *Demonstrated financial need* **means that you have proven you need financial aid according to a certain formula,** such as the Congressional Methodology. To begin to apply for need-based financial aid, you must ask your institution for an application form called a needs analysis document. **The *needs analysis document* is a form for helping people prove their financial need to their schools.** The *two federal forms you are most likely to encounter are the FAF and the FAFSA.*

Financial aid is available regardless of whether you are getting money from your family. It is also available whether you are going it alone as a young person or are going back to school as an older person.

- *Aid for parents of students:* The Congressional Methodology formula considers your family's size, income, net worth, and number of members now in higher education. It then considers your anticipated costs of attending a particular school. From these two factors, the formula arrives at an estimated family contribution. Schools then make their own calculations based on this formula. If the results show your family's resources insufficient, you'll get some help.

- *Aid for self-supporting students under 24:* If you're self-supporting, the Congressional Methodology formula counts just your income and assets, not your family's. You must show that you are single, under age 24, and without dependents. You must also show you have not been claimed as a dependent by your parents for two years. Finally, you must show that you have had annual resources of at least $4,000 during each of these two years.[49]

- *Aid for returning adult students:* Even returning adult students can obtain financial aid based on need. It's a matter of minimizing one's income and assets.

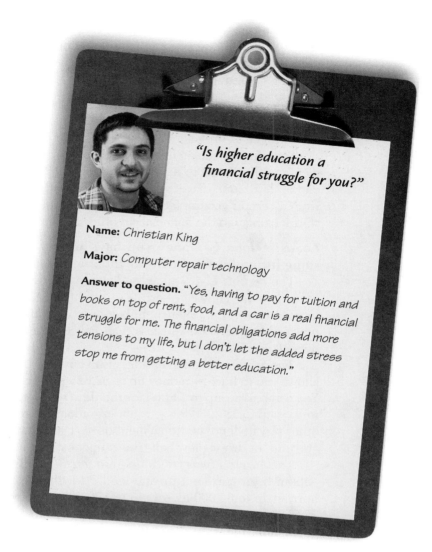

"Is higher education a financial struggle for you?"

Name: Christian King

Major: Computer repair technology

Answer to question. "Yes, having to pay for tuition and books on top of rent, food, and a car is a real financial struggle for me. The financial obligations add more tensions to my life, but I don't let the added stress stop me from getting a better education."

(For example, older people can move their savings into retirement plans, which are sheltered from financial aid computations.) Believe it or not, it may also help to apply to an expensive institution, according to one piece of advice. The reason is that the more expensive the school is, the more aid students are eligible for.[50]

TYPES OF FINANCIAL AID. We may classify financial aid as grants, scholarships, loans, and work. These are available from several sources: federal, state, school, and private.

- *Grants: Grants* **are gifts of money;** they do not have to be repaid.

    One large need-based grant program from the federal government is the *Pell Grants,* given to undergraduates on the basis of need. Normally Pell Grants are given to families with an annual income of less than $25,000, although there are special exceptions. You should apply in any case. Many institutions will not consider you for other grants unless you've been turned down for a Pell Grant.

    Another need-based federal grant program is the *Supplemental Educational Opportunity Grants (SEOG), which are designed to augment other forms of financial aid.*

Some companies also offer their employees grants in the form of educational benefits that allow them to attend school while working. For example, a hospital may pay one of its employees to go to nursing school while he or she continues working.

- ***Scholarships: Scholarships are usually awarded on the basis of merit,*** often academic merit. Sometimes the scholarships are for merit in other areas as well, such as proficiency in a certain sport or musical activity.

    Sometimes scholarships are available for reasons you couldn't possibly predict, and they seem to have nothing to do with merit. For instance, you have a certain last name, have a parent who worked for a certain organization, or are from a certain geographical area. You'll never know what these are unless you start looking. Go the financial aid office or library and ask for help.

- ***Loans: A loan is money you have to pay back, either as money or in some form of work.*** There are three well-known federal loan programs.

    The *Perkins Loans* allow students to borrow up to $4,500 for their first and second years. They can borrow up to $9,000 for all undergraduate years. The interest rate is 5%. Repayment begins nine months after graduation (unless you quit or become a student less than half time). The repayment may be spread over 10 years.

    The *Stafford Loan Program,* also known as the Guaranteed Student Loans, allows you to borrow money up to $2,625 per year for the first and second year. You can borrow up to $4,000 for the third year and beyond. Thus, you can accumulate up to $17,250 for your undergraduate years. Loans are made by banks or other private lenders. Repayment doesn't start until six months after you graduate, quit, or drop below half-time student status.

    The *Parent Loans for Undergraduate Students (PLUS)* program allows parents to borrow from a private lender for their children's education. They can borrow up to $4,000 a year, up to $20,000 for each student and at a rate up to 12%. To be eligible, you have to have applied for a Pell or Stafford first. Parents begin repayment 60 days after receiving the money. Students taking out the loan may wait until 60 days after quitting or graduating from school before beginning repayment.

    A more recent kind of loan is a direct-loan program by the U.S. government, designed to cut out bankers' profits, streamline procedures, and help students predict and organize their debts. Depending on their circumstances, graduates can repay their debt over 10 to 30 years. (Most student loans are structured for repayment over 10 years.)[51]

- ***Work:*** Many schools offer part-time work opportunities, usually on campus, for money or for room and/or board. Of course, you may also be able to line up part-time work off campus. In addition, a federally funded need-based program called *College Work-Study* helps schools set up jobs for students. Typically College Work-Study covers 12–15 hours a week, or up to 40 hours a week during the summer.

    Cooperative education programs allow you to improve your marketability on graduation by giving you work experience in your major. The work may go on at the same time as the course work or as part-time school and part-time work. Or the work may alternate with course work—for example, one semester in school and the next semester at work. Pay is often modest, but the experience is what counts. Cooperative education programs are offered at about 1,000 schools.

Onward

| PREVIEW | Personal growth is a lifelong process.

Most people find that concerns about stress, relationships, and money continue after they're out of school. Thus, like other skills in this book, the techniques described here are not just things you need to know for the short run. They are lifelong skills that will benefit you no matter what kind of degree you hold.

NOTES

1. The perils of burnout. (1987, October). *Newsweek on Campus.*

2. Lazarus, R. S. (1981, July). Little hassles can be hazardous to health. *Psychology Today,* p. 61.

3. Selye, H. (1974). *Stress without distress.* New York: Lippincott, pp. 28–29.

4. Holmes, T. H., & Rahe, R. H. (1967). The social readjustment rating scale. *Journal of Psychosomatic Research,* 11, 213–218.

5. Selye, 1974, p. 27.

6. Lazarus, R. S., & Forlman, S. (1982). Coping and adaptation. In W. D. Gentry (Ed.), *Handbook of behavioral medicine.* New York: Guilford Press.

7. Hinkle, L. E., Jr. (1987). Stress and disease: The concept after 50 years. *Social Science & Medicine,* 25, 561–566.

8. Kiecolt-Glazer, J., & Glaser, R. (1988). Major life changes, chronic stress, and immunity. *Advances in Biochemical Psychopharmacology,* 44, 217–224.

9. Kiecolt-Glazer, J. et al. (1987, August) Stress, health, and immunity: Tracking the mind/body connection. Presentation at American Psychological Association meeting, New York.

10. Kannel, W. B. (1990). CHD risk factors: A Framingham study update. *Hospital Practice,* 25, 119.

11. Eliot, R., & Breo, D. (1984). *Is it worth dying for?* New York: Bantam Books.

12. McCulloch, A., & O'Brien, L. (1986). The organizational determinants of worker burnout. *Children & Youth Services Review,* 8, 175–190.

13. Girdano, D. A., & Everly, G. S., Jr. (1986). *Controlling stress and tension.* Englewood Cliffs, NJ: Prentice-Hall.

14. Matthews, A. (1993, March 7). The campus crime wave. *New York Times Magazine,* pp. 38–42, 47.

15. Dear diary (1987, August). *American Health.*

16. Mee, C. L., Jr. (Ed.). (1987). *Managing stress from morning to night.* Alexandria, VA: Time-Life Books.

17. Zajonc, R. B. (1985). Emotion and facial efference: A theory reclaimed. *Science*, 228, 15–21.

18. Adelmann, P. K., & Zajonc, R. B. (1989). Facial efference and the experience of emotion. *Annual Review of Psychology*, 40, 249–280.

19. Zajonc, R. Cited in Goleman, D. (1989, June 29). Put on a happy face—it really works. *San Francisco Chronicle*, p. C10. Reprinted from *New York Times*.

20. Donahue, P. A. (1989). Helping adolescents with shyness: Applying the Japanese Morita therapy in shyness counselling. *International Journal for the Advancement of Counselling*, 12, 323–332.

21. Zastrow, C. (1988). What really causes psychotherapy change? *Journal of Independent Social Work*, 2, 5–16.

22. Braiker, H. B. (1989, December). The power of self-talk. *Psychology Today*, p. 24.

23. Cousins, N. (1979). *Anatomy of an illness*. New York: Norton.

24. Dillon, K. M., Minchoff, B., & Baker, K. H. (1985–1986). Positive emotional states and enhancement of the immune system. *International Journal of Psychiatry in Medicine*, 15, 13–18.

25. Long, P. (1987, October). Laugh and be well? *Psychology Today*, pp. 28–29.

26. Siegel, B. (1986). *Love, medicine, and miracles*. New York: Harper & Row.

27. Reifman, A., & Dunkel-Schetter, C. (1990). Stress, structural social support, and well-being in university students. *Journal of American College Health*, 38, 271–277.

28. Leerhsen, C., et al. (1990, February 5). Unite and conquer. *Newsweek*, pp. 50–55.

29. Snyder, M. (1988). Relaxation. In J. J. Fitzpatrick, R. L. Taunton, & J. Q. Benoliel (Eds.), *Annual review of nursing research*, 8, 111–28. New York: Springer.

30. Benson, H. (1989). Editorial: Hypnosis and the relaxation response. *Gastroenterology*, 96, 1610.

31. Weiten, W., Lloyd, M. A., & Lashley, R. L. (1991). *Psychology applied to modern life: Adjustment in the 90s* (3rd ed.). Pacific Grove, CA: Brooks/Cole.

32. Weiten, Lloyd, & Lashley, 1991, p. 179.

33. Burns, D. D. (1989). *The feeling good handbook*. New York: Plume.

34. Burns, 1989, p. 371.

35. Beck, A. (1989). *Love is never enough*. New York: HarperPerennial.

36. Burns, 1989, p. 379.

37. Crooks, R., & Baur, K. (1990). *Our sexuality* (4th ed.). Redwood City, CA: Benjamin/Cummings, p. 268.

38. Alberti, R. E., & Emmons, M. L. (1970). *Your perfect right: A guide to assertive behavior*. San Luis Obispo, CA: Impact.

39. Alberti, R. E., & Emmons, M. L. (1975). *Stand up, speak out, talk back!* New York: Pocket.

40. Jakubowski-Spector, P. (1973). Facilitating the growth of women through assertive training. *Counseling Psychologist, 4,* 75–86.

41. Weiten, Lloyd, & Lashley, 1991.

42. Gottesman, G. (1991). *College survival.* New York: Prentice Hall Press, pp. 13–14.

43. Gottesman, 1991, pp. 196–197.

44. Credit cards become big part of life. (1991, February 9). *New York Times,* p. 16.

45. Brookes, A. (1994, November 5). Lesson for teen-agers: Facts of credit-card life. *New York Times,* p. 31.

46. Foren, J. (1991, December 1). College students piling on credit card debt. *San Francisco Examiner,* p. E-9.

47. Warner, J. (1992, July 20). It's chic to be cheap: A penny-pincher's primer. *Business Week,* pp. 94–95.

48. Madden, M. (1996, August 5). Colleges tighten belts. *USA Today,* p. 9B; citing report by American Council on Education, *Campus Trends 1996.*

49. *Success with your money.* (1988). Washington, DC: Kiplinger's Changing Times, p. 132.

50. Nemko, M. (1992, June 28). A grown-up's guide to financial aid. *This World, San Francisco Chronicle,* pp. 11–12.

51. Manegold, C. S. (1994, September 19). U.S. has high hopes for a revamped student loan program. *New York Times,* p. A10.

Classroom Activities: Directions to the Instructor

1. ***How much stress do you have in your life?*** Ask students to complete Personal Exploration #10.1, "The Student Stress Scale." Each student should list on a sheet of paper his or her Top Ten Stressors, drawing on this Personal Exploration, if necessary.

   Students should then meet in a small group (three to five students), designate a secretary or recorder, and develop a master list from their separate lists. After identifying the top five stressors for the group, students should discuss how the stressors affect their behaviors and feelings and how they have ineffectively coped with such stressors in the past. They should then discuss how they would hope to deal with them in the future.

   If time permits, students may share their experiences with the class as a whole.

2. ***Practicing a relaxation technique.*** The instructor should select *one* of the three relaxation techniques described in this chapter—*progressive muscular relaxation, mental imagery,* or *meditation*—for 10 minutes of practice by the class as a whole. Read aloud from this book the steps for the particular method.

Important: Tell students that whenever everyday thoughts occur they are to disregard them and return to the relaxation procedure.

After the 10 minutes are up, ask students to discuss their experience. Questions for discussion: Do you actually feel more relaxed? Did you almost fall asleep? Was it difficult to disregard the intrusion of everyday thoughts? Were you too aware of others in the room? Do you think the technique might work in private?

3. ***What are your feelings about conflict?*** Ask students to refer to Practical Exploration #10.2, "What Are Your Feelings About Conflict?" Ask them to discuss (in a small or large group) which style of conflict they seem to gravitate to.

   Questions for discussion: How well does this seem to work for you? As a regular way of operating, what kinds of frustrations does it produce for you? for the people with whom you're in conflict? What alternative style of conflict can you see yourself doing?

4. ***Practicing assertiveness.*** Have students form groups of three people each. Students should then take turns describing situations in which they were *nonassertive* (passive). They should describe who was involved in the interaction, how they felt about that person or persons, and their feelings about themselves as a result of their nonassertiveness.

   Next, students should give the same attention to situations in which they behaved *aggressively.* Finally, they should apply the same considerations to situations in which they were *assertive* in their communication style.

   Ask students to choose one of the incidents in which they behaved nonassertively or aggressively and, with a second group member role-playing the other person, practice behaving assertively in the same situation. The third person in the group should act as observer, monitoring eye contact, voice tone, body posture, and other signs of assertiveness.

   In the group or with the class as a whole, students should discuss what kinds of situations give them the most trouble in being assertive. Ask them to state whether these situations involve authority figures, strangers, or people close to them. Have them identify role models who might help them become assertive and state what they notice about their behavior.

5. ***What are common concerns about money?*** Have each student write down on a sheet of paper five principal thoughts or worries he or she has about money. Be sure to tell students *not* to put their names on the paper, but to fold it up for collection by the instructor.

   Read aloud some of the responses to the class for discussion purposes. Questions to consider: How common are some of these concerns? What can you do about them? Does it make you feel better knowing that others have the same worries you have?

6. ***The credit card hassle.*** In the class at large, ask students to discuss the problems of credit cards. Questions to consider: What is the psychology behind credit cards that makes them irresistible to use? Suppose instead of using a credit card you had to go apply for a bank loan every time you wanted to buy something. Would you do it? If you have credit cards, do you know what their interest rates and charges are? How much does that work out to per month on the unpaid balance? Could you cut up your credit cards today and get through the rest of the school year?

The Examined Life:
Student Assignments for Journal Entries

JOURNAL ENTRY #10.1: HOW DO YOU REACT TO STRESS? When you experience stress, what kinds of psychological reactions do you have (for example, irritability, impatience, depression)? What kinds of physiological reactions do you have to stress (for example, insomnia, upset stomach, tiredness)? List your reactions and compare them to the reactions of other people you know.

_____

_____

_____

_____

_____

_____

_____

JOURNAL ENTRY #10.2: HOW DO YOU DEAL WITH STRESS? What kinds of things do you do to reduce your feelings of stress? What kinds of things _could_ you do? Give some thought to the whole matter of "partying," or heavy drinking and/or drugging. How much of it do you see around you? Have you been affected by it? Is stress a contributor?

_____

_____

_____

_____

_____

_____

_____

JOURNAL ENTRY #10.3: HOW DO YOU HANDLE CONFLICT? Write a page or two of detail about an important relationship (as with parents, boyfriend/girlfriend, spouse, children, professor, boss). Are you satisfied with this relationship? What have you learned in this chapter that might help you to improve it?

_____

_____

_____

_____

_____

_____

JOURNAL ENTRY #10.4: **ARE YOU PASSIVE OR AGGRESSIVE?** Do you feel you're inclined to be aggressive or to be passive in conflict situations? Imagine yourself having a disagreement with someone (such as an instructor about a grade on a paper or a roommate about living arrangements). Write out a little script about some things you might say to express your point of view without hurting the other person or hurting yourself.

_____

_____

_____

_____

_____

_____

_____

JOURNAL ENTRY #10.5: **WHAT IS UPSETTING ABOUT MONEY?** What do you find particularly upsetting to you about money? What does this chapter suggest you might be able to do about it?

_____

_____

_____

_____

_____

_____

JOURNAL ENTRY #10.6: **WHAT DO YOU KNOW ABOUT STUDENT LOANS?** Some students talk almost like bankers, computing which loans and repayment schedules are better than others. Have you done comparisons of the various loans available? If not, what kind of action might you take here?

_____

_____

_____

_____

_____

_____

CHAPTER ELEVEN

CAREER & WORK
Vocational direction,
job hunting, résumés, & interviewing

IN THIS CHAPTER: What will you do when you get out of school? What would you *like* to do? Is there necessarily a relationship between your academic career field or major and your actual career? These are some of the most important questions you'll ever have to consider.
In this chapter, we consider the following:

■ **Your future:** What do you want to do when you get out of school, and how can you get career advice?

■ **Vocational tests:** What vocational tests can help point you toward a career?

■ **Job hunting:** What are the best ways to find a good job? How does networking help? How can you use a computer to help you in a job search? What are the best ways to write a résumé? What are some techniques for interviewing?

▪When we go to our jobs, what is it that we are trading for money?

The answer is, simply, our *life energy.*

"Our life energy," explain Joe Dominguez and Vicki Robin, authors of *Your Money or Your Life,* "is our allotment of time here on earth, the hours of precious life available to us." Life energy is all we have. "It is precious because it is limited and irretrievable and because our choices about how we use it express the meaning and purpose of our time here on earth."[1]

Thus, they say, in considering what to do for a living, two questions become important:

▪ Are you receiving satisfaction and value in proportion to your life energy expended?

▪ Is the expenditure of life energy in alignment with your values and purpose?

Considering all the ways you might spend your future days, then, what would make you *feel most fulfilled while trading your irretrievable life energy?*

Unfortunately, for a great many people, work does not give them this sense of purpose. According to a Gallup poll, only 41% of the respondents consciously chose the job or career they are in. Of the rest, 18% got started in their present job through chance circumstances, and 12% took the only job available. The remainder were influenced by relatives or friends.[2]

Perhaps the most important finding was this: *Nearly two thirds said that, given a chance to start over, they would try to get more information about career options.*

Maybe, then, you are in a good position to take advantage of others' hindsight: Get as much information as you can about careers and jobs.

What Do You Want to Be After You Graduate?

PREVIEW Some careers have a relationship to one's academic career field, but many others do not. Other competencies related to a career are related work experience; personal discipline; information-handling skills; and political, networking, and teamwork skills. It's best to decide on a career before picking an academic career field or major; advice can be obtained at the school's career counseling and job placement center.

In urging you to get career information, we also need to say this: Don't be afraid about making a mistake in a career choice. People make career changes all the time, in all phases of life. Moreover, in the beginning, it's natural to go through some trial and error until you find what suits you. Indeed, columnist and business consultant Jack Falvey points out that most people do some casting about: "It is a rare person who knows with certitude what he [or she] wants to be and then follows that dream into the sunset for a lifetime. It is unrealistic to set that [ideal] as a standard."[3]

In fact, in the future, the average person is expected to have *four career changes*—and several job changes within each career.[4] Statistically, people

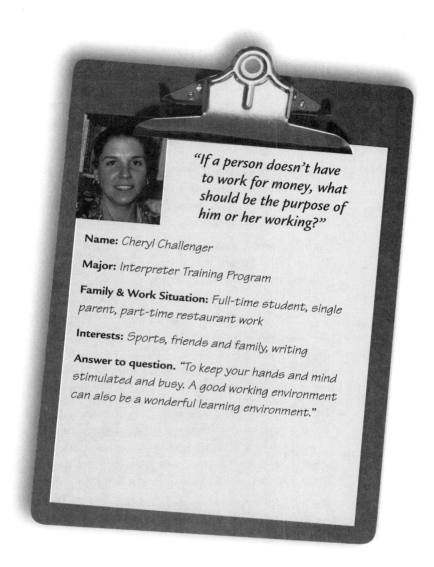

"If a person doesn't have to work for money, what should be the purpose of him or her working?"

Name: Cheryl Challenger

Major: Interpreter Training Program

Family & Work Situation: Full-time student, single parent, part-time restaurant work

Interests: Sports, friends and family, writing

Answer to question. *"To keep your hands and mind stimulated and busy. A good working environment can also be a wonderful learning environment."*

change jobs or assignments every 2½ years.[5] The best approach you can take, then, is to be flexible.

IS THERE A RELATIONSHIP BETWEEN ACADEMIC CAREER FIELD OR MAJOR & YOUR CAREER? Many career students assume that to enter most careers you must have the appropriate academic preparation. There are three possibilities here:

- ■ *Relationship between academic preparation and career:* For most career and vocational-technical students, there clearly *is* a relationship between the academic preparation they do and their careers. To be a computer technician, medical assistant, or paralegal, for example, you should study these fields in school. This is because the training for the occupation is so specific.

- ■ *No relationship between academic preparation and career:* A great many fields require no specific major or academic preparation at all. You can be a sales representative or a store manager, for example, without necessarily taking business courses, although they help.

Quite apart from considering your career, however, is another important question: What do you want to *study*? For many people, higher education is a once-in-a-lifetime activity. Regardless of what you're going to do for a living, now is also the time to take a few courses in those subjects you're curious about.

OTHER COMPETENCIES NEEDED FOR A CAREER. It's important to realize that academic preparation and a certificate or degree are only a *start* toward a career. Besides these, you need other competencies appropriate to the work you choose. Examples are:

- *Related work experience:* It greatly helps to have acquired some skills related to the line of work you're entering. Such skills may be obtained from part-time work, internships, work-study programs, cooperative educational experiences, and co-curricular activities. These are matters we would strongly recommend looking into with a career counselor and/or your academic advisor.

- *Personal discipline:* You need to know how to dress appropriately, get to work on time, and be pleasant to co-workers and clients. You also need to be able to persist in completing your assignments, come hell or high water. (You might not *want* to make 100 telephone calls a day, but it might be required in your job.)

- *Information-handling and communication skills:* Most jobs these days that have a future to them require that you know how to handle information and communicate it. This means knowing how to write a report, how to give a speech or presentation, and how to participate in a meeting. It probably also means knowing how to handle a computer (to do word processing, say).

- *Political, networking, and teamwork skills:* Knowing how to handle office politics (otherwise known as "organizational dynamics") is an important aspect of most career building. So is networking—the making, nurturing, and maintaining of personal contacts with people who can assist you. Indeed, developing these skills while you are in school can help you get your foot in the door for a new career. (For example, you might get to know an instructor or fellow student who has connections to an industry you're interested in.) All of these activities contribute to teamwork skills, which are necessary in the pursuit of a career.

WHAT DO YOU WANT TO DO FOR A CAREER? How do you find which might be best for you? You can just leave things to chance, as many people do. Indeed, one out of three students in higher education puts off making a career decision until after graduation.[6] Then you can take whatever comes along, hoping everything will just work out for your future happiness.

But consider what it is that makes people want to succeed. University of Rochester psychology professor Edward L. Deci has studied human motivation for many years. According to his research, people do better when they are encouraged to pursue a task for its own sake. They also enjoy it more than those told to do the task for a reward. Or those told they will be punished if they don't perform correctly.[7] Clearly, then, it's worth your while to seek out a career that you really want to do.

CAREER COUNSELING & JOB PLACEMENT CENTER. Career guidance starts with a visit to the career counseling center, which most schools have. Often the center is coupled with the job placement office.

Basically, the career counseling and job placement center offers the following services:

- *Vocational testing:* Tests such as those described in the next section ask you questions about your interests, abilities, and values. They also make suggestions about possible career areas that might interest you.

- *Career counseling:* Career counseling offices usually have lots of information about what occupational fields are expanding. They also can tell you where the jobs tend to be concentrated geographically, the salary levels, and the training required.

  You may get one-on-one advice from career advisors. Or you may be steered to job fairs attended by prospective employers or be introduced to graduates of your school who are working in fields you're considering.

- *Information about advanced training:* Some careers may require a degree from a four-year institution or even a graduate degree. Often the career counseling office provides information on these programs and their admissions requirements and costs.

- *Job placement:* Students of the traditional college age (18–24 years old) may think of part-time or summer jobs as simply ways of making money to help get them through school. However, these jobs can also provide valuable work experience that you can leverage later when you're trying to obtain a career-path type of job. The job-placement office can also help you find out about internships or fieldwork jobs associated with your career field or major.

Tests to Help Establish Career Interests

PREVIEW Vocational tests can help people establish their career interests and abilities. One presented here is the "career video" exercise. More formal tools include the Strong/Campbell Interest Inventory and the Edwards Personal Preference Schedule. Visiting the career counseling and job placement office can be a valuable and ultimately time-saving experience.

How can you identify the occupations that might suit your abilities and interests? One way to do this is through vocational testing offered by career counselors. Let's consider some of these tests.

THE "CAREER VIDEO" EXERCISE. John Holland is a psychologist at Johns Hopkins University who has developed a system that divides career areas into six categories based on different interests and skills.[8] Here let us suppose that Holland's six career categories have been produced as a series by a "career introduction video service." (This is sort of a variation on those video dating services you may have seen ads for.) To see which careers appeal to you, try Practical Exploration #11.1.

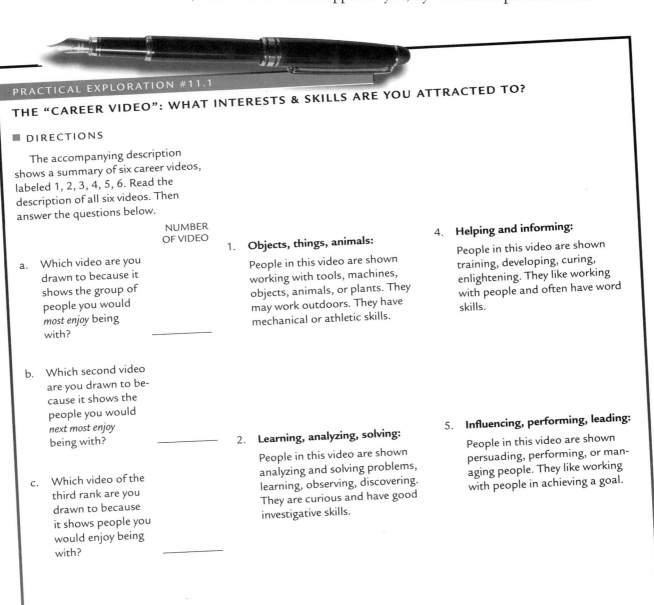

PRACTICAL EXPLORATION #11.1
THE "CAREER VIDEO": WHAT INTERESTS & SKILLS ARE YOU ATTRACTED TO?

■ DIRECTIONS

The accompanying description shows a summary of six career videos, labeled 1, 2, 3, 4, 5, 6. Read the description of all six videos. Then answer the questions below.

NUMBER OF VIDEO

a. Which video are you drawn to because it shows the group of people you would *most enjoy* being with?   _____

b. Which second video are you drawn to because it shows the people you would *next most enjoy* being with?   _____

c. Which video of the third rank are you drawn to because it shows people you would enjoy being with?   _____

1. **Objects, things, animals:**

   People in this video are shown working with tools, machines, objects, animals, or plants. They may work outdoors. They have mechanical or athletic skills.

2. **Learning, analyzing, solving:**

   People in this video are shown analyzing and solving problems, learning, observing, discovering. They are curious and have good investigative skills.

3. **Innovating and creating:**

   People in this video are shown being intuitive, creative, imaginative, and artistic. They like to operate in unstructured environments.

4. **Helping and informing:**

   People in this video are shown training, developing, curing, enlightening. They like working with people and often have word skills.

5. **Influencing, performing, leading:**

   People in this video are shown persuading, performing, or managing people. They like working with people in achieving a goal.

6. **Data and details:**

   People in this video are shown executing tasks, following instructions, and working with numbers and facts. They like working with data.

   (continued on next page)

THE "CAREER VIDEO": WHAT INTERESTS & SKILLS ARE YOU ATTRACTED TO?

■ INTERPRETATION

The video numbers represent the following:

1 = *Realistic*
2 = *Investigative*
3 = *Artistic*
4 = *Social*
5 = *Enterprising*
6 = *Conventional*

In general, the closer the types, the less the conflict among the career fields. Here's what the six fields mean.

1. **Realistic:** People in this video consider themselves "doers." They are practical, down-to-earth, mechanically inclined, action-oriented, interested in physical activity.

   Interests may be mechanical or scientific. Examples of occupations: coach, computer graphics technician, electrical contractor, electronics technician, farmer, fitness director, health and safety specialist, industrial arts teacher, jeweler, navy officer, physical education teacher.

2. **Investigative:** If you're this type, you consider yourself a problem solver. You're probably rational and analytical, valuing intellectual achievement. You're thought-oriented rather than action-

oriented. You may not be very people-oriented, indeed may be a loner.

   Sample occupations: cattle breeder, college professor, computer programmer, engineer, environmentalist, flight engineer, physician, scientist, urban planner.

3. **Artistic:** As might be expected, artistic people describe themselves as creative. They also consider themselves independent, unconventional, and emotional, valuing self-expression and disliking structure.

   Careers are apt to be in visual or performing arts. Examples of occupations: actor, architect, cartoonist, communications specialist, editor, illustrator, interior decorator, jewelry designer, journalist, librarian, orchestra leader, photographer, public relations person, sculptor.

4. **Social:** Social people value helping others and consider themselves socially concerned and caring and understanding of other people. They are drawn to associating with others in close personal relationships.

   Some careers: career specialist, caterer, convention planner, counselor, home economist, insurance claims specialist, minister, nurse, teacher, travel agent.

5. **Enterprising:** If you consider yourself adventurous, assertive, risk-taking, outgoing, and persuasive, you may be of the enterprising type. Power and prestige are important to you, and you prefer leadership to supporting roles.

   Examples of occupations: banker, city manager, FBI agent, labor negotiator, lawyer, marketing specialist, politician, promoter, real-estate developer, sales representative, television announcer or producer.

6. **Conventional:** Conventional types see themselves as enjoying routine, order, neatness, detail, and structure, as well as prestige and status. They are self-controlled and skilled in planning and organizing.

   Some occupations: accountant, auditor, database manager, hospital administrator, indexer, information consultant, insurance administrator, legal secretary, office manager, personnel specialist, statistician.

   Most people are not one distinct type but rather a mixture of types. This is why this Personal Exploration offers second and third choices.

   These interpretations may help suggest possible directions for you to pursue for your major and career.

OTHER TESTS FOR CAREER DECISION MAKING. A more sophisticated version of the "career video" test is available under the name of the *Vocational Preference Inventory*, developed by John Holland. Holland has also written a *Self-Directed Search Assessment Booklet.* This contains a self-marking test that you can use to examine what occupations you might begin to investigate. A career counselor can give you a further explanation of these valuable tests.

Two other tests used by career counselors are the Strong/Campbell Interest Inventory (SCII) and the Edwards Personal Preference Schedule (EPPS). The Strong/Campbell test enables students to compare their interests to those of people in various occupations. The Edwards test allows students to discover what their personal needs and preferences are—such as need for order, dominance, helping others, and social orientation.

GOING FOR AN APPOINTMENT AT CAREER COUNSELING. Visiting a career counseling center and taking a vocational test might require most of an afternoon, but the experience may save you months or even years of wasted effort. To get started on establishing your career path, do Practical Exploration #11.2.

PRACTICAL EXPLORATION #11.2

WHAT CAN YOU LEARN FROM A VISIT TO THE CAREER COUNSELING & JOB PLACEMENT OFFICE?

The purpose of this assignment is to get you into the Career Counseling and Job Placement Office and have you talk to one of the counselors.

■ **DIRECTIONS**

Call the Career Counseling Center (or its equivalent on your campus) and make an appointment to come in. Explain to the counselor that you are doing a class assignment for this course. Ask if he or she can spare 15–20 minutes of time for a brief interview. Make an appointment to meet.

My appointment is at (date and time)

_____

_____

with (name of counselor)

_____

_____

at (location)

_____

_____

■ **QUESTIONS FOR THE VISIT**

Review the interview questions below and add two of your own. Ask the following questions and fill in the blanks.

1. What kind of career counseling services do you offer?

_____

_____

2. What kind of information do you have about occupational fields?

_____
_____
_____
_____
_____
_____
_____
_____
_____
_____
_____

3. What kind of vocational tests do you offer? How long do they take?

_____
_____
_____
_____
_____
_____
_____
_____
_____

4. What kind of information do you have, if any, about graduate and professional schools?

_____
_____
_____
_____
_____
_____
_____
_____
_____
_____

5. If this office has a job placement component, what kind of services does it offer? Does it help students get internships or fieldwork placements?

_____
_____
_____
_____
_____
_____

The Job of Looking for a Job

PREVIEW Everyone should train in the job of looking for a job. Three ways to connect with jobs are networking, the informational interview, and internships. The computer can also be a job-search tool, as in hunting for online job openings and putting your résumé in an online database. It helps to know techniques for writing résumés, both recruiter-friendly and computer-friendly, chronological and functional. It's also important to know how to write a cover letter to accompany the résumé and how to behave in an interview.

"The average person will go job hunting *eight* times in his or her life," says Richard Bolles. A former clergyman, Bolles is author of *What Color Is Your Parachute?* and other writings about career searching.[9–11] Thus, today one needs to train for the task of *finding and getting* a job as much as for the ability to do the job itself.

Bolles offers several insights on finding that "lucky" job.[12] Luck, he says, favors people who

- Are going after their dreams—the thing they really want to do most in the world.

- Are prepared.

- Are working hardest at the job hunt.

- Have told the most people clearly and precisely what they are looking for.

- Treat others with grace and dignity, courtesy and kindness.

THREE WAYS OF LOOKING FOR JOBS. Listing the various ways of finding jobs would take a book in itself. Our suggestion is to go through the Career Counseling Center and find out everything you can about this subject.

Three ways of making connections are as follows:

- **Networking:** We would agree with Jack Falvey when he says that contacts are everything. This means learning to "network" as a way of developing relationships that could pay off in a job. **Networking is making contacts, and making use of existing contacts, with people to find work and advance your career.**

  Suppose you're a bank manager looking to fill entry-level jobs such as teller, personal banker, and mortgage consultant. Whom would you be more apt to hire—applicants who were referred by your own employees or applicants who weren't? A two-year study of one large bank found that although applicants with referrals made up only 8% of all applicants, four out of five of them were interviewed and they received 35% of the jobs.[13] Why? First, the applicants who knew someone in the bank had important information about the bank and the skills it wanted. Second, it's more difficult for a manager to assess such qualities as dependability when he or she can't check out an applicant with other employees first.[14]

  Networking can be *formal*, as when you make a point of getting to know instructors or others (as through internships or social organizations) in the industry in which you're interested in finding work. Or it can be *informal*, as when you're able to call on friends, fellow students, or co-workers to help you make connections (as through a relative) to a possible job.

Many people may wince at the mere mention of the word "networking," in part, according to one career consultant, because it goes back to one of the guiding principles of childhood: Don't talk to strangers. We may also be resistant because we want to feel it's not *who* we know but *what* we know in developing our careers.[15] Nevertheless, networking is important. "Part of an aggressive career strategy is making sure your accomplishments and skills are known within your company and within your industry," says the president of one national executive recruiting firm.[16]

■ ***The informational interview:*** Students have a somewhat privileged status just by being students. Everyone knows that they are in a temporary position in life, that of *learning.* Consequently, it is perfectly acceptable for you to write a letter to a high-level executive asking for an *informational interview.* The letter should be written on high-quality paper stock, perhaps even on a letterhead printed with your name and address. *(See ■ Panel 11.1.)*

"You may find it hard to believe that some senior management types would clear their calendars for an hour or two just to talk to a student," Falvey

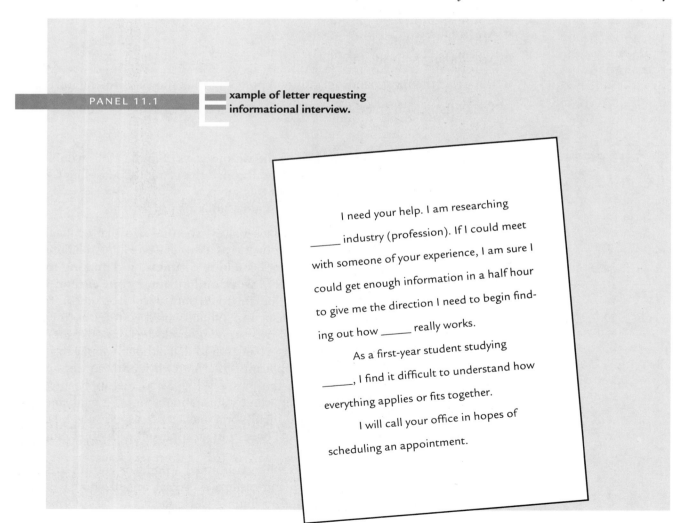

PANEL 11.1   Example of letter requesting informational interview.

> I need your help. I am researching _____ industry (profession). If I could meet with someone of your experience, I am sure I could get enough information in a half hour to give me the direction I need to begin finding out how _____ really works.
>
> As a first-year student studying _____, I find it difficult to understand how everything applies or fits together.
>
> I will call your office in hopes of scheduling an appointment.

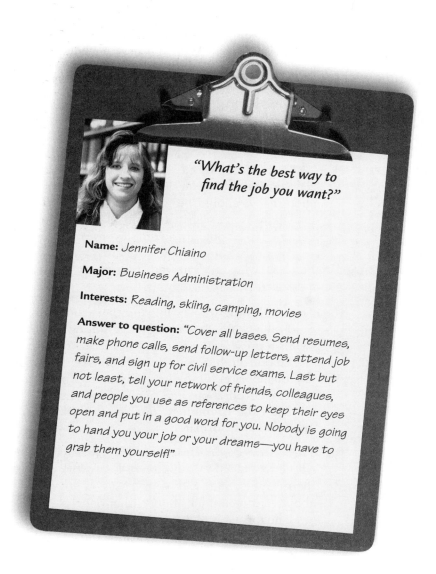

"What's the best way to find the job you want?"

Name: *Jennifer Chiaino*

Major: *Business Administration*

Interests: *Reading, skiing, camping, movies*

Answer to question: *"Cover all bases. Send resumes, make phone calls, send follow-up letters, attend job fairs, and sign up for civil service exams. Last but not least, tell your network of friends, colleagues, and people you use as references to keep their eyes open and put in a good word for you. Nobody is going to hand you your job or your dreams—you have to grab them yourself!"*

observes, "but they do it all the time.[17] After sending the letter, you can make the follow-up phone call. This will probably connect you with a secretary who handles the appointment calendar. Simply remind him or her that you had written to set up a meeting and ask how the executive's calendar looks.

■ **Internships:** Summer interns are a segment of the labor force that, according to one report, "in a generation, has grown to encompass roughly a third of college students."[18] Essentially **an *internship* is a temporary stint of on-the-job training that allows you to gain inside professional experience within a particular company or organization.** What the company gets in return is your labor (sometimes for a modest salary, sometimes for no salary). It also gets the opportunity to bid for your services after you graduate if the people there decide they like you—an example of networking at work.

Internships—sometimes called field experiences or cooperative educational experiences—may be as short as a few days during semester break or as long as a complete summer or school term. You can locate them through the career counseling center, of course. You can also simply ask guest speakers or other campus visitors about them. You might even be able to create your own internship, as by asking an executive during an informational interview.

WRITING A RECRUITER-FRIENDLY RÉSUMÉ. Writing a résumé is like writing an ad to sell yourself. However, it can't just be dashed off or follow any format of your choosing. It should be carefully designed to impress a human recruiter, who may have some fairly traditional ideas about résumés. (It should also be designed to be put into an employer's computerized database, as we'll describe.)

Here are some tips for organizing résumés, offered by reporter Kathleen Pender, who interviewed numerous professional résumé writers.[19] *(See ■ Panel 11.2.)*

- **The beginning:** Start with your name, address, and phone number.

   Follow with a clear objective stating what it is you want to do. (Example: "Sales representative in computer industry.")

   Under the heading "Summary" give three compelling reasons why you are the ideal person for the job. (Example of one line: "Experienced sales representative to corporations and small businesses.")

   After the beginning, your résumé can follow either a *chronological* format or a *functional* format.

- **The chronological résumé:** The chronological résumé works best for people who have stayed in the same line of work and have moved steadily upward in their careers. Start with your most recent job and work backward, and say more about your recent jobs than earlier ones.

   The format is to list the years you worked at each place down one side of the page. Opposite the years indicate your job title, employer name, and a few of your accomplishments. Use action words ("managed," "created," "developed"). Omit accomplishments that have nothing to do with the job you're applying for.

- **The functional résumé:** The functional résumé works best for people who are changing careers or are re-entering the job market. It is also for people who want to emphasize skills from earlier in their careers or their volunteer experience. It is particularly suitable if you have had responsibilities you want to showcase but have never had an important job title.

   The format is to emphasize your skills, then follow with a brief chronological work history emphasizing dates, job titles, and employer names.

- **The conclusion:** Both types of résumés should have a concluding section showing school, degree, and graduation date and occupational credentials or licenses. They should also include affiliations and awards if they are relevant to the job you're seeking.

- **The biggest mistakes on résumés:** The biggest mistake you can make on a résumé is to *lie*. Sooner or later a lie will probably catch up with you and may get you fired, maybe even sued.

   The second biggest mistake is to have *spelling errors*. Spelling mistakes communicate to prospective employers a basic carelessness.

Example of a basic résumé.

771 Randall Avenue
San Jose, CA 95190

(408) 555-4567

STACEY S. WILLIAMS

OBJECTIVE:

Sales representative in an electronics company in an entry-level position.

SUMMARY OF QUALIFICATIONS:

Experienced with working with general public and in retail selling during summer and Christmas jobs. Superb writing skills developed through college courses and extracurricular activities. Active volunteer in literacy program and discussion forums. Knowledge of Spanish.

BUSINESS EXPERIENCE:

Nov. 22–Dec. 24, 1998   FRY'S ELECTRONICS, San Jose, CA

SALESPERSON, television sets and VCRs.

Nov. 22–Dec. 24, 1997   MACYS, San Jose, CA

SALESPERSON, video games.

SUMMER JOBS:

1993–1997   DEPT. OF PARKS & RECREATION, San Jose, CA

June—Sept. 1997, GATE ATTENDANT, pool area; June—Sept. 1996, GATE ATTENDANT, pool area; June—Sept. 1995, LOCKER ROOM ATTENDANT; June—Sept. 1994, LOCKER ROOM ATTENDANT; June—Sept. 1993, PARK ATTENDANT. Collected tickets, checked residency, painted, cleaned pool area.

EDUCATION:

A. A. in International Business, minor in Journalism, San Jose Career College, San Jose, CA, 1998.

Dean's List, 2 years.

Courses in International Relations: U.S., European, Latin America.

Additional courses in: Principles of Journalism, Feature Writing, Fundamentals of Public Speaking, Principles of Economics, Introduction to Business.

EXTRACURRICULAR ACTIVITIES:

Editor and reporter, college newspaper.

Member, debate team.

Volunteer, Project READ, a literacy program, and of National Issues Forums, network of forums to discuss national issues.

REFERENCES AVAILABLE ON REQUEST

PANEL 11.3   **R**ésumé dos and don'ts.

There are no hard and fast rules to résumé writing, but these are a few points on which the majority of experts would agree.

DO . . .

- Start with a clear objective.
- Have different résumés for different types of jobs.
- List as many relevant skills as you legitimately possess.
- Use jargon or buzzwords that are understood in the industry.
- Use superlatives: biggest, best, most, first.
- Start sentences with action verbs (organized, reduced, increased, negotiated, analyzed).
- List relevant credentials and affiliations.
- Limit your résumé to one or two pages (unless you're applying for an academic position).
- Use standard-size, white or off-white heavy paper.
- Use a standard typeface and a letter-quality or laser-jet printer.
- Spell check and proofread, several times.

DON'T . . .

- Lie.
- Sound overly pompous.
- Use pronouns such as I, we.
- Send a photo of yourself.
- List personal information such as height, weight, marital status or age, unless you're applying for a job as an actor or model.
- List hobbies, unless they're directly related to your objective.
- Provide references unless requested. ("References on request" is optional.)
- Include salary information.
- Start a sentence with "responsibilities included:"
- Overuse and mix type styles such as bold, underline, italic, and uppercase.

Other résumé dos and don'ts appear in the above box. *(See ■ Panel 11.3.)*

■
WRITING A COMPUTER-FRIENDLY RESUME. Once upon a time, an employer would simply throw away old résumés or file them and rarely look at them again. Now a company may well use a high-tech résumé-scanning system such as Resumix.[20] This technology uses an optical scanner to input 900 pages of résumés a day, storing the data in a computerized database. The system can search for up to 60 key factors, such as job titles, technical expertise, education, geographic location, and employment history. Resumix can also track race, religion, gender, and other factors to help companies diversify their workforce. These descriptors can then be matched with available openings.

Such résumé scanners can save companies thousands of dollars. They allow organizations to search their existing pool of applicants more efficiently before turning to advertising or other means to recruit employees. For applicants, however, résumé banks and other electronic systems have turned job hunting into a whole new ball game. The latest advice is as follows:

| PANEL 11.4 | **T**ips for preparing a computer-scannable résumé. Resumix Inc., maker of computerized résumé-scanning systems, suggests observing the following rules of format for résumé writing: |

- Exotic typefaces, underlining, and decorative graphics don't scan well.

- It's best to send originals, not copies, and not to use a dot-matrix printer.

- Too-small print may confuse the scanner; don't go below 12-point type.

- Use standard 8½ × 11-inch paper and do not fold. Words in a crease can't be read easily.

- Use white or light-beige paper. Blues and grays minimize the contrast between the letters and the background.

- Avoid double columns. The scanner reads from left to right.

- *Use the right paper and print:* In the past, job seekers have used tricks such as colored paper and fancy typefaces in their résumés to catch a bored personnel officer's eye. However, optical scanners have trouble reading type on colored or gray paper and are confused by unusual typefaces. They even have difficulty reading underlining and poor-quality dot-matrix printing.[21] Thus, you need to be aware of new format rules for résumé writing. (*See* ■ *Panel 11.4.*)

- *Use keywords for skills or attributes:* Just as important as the format of a résumé today are the *words* used in it. In the past, résumé writers tried to present their skills clearly. Now it's necessary to use, in addition, as many of the buzzwords or keywords of your career field or industry as you can.

  Action words should still be used, but they are less important than nouns. Nouns include job titles, capabilities, languages spoken, type of degree, and the like ("sales representative," "Spanish," "A.A. degree"). The reason, of course, is that a computer will scan for keywords applicable to the job that is to be filled.

  Because résumé-screening programs sort and rank keywords, résumés with the most keywords rise to the top of the electronic pile. Consequently, it's suggested you pack your résumé with every conceivable kind of keyword that applies to you. You should especially use those that appear in help-wanted ads.[22]

  If you're looking for a job in desktop publishing, for instance, certain keywords in your résumé will help it stand out. Examples might be *Adobe Illustrator, Pagemaker, PhotoShop, Quark.*

USING THE COMPUTER TO LOOK FOR JOBS. Today there are many computer-related tools you can use to help you in your job search. These range from résumé-writing software to online databases on which you can post your résumé or look for job listings.[23–31] Two types of online job-hunting tools are as follows:

■ ***Online job openings:*** You can search online for lists of jobs that might interest you. This method is called the "armchair job search" by careers columnist Joyce Lain Kennedy, coauthor of *Electronic Job Search Revolution*.[32] With a computer you can prowl through online information services, online job ad services, or newspaper online information services. (Examples of online information services are America Online, CompuServe, Prodigy, and Microsoft Network.)

■ ***Résumé database services:*** You can put your specially tailored résumé in an online database, giving employers the opportunity to contact you. Among the kinds of resources for employers are databases for students in higher education and databases for people with experience.

You may wish to try Practical Exploration #11.3 to draft a résumé using some of the principles just described.

WRITING A GOOD COVER LETTER. Write a targeted cover letter to accompany your résumé. This advice especially should be followed if you're responding to an ad.

Most people don't bother to write a cover letter focusing on the particular job being advertised. Moreover, if they do, say San Francisco employment experts Howard Bennett and Chuck McFadden, "they tend to talk about what *they* are looking for in a job. This is a major turn-off for employers."[33] Employers don't care very much about your dreams and aspirations, only about finding the best candidate for the job.

Bennett and McFadden suggest the following strategy for a cover letter:

■ ***Emphasize how you will meet the employer's needs:*** Employers advertise because they have needs to be met. "You will get much more attention," say Bennett and McFadden, "if you demonstrate your ability to fill those needs."

How do you find out what those needs are? *You read the ad.* By reading the ad closely you can find out how the company talks about itself. You can also find out what attributes it is looking for in employees and what the needs are for the particular position.

■ ***Use the language of the ad:*** In your cover letter, use as much of the ad's language as you can. "Use the same words as much as possible," advise Bennett and McFadden. "Feed the company's language back to them." This will produce "an almost subliminal realization in the company that you are the person they've been looking for."

■ ***Take care with the format of the letter:*** Keep the letter to one page and use dashes or asterisks to emphasize the areas where you meet the needs described in the ad. Make sure the sentences read well and—very important—that no word or name is misspelled.

THE INTERVIEW. The intent of both cover letter and résumé is to get you an interview. The act of getting an interview itself means you're probably in the top 10%–15% of candidates. Once you're into an interview, a different set of skills is needed.

You need to look clean and well groomed, of course. You also need to learn as much as you can about the employing organization and its needs so that you can show why you're better than other candidates. Richard Bolles, for instance, suggests that you need to be able to say what distinguishes you from the 20 other

PRACTICAL EXPLORATION #11.3

HOW CAN YOU BUILD AN IMPRESSIVE RÉSUMÉ?

For this exercise, it doesn't matter whether you're of traditional college age or are a returning adult student. Its purpose is to get you accustomed to thinking about one important question: *What kinds of things might you be doing throughout your school years in order to produce a high-quality résumé?*

Fill in the lines below with your *present* experience. Then add ideas about *experience you might acquire* that would help you in the next few years.

■ 1. MY PRESENT EDUCATION:

_____
_____
_____
_____

Highlights of my present education (your most impressive accomplishments):

_____
_____
_____
_____
_____

■ MY FUTURE EDUCATION:

_____
_____
_____
_____
_____

Highlights of my education (impressive accomplishments you would like to be able to list):

_____
_____
_____
_____

■ 2. MY PRESENT WORK EXPERIENCE:

_____
_____

_____
_____
_____

Highlights of my present work experience (your most impressive accomplishments):

_____
_____
_____
_____

■ MY FUTURE WORK EXPERIENCE:

_____
_____
_____

Highlights of my work experience (impressive accomplishments you would like to be able to list):

_____
_____
_____

■ 3. MY PRESENT CO-CURRICULAR ACTIVITIES:

_____
_____
_____

Highlights of my present co-curricular activities (your most impressive accomplishments):

_____
_____
_____
_____

■ MY FUTURE CO-CURRICULAR ACTIVITIES:

_____
_____
_____
_____

Highlights of my co-curricular activities (impressive accomplishments you would like to be able to list):

_____
_____
_____

■ 4. MY PRESENT HONORS AND AWARDS:

_____
_____
_____
_____

■ MY FUTURE HONORS AND AWARDS:

_____
_____
_____
_____

people the employer is interviewing. "If you say you are a very thorough person, don't just say it," suggests Bolles. "Demonstrate it by telling them what you know about their company, which you learned beforehand by doing your homework."[34]

Still, you shouldn't try to smooth-talk your way through the interview, suggests Max Messmer, head of Robert Half International, a big staffing services firm. Honesty counts, and you should mean what you say. Because personal references for job candidates are becoming more difficult to obtain, interviewers are now scrutinizing candidates more carefully for character and candor. Indeed, a survey by the firm found that nearly one-third of executives polled rated honesty and integrity as the most critical qualities in a job candidate. "Without such attributes as trustworthiness and integrity, even the most highly skilled and articulate job seeker or employee will have limited success," says Messmer.[35]

Terry Mullins, dean of the School of Business Administration at the University of Evansville in Indiana, points out that most successful interviews follow a three-scene script. If you plan your moves to cooperate with the script, you'll increase your chances of being hired.[36]

- **Scene 1: The first three minutes—small talk and the "compatibility" test:** The first scene of the interview, lasting about three minutes, consists of small talk. This is really a compatibility test. Thus, as you shake hands, you should make eye contact and smile. Wait to be invited to sit down. Comment on office decorations, photographs, or views. Ask after objects in the interviewer's office that may reflect his or her personal interests. Show that you are at ease with yourself and the situation.

- **Scene 2: The next 15–60 minutes—telling your "story":** Even though you may be uncomfortable about self-promotion, it's expected at a job interview. Indeed, employers estimate future accomplishments by past successes. Thus, before the interview you should have spent considerable time studying your accomplishments to reveal the best of your skills. You should examine your experience in terms of goals achieved, abilities developed, lessons learned—and then get comfortable practicing your "story."

  In scene 2 of the interview, which may last anywhere from 15 minutes to an hour or more, you should explain your accomplishments, abilities, and ambitions, emphasizing your ability to add value to the employer. If you can claim credit for reducing costs, increasing sales, or improving quality in your previous jobs, you should stress this now. Also, if you have any blemishes on your record or holes in your experience, this is the time to explain them. As you come to the end of this scene, Mullins suggests, you should emphasize your willingness and capacity to perform at the highest level for your new employer.

- **Scene 3: The final 1–2 minutes—closing the interview and setting up the next steps:** The end of the interview, which may last only a minute or two, is crucial, Mullins says. You don't want the interviewer to control the situation by closing with the customary "We'll be in touch with you when we decide something." This statement takes away your power to influence the decision.

  Instead, Mullins advises, you should end the interview by saying, "I'll keep you posted about developments in my job search." This final remark keeps you in control and enables you to follow up with additional information—such as a letter restating some of your accomplishments or providing news of other job offers—that may improve your prospects.

THE FOLLOW-UP LETTER. Regardless of how well or how poorly you felt the interview went, afterward you should always send a short thank-you note. The letter, advises Max Messmer, should accomplish three things:[37] (1) It should express your gratitude. (2) It should reinforce your interest in the job. (3) It should recap the two or three strongest points working in your favor.

Onward

PREVIEW Life is an endless process of self-discovery.

"Life isn't a mountain that has a summit . . . ," says John Gardner, the founder of Common Cause, "nor a game that has a final score." Rather, "Life is an endless unfolding and—if we wish it to be—an endless process of self-discovery, an endless and unpredictable dialogue between own potentialities and the life situations in which we find ourselves." A person's potentialities, Gardner says, include not just intellectual gifts. They cover "the full range of one's capacities for learning, sensing, wondering, understanding, loving, and aspiring."[38]

This, then, is not the end. It is the beginning.

NOTES

1. Dominguez, J., & Robin, V. (1992). *Your money or your life*. Bergenfield, NJ: Penguin.

2. Gallup Organization October 1989 survey for National Occupational Information Coordinating Committee. Reported in Associated Press (1990, January 12). Working at the wrong job. *San Francisco Chronicle*, p. C1.

3. Falvey, J. (1986). *After college: The business of getting jobs*. Charlotte, VT: Williamson.

4. Yate, M. J. Quoted in McIntosh, C. (1991, May). Giving good answers to tough questions. *McCall's*, pp. 38, 40.

5. Falvey, 1986.

6. Shertzer, B. (1985). *Career planning* (3rd ed.). Boston: Houghton Mifflin.

7. Deci, E. L., & Flaste, R. (1995). *Why we do what we do: The dynamics of personal autonomy*. New York: Grosset/Putnam.

8. Holland, J. (1975). *Vocational preference inventory*. Palo Alto, CA: Consulting Psychologists Press.

9. Bolles, R. N. Quoted in Rubin, S. (1994, February 24). How to open your job 'parachute' after college. *San Francisco Chronicle*, p. E9.

10. Bolles, R. N. (1994). *What color is your parachute?* Berkeley, CA: Ten Speed Press.

11. Bolles, R. N. (1990). *The 1990 quick job-hunting (and career-changing) map: How to create a picture of your ideal job or next career*. Berkeley, CA: Ten Speed Press.

12. Bolles, R. N. Cited in Minton, T. (January 25, 1991). Job-hunting requires eyes and ears of friends. *San Francisco Chronicle*, p. D5.

13. Study by Stanford and Columbia universities. Reported in Koss-Feder, L. (1997, January 5). In a job hunt, it often *is* whom you know. *New York Times*, sec. 3, p. 8.

14. Popp, A. L. (1997, January 26). Getting a foot in the door: The fruits of networking [letter]. *New York Times*, sec. 3, p. 38.

15. Steinkirchner, K. Reported in The 'N' word. (1994, August). *Psychology Today*, p. 13.

16. Judge, L. Quoted in Ross, S. (1997, June 15). Don't hide your light under a bushel: Network. *San Jose Mercury News*, p. 2PC.

17. Falvey, 1986.

18. For students, internships becoming rite of passage. (1996, July 18). *San Francisco Chronicle*, p. A7; reprinted from *Los Angeles Times*.

19. Pender, K. (1994, May 16). Jobseekers urged to pack lots of 'keywords' into resumes. *San Francisco Chronicle*, pp. B1, B4.

20. Howe, K. (1992, September 19). Firm turns hiring into a science. *San Francisco Chronicle,* pp. B1, B2.

21. Bulkeley, W. M. (1992, June 23). Employers use software to track resumes. *Wall Street Journal,* p. B6.

22. Kennedy, J. L., & Morrow, T. J. (1994). *Electronic resume revolution: Create a winning resume for the new world of job seeking.* New York: Wiley.

23. Palladino, B. (1992, Winter). Job hunting online. *Online Access,* pp. 20–23.

24. Online information. (1992, October). *PC Today,* p. 41.

25. Strauss, J. (1993, October 17). Online database helps job seekers. *San Francisco Sunday Examiner & Chronicle,* Help wanted section, p. 29.

26. Murray, K. (1994, January 2). Plug in. Log on. Find a job. *New York Times,* sec. 3, p. 23.

27. Mannix, M. (1992, October 26). Writing a computer-friendly resume. *U.S. News & World Report,* pp. 90–93.

28. Bulkeley, W. M. (1992, June 16). Job-hunters turn to software for an edge. *Wall Street Journal,* p. B13.

29. Anonymous. (1992, June). Pounding the pavement. *PC Novice,* p. 10.

30. Anonymous. (1993, September 13). Personal: Individual software ships ResumeMaker with career planning. *EDGE: Work-Group Computing Report,* p. 3.

31. Mossberg, W. S. (1994, May 5). Four programs to ease PC users into a job search. *Wall Street Journal,* p. B1.

32. Kennedy, J. L., & Morrow, T. J. (1994). *Electronic job search revolution: Win with the new technology that's reshaping today's job market.* New York: Wiley.

33. Bennett, H., & McFadden, C. (1993, October 17). How to stand out in a crowd. *San Francisco Sunday Examiner & Chronicle,* Help wanted section, p. 29.

34. Bolles. Quoted in Rubin, 1994.

35. Messmer, M. Quoted in Honesty counts in job interviews. (1997, July-August). *The Futurist,* p. 49.

36. Mullins, T. Reported in How to land a job. (1994, September/October). *Psychology Today,* pp. 12–13.

37. Messmer, M. (1995). *Job hunting for dummies.* Foster City, CA: IDG Books, p. 307.

38. Gardner, J. W. 1991 commencement address, Stanford University, June 16, 1991. Quoted in Gardner, J. W. (1991, May–June). You are what you commit to achieve. *Stanford Observer,* pp. 10–11.

Classroom Activities: Directions to the Instructor

1. ***What would you like to spend your life doing?*** Ask students to write down on a sheet of paper three things that (whether working or not working) they would like to spend their lives doing if they had a reasonably modest income and didn't have to work. (These are supposed to express their dreams, so tell students to make them as detailed as possible.)

   Now ask them to write down three more things they would like to do for their work or career if money were no object.

   In a small group or classroom setting, have students discuss their choices. Questions to consider: Why would you choose these directions? Do you think you could achieve any of these? How might you go about it?

2. ***What interests and skills are you attracted to?*** Ask students to complete Practical Exploration #11.1, "The 'Career Video.'" When everyone has finished, ask each student to join with others in a group that corresponds to your first choice of career video. (If a student turns out to be the only one in a group, he or she should join the second-choice group.)

   Within each group, students should discuss the following questions: What qualities led you to this choice? What kinds of occupations mentioned above seem attractive to you? Does the career field(s) or major(s) you're contemplating lead in this direction?

   Now ask each student to join with others in his or her second choice of career video. Discuss the same questions. If there's time, have students join the group of their third choice. Questions to consider: Do you find yourself assembling with most of the same people as before? If not, what seems to account for the differences? What information of personal value to you can you take away from this?

3. ***Visiting the career counseling and job placement office.*** Have students complete (out of class) Practical Exploration #11.2, "What Can You Learn from a Visit to the Career Counseling & Job Placement Office?" Have them discuss the results of their investigations in class. Then ask them to make an appointment to follow up on one of the components (such as taking a vocational test). Suggest that students write a one-page report on their follow-up investigation to turn in to the instructor.

4. ***How can you build a great résumé?*** In small groups have students complete Practical Exploration #11.3, "How Can You Build an Impressive Résumé?" Brainstorming may help in putting together a résumé. Have students talk through their responses to the Personal Exploration and take turns asking for feedback and suggestions.

5. ***The informational interview.*** Have students look back at the heading "Ways of Looking for Jobs" and the discussion of informational interviews. Instruct them to obtain an informational interview with someone (preferably an executive or administrator) in an organization for which they might be interested in working, either as an intern or in a possible career capacity. Have them prepare a list of questions to ask the person they'll be interviewing.

   After the interview, the student should write a one-page paper reporting on his or her experience for submission to the instructor.

The Examined Life:
Student Assignments for Journal Entries

JOURNAL ENTRY #11.1: DREAMING WHAT YOU'D LIKE TO STUDY. The best way to start thinking about your prospective career field or major is to dream your dreams. Your journal is the place to do this. Take 15 minutes to free-associate, and write as quickly (but legibly) as you can all your desires about things you're curious about or enjoy and would like to study. Then state what fields of study or majors might best serve your wishes.

_____

_____

_____

_____

_____

_____

_____

JOURNAL ENTRY #11.2: DREAMING YOUR CAREERS. You go through life only once. Yet it's possible to have more than one career—be a salesperson/musician, a travel agent/travel writer, a nurse/social activist, for example. Or you might have successive careers, each one different. When you "dream the impossible dream," what careers come to mind?

_____

_____

_____

_____

_____

_____

_____

JOURNAL ENTRY #11.3: GETTING GOOD AT JOB INTERVIEWS. Interviewing for jobs is a skill all by itself. This book did not have space to give this subject the coverage it deserves. What kinds of skills do you think are needed for interviewing? What books can you find in the library that might help you refine your interviewing techniques?

CHAPTER TWELVE

_____

_____

_____

_____

_____

_____

RESOURCES
Assistance, opportunity, & diversity

IN THIS CHAPTER: Discover the treasure trove to be found on your campus in three important areas:

- **_Assistance:_** How to find help—for your studies, health, emotions, finances, and other matters.

- **_Opportunity:_** How to get extra value with your education—in activities, student life, and living arrangements.

- **_Diversity:_** How to see through the eyes of people different from you—in gender, age, race, ethnicity, nationality, religion, and ability.

■ HELP!

That's a word we've all used at some point. Or certainly wanted to.

Often help is easy to ask for and easy to get. ("Am I in the right line?")

At other times, however, *Help!* may be the silent cry of a student overwhelmed by confusion, loneliness, test anxiety, family problems, or money worries. Is help available for these sorts of matters? The answer is: You bet!

Unfortunately, sometimes people with a problem can't imagine there's a way out. Or they're too timid or too proud to ask for help. That's why we put this chapter in the book. Its purpose is to show what kind of assistance is available when you need it.

In addition, we want to give you the chance to find out what a gold mine higher education is outside the classroom. For instance, many former career and vocational-technical students value lifelong friendships and job contacts they made while in school. To help you realize the same benefits, we will look at opportunities that school gives you.

Finally, it looks as though people in the 21st century will be exposed to far more cultural diversity than has been the case in the past. Thus, we will look at ways you can use your time in school to learn to get along with people different from you. By "different," we mean different in all ways—in dress, gender, age, religion, skin color, nationality, sexual preference, cultural tastes, and so on.

A Look Around the Campus

PREVIEW The orientation program for new students is a good way to start finding out about campus services. Helpful publications include the school's catalog, campus map, student handbook, bulletins, course lists, and brochures, flyers, and posters. Areas of assistance include academic help; physical and emotional help; other campus help; activities and campus life; and community services.

What do you usually do first after getting off a bus or parking your car in an unfamiliar neighborhood?

You take a quick look around.

You check out the area to get a sense of the layout of things. You get a picture of what your options are.

That's what we're going to do in this chapter—take a quick look around the campus so you can see what your options are. We will show you how to check out various campus facilities to find out what services and opportunities are available to help you survive, enjoy, and profit from school.

THE ORIENTATION PROGRAM. Many career or vocational-technical schools offer an orientation program and tour of the campus for new students. However, some facilities and services may be left off the tour (because of time). Or you may not find some of them personally interesting or presently valuable to you. Still, if you have a chance to take the tour, we urge you to do so. You may sometime need to know where to go to waive a course or get into one already filled, where to get information to seek employment, and so on.

Obviously, if you've already had a campus tour or gone through an orientation program for new students, you're ahead of the game.

PUBLICATIONS: INSTRUCTION MANUALS FOR HIGHER EDUCATION. Many jobs have instruction manuals, briefing books, and similar publications to help employees understand what they are supposed to do. Career and vocational-technical schools have them too, as follows:

- *School catalog:* Publications are a great way to find out all aspects of campus life. Probably the most valuable is the school's catalog, which is the playbook or rule book for the game of higher education. **The *catalog* contains requirements for graduation, requirements for certificate or degree programs, and course descriptions.** It also may contain a history of the school, information about faculty, and various programs and services. In addition, it may contain information about financial aid.

  The catalog is most likely available in the Admissions Office, Counseling Office, or campus bookstore.

- *Campus calendar:* Of particular value is the ***campus calendar,* which lists the deadlines and dates for various programs.** You'll particularly want to take note of the last days when you can *enroll* in a new course and when you can *drop* a course without penalty. You should highlight important dates on the calendar and post it in a prominent place, such as over your desk at home.

- *Campus or school map:* Many catalogs include a map of the campus or school, but if yours does not, pick up one. You might wish to have a one-page map anyway because it's easier to carry around.

- *Student handbook:* Some institutions publish a **student handbook, which summarizes many of the school's policies and regulations.** This may be the same information contained in the catalog but written in a way that is more readable or accessible to students.

- *Campus bulletins and newspaper:* On some campuses, there may be **a *student bulletin* or *campus bulletin*, which is helpful in keeping you informed of school activities and events,** as well as other matters. This periodical, which may appear from time to time throughout the school term, may be published by an office of the administration.

  The *campus newspaper* is a student-run news publication that is published on some campuses, especially the larger ones. The campus newspaper may be the single best source of ongoing information. Depending on the school, it may be published twice a week, weekly, or every two weeks. Because its readership is the entire school community—not only students but also staff, faculty, and possibly townspeople—the news in the paper may cover topics of broad interest. In addition, some schools publish a special "Orientation Edition" of the paper as a service to new students.

- *Course lists:* **The *course list* is simply a list of the courses being taught in the present school term.** Published prior to each new term, the course list states what courses are being taught, on what days at what times, for how many units, by what instructor. Sometimes the instructor is simply listed as "Staff." This may mean he or she is a teaching assistant. Or it may mean that the instructor was simply unassigned at the time the course list was printed. Call the department if you want to know who the instructor is.

- *Brochures, flyers, and posters:* Especially during orientation or when registering, you may find yourself flooded with brochures. You may also see flyers and posters on campus bulletin boards.

  Some of these may be on serious and important personal subjects: security and night escorts to parked cars, alcohol and drug abuse, date rape, and so on. Some may be on campus events and club offerings. Some may simply list apartments to share or rides wanted. Some may list upcoming job fairs, concerts, political events, or films.

  Most of this kind of information has to do with the informal or extracurricular side of your school experience. Much is as important as the purely academic part. Indeed, many prospective employers look at this extracurricular side to see how well rounded a student's educational experience has been.

  You may want to make a portfolio or folder containing all this printed information relevant to your school career so it will all be in one place. In addition, it's particularly important to study the school catalog, as you can find yourself unnecessarily frustrated at times if you are ignorant of school policies and procedures. Learn where to go for official information. Familiarize yourself with the campus "chain of command" for presenting concerns, complaints, and appeals.

  To begin getting familiar with the catalog, do Practical Exploration #12.1.

LEARNING TO USE YOUR SCHOOL'S CATALOG

Obtain a copy of your school's catalog. Fill in the answers in the following lines.

■ A. GENERAL

1. How many undergraduate students are enrolled?_____

2. When was the school founded?_____

3. What is the mission, orientation, or specialization of the school? (Examples: electronics.)
   _____
   _____
   _____
   _____

4. How is the institution organized? (Example: schools, with divisions and departments.)
   _____
   _____
   _____
   _____

5. What are some other campuses or sites the institution has, including extension divisions, if any?
   _____
   _____
   _____
   _____

6. Look at the lists of majors or career fields offered by the college. Which three might interest you?
   _____
   _____
   _____
   _____

7. Is it possible to graduate with more than one major? If so, which two might interest you?
   _____
   _____
   _____
   _____

■ B. THE CAMPUS CALENDAR

1. *Cut-off dates:* What is the last date this semester on which you may … (specify month and day)

   Add a course?_____

   Drop a course?_____

   Drop a course and receive partial tuition refund?_____

   Ask for a grade of "Incomplete," if offered?_____

   Withdraw from a course?_____

2. *Holidays:* On what holidays is the school closed this semester?
   _____
   _____
   _____
   _____

3. *Registration:* What are the dates for registration for next semester?
   _____
   _____

4. *Exams:* When are final exams scheduled for this semester?
   _____
   _____

5. *Class end and start dates:*

   What is the last day of classes for this semester?_____

   What is the first day of classes for next semester?_____

■ C. TUITION & FINANCIAL AID

1. What is the annual tuition for students at the school?

2. What financial aid is available? (Examples: loans, scholarships, work/study.)
   _____
   _____
   _____

■ D. GRADES

1. Grades instructors give (such as A, B, C, D, F) and what they mean:
   _____
   _____
   _____

2. Meaning of "Pass/fail," if offered:
   _____
   _____
   _____

3. Meaning of "Incomplete," if offered:
   _____
   _____

4. Meaning of "Audit":
   _____
   _____
   _____

5. What minimum grade-point average do you need to maintain in order to be considered in satisfactory academic standing?
   _____
   _____

6. What happens if you fall below that minimum?
   _____
   _____

■ E. CREDITS

1. What is the definition of a credit (or unit)?
   _____
   _____
   _____

2. Does your school give credit for advanced courses taken in high school? _____ For courses taken at other institutions? _____

   For some life experience outside of school? _____

   (continued on next page)

■ F. GRADE-POINT AVERAGE & GRADUATION REQUIREMENTS

1. Explain the formula for computing students' grade-point average:

_____

_____

_____

_____

2. List the courses you are taking this semester or quarter and the number of credits (units) for each.

_____

_____

_____

_____

_____

For each course assign a hypothetical grade according to the following formula: A = 4.0, B = 3.0, C = 2.0, D = 1.0, F = 0.0. Then compute the grade points earned for each course. (Example for one course: "First-Year Experience, 3 credits, grade of A = 4.0; 4.0 × 3 credits = 12 grade points.")

Now add up your grade points earned for all courses. Finally, divide them by the total number of credits (units) attempted to derive your hypothetical grade-point average for the semester or quarter.

_____

_____

_____

_____

_____

_____

3. What minimum grade-point average is required for graduation?

_____

4. Besides completing a major, what are the other requirements for graduation?

_____

_____

_____

_____

■ G. MISCONDUCT

1. *Academic matters:* How does the school deal with cheating and plagiarism? (Plagiarism is passing off someone else's work as your own, as when writing a paper.)

_____

_____

_____

2. *Nonacademic matters:* How does the school deal with nonacademic matters such as sexual harassment, drunkenness, property damage, or off-campus arrests?

_____

_____

_____

_____

_____

■ H. SPECIAL PROGRAMS

1. *Academic honors:* What forms of recognition does the school offer for academic excellence? What are the standards for achieving such honors? (Examples: honors programs, dean's list, scholarships.)

_____

_____

_____

_____

2. *Other special programs:* What other special programs are offered, and what are the criteria for participation? (Example: internships.)

_____

_____

_____

_____

_____

SOME PARTICULARLY IMPORTANT PLACES TO KNOW ABOUT. There are three places on campus that, in our opinion, a newcomer should get to know right away:

- ***The library:*** Most new students don't understand how to use the library and are unaware of the scope of its services. When it comes to writing papers, this is the place to know about. Make it a point to find out when the library offers orientation and research training. Keep any handouts available.

- ***The learning center:*** This is the place for learning specific subjects or skills (for example, word processing or math help). It's an invaluable resource.

■ *The career center:* If you're undecided about your career direction or major, the career center is the place to go. This can save you from going down a lot of blind alleys. Even students who have already chosen a career direction or major can benefit from this place, which can help you focus your efforts.

FIVE ADDITIONAL IMPORTANT SERVICES OR CENTERS. There are five additional areas of services or centers, as described in this chapter.

■ *Academic help:* Examples are instructors, academic advisors and counselors, librarians, and tutors.

■ *Physical, emotional, and spiritual help:* Examples are health and fitness professionals, counselors, psychotherapists, security personnel, chaplains, and support groups (for adult returning students or single parents, for example).

■ *Other help:* Examples are financial affairs, housing office, career counseling and placement, child care, transportation, and legal services. There are also various community services, such as post office, laundry, and bank.

■ *Activities and campus life:* Examples are athletics, clubs, bands, student government, and academic advisory boards. (Some career and vocational-technical schools have a lot of these offerings, some have almost none.)

■ *Multicultural centers:* Examples are centers for racial and ethnic groups, women, students with children, international students, gays and lesbians, nontraditional students, and students with disabilities. (Again, some campuses will have these, some won't.)

Academic Help

PREVIEW People who can assist you with academic problems are academic advisors, instructors, librarians and media center staff, tutors and study-skills staff, some other academic services (such as the computer center), and the Dean of Students office. Academic advising—which is principally about certificates, degrees, majors, and courses but also other information—is extremely important because it affects your school, career, and life plans.

Obtaining a certificate or degree is the goal, of course, of the academic part of school. This piece of paper signifies that you have passed certain courses with a minimum grade. Completing the courses means that you have passed tests, written research papers, done projects, and so on. To accomplish all these, you must have attended classes, listened to lectures, gone to the library, and read a lot. Hopefully, while you're having to jump through all these hoops, learning is also taking place.

POSSIBLE ACADEMIC DIFFICULTIES. As you try to accomplish all these tasks, there are any number of places where hangups and glitches can occur—and where you might need some help. Here are some possibilities: You can't get the classes you want.

You wonder if you can waive some prerequisites. You don't know what you still need to do in order to graduate. You're having trouble with your writing, or math, or study skills. You're sick and can't finish your courses. You don't know how to compute your grade-point average. You need recommendations for an employer.

Knowing where to go for help, getting good advice, cutting through bureaucratic red tape—these are skills you won't discard after you get out of school. They are part and parcel of being A Person Who Can Get Things Done, which is what all of us wish to be. Learning how to find your way around the academic system, then, is training for life. In the world outside school, these skills are called *networking* and *troubleshooting*—and they are invaluable in helping you achieve where you want to go in your career.

The academic services or people we will describe are:

■ Academic advisors

■ Instructors

■ Librarians and media center staff

■ Tutors and study-skills staff

■ Some other academic services

■ When all other help fails: the Dean of Students office

ACADEMIC ADVISORS. What people will you deal with most on the academic side? Probably your instructors. But there is another individual who, in the grand scheme of things, could be *more* important: the academic advisor. Why? For most first-year students, the first year of higher education "is both exciting and crisis oriented," says one pair of writers. "New students are unfamiliar with [school] resources, their major field, the faculty, course work, academic expectations, and career applications of their major."[1] Thus, *academic advising is extremely important because it affects your planning for school and beyond that for your career and for your life.*

The *academic advisor* counsels students about their academic program. The academic advisor is either a full-time administrative employee or a faculty member, often in the career field you intend to pursue. What does he or she do that we think is so important? There are two principal activities:

■ *Gives information about certificates, degrees, majors, and courses:* The academic advisor explains to you what courses are required in your *certificate program* or *degree program*—**all the courses you must take to obtain a certificate or degree in a specific field.** Courses will be of two types:

(1) *General education courses* are those specified in the school's catalog which most or all students have to take to obtain a degree. Examples are a choice, from a list, of a couple of social science courses (for instance, economics or psychology) or a couple of humanities courses (for instance, English or speech).

(2) *Courses in your major or career field* will be those, from another list, that are needed for you to complete your ***major* or *career field*—your field of specialization.** Perhaps a third of the courses you need to graduate will be in this category. Some institutions also require a ***minor,* a smaller field of specialization,** which will entail fewer courses.

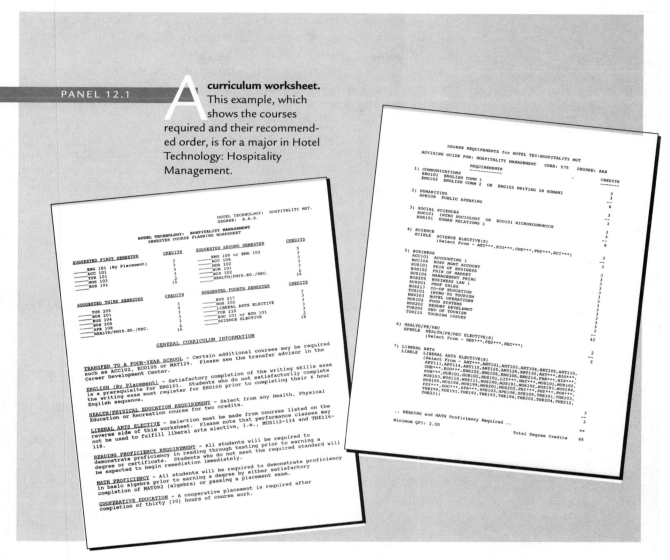

PANEL 12.1

A **curriculum worksheet.** This example, which shows the courses required and their recommended order, is for a major in Hotel Technology: Hospitality Management.

Both general-education courses and the courses for your major or career field often are identified on what is called a *curriculum worksheet,* which both you and your advisor have access to. **The *curriculum worksheet*—also known as the *audit sheet* or the *degree plan*—lists all the courses required for the major and the semesters in which it is recommended you take them.** You should always keep an updated copy of your curriculum worksheet so you can tell at a glance what courses you still need to take and where you are in the Big Picture in relation to graduation.

The accompanying example shows a curriculum worksheet for Hotel Technology: Hospitality Management. *(See ■ Panel 12.1.)*

■ ***Provides information, advice, and support in general:*** Academic advisors are usually also available to talk about other matters important to you. These include problems in keeping up with course work, indecisiveness about what career or major to focus on, concern over whether you are being fairly treated by an instructor, and personal stresses. Adult students dealing with "juggler's syndrome" (juggling school, work, and family) often find their academic advisor very understanding.

If an advisor does not feel capable of helping you directly, he or she will certainly have some thoughts about where to turn (perhaps to a counselor, who is different from an advisor).

Here's an important fact: *poor academic advising is a major reason students drop out of higher education.*[2] Conversely, students who receive good academic advising not only are more apt to graduate but are also happier while they are in school.

The most effective way to work with your academic advisor is to *know your catalog and degree requirements.* If you understand and follow the requirements listed in your catalog instead of making a lot of substitutions in your courses, the process should be simple. However, the bottom line is this: Learn your degree requirements, and if you have questions, *ask them.*

When you first enroll in your institution, your academic advisor will be assigned to you. Later, if you change majors or career fields, or if you go from being "Undecided" or "Undeclared" to declaring your major, you may change advisors.

Students should see their academic advisor *at least* once a semester or quarter. You should also see him or her whenever you have any questions or important decisions to make about your school career. (*See ▪ Panel 12.2.*)

PANEL 12.2   **U**sing your advisor for academic success.

Like everything else in higher education, you get out of academic advising what you put into it. Here are some tips for using your advisor to make school work best for you:

Be aware of the advising period—see the catalog: The school requires students at least once a semester or quarter to see their advisors about which courses they will take the next term. The period for doing this, often about two weeks, is usually listed on the academic calendar in the school catalog and is announced in campus notices. *Put the dates of the advising period on your personal calendar and be sure to make an appointment to see your advisor.*

See your advisor more than once a term to establish a relationship: Your advisor is not just a bureaucrat who has to sign off on your courses and should not be treated as such. See him or her at least one other time during the semester or quarter to discuss problems and progress. Ask about interesting courses, interesting instructors, any possible changes in major, and difficult courses and how to handle them. Discuss any personal problems affecting your life and work. *In short, if possible, make your advisor a mentor—a person you can trust.*

If your advisor isn't right for you, find another one: If you feel your advisor is distant, uncaring, arrogant, ignorant, or otherwise unsuitable, don't hesitate to make a change. You have this right, although you have to be your own advocate here. *To make a change, ask another instructor or staff person to be your advisor.* Depending on the arrangements on your campus, you may get another advisor by going to the Advisement Center, the Registrar, the Office of Student Services, or the Dean of Students.

INSTRUCTORS. You will have many instructors, and they can be valuable resources to you. Instructors in higher education and high school teachers often have different kinds of training, as follows:

- *Training in teaching:* You may have been bored by some of your high school teachers, but, believe it or not, all such teachers have actually had training in how to teach. Instructors in higher education, on the other hand, often have not, unless they are former high school teachers.

- *Years of study:* Most high school teachers have earned a teaching credential on top of a bachelor's degree (B.A. or B.S.), representing a minimum of four to five years of schooling.

    Many of the full-time instructors with whom you will study now will have a master's degree (M.A. or M.S.), which represents one or two years of study after the bachelor's degree. These instructors may be addressed as "Mr." or "Ms." or "Professor." (Sometimes instructors will invite students to address them by their first names.)

    Some instructors—those you might address as "Doctor"—have a *doctorate* or *Ph.D.* or *Ed.D.* degree. (Ph.D. stands for "Doctor of Philosophy," although the degree is given for all subject areas in addition to philosophy. Ed.D. stands for "Doctor of Education.") To earn this degree, they have spent several years researching and writing a doctoral dissertation, a book-length investigation of a specific subject.

    Other instructors in career or vocational-technical education may have advanced degrees or they may not, but their years of work experience in a particular career field give them mastery over their subject matter.

The biggest difference between taking a course in high school and taking one in community college, career, or vocational-technical school is this: *More is now expected of you.* Higher education, after all, is designed to treat you as an adult. Thus, you have more adult freedoms than were probably allowed you in high school. For example, many instructors do not take daily attendance. Moreover, they may not check your assignments on a daily basis. Thus, you are expected to do more of your work on your own.

Still, instructors are among the academic resources available to you. In most institutions, instructors are required to be in their offices during certain hours (posted on their office doors and/or available through the department secretary). In addition, many are available for questions a minute or so after class. You may also be able to make appointments with them at other times. (Be sure to make a note of the time of the appointment. Telephone the instructor if you can't keep it.)

The instructor is the one to see if you have a question or problem about the course you are taking. These include which books and supplies to buy, what subjects in a text will be covered on a test, anything you don't understand about an assignment or test question. Don't be afraid to ask. And if you begin to have trouble in a course, don't wait until the test. See your instructor as soon as possible.

LIBRARIANS & MEDIA-CENTER STAFF. Perhaps you think the library is just a quiet place with books and magazines where you can go to study. Actually, there is more to it than that. *One of the first things you should do is find out how to use a library.* Often the library has a room or section in it called the media center.

The library is one of the most important buildings on campus. Don't be intimidated by all the staff, books, and machines (computer terminals, microfilm readers). Instead, we suggest doing the following:

■ ***Tour the facilities:*** Go to the library/media center and simply walk around every place you are allowed to go. *Actively* scan the titles on the shelves, looking for books or magazines you're interested in. *Actively* take note of the desks and study areas available, picking out a couple of spots you might favor using later. *Actively* read the directions on how to use machines, such as computers, microfilm readers, and copiers.

■ ***Ask how to use the facilities:*** Have you ever noticed how some people are so concerned with how they look to others or how others will react to them that they never ask directions? Some drivers, for instance, would rather "figure it out for themselves" than stop and ask a local person how to get somewhere.

These folks really limit themselves. People shut off a major source of personal growth when they can't ask for assistance or help.

If you're the kind of person who's reluctant to seek help, here's a good exercise. Ask the librarians or media center staff for a *demonstration* on how to use the facilities to do research. Sometimes there is a standard guided tour. Ask how to use the computerized catalog for books and periodicals and how to use microfilm equipment. Ask how to play videotapes or audiotapes in the media center. Ask about other research libraries and facilities on campus. Ask, ask, ask! Librarians are there precisely to answer questions.

We looked at libraries and media centers in more detail in Chapter 7, "Writing & Speaking."

TUTORS & STUDY-SKILLS STAFF. *This is an important, probably underused resource.*

Most institutions offer courses or services for improving your reading, writing, math, or study skills. The place for doing this may be located in a **learning center, or *learning lab*, a special center where you go to learn a specific subject or skill.** Sometimes learning centers are located in a special building or room on campus. Sometimes they are attached to various departments, such as the English department. For example, some foreign-language learning centers may offer a computer terminal or a booth with television monitor and earphones, which allows you to practice the language.

In addition, you can arrange, either through the learning center or through academic departments (ask an instructor or the department secretary), for the help of a tutor. **A *tutor* is essentially a private teacher or coach.** This person will help you, through a series of regularly scheduled meetings, to improve a particular skill. In some instances, tutoring may be free. In other instances, as with private tutors, a small fee may be required, but the result is usually worth the cost.

SOME OTHER ACADEMIC SERVICES. There are several other on-campus services available to help you with the academic side of school, ranging from photocopiers to computer practice rooms. For example, some campuses have a computer or lab in which you may use a personal computer for such tasks as writing papers (word processing), doing calculations (using spreadsheets), doing computer

"Where's the best place to go for help when you're having academic difficulties, and why?"

Name: Victoria Boley

Major: Human Resources

Interests: Helping people

Answer to question: "I have found that the best place to go for help when I am having academic difficulties are the professors, because they are the ones I have trouble understanding. When I tell them I don't understand something, they can explain it better one on one."

graphics, and the like. Courses teaching valuable computer skills, such as word processing, are offered through this center or through academic courses.

WHEN ALL OTHER HELP FAILS: THE DEAN OF STUDENTS OFFICE. If you can't seem to find help for whatever your difficulty is, try the Dean of Students office. It is the *job* of the staff here to see that you are well taken care of in school. If they can't handle the problem themselves, they will find someone who will.

Physical & Emotional Help

PREVIEW People to help you take care of your physical and emotional well-being may be found in several places. They include the health service, counseling center, security office, wellness/fitness services, and on-campus and off-campus support groups.

The academic help we described has to do with taking care of your mind. Now let's consider the services that may be offered to take care of your body and heart. (These are more apt to be found in institutions with large enrollments.) Some basic facilities and services are:

■ Health service

■ Counseling center

■ Security office

■ Wellness/fitness services

■ Support groups

HEALTH SERVICE. Many institutions of higher learning, such as community colleges, have some sort of health or medical service, ranging from clinic or health-care center to nurse's office. Treatment is often free or low cost for minor problems.

Your institution may assume that most students' health care will be handled by community hospitals and other resources. However, there is probably some office that can at least provide you with first aid, aspirin, and advice and referrals.

This office is a good place to go to if you need help or information about physical problems, anxiety, birth-control information, sexually transmitted diseases, or alcohol or other drug problems. If your campus does not offer health care services, consider checking out the city or county public health department.

COUNSELING CENTER: PSYCHOLOGICAL SERVICES. All of us have stresses in our lives, and higher education unquestionably adds to them. If you find yourself overwhelmed with test anxiety, if you're sleeping through classes because you have a resistance to the subject, if you feel you're on the verge of flunking for whatever reason, *don't be the least bit hesitant about seeking help at the counseling center.* Such counseling is often free or low cost.

In addition, problems arise that may not have much to do with the academic side of school: love relationships, problems with parents and with self-esteem, "Who am I?" identity concerns, pregnancy, worries about sexually transmitted diseases, and so on. Most psychological counselors are familiar with these problems and are able to help.

Psychological distress is as real as physical distress and should not be ignored. Some students worry that it is not cool or it will be seen as an admission of weakness to seek counseling help. Nothing could be further from the truth. People who are unwilling to admit they need help often find that their problems "leak out" in other ways. These could include oversleeping, alcohol or other types of drug abuse, or anger toward family members. By refusing to get help, they compound their problems until they need help even more.

If a counseling "center" doesn't exist on your campus, there is certainly someone designated to handle crisis intervention and offer referral information.

SECURITY OFFICE. The campus security personnel or police may be most visible in their roles of enforcing parking control—a problem with almost every campus of higher learning, regardless of kind. However, they do far more than that.

Afraid to walk across campus to your car after a night class? Call campus security to ask for an escort. It's done all the time on many urban campuses. Locked out of your car or locker? Call the campus police. Lost your watch, had something stolen, been hassled by a drunk, or found yourself dealing with someone who has been raped? Such problems are the reasons, unfortunately, that campus security exists. *(See ■ Panel 12.3.)*

PANEL 12.3   **Tips for staying safe.**

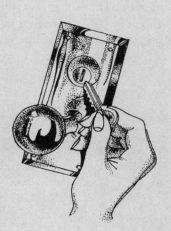

Safety is a major issue on many campuses. At your school, you may see posters, brochures, and newspaper articles concerned with such matters as use of nighttime escorts to parked cars. The basic piece of advice is: Use common sense about your safety; be alert for trouble. Other safety tips are as follows:

WHEN WALKING, TRAVELING, OR OUT IN PUBLIC:

1. At night or early morning, don't walk alone or jog alone. Stay with groups. Take advantage of campus escort services. Travel in well-populated, well-lighted areas.

2. Don't show money or valuables in public. Discreetly tuck away your cash after using an automated teller machine.

3. On foot: Walk rapidly and look as though you're going somewhere; don't dawdle. If someone makes signs of wanting to talk to you, just keep on going. It's less important that you be polite than that you be safe.

4. In a car: Make sure all doors are locked. Don't open them for anyone you don't know.

5. Don't leave backpacks, purses, or briefcases unattended.

WHEN IN YOUR RESIDENCE:

1. Lock your residence doors at all times.

2. Don't let strangers into your residence. Ask any stranger the name of the person he or she wants to see.

IF YOU SENSE YOU MIGHT BE ATTACKED:

1. If you are facing an armed criminal, the risk of injury may be minimized by cooperating with his or her demands. Avoid any sudden movements and give the criminal what he or she wants.

2. If you sense your life is in immediate danger, use any defense you can think of: screaming, kicking, running. Your objective is to get away.

3. In a violent crime, it is generally ineffective for the victim to cry or plead with the attacker. Such actions tend to reinforce the attacker's feeling of power over the victim.

WELLNESS/FITNESS SERVICES. Some smaller career or vocational-technical schools will have no fitness or athletic facilities at all. Others, however, allow you to use not only lockers, showers, and spas but also pools, fitness centers, weight-training equipment, basketball courts, and so on.

SUPPORT GROUPS. Most institutions offer some sort of connection or referral to support groups of all kinds. There are, for example, support groups for people having difficulties with weight, alcohol, drugs, gambling, incest, spouse abuse, or similar personal problems. There are also support groups or "affinity" groups. They may exist for women, men, physically challenged individuals, gays, ethnic and racial minorities, older students, international students, and so on. The counseling center can probably connect you with a support group of interest to you. Or you may see meeting announcements on bulletin boards or in campus publications.

Other Kinds of Assistance

PREVIEW Questions about your academic record can be resolved at the registrar's office. Other on-campus assistance is often available to assist you with financial aid, housing, transportation, check cashing (cashier or business office), job placement, career counseling, day care, and legal services. Services not found on campus are usually available in the nearby community.

Whether your career or vocational-technical education takes place on a large campus or in a single building, the experience can almost be like coming into a different town or village—except that the town's main industry is education. Fortunately, the town's administrators also care about students, and they have set up several services to deal with your needs that are neither academic on the one hand nor physical and emotional on the other.

Among the departments and services available are the following:

- Registrar
- Financial aid
- Housing
- Transportation
- Cashier/Business office
- Job placement or career services
- Career center
- Day care
- Legal services
- Community services

REGISTRAR. **The *registrar* is responsible for keeping all academic records.** This is the office you need to seek out if you have questions about whether a grade was recorded correctly (after asking your instructor). The people there can also answer your inquiries about transcripts, graduation, or transfer from or to another institution or college.

FINANCIAL AID. One of the most important offices on the campus is the office of financial aid. If you're putting yourself through school or your family is unable to pay your way entirely, you really need to get to know this office. Just as its title indicates, **the *financial aid office* is concerned with finding financial aid for students.** Such help can consist of low-interest loans, scholarships, part-time work, and other arrangements.

The workings of financial aid were discussed in Chapter 10, "Personal Growth."

HOUSING. No doubt you already have a roof over your head for the present semester or quarter, but if you're not satisfied with it, you might try going to the housing office, if your school has one. **The *housing office* helps students find places to live while they're going to school.** It provides listings of off-campus rooms, apartments,

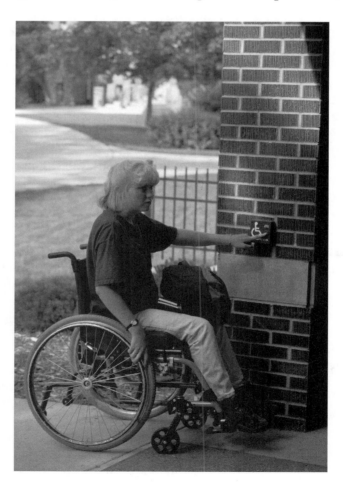

and houses for rent in the community. Because landlords listed with this office probably have to meet certain standards of safety and cleanliness, the housing office is often a better source than rentals advertised in classified ads or on bulletin boards.

TRANSPORTATION. The transportation office may be part of campus security or the campus police. **The *transportation office* issues permits for parking on or near the campus and gives out information on public transportation and car pools.**

CASHIER/BUSINESS OFFICE. **The *cashier's office* or *business office* is where you go to pay school fees or tuition.** On some campuses you may also be able to cash checks here.

JOB PLACEMENT. **The *job placement office* or *employment office* provides job listings from employers who are looking for student help.** Many of the jobs are part time. They may range from waiting tables, to handing out equipment in an electronics lab, to working behind a counter in a store.

CAREER CENTER. **The *career center* is the place to find help if you're having trouble deciding on career goals or a major.** (It may also be called the *career development center* or the *career counseling center*.) We considered the process of selecting a major or career field in Chapter 11, "Career & Work."

CHILD CARE. Some schools offer, or offer referrals to, child-care or day-care facilities for children of adult students and faculty. The centers are usually staffed by professional child-care specialists who may be assisted by student interns or helpers studying child-related disciplines, such as education or psychology. As many as a quarter of career-education students are parents, so child care is an important resource. Sometimes students with children get together with similar students for cooperative child-care arrangements.

LEGAL SERVICES. Some schools, particularly larger ones, have a legal-services office to provide information and counseling to students. Naturally, we hope you'll never have to use it. Still, it's good to know where to call if problems such as landlord-tenant disputes, auto accidents, drunk driving, or employment discrimination arise.

COMMUNITY SERVICES. You'll probably want such services as the post office, copy centers, automated teller machines, eating places, and service stations. These may exist right on campus, at least at larger schools. If not, you may be able to find them close by the campus or in the community that you commute from. You may also be able to find help in consumer organizations, political and environmental organizations, city or county recreation departments, and YMCAs and YWCAs. Finally, you may need to find such services as off-campus counseling, child care, legal assistance, and food and clothing banks.

Activities & Campus Life

PREVIEW A great deal of student life centers on the student union, the bookstore, and clubs and activities.

Some smaller career or vocational-technical schools may have only lecture halls, laboratories, and libraries. Larger schools, however, may offer student-centered places such as the student union, the bookstore, and other centers of student life.

STUDENT UNION. This is often the "crossroads of the campus," the place where you go to hang out after class, where you are apt to run into your friends. **The *student union*, often called the *student center* or *campus center*, is different on every campus. However, even many smaller schools offer a cafeteria or dining hall and some recreation areas.** Recreation may include television rooms,

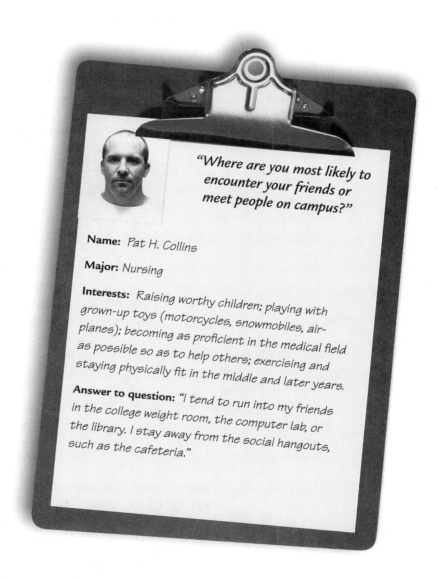

"Where are you most likely to encounter your friends or meet people on campus?"

Name: Pat H. Collins

Major: Nursing

Interests: Raising worthy children; playing with grown-up toys (motorcycles, snowmobiles, airplanes); becoming as proficient in the medical field as possible so as to help others; exercising and staying physically fit in the middle and later years.

Answer to question: "I tend to run into my friends in the college weight room, the computer lab, or the library. I stay away from the social hangouts, such as the cafeteria."

Ping-Pong tables, pool tables, and video games. On larger campuses, there may also be a bookstore, study lounges, a post office, convenience store, barbershop or hairdresser, and bank or automated teller machine. Here's where you will find bulletin boards advertising everything from rental housing to shared rides.

BOOKSTORE. Often located in the student center, the campus bookstore's main purpose is to make textbooks and educational supplies available for students. Beyond that, it may carry anything from candy, coffee mugs, and sweatshirts on the one hand to general-interest books and personal computers on the other. The bookstore also often sells the school's *catalog* and the *course list* (if these are not free).

In most campus bookstores, you can find textbooks for the courses you have signed up for by looking for the course number on the shelves. Here are three tips regarding textbooks:

- ***Check out the books for your courses:*** If ever there was a way of getting a preview of your academic work, it is here. Want to know how hard that course in physics or accounting is going to be? Go to the bookstore and take a look through the textbooks.

- ***Buy the books early:*** Because many students do a lot of course adding and dropping at the beginning of the school term, they may wait to buy their textbooks until they are sure what their classes are. Big mistake. Books may be sold out by the time they make up their minds, and it can take a few weeks for the store to get new ones in. A better plan is to buy the texts, but don't write in them. Hang on to your receipts so you can return the books later, if necessary, and get your money back.

- ***Buy the right edition:*** As material becomes outdated, publishers issue new editions of their books. If you buy a used version of the assigned text, make sure you get the most recent edition. An out-of-date edition won't have all the facts you need to know. This is an especially important consideration for career or vocational-technical students, who are often studying in fields that change rapidly.

STUDENT LIFE. Whatever your background or interest, there may be some club or activity or association on campus or nearby that will be of interest to you. This is especially true of larger campuses. Through these you can continue interests developed earlier, such as music or sports. You can also use them to *develop* talents and interests, such as those in computing, politics, or camping.

You can join groups not only simply to have fun but also for two other important reasons: (1) to make friends, and (2) to get some experience related to your career field. For instance, if your career interest is computer repair, you may want to join a computer users' group. This is not just "pretend" stuff; it is valid experience that you'll want to put on your career résumé when you go job hunting later.

The Multicultural "Salad Bowl":
Diversity of Genders, Ages, Cultures, Races, & So On

PREVIEW Because of the changing "melting pot," global economy, and electronic communications, you will live in a world that is increasingly culturally and racially more diverse. Higher education gives you the opportunity to learn to live with diversity in gender and sexual orientation, age, race and culture, and disabilities.

Three developments ensure that the future will not look the same as the past:

- ***Changing "melting pot" (or "salad bowl"):*** By the year 2000, it is estimated that white males will make up less than 10% of newcomers to the American workforce. Most new workers will be women, minorities, and recent immigrants.[3] America has always been considered a "melting pot"—or maybe "salad bowl" is a better description—of different races and cultures. However, the country will probably become more so in the near future.

- ***Changing world economy:*** The American economy is becoming more a part of the world economy. "We are in an unprecedented period of accelerated change," point out John Naisbitt and Patricia Aburdene. Perhaps the most breathtaking, they say, is "the swiftness of our rush to all the world's becoming a single economy."[4] The American economy is now completely intertwined with the other economies of the world—and therefore with the world's people.

- ***Changing electronic communications:*** Electronic communications systems—telephones, television, fax machines, computers—are providing a wired and wireless universe that is bringing the cultures of the world closer together. For example, 12 million people already communicate with each other through the Internet. The *Internet* is a global computer-linked network tying together thousands of smaller computer networks.

Many people are not prepared for these changes. Fortunately, many institutions of higher education are ***multicultural, or culturally and racially diverse places. Diversity means variety—in race, gender, ethnicity, age, physical abilities, and sexual orientation.*** Higher education gives you the opportunity to learn to study, work, and live with people different from you. While you need not approve of other people's lifestyles, it's in your interest to display respectful behavior toward others. In this way you prepare yourself for life in the 21st century.

In this section, we look at the following kinds of diversity:

- Gender and sexual orientation

- Age

- Race and culture

- Disabilities

GENDER & SEXUAL ORIENTATION. After steady increases over two decades, enrollments of women in higher education now greatly exceed those of men. In 1970, women made up 42% of students in higher education. By 1990, however, that figure had risen to 55%. Why the dramatic change? One reason, perhaps, is the surge of interest among older women who postponed or never considered higher education and are now enrolling. Indeed, 49% of women in higher education are over 24 years old, compared with 24% of men.[5]

Women have reasons to feel proud of their accomplishments. They get higher grades on the average than men do, are awarded more scholarships, and complete degrees at a faster pace.[6] However, traditionally they also suffer lower pay and slower advancements after leaving school. Still, with so many women in higher education, the increased numbers of female graduates could put pressure on employers to change.

Colleges and technical schools have experienced considerable pressures to develop policies for countering sex stereotypes, sexism, and sexual harassment:

- **Stereotype: A _stereotype_ is an expected or exaggerated expectation about a category of people, which may be completely inaccurate when applied to individuals.** For example, a stereotype is that men are better than women in math and science, or women are better than men in cooking.

- **Sexism: _Sexism_ is discrimination against individuals based on their gender.** An example is the behavior of instructors who call more often on men than women (as is frequently the case) to answer questions in class.

- **Sexual harassment: _Sexual harassment_ consists of sexually oriented behaviors that adversely affect someone's academic or employment status or performance.** Examples are requests for sexual favors, unwelcome sexual advances, or demeaning sexist remarks.

Higher education has also been trying to improve the climate for homosexuals, or gays and lesbians. In recent times, surveys have found first-year students more accepting of gay rights. For example, in 1987, 60% of male freshmen said there should be laws prohibiting homosexuality, but four years later only 33% of them still supported such laws.[7]

Most students keep their views on homosexuality to themselves. However, on some campuses, homophobia still exists and may be expressed in active ways. **_Homophobia_ is fear of, or resistance to, the idea of homosexuality or of homosexuals.** Students may express their opposition by harassing gay rights activists or even physically assaulting students whose sexual orientation they do not accept. In many states, the law now allows prosecutors to file charges against those accused of such harassment.

AGE. About 17 million Americans are taking higher-education courses of one form or another. However, only 6 million are so-called **_traditional students_—that is, students between 18 and 24 years old**.[8] The dramatic shift from students in their late teens and early twenties occurred because of the rising number of nontraditional students. **_Nontraditional students_—sometimes called adult students or returning students—are those who are older than 24.** As mentioned, nearly half the women students and nearly a quarter of the men students in higher education are over age 24. Many of these also attend school part time. (Actually, about half the students in higher education, regardless of age, are enrolled part time.)

Who are these nontraditional students? There is no easy way to categorize them. Large numbers are women entering the labor force, displaced workers trying to upgrade their skills, people switching careers, managers taking courses to gain advancement, others seeking intellectual stimulation. Some are retirees: In a recent year, according to the Census Bureau, 320,000 Americans age 50 and over were enrolled in higher-education courses.[9]

Whatever their reasons, nontraditional students often bring a high level of motivation, a wealth of life experience, and a willingness to work hard. Younger students often find that adult students make valuable team or study-group members.

Nontraditional students also bring a number of concerns. They worry that their skills are rusty, that they won't be able to keep up with younger students. They worry that their memory is not as good, that their energy level is not as high. Single parents worry that they won't be able to juggle school and their other responsibilities. They are concerned about scant or nonexistent child care. They may feel greater pressure regarding employment security.

Fortunately, most campuses have someone whose job it is to support adult students. There are also a number of other strategies that adult learners can employ. (See ■ Panel 12.4.)

PANEL 4.1   **S**trategies for adult learners.

Some strategies for students who are over age 24 or attending school part time:

Ask for support: Get your family involved by showing them your textbooks and giving them a tour of the campus. Hang your grades on the refrigerator right alongside those of the kids. Or get support from friends (such as other adult students), a counselor, or an instructor. See if the school sponsors an adult support group.

Get financial aid: See Chapter 10's section on money. You may be able to get loans, scholarships, or fellowships.

Enroll parttime: Going part time will ease the stresses on your time and finances. Start with just one course to test the waters.

Arrange for child care: If you have young children, you'll need child care not only for when you're away at class but also when you're home doing homework.

Learn time-management skills: See the other chapters in this book, particularly Chapter 3, on how to manage your time.

Get academic support: If you're worried about being rusty, look for review courses, one-on-one free tutoring, and similar support services.

Avoid grade pressure: Unless you're trying to get into a top college, don't put yourself under undue pressure for grades. Just do the best you can in the time you have to devote to school.

Have fun: School should also be enjoyable for itself, not just a means to a better life. If you can't spare much time for campus activities, at least spend some time with other nontraditional students. Some campuses, for example, even have a "resumers lounge." Or experiment with your image, dressing in ways (hip? professional? sexy?) that will allow you to reinvent yourself a bit.

Form or join a returning students group: Get together with others in your classes who seem to be in similar circumstances for study and other mutual support.

RACE & CULTURE. Past generations of the dominant culture in the United States felt threatened by the arrival of Irish, Italians, Germans, Eastern Europeans, Catholics, and Jews. (And some people are still uncomfortable with them today.) Now the groups considered prominent racial minorities are people of African, Hispanic, and Asian descent or Native Americans and Alaskan Natives. Indeed, four of these groups (African-Americans, Hispanic-Americans, Native Americans, and Alaskan Natives) presently make up 20% of Americans. By the year 2000, they are expected to make up nearly a third of the students in higher education.

Let us briefly consider some of these groups:

■ *African-Americans:* The largest nonwhite minority, African-Americans make up 12% of the population of the United States, comprising 30 million people. By almost any measure, African-Americans continue to face disadvantages resulting from the burden of slavery and three centuries of racial discrimination. Indeed, one survey found that 80% of African-Americans who responded reported having experienced some form of racial discrimination during their years in higher education.[10]

Gains in civil rights and voting rights during the 1960s increased the numbers of African-Americans in elective office sixtyfold during the last 30 years. Outlawing discrimination in education and employment has helped establish a third of African-Americans in the middle class (up 10% from the 1960s). Even so, unemployment rates for African-Americans continue to be double those of whites. Moreover, they continue to suffer disproportionately from serious health problems, crime, and poverty.

Many African-Americans go to school in the large system of black colleges and other black institutions of higher learning. Still, perhaps 80% of African-American students attend institutions of higher education in which the majority of students are white.[11]

■ *Hispanic-Americans:* People from Spanish-speaking cultures make up the second largest minority group in the United States (at 9% of the population, or 22 million). They make up more than 10% of the population of Colorado, Florida, and New York. They constitute nearly a fifth of the population of Arizona, more than a quarter of the people in California and Texas, and more than a third of those in New Mexico.

Two-thirds of Hispanics are Mexican-Americans, which, after African-Americans, represent the second largest disadvantaged minority group. Puerto Ricans and Cubans are the next largest groups of Hispanics, followed by others from Caribbean, Central American, and South American countries.

■ *Asian-Americans:* There are 28 separate groups of Asian-Americans, according to census studies, ranging from Chinese to Japanese to Pacific Islanders. Asian-Americans are the fastest-growing minority in the United States, with 40% living in California and most of the rest in Hawaii and New York.[12] The two largest groups are Chinese and Filipino who, along with the Japanese, are descendants of earlier tides of immigration. However, the fastest-growing groups of recent years have been those from Vietnam, India, Korea, Cambodia (Kampuchea), and Laos. Asian-Americans continue to suffer discrimination, as reflected in lower income levels compared to those of whites.

■ *Other races, cultures, religions:* Of course there are many other groups of ethnic and religious minorities. Those with the longest history of habitation in the United States are the people considered native—Indians, Alaskans, and Hawaiians. In 1990, there were nearly 2 million Native Americans and Alaskan Natives, according to the U.S. census. Since 1968, 24 institutions of higher education have been established in the United States that are owned and operated by Native Americans.[13]

The dominant religion in the United States is Protestant. Nevertheless, there are numerous minority religions: Catholic, Jewish, Muslim, Buddhist, Hindu, and so on. And, of course, many people espouse no formal religion or no religion at all.

■ *International students:* Many campuses are enriched by the presence of international students. These are foreign visitors who have come to the United States to pursue a course of study. Some of them may find themselves especially welcome. Others, however, may find that their skin color, dress, or accent exposes them to no less bias than American-born minorities experience. Some Americans worry that, with so much overseas talent in science and engineering programs, we are offering a kind of foreign aid. In fact, however, over half of all foreign graduate students in science and engineering choose to remain in the United States after completing their schooling. Thus, they form an important part of our high-tech work force.[14]

DISABILITY. Nearly one in eleven first-year students in higher education reports some kind of physical disability.[15] **A *physical disability* is a health-related condition that prevents a person from participating fully in daily activities,** including school and work. As a result of the 1990 Americans with Disabilities Act, colleges and technical schools have had to change policies and remodel buildings to accommodate students with disabilities. For instance, the law bars discrimination against the disabled in public accommodations and transportation. This provision means that new and renovated buildings and buses must be accessible to people with handicaps.

People with disabilities are not only those who are physically handicapped (for example, wheelchair users) or the visually or hearing impaired. They are also those with any type of learning disability. For example, people with dyslexia have difficulty reading. Whatever their impairment, people with disabilities resent words that suggest they're sick, pitiful, childlike, or dependent or, conversely, objects of admiration. They also object to politically correct euphemisms such as the "differently abled," "the vertically challenged," or the "handi-capable."[16]

Onward

PREVIEW Don't always pretend "everything's cool" when it's not.

Often people wear a mask to hide their feelings. Sometimes it's an "Everything's cool" expression. Sometimes it's a stone-faced "Don't mess with me" look. However, *we* know and *you* know that behind the mask is often a human being in need of help and friendship.

When the pressures of school begin to be overwhelming, that's the time to take another look at this chapter. It's clear that all kinds of support are available to students. The main thing is to decide that *you're not alone* and go after it.

The principal lesson of this chapter has a great deal of value outside of school. That lesson is this: *Find out everything you can about the organization you're in.* The more you understand about the departments and processes of your work world, for instance, the better you'll be able to take control of your own life within it. The same is true with the world outside of work.

NOTES

1. Kramer, G. L., & Spencer, R. W. Academic advising, in Upcraft, M. L., Gardner, J. N., & Associates (Eds.). (1990). *The freshman year experience: Helping students survive and succeed in college* (p. 97). San Francisco: Jossey-Bass.

2. Crockett, D. S. Academic advising, in Noel, L., Levitiz, R., & Saluri, D., & Associates (Eds.). (1985). *Increasing student retention* (pp. 244–263). San Francisco: Jossey-Bass.

3. Hudson Institute, Workforce 2000, U.S. Bureau of Labor Statistics, in Jobs for women in the nineties (1988, July). *Ms,* p. 77.

4. Naisbitt, J., & Aburdene, P. (1990). *Megatrends 2000.* New York: Morrow, p. 19.

5. Freedberg, L. (1993, November 12). Women outnumber men at college. *San Francisco Chronicle,* pp. A1, A9.

6. Adelman, C., U.S. Department of Education. *Women at thirtysomething.* Cited in Stipp, D. (1992, September 11). The gender gap. *Wall Street Journal.*

7. Cage, M. C. (1993, March 10). Openly gay students face harassment and physical assaults on some campuses. *Chronicle of Higher Education,* pp. A22–A24.

8. Freedberg, L. (1992, June 28). The new face of higher education. *This World, San Francisco Chronicle,* p. 9.

9. Beck, B. (1991, November 11). School day for seniors. *Newsweek,* pp. 60–65.

10. Simpson, J. C. (1987, April 3). Campus barrier? Black college students are viewed as victims of a subtle racism. *Wall Street Journal.*

11. Evans, G. (1986, April 30). Black students who attend white colleges face contradictions in their campus life. *Chronicle of Higher Education,* pp. 17–49.

12. Barringer, F. (1991, June 12). Immigration brings new diversity Asian population in the U.S. *New York Times,* pp. A1, D25.

13. Marriott, M. (1992, February 26). Indians turning to tribal colleges for opportunity and cultural values. *New York Times,* p. A13.

14. Kotkin, J. (1993, February 24). Enrolling foreign students will strengthen America's place in the global economy. *Chronicle of Higher Education,* pp. B1–B2.

15. Jaschik, S. (1993, February 3). Backed by 1990 law, people with disabilities press demands on colleges. *Chronicle of Higher Education*, p. A26.

16. Shapiro, J. P. (1993). *No pity: People with disabilities forging a new civil rights movement*. New York: Times Books.

Classroom Activities: Directions to the Instructor

1. ***What are you unsure about?*** Ask students to write down on a piece of paper some aspect of higher education they're not quite clear on. Also have them list some resources they might be interested in. They may include matters related to grades, career interests or majors, and graduation. They may also include nonacademic matters that will help them benefit from their career-education experience.

   In a small-group setting (in a group of 3 to 6 students), have students discuss anything they're still unsure or confused about. Also have them discuss those matters they would like to investigate further.

   Which things that came out of each small group's discussion are particularly interesting or noteworthy? Have the group designate someone to describe them to the class as a whole.

2. ***How do you make friends on campus?*** Because students in career programs often have so many other commitments, making friends on campus may be a low priority. Yet studies show that having friends on campus is important for keeping students in school. The goal of this activity is to help students become acquainted with others, with the goal of developing possible friendships.

   Have everyone in the class write down on a piece of paper five ways they can think of to meet people on campus. Also have them describe the primary hindrance to making friends. (Examples: shyness, not enough time.) Call on people to discuss their thoughts and suggestions.

3. ***What off-campus resources does your community offer?*** When considering the topic of helpful resources, many students consider only those available on campus. The advantage of commuting from somewhere else, however, is that it is apt to offer additional resources not found at the school.

   Have students list as many off-campus and community resources they can think of that might assist them while in school. Call on people to discuss their ideas.

4. ***What is real diversity?*** In class discussion, ask students to explain why diversity is important.

   Questions for discussion: Is diversity more than just having numerous people from various minority backgrounds working for a company or attending a technical school or college? Is diversity really about how a person thinks and feels about others? How realistic are the mass media in portraying minorities? Give examples. Have there been times in your life when you have been a victim of prejudice and discrimination? Is society becoming more or less tolerant and accepting of diversity? What examples of tolerance and diversity in this country would you be proud to show a foreign visitor?

The Examined Life:
Student Assignments for Journal Entries

JOURNAL ENTRY #12.1: **WHAT PROBLEM MIGHT YOU NEED HELP SOLVING?** What problem can you think of that might occur during school for which you might need help? It could be lack of money, conflicts in a personal relationship, dealing with child care, or difficulty in keeping up with a course. What kind of assistance could you get to ease the problem?

_____
_____
_____
_____
_____
_____

JOURNAL ENTRY #12.2: **FINDING IMPORTANT SCHOOL SERVICES.** Find the following places and write down the location and the telephone number for contacting them. (If these places do not exist on your campus, indicate *None* in the space.) Unless your instructor asks you to turn this in, post the list over your desk or near your bed.

Services	Building name & room number	Telephone
Learning/tutoring center		
Library/media center		
Your academic advisor		
Dean of students		
Health service or infirmary		
Counseling center		
Security or campus police		
Registrar		
Financial aid office		
Transportation office		
Cashier/business office		
Job placement center		
Adult services		
Career center		
Child care		
Legal services		
Student union or center		

JOURNAL ENTRY #12.3: GETTING TO KNOW AN INSTRUCTOR. You never know when you will need the help of an instructor—to explain a homework problem, to clarify an exam question, to give you a reference, or just be a good friend.

Select an instructor, such as one from a course you are now taking or from a field you are considering majoring in, or your faculty advisor. Telephone that instructor, explain you are doing a class assignment, and ask if he or she can spare 10 minutes for a brief interview. Make an appointment to meet.

1. Name of instructor being interviewed: _____

2. Department in which instructor teaches (example: Computer Information Systems): _____

3. What is your area of specialization or research? _____
   _____

4. What kinds of undergraduate and graduate degrees do you have and where did you receive them? _____
   _____
   _____

5. Why did you decide to teach at this institution? _____
   _____
   _____

6. *Ask a question of your own.* (Example: "What do you think are the characteristics of a good student?")
   Your question: _____
   _____
   _____

   The instructor's answer: _____
   _____
   _____

JOURNAL ENTRY #12.4: WHAT IS YOUR CULTURAL HERITAGE? Many people have never taken the time to learn about their cultural heritage. Using library research and interviews with family members and relatives, answer the following questions:

1. What are the unique characteristics of your cultural background?
   _____
   _____
   _____
   _____

2. What would you like others to know about your cultural background that you feel they don't understand?
   _____
   _____
   _____
   _____

Sources & Credits

TEXT SOURCES & CREDITS

CHAP. 2: **Prac Expl #2.3** adapted from Nowicki-Strickland Scale and results from Nowicki, S. Jr. & Strickland, B. R. (1973, February). A locus of control scale for children. *Journal of Consulting & Clinical Psychology, 40*(1), 148–54. Copyright © 1973 by the American Psychological Association. Adapted by permission. **Panel 2.1** adapted from McGinnis, A. L. (1990). *The power of optimism.* San Francisco: Harper & Row, p. xiv. **CHAP. 3:** **Panel 3.7** Adapted from Sapadin, L. Reported in Peterson, K. S. (1997, July 22). Helping procrastinators get to it. *USA Today,* p. 7D. Based on Sapadin, L. (1997). *It's about time.* New York: Penguin. **CHAP. 4:** **Prac Expl #4.1 and Prac Expl. #4.2** adapted from "Modality Inventory" by Ducharme, A., & Watford, L., Middle Grades Department, Valdosta State University, Valdosta, GA 31698. Reprinted with the kind permission of Dr. Adele Ducharme and Dr. Luck Watford. **Panel 4.1** adapted from Lindgren, H. C. (1969). *The psychology of college success: A dynamic approach.* New York: Wiley. **CHAP. 5:** **Panel 5.1** from Weiten, W. (1989). *Psychology: Themes and variations.* Pacific Grove, CA: Brooks/Cole, p. 254. Used with permission. Based on material from D. van Guilford, Van Nostrand, 1939. **Pages 106–107,** material beginning "A Rustler . . .; from Weiten, W., Lloyd, M. A., & Lashley, R. L. (1990). *Psychology applied to modern life: Adjustment in the 90s* (3rd ed.). Pacific Grove, CA: Brooks/Cole, p. 24. Adapted from Bower, G. H., & Clark, M. C. (1969). Narrative stories as mediators of social learning. *Psychonomic Science, 14,* 181–82. Copyright © 1969 by the Psychonomic Society. Adapted by permission of the Psychonomic Society. **Prac Expl #5.1** adapted from Cortina, J., Elder, J., & Gonnet, K. (1992). *Comprehending college textbooks: Steps to understanding and remembering what you read* (2nd ed.). New York: McGraw-Hill, pp. 3–4. By permission of McGraw-Hill. **Panel 5.2** reproduced from Weeks, J. R. (1992). *Population: An introduction to concepts and issues* (5th ed.). Belmont, CA: Wadsworth. **Panel 5.3,** page reproduced from Biagi, S. (1994). *Media/Impact: An introduction to mass media,* updated second edition. Belmont, CA: Wadsworth, p. 180. **CHAP. 8:** **Prac Expl #8.1** adapted from Adams, J. L. (1974). *Conceptual blockbusting.* Stanford, CA: Stanford Alumni Association (The Portable Stanford), p. 106. **CHAP. 9:** Chapter adapted from Williams, B. K., Sawyer, S. C., & Hutchinson, S. E. (1995). *Using information technology: A practical introduction to computers & communications.* Burr Ridge, IL: Irwin. Used with permission of Richard D. Irwin, a Times Mirror Higher Education Group, Inc., company. **Panel 9.1** adapted from the Editors of *PC World Magazine* (1992, November 13). Mobile computing, special pullout section sponsored by Intel. *Newsweek,* p. N26. **Panel 9.2** from Williams, Richard. (1993, April 10). On the hunt for a used computer. *The Globe & Mail* (Toronto), p. B13. **CHAP. 10:** Portions of chapter adapted from Williams, B. K., & Knight, S. M. (1994). *Healthy for life: Wellness and the art of living* (Pacific Grove, CA: Brooks/Cole), especially Unit 2. Used with permission. **Prac Expl #10.1** from Mullen, Cathleen, & Costello, Gerald. (1981). *Health awareness through self-discovery.* Edina, MN: Burgess International Group. **Panel 10.2** from Benson, H. (1989). Editorial: Hypnosis and the relaxation response. *Gastroenterology, 96,* 1610. **Prac Expl #10.2** from Sternberg, R. J., & Soriano, L. J. (1984). Styles of conflict resolution. *Journal of Personality & Social Psychology, 47,* 115–26; Weiten, W., Lloyd, M. A., & Lashley, R. L. (1991). *Psychology applied to modern life: Adjustment in the 90s* (3rd ed.). Pacific Grove: CA: Brooks/Cole; Williams, B. K., & Knight, S. M. (1994). *Healthy for life: Wellness and the art of living* (Pacific Grove, CA: Brooks/Cole), pp. 8.36–8.39. **Prac Expl #10.3** from Lazarus, A. A. (1971). Assertiveness questionnaire, in *Behavior therapy and beyond.* New York: McGraw-Hill. By permission of Arnold A. Lazarus, Ph.D. **CHAP. 11:** **Prac Expl #11.1** adapted and reproduced by special permission of the Publisher, Psychological Assessment Resources Inc., Odessa, FL 33556, from the *Self-Directed Search Assessment Booklet* by John L. Holland, Ph.D. Copyright 1970, 1977, 1985, 1990, 1994 by PAR, Inc. Further reproduction is prohibited without permission from PAR, Inc. The Self-Directed Search materials are available for purchase through PAR, Inc. by calling 1-800-331-8378. **Panel 11.1** from Falvey, J. (1986). *After college: The business of getting jobs.* Charlotte, VT: Williamson Publishing, p. 37. **Panel 11.3** from Pender, K. (1994, May 16). Résumé dos and don'ts. *San Francisco Chronicle,* p. B4. © San Francisco Chronicle. Reprinted by permission. **CHAP. 12:** **Panel 12.1** courtesy Genesee Community College. **Panel 12.3** adapted from San Jose State University Police Department (1989). *Safety and security at San Jose State.* San Jose, CA: San Jose State University, Police Department, Investigations/Crime Prevention Unit.

PHOTO SOURCES & CREDITS

Photos on following pages by Michael Garrett, Genesee Community College: 7 (right), 9, 13, 25, 33, 51, 54, 64, 69, 91, 93, 111, 118, 122, 123, 140, 159, 170, 173, 175, 192, 196, 199, 211, 217, 229, 245, 253, 277, 287, 295, 311, 321, 327, 332, 335. Photos on following pages from PhotoDisc, Inc.: 1, 3, 10 (all), 15, 16, 23, 34, 36, 37, 49, 52, 66 (both), 73, 74, 77, 81, 85, 99, 104, 106, 124, 125, 135, 136, 142, 145, 149, 163, 164, 149, 178, 190, 202, 207, 209, 219, 231, 235, 237, 240, 247, 251, 259, 264, 266, 279, 289, 303, 309, 325, 328, 333. Images copyright 1998 PhotoDisc, Inc.

Glossary/Index

Abbreviations, 88

Absolute qualifier words, 148

Abstracts are brief summaries of journal articles along with bibliographic information about them, 184

Academic advisor is a school employee or faculty member assigned to counsel students about their academic program, 316–318

Academic calendar, 53

Academic dishonesty, 159–164
   alternatives to, 164
   penalties for, 163
   reasons for, 162
   self-evaluation on, 160, 162–163
   types of, 159, 161

Academic help, 315–321
   from academic advisors, 316–318
   from the Dean of Students office, 321
   from instructors, 319
   from librarians, 319–320
   from tutors, 320

Academic skills
   career skills and, 5–7
   school dropouts and, 17
   upgrading, 10–11

Accommodation, 263

Actions for goal-achievement, 40–43

Active aggression, 265

Active listening, 92–94

Active reading, 118–119

Adaptation is a way of dealing with stress where you do not change the stressor or the stress, 256, 257

Adult learners, 331

Advance organizers are mental landmarks under which facts and ideas may be grouped and organized in your mind, 115–116

African-American students, 332

Age diversity, 330–331

Aggressive behavior means you vehemently expound your opinions, accuse or blame others, and hurt others before hurting yourself, 268
   active vs. passive aggression, 265

Alcohol use, 257

Almanacs, 183, 185

Analytical graphics are graphical forms that make numeric data easier to analyze than when it is in the form of rows and columns of numbers, 240

Anxiety
   expressions of, 254–255
   about higher education, 28–30, 252
   about public speaking, 200–201
   steps for reducing, 124–125
   test, 141–143

Appeal to authority argument uses an authority in one area to pretend to validate claims in another area in which the person is not an expert, 215–216

Appeal to pity argument appeals to mercy rather than arguing on the merits of the case itself, 216

Appendix is a section in the back of the book containing supplementary material, material of optional or specialized interest, such as tables and charts, 114, 115

Arguments consist of one or more premises, or reasons, logically supporting a result or outcome called a conclusion, 214

Asian-American students, 333

"As if" technique, 50

Assertiveness is defined as acting in your own best interest by expressing your thoughts and feelings directly and honestly. It means standing up for yourself and openly expressing your personal feelings and opinions, yet not hurting either yourself or others, 268–270
   developing, 270
   personal exploration on, 269

Association is a strategy of memorizing in which one idea reminds you of another, 100

Attendance, class, 83–84

Attention
   audience, 199–200
   memory and, 104

Auditory learners use their voices and their ears as their primary means of learning, 80
   lectures and, 81

Audit sheet. *See* Curriculum worksheet

Automated teller machines (ATMs), 273

Automobiles
   expenses associated with, 272
   insurance required for, 275

Avoidance, conflict, 263

Banks, 273

Bell cue is an action or gesture that indicates important points, 93, 138

Bell phrase is an indicator of an important point. Bell phrases are important because they indicate you should note what comes after them and remember them, 93, 138

Bibliography, or "Notes" section, lists sources or references used in writing the text, 114, 115

Blue books, 139

Body care, 260

Boldface type, 116, 138

Books
   researching, 180–183
   surveying, 115, 117

Books in Print, 182

Bookstore, campus, 328

Boredom
   classroom, 91–94
   methods for fighting, 68, 92–95
   overpreparedness and, 17
   study assignments and, 68

Brainstorming means jotting down all the ideas that come to mind about a particular matter, 154, 178, 218
   rules for, 218–219

Breaks, study, 65, 126

Brochures, 312

Bulletin board services (BBSs), 244

Burnout, 255

Business office is the campus office where students go to pay school fees or tuition, 326

Calendar, creating, 53–56
Campus activities, 327–328
Campus bulletin is a periodical that informs students of campus activities and events, 312
Campus calendar is a publication listing the deadlines and dates for various programs during the academic year, 311
Campus center. *See* Student union
Campus map, 312
Campus newspaper is a student-run news publication that is published on some campuses, 312
Campus resources
    academic help, 315–321
    important places, 314–315
    miscellaneous services, 315, 324–326
    orientation program, 310–311
    physical and emotional help, 321–324
    publications, 311–314
"Canned" term papers, 171
Card catalogs contain information about each library book, typed on a 3-by-5 inch card, and stored in wooden file drawers, 180, 181
Career. *See also* Employment; Work
    competencies needed for, 288
    deciding on, 288–289
    interview skills and, 300, 302
    job-hunting skills and, 293–303
    relationship of major to, 287–288
    relevance of higher education to, 3–7
    résumé writing and, 296–299
    vocational tests and, 289–292
Career center is the campus office that helps students with decisions about career goals and majors, 315, 326
Career counseling, 289, 292
Career education, 2. *See also* Higher education
Career student, 2–3. *See also* Practical student
"Career video" exercise, 290–291
Cars. *See* Automobiles
Cashier's office is the campus office where students go to pay school fees or tuition, 326
Cassette tapes, 128
CD-ROM catalogs look like music CDs, except that they are used to store text and images. CD-ROM

stands for Compact Disk–Read Only Memory, 180, 182
Certificate program is a list of courses a student must take to obtain a certificate in a specific field, 316
Chapter summary, 116
Chapter table of contents, 115
Charge cards are those that require that the bill be paid off every month, 273
    disadvantages of, 274
Chat rooms, 244
Cheating is using unauthorized help to complete a test, practice exercise, or project, 161
    alternatives to, 164
    penalties for, 163
    reasons for, 162
Children
    day-care facilities for, 326
    school responsibilities and, 14–15
Chronological résumé, 296
Circular reasoning argument rephrases the statement to be proven true. It then uses the new, similar statement as supposed proof that the original statement is in fact true, 216
Classes
    attendance at, 83–84
    evaluating performance in, 82–83
    fighting boredom and fatigue in, 91–94
    overcoming obstacles in, 95
    participation in, 85, 94
    time needed for, 63
Clothing expenses, 273
College Work-Study program, 278
Commitment, 32
Communication
    bad, 265
    conflict and, 262–265
    good, 265–266
    listening and, 266–267
    self-expression and, 267
Communications software manages the transmission of data between computers, 241
Communications technology, 242–246
    Internet and World Wide Web, 244–246
    online information services, 243–244
    telephone-related services, 242–243
Community services, 326
Commuting
    balancing with school and work, 12

expenses associated with, 272
    making friends and, 11–12
    time needed for, 63
Comparison charts are useful for studying several concepts and the relationships between them, 128, 129
Compromise, 264
Computer networks, 183, 185
Computers. *See* Personal computers
Computer-scannable résumés, 298–299
Concept maps are visual diagrams of concepts, 128, 129
Conceptual blocks, 218
Conflict
    areas of, 264
    personal exploration on, 263
    in relationships, 265
    styles of dealing with, 263–264
Control, personal sense of, 30–32
Conversation starters and stoppers, 266
Cooperative education programs allow you to improve your marketability upon graduation by giving you work experience in your major, 278
Coping is a way of dealing with stress where you change the stressor or your reaction to it, 257
    with stress, 257–262
    with test anxiety, 141–143, 165
Copyright page (on the back of the title page) gives the date the book was published, 112, 113
Cornell method of note taking, 87
Counseling center, 322
Counselors, 260
Course list is a list of the courses being taught in the current school term, 312
Courses
    identifying for goal-achievement, 40–41
    syllabus for, 54
Cover letter, 300
Cramming is defined as preparing hastily for an examination, 100
    problems with, 72–73, 100–101
Creative thinking consists of imaginative ways of looking at known ideas, 217–221
    brainstorming and, 218–219
    mind mapping and, 219
    sensory images and, 220
    serendipity and, 221
    stereotyping and, 218

Creativity refers to the human capacity to express ourselves in original or imaginative ways, 34

Credit cards are those that allow the charges to be paid off in installments plus interest, provided you make a minimum payment every month, 273
  disadvantages of, 274

Crisis is an especially strong source of stress, 253

Crisis makers, 70

Critical thinking means clear thinking, skeptical thinking, active thinking. It involves actively seeking to understand, analyze, and evaluate information in order to solve specific problems, 210–216
  mind-sets and, 210–211
  reasoning and, 214–216
  reducing errors through, 211–212
  steps in, 210, 212–213

Criticism, expressing, 267

Cultural diversity, 332–334

Curriculum worksheet is a list of courses required for the major and the semesters in which it is recommended the students take them, 317

Database is a collection of interrelated files in a computer system. These computer-based files are organized so that those parts that have a common element can be retrieved easily, 239

Database management system (DBMS) is a program that controls the structure of a database and access to the data, 239–240

Dean of Students office, 321

Debit cards enable you to pay for purchases by withdrawing funds electronically directly from your savings or checking account, 274

Dedicated fax machines are specialized devices that do nothing except send and receive documents over transmission lines from and to other fax machines, 242

Deductive argument is defined as follows: If its premises are true, then its conclusions are also true, 214

Defiers, 70

Degree plan. *See* Curriculum worksheet

Degree program is a list of courses a student must take to obtain a degree in a specific field, 316

Delaying tactics, 68–69

Demonstrated financial need means that you have proven you need financial aid according to a certain formula, 276

Depth-of-processing principle states that how shallowly or deeply you hold a thought depends on how much you think about it and how many associations you form with it, 105–106

Desktop accessory/organizer is a software package that provides an electronic version of tools or objects commonly found on a desktop: calendar, clock, card file, calculator, and notepad, 236

Desktop computers, 230

Diagrams, study, 128

Dictionaries, 183, 185

Diplomacy, 267

Directories, online. *See* Web directories

Disabled students, 334

Disarming technique, 267

Discipline, 44

Dishonesty in education. *See* Academic dishonesty

Disorder, 218

Distractions, 66–68

Distress is the effect when stress occurs owing to a negative event, 254

Distressor is the source of stress as a negative event, 254

Distributed practice is when the student distributes study time over several days. It is more effective for retaining information, 105

Diversion, 265

Diversity means variety—in race, gender, ethnicity, age, physical abilities, and sexual orientation, 329
  age, 330–331
  gender, 329–330
  physical disability, 334
  racial/cultural, 332–334
  sexual orientation, 330

Documentation style, 194–195

Domination, 263

Dreamers, 70

Dropout rate, 17

Drug use, 257

"Dumb" questions, 219

Earnings, lifetime, 4

Eating
  stress-release through, 257
  time needed for, 63

Editing term papers, 193–195

Edwards Personal Preference Schedule (EPPS), 291

Electronic distractions, 67

Electronic spreadsheet allows users to create tables and financial schedules by entering data into rows and columns arranged as a grid on a display screen, 238–239

Electronic study guide is a floppy disk that students can use on their personal computer to rehearse practice questions and check their answers, 138

E-mail (electronic mail) links computers by wired or wireless connections and allows users, through their keyboards, to post messages and to read responses on their display screens, 242–243
  on the Internet, 244

Emotional intelligence is the ability to cope, empathize with others, and be self-motivated, 209

Emotions
  denying, 265
  expressing, 258, 265–266, 267
  managing, 258

Employment. *See also* Career; Work
  follow-up letter for, 303
  interview for, 300, 302
  online tools for finding, 299–300
  process of looking for, 293–303
  relevance of higher education to, 3–7
  résumé writing and, 296–299

Employment office is a campus office that provides job listings from employers who are looking for student help, 326

Encyclopedias, 183, 185

Environment
  for studying, 67
  for taking tests, 140
  for writing, 188

Errors
  admitting and reducing, 211–212
  fear of making, 218

Essays, 151–158
   long-answer, 151, 152–158
   short-answer, 151–152
"Essentials for Time & Life Management" program, 35–43, 52–61
Eustress is the effect when stress occurs owing to a positive event, 254
Eustressor is the source of stress as a positive event, 254
Examinations. *See* Tests
Expenses, controlling, 272–273
Expressing emotions, 258, 265–266, 267
Expressive writing, 171
Expulsion means you are kicked out of school permanently; you are not allowed to return, 163
External locus of control is the belief that rewards and punishments are controlled mainly by outside forces and other people, 30

Failure
   cheating and, 163
   meaning of, 35
Fakery is when a person makes up or fabricates something, 161
Fallacies are patterns of incorrect reasoning, 215–216
False cause is a type of fallacy in which the conclusion does not follow logically from the supposed reasons stated earlier, 215
Family, and school responsibilities, 14–15
Fatigue, 91–94
Fax stands for "facsimile transmission" or reproduction, 242
Fax modem, which is installed as a circuit board inside a computer's cabinet, is a modem with fax capability, 242
Fear
   of higher education, 28–30
   of making mistakes, 218
   of public speaking, 200–201
Feelings. *See* Emotions
Fill-in-the-blank questions require you to fill in an answer from memory or to choose from options offered in a list, 150
Finances, personal. *See* Money
Financial aid refers to any kind of financial help you get to enable you to pay for higher education, 275–278

demonstrating the need for, 276–277
   types of, 277–278
Financial aid office is a campus office to help students find financial aid opportunities to pay for their studies, 325
Fitness services, 324
5R steps is a system of note taking and note learning consisting of the steps: Record, Rewrite, Recite, Reflect, Review, 86–90
Flash cards are cards bearing words, numbers, or pictures that are briefly displayed as a learning aid. One side of the card asks a question, the other side provides the answer, 71–72, 127, 138
Follow-up letter, 303
Food
   dealing with stress through, 257
   as monthly expense, 273
Forgetting curve, 102–103
Formal networking, 293
Friends
   emotional support from, 259–260
   making on campus, 11–12
   school responsibilities as strain on, 15
Functional résumé, 296

Gender diversity, 329–330
Genius, use of term, 208
Gift assistance is financial aid you do not have to pay back, 276
Glossary is an alphabetical list of key terms and their definitions, as found in the text, 114, 115
Goals
   actions for achieving, 40–43
   intermediate-range, 39–40
   long-range, 38
   plan for determining, 38–40
   translating into daily tasks, 36, 52
Government publications, 183, 185
Grades
   class attendance and, 83–84
   penalties for cheating and, 163
   on term papers, 171–173
Grammar
   software for checking, 237
   in term papers, 173
Grants are gifts of money, 277
Graphics software, 240–241
Guessing strategies, 147, 149
Guided imagery is a procedure in which you essentially daydream

an image or desired change, anticipating that your body will respond as if the image were real, 261
Guiding words are common words that instruct you in the tasks you are to accomplish in your essay-question answer, 152–154

Handbooks, 183, 185
Handouts, 137
Happiness, 5
Hard-disk storage, or "hard-drive" storage, is your computer's filing cabinet, which allows you to permanently store all your data, as well as your software, 231
Hardware, computer, 231
Hassles are simply frustrating irritants, 253
Hasty generalizations, 215
Health insurance, 274
Health service, 322
Higher education
   compared to high school, 8–10
   fears about, 28–30
   happiness and, 5
   income and, 4
   instruction manuals for, 311–314
   life goals and, 36–38
   methods of instruction and, 6–7
   personal development and, 5
   school dropouts and, 17–18
   survival skills for, 30–35
   values about, 25–27
Highlighting
   lecture notes, 89
   textbooks, 122
Hispanic-American students, 333
Homework. *See also* Study
   preparedness for lectures and, 85, 94, 95
   scheduling time for, 58
Homophobia is fear of, or resistance to, the idea of homosexuality or of homosexuals, 330
Honesty, academic, 159–164
Hopelessness, 265
Housing expenses, 272
Housing office is a campus office to help students find housing either on or off campus, 325–326
Humor, 258

IBM-style computers, 228–229
Idea cards, 187

Immediate perceptual memory is defined as a reflex memory in which an impression is immediately replaced by a new one, 101

Income, lifetime, 4

Incubation technique, 221

Index is an alphabetically arranged list of names and subjects that appear in the text, giving the page numbers on which they appear, 114, 115

of periodicals, 183, 184

Index cards, 186–187, 197

Inductive argument is defined as follows: If the premises are true, the conclusions are *probably* true, but the truth is not guaranteed, 214

Informal networking, 293–294

Information

high-tech ways of collecting, 187–188

low-tech ways of collecting, 185–187

online sources of, 185

Informational interview, 294–295

Information cards, 187

Information technology, 228–247

communications tools, 242–246

computer software, 234–241

personal computers, 228–234

Initial research, 176–177

Inner voice, 124

Instruction, principle methods of, 6–7

Instructors

academic help from, 319

negotiating with, 164

term paper topics and, 175, 176

test preparation and, 137–138

Insurance, 274–275

Integrated software packages combine the features of several applications programs into one software package, 241

Integration, conflict, 264

Integrity, academic, 159–164

Intelligence

creative thinking and, 217–221

critical thinking and, 210–216

emotional, 209

seven kinds of, 208–209

Interference is the competition among related memories, 105

Interlibrary loan is a service that enables you to borrow books from other libraries, 180

Intermediate-range goals, 39–40

Internal locus of control is the belief that rewards and punishments are due to one's own behavior, character, or efforts, 31

International students, 334

Internet is an international computer network connecting approximately 36,000 smaller networks, 244–246

Internet service providers (ISPs) are companies that will provide public access to the Internet for a fee, 246

Internship is a temporary stint of on-the-job training that allows you to gain inside professional experience within a particular company or organization, 295–296

Interviews

employment, 300, 302

follow-up letter to, 303

informational, 294–295

Irrelevant attack on an opponent attacks a person's reputation or beliefs rather than his or her argument, 216

Irrelevant reason is a type of fallacy in which the conclusion does not follow logically from the supposed reasons stated earlier, 215

Italic type, 116, 138

Job-placement office is a campus office that provides job listings from employers who are looking for student help, 326

services offered by, 289

Jobs. *See* Career; Employment; Work

Journal entries, 21

Journal research, 183–184

Jumping to conclusions is a type of fallacy. It happens when a conclusion has been reached when not all the facts are available, 215

Key terms

in lecture notes, 89–90

in textbooks, 116

Keywords are important terms or names that you are expected to understand and be able to define, 182

in computer-scannable résumés, 299

Kinesthetic learners learn best when they touch and are physically involved in what they are studying, 80

Laboratory assignments

career skills and, 6

usefulness of, 126

Laptop computers, 230

Learning

demonstration of, 172

difficult subjects, 123–128

note-taking system for, 86–90

reading for, 110

tools for aiding, 127–128

Learning center is a special center where students go to learn a specific subject or skill, 314, 320

Learning lab. *See* Learning center

Learning objectives are topics the student is expected to learn, which are listed at the beginning of each chapter, 116

Learning styles are the ways in which people acquire knowledge, 78

lectures and, 80, 81

personal exploration of, 78–79

textbooks and, 80

types of, 80–81

Lectures

attendance at, 83–84

career skills and, 6, 95

fighting boredom and fatigue in, 91–94

learning styles and, 80, 81

note-taking system for, 86–90

overcoming obstacles in, 95

participation in, 85, 94

taping, 72, 95

Legal-services office, 326

Librarians, 319–320

Library research, 179–188, 314, 320

book resources and, 180–183

collecting information for, 185–188

computer networks and, 183, 185

government literature and, 183, 185

periodical resources and, 183–184

practical exploration exercise, 189

reference materials and, 185

Life goals

examples of, 37

higher education and, 36–38

plan for determining, 38–40

translating into daily tasks, 36, 52

Lifted term papers, 171

Listening
   active, 92–94
   guidelines for, 266–267
Loan is money you have to pay back, either as money or in the form of some work, 278
Locus of control refers to one's beliefs about the relationship between one's behavior and the occurrence of rewards and punishment, 30
   personal exploration of, 31–32
Long-answer essay generally requires three or more paragraphs to answer, 151
   strategy for handling, 152–158
Long-range goals, 38
Long-term memory entails remembering something for days, weeks, or years, 102
   cramming and, 100–101
   forgetting curve and, 102–103
   reading and, 111
   strategies for improving, 103–108
Lying is simply misrepresentation of the facts. It can occur by omission or by commission, 161
   reasons for, 162

Macintosh-style computers, 229–230
Magazine research, 183–184
Mail-merge program, 237
Major is a student's field of specialization, 316
   deciding on, 18, 39
   relationship to career, 287–288
Management
   stress, 256–262
   time, 50–73
Margins
   using for taking notes, 87, 89–90
   using in 3Rs reading system, 121
Martyrdom, 265
Massed practice is putting all your studying into one long period of time, 105
Master timetable, 53–56
Matching questions require you to associate items from one list with items from a second list, 150
Math anxiety, 124
Media center, 319–320
Meditation is concerned with directing a person's attention to a single, unchanging, or repetitive stimulus. It is a way of quelling the "mind chatter," 262

"Melting pot," 329
Memory is defined as a mental process that entails three main operations: recording, storage, and recall, 100
   cramming and, 100–101
   forgetting curve and, 102–103
   learning styles and, 80–81
   reading and, 111
   strategies for improving, 103–108
   types of, 101–102
Memory (computer) is the internal memory, often called "RAM", for Random Access Memory, that the computer uses for temporary storage in order to do quicker, more seamless processing, 231
Mental imagery is a procedure in which you essentially daydream an image or desired change, anticipating that your body will respond as if the image were real, 261
Menus (software), 235
Merit-based financial aid is based on some kind of superior academic, music, sports, or other abilities, 276
Messiness, 218
Method of loci is a memory technique that involves memorizing a series of places and then using a different vivid image to associate each place with an idea or a word you want to remember, 108
Mind mapping is brainstorming by yourself with the help of pencil and paper, 219
Mind-sets, 210–211
Minor is a smaller field of specialization chosen by the student, 316
Mistakes
   admitting and reducing, 211–212
   fear of making, 218
Mixed-modality learners are able to function in any of three learning styles or "modalities"—auditory, visual, and kinesthetic, 80
Mnemonic devices are tactics for making things memorable by making them distinctive, 106–108
Modems are hardware devices needed to send messages from one computer to another via a phone line, 232, 241

Moderating qualifier words, 148
Money, 270–278
   banks and, 273
   charge, credit, and debit cards, 273–274
   controlling spending of, 272–273
   financial aid, 275–278
   insurance, 274–275
   personal diagnostic report, 271
Motivation, 24
Multiculturalism refers to cultural and racial diversity, 329
Multiple-choice questions allow you to pick an answer from several options offered, 148–149

Narrative story method is a memory technique that involves making up a narrative, or story. It helps students recall unrelated lists of words by giving them meaning and linking them in a specific order, 107
Need-based financial aid requires you or your parents to fill out forms stating your resources. The school then determines how much aid needs to be made up from somewhere else, 276
Needs analysis document is a form for helping people prove their financial need to their schools, 276
Negative thoughts, 124
Negotiations, instructor, 164
Nervousness
   expressions of, 254–255
   reducing, 200–201, 202
Networking is making contacts, and making use of existing contacts, with people to find work and advance your career, 293–294
Newsgroups, 245–246
Newspaper research, 183–184
Nonacademic activities, 41
Nonassertive behavior means consistently giving in to others on points of difference. It means agreeing with others regardless of your feelings, not expressing your opinions, hurting yourself to avoid hurting others, 268
Nontraditional students, sometimes called adult students or returning students, are post-secondary students who are older than 24 years, 330–331

"No shame, no blame" approach to mistakes, 211–212
Notebook computers, 230
  considerations for buying, 232
Notes
  5R system for taking, 86–90
  leaving spaces in, 95
  preparing for oral presentations, 197
  sorting for term papers, 188, 190
  trading with classmates, 95

Objective questions are those that are true-false, multiple-choice, matching, and fill-in, 145, 146–150
  fill-in-the-blank questions, 150
  matching questions, 150
  multiple-choice questions, 148–149
  strategies applicable to, 147
  true-false questions, 147–148
Obstacles to goal-achievement
  identifying, 39
  overcoming, 41
Online computerized catalogs require that you use a computer terminal or microcomputer that has a wired connection to a library database, 182
Online information services, 185, 243–244, 246
Optimism, 33–34
Oral presentations, 196–202
  audience attention in, 199–200
  career skills and, 170
  delivering, 201–202
  preparing notes for, 197
  reducing nervousness in, 200–201, 202
  stages in, 197–199
Orientation program, 310–311
Originality, 171–172
Outlines
  for long-answer essays, 154, 155
  for oral presentations, 197
  software for creating, 237
  for term papers, 177–178, 188, 190
Overdoers, 70
Overlearning is defined as continued rehearsal of material after you first appeared to have mastered it, 104, 139

Papers. *See* Term papers
Parent Loans for Undergraduate Students (PLUS), 278
Parents, living with, 14

Participation, class, 85, 94
Part-time work, 276, 278
Passive aggression, 265
Passive behavior means consistently giving in to others on points of difference. It means agreeing with others regardless of your feelings, not expressing your opinions, hurting yourself to avoid hurting others, 268
Passive reading, 118
Pell Grants, 277
Penalties for cheating, 163
People distractions, 68
Perfectionists, 70
Periodical research, 183–184
Perkins Loans, 278
Persistence
  importance of, 209
  incubation as form of, 221
  locus of control and, 32
  values about, 27
Personal associations, 90
Personal computers (PCs) are desktop or portable computers that can run easy-to-use, personal assistance software such as word-processing programs, 228–234
  communications tools for, 242–246
  desktop vs. laptop, 230
  IBM-style vs. Macintosh-style, 228–230
  job hunting with, 299–300
  minimum system for, 232
  modems for, 232
  power needed in, 231
  purchasing, 232–234, 272
  software for, 234–241
  upgradability of, 231
Personal development
  as lifelong process, 279
  practical education and, 5
Personal information manager (PIM) is a combination word-processor, database, and desktop accessory program that organizes a variety of information, 236, 238
Personal support system, 18
Photocopiers, 187
Physical disability is a health-related condition that prevents a person from participating fully in daily activities, 334
Physical help, 321–324
Plagiarism means presenting another person's ideas as one's own, 161

of term papers, 171–172
Planning process
  actions based on, 40–43
  life/career goals and, 38–40
Pleasure reading, 110
Portable computers, 230
  for collecting library information, 187–188
  considerations on buying, 232
Positive self-talk consists of giving yourself positive messages, 124
  test anxiety and, 142–143
Practical student. *See also* Students
  profile of, 2–3
  seven challenges for, 8–18
  survival skills for, 30–35
  values assessment for, 24–28
Praise, expressing, 267
Preface tells the reader the intended audience for the book, the author's purpose and approach, why the book is different, and perhaps an overview of the organization, 112, 113
Preparation
  for lectures, 85, 94, 95
  for oral presentations, 200–201
  for tests, 138–139, 164
Presentation graphics are graphics used to communicate or make a presentation of data to others, 240–241
Priority setting, 61
Problem solving
  creative thinking for, 217–221
  critical thinking for, 210–216
  incubation technique for, 221
Process diagrams are useful for representing the steps in a process, 128, 129
Procrastination is defined as putting off things intentionally and habitually, 70
  fighting, 70–71
  types of, 70
Progressive muscular relaxation consists of reducing stress by tightening and relaxing major muscle groups throughout your body, 260–261
Proofreading
  term papers, 195
  test answers, 146, 158
Psychological reactions to stress, 254–255
Psychological risks, 35

Psychological services, 322
Public speaking. *See also* Oral presentations
    reducing your fear of, 200–201

Qualifier words, 148
Questionable statistics, 216
Questions
    answering on tests, 144–146
    asking in class, 94, 95
    conversational, 266–267
    objective, 145, 146–150
    practice, 138
    review or discussion, 116
    SQ3R reading system and, 117–118
    subjective, 144, 145
    3Rs reading system and, 121
Racial diversity, 332–334
RAM (Random Access Memory), 231
Reader's Guide to Periodical Literature, 177
Reading
    active vs. passive, 118–119
    career skills and, 6
    long-term memory and, 111
    personal exploration of, 109
    SQ3R system of, 117–120
    of textbooks, 112–116
    3Rs system of, 120–123
    two types of, 110
Reasoning means giving reasons in favor of this or that assertion, 214
    deductive and inductive, 214
    incorrect, 215–216
Recitation
    of lecture notes, 90
    in SQ3R reading system, 119–120
    in 3Rs reading system, 122–123
Recording
    of lecture notes, 87–88
    in 3Rs reading system, 121–122
Reference materials, 185
Reflecting on lecture notes, 90
Registrar is the campus office responsible for keeping track of grades, transcripts, and other academic records, 325
Rehearsing a speech, 200–201
Reinforcements, goal, 39
Relationships
    conflict in, 265
    school responsibilities and, 15–16
Relaxation techniques
    coping with stress through, 260–262
    memory and, 104

for public speaking, 200–201
    for test anxiety, 141–142
Religions, 333
Reminders, daily, 60
Reorganizing term papers, 194
Repetition, 102, 104
Research
    collection methods, 185–188
    initial, 176–177
    library, 179–188, 189
Responsibility, personal, 30–32
Résumés
    computer-scannable, 298–299
    cover letter with, 300
    database services for, 300
    exercise on creating, 301
    tips on writing, 296–298
Reviewing
    lecture notes, 90
    in SQ3R reading system, 120
    as test preparation strategy, 139
Revising term papers, 193–194
Rewards, 65
Rewriting lecture notes, 89–90
Rhymes, 102, 107
Risks, psychological, 35
Rites of passage, 20

Safety tips, 323
Scholarships are usually awarded on the basis of merit, 278
School. *See also* Higher education
    balancing with commuting and work, 12–13
    campus resources at, 310–315
    making friends at, 11–12
School catalog contains requirements for graduation, requirements for certificate or degree programs, and course descriptions, 311
    learning to use, 313–314
Search engines. *See* Web search engines
Security office, 322–323
Selective perception, 218
Self-blame, 265
Self-expression, 267
Self-help assistance is financial aid that requires something in return, 276
Self-study practice sessions, 138
Seminars, 6
Sensory images, 220
Sentence-completion questions, 150
Serendipity, 221

Sexism is discrimination against individuals based on their gender, 330
Sexual harassment consists of sexually-oriented behaviors that adversely affect someone's academic or employment status or performance, 330
Sexual orientation, 330
Short-answer essay may be a brief one-word or one-sentence answer to a short-answer question, a one- or two-paragraph essay, or a list or diagram, 151
    strategy for handling, 151–152
Short-term memory is defined as recording seven elements for a maximum of 30 seconds, 101–102
Shyness, 71
Signal word or phrase. *See* Bell phrase
Six-step examination approach, 143–146
Sleep
    dealing with stress through, 257
    time needed for, 63
Slippery slope argument is a failure to see that the first step in a possible series of steps does not inevitably lead to the rest , 216
Social support systems, 259–260
Social withdrawal, 257
Soft skills, 170
Software, 234–241
    communications, 241
    database management, 239–240
    desktop accessory/manager, 236
    graphics, 240–241
    integrated packages, 241
    personal information manager, 236, 238
    power or flexibility of, 231
    spreadsheet, 238–239
    suites, 241
    word processing, 235–236
Sorting your notes, 188, 190
Source cards, 186
Speeches. *See* Oral presentations
Spelling
    software for checking, 237
    in term papers, 173
Spousal responsibilities, 14
Spreadsheet software allows users to create tables and financial schedules by entering data into rows and columns arranged as a grid on a display screen, 238–239

SQ3R reading system has five steps: Survey, Question, Read, Recite, Review, 117–120, 126

Stafford Loan Program, 278

Stage fright, 200–201

Statistics, questionable, 216

Stereotypes are exaggerated expectations about a category of people, which may be completely inaccurate when applied to individuals, 330

   as conceptual block, 218

Straw man argument is when you misrepresent your opponent's position to make it easier to attack, or when you attack a weaker position while ignoring a stronger one, 216

Stress is the reaction of our bodies to an event, 252–262

   causes and manifestations of, 252–255

   coping strategies for, 257–262

   difficult subjects and, 125

   managing, 256–262

   nonproductive ways of handling, 257

   relaxation techniques for, 260–262

   Student Stress Scale, 255

   test anxiety and, 141–143, 165

   types of, 254–255

   worries of students and, 252

Stressors are the source of stress, 252–253

   characteristics of, 253–254

   reducing, 257–258

Stress site, 254

Strong/Campbell Interest Inventory (SCII), 291

Strong stressor is a powerful, ongoing source of extreme mental or physical discomfort, 253

Student bulletin is a periodical that informs students of campus activities and events, 312

Student handbook is a guide that summarizes many of the school's policies and regulations, 312

Students. *See also* Practical student

   academic help for, 315–321

   activities and campus life for, 327–328

   benefits of higher education for, 3–7

   campus resources for, 310–315

   diversity issues for, 329–334

   fear of higher education in, 28–30

   financial aid for, 275–278

   international, 334

   miscellaneous assistance for, 324–326

   physical and emotional help for, 321–324

   principal worries of, 252

   survival skills for, 30–35

   traditional vs. nontraditional, 330–331

   values assessment for, 24–28

Student Stress Scale, 255

Student union is a meeting place for students. It has a cafeteria or dining hall and often recreational areas as well, 327–328

Study

   cramming vs., 72–73, 100

   delaying tactics and, 68–69

   distractions from, 66–68

   procrastination and, 70–71

   scheduling time for, 65–66

   time required for, 50–51, 58, 64, 125–126

   tools for aiding, 127–128

   using waiting time for, 71–72

Study diagrams are literal representations of things from real life, which you have rendered in your own hand, 128, 129

Study group is a group of classmates that gets together to share notes and ideas, 69

   test preparation and, 138

Study guide is a booklet that contains practice questions, along with their answers, covering material in the textbook, 138

Style books, 185

Subjective questions are those that generally require long-answers, such as essay-type questions or those requiring lists as answers, 144, 145

Subjective tests, 152–158

Submissive behavior means consistently giving in to others on points of difference. It means agreeing with others regardless of your feelings, not expressing your opinions, hurting yourself to avoid hurting others, 268

Subnotebook computers, 230, 232

Subvocalizing, 119

Suites (software) are applications—like spreadsheets, word processing, graphics, and communi-cations—that are bundled together and sold for a fraction of what the programs would cost if bought individually, 241

Supplemental Educational Opportunity Grants (SEOG), 277

Support groups, 260, 324

Support systems, 259–260

Survey is an overview, 115, 117

Suspension means you are told you cannot return to school for a given amount of time, usually a semester or a year, 163

Syllabus is a course outline or guide that tells the student what reading assignments are required, what assignments are due when, and when examinations are scheduled, 54, 85

   test preparation and, 137

Table of contents lists the principal headings in the book, 112, 113

Tact, 267

Taping lectures, 72, 95, 128

Tasks

   breaking assignments into, 68–69

   prioritizing, 69

Teachers. *See* Instructors

Telephone

   distractions, 67

   expenses, 272

Telephone-related communications services, 242–243

Television, time spent watching, 63–64

Tenant's insurance, 274–275

Term papers, 171–195

   academic dishonesty on, 161

   career skills and, 170

   documentation style in, 194–195

   editing, 193–194

   finalizing, 194–195

   first draft of, 190–191

   five phases in producing, 173–195

   grading of, 171–173

   initial research for, 176–177

   library research for, 179–188

   making a copy of, 195

   outline for, 177–178, 190

   picking topics for, 174–176

   plagiarism of, 171–172

   proofreading, 195

   revising, 193–194

   sorting your notes for, 188

   typing, 195

   writing tips for, 191–192

Test anxiety consists of thoughts and worries (the mental component) and feelings and sensations (the physical component) of stress linked to test taking, 141
  coping with, 141–143, 165
Tests, 136–165
  academic honesty and, 159–164
  becoming expert at taking, 136–140
  coping with anxiety about, 141–143, 165
  cramming for, 100
  environment for taking, 140
  essay questions on, 151–158
  items to bring to, 139–140
  objective questions on, 145, 146–150
  preparation strategies for, 138–139
  proofreading answers on, 146
  psyching out the instructor on, 137–138
  six-step examination approach for, 143–146
  subjective questions on, 144, 145
Textbooks
  advance organizers in, 115–116
  basic features of, 112–115
  bringing to class, 85
  learning styles and, 80
  tips on using, 112
Thesaurus lists synonyms, or words with similar meanings, 185
  computer program, 237
Thesis statement is a concise sentence that defines the purpose of your paper, 190
Thinking
  creative, 217–221
  critical, 210–216
  positive, 124
  strategies for test questions, 148
  using spare time for, 72
3Rs reading system has three steps for mastering textbooks: Read, Record, Recite, 120–123, 126
Time
  log-keeping exercise, 62
  required for study, 50–51, 58, 64, 125–126
  weekly use of, 63–64
Time lines are sketches representing a particular historical development, 128, 129
Time management, 50–73
  boosting performance through, 71–72
  as career skill, 7
  delaying tactics and, 68–69

  distractions and, 66–68
  master timetable and, 53–56
  procrastination and, 70–71
  six-step program for, 35–43, 52–61
  steps for improving, 52–61
  study time and, 50–51, 65–66
  time wasters and, 61–72
  "To Do" lists and, 60–61
  weekly timetable and, 57–60
Timetables
  master, 53–56
  weekly, 57–60
Title page gives the title, edition number (if later than the first edition), author, and publisher, 112, 113
"To Do" lists, 60–61
Topics, term paper, 174–176
Traditional students are post-secondary students between the ages of 18 and 24 years, 330
Transportation expenses, 272
Transportation office is the office that issues permits for parking on campus and gives out information on public transportation and car pools, 326
Travel time requirements, 63
True-false questions are statements that you must indicate are either correct or incorrect, 147–148
Tutor is a private teacher or coach who's purpose is to help an individual student improve a particular skill, 320
Typing term papers, 173, 195

Unconscious mind, 219
Uncritical thinking, 210–211
Underlining key information, 121, 122
Unloading means taking 2–3 minutes to jot down on the back of the exam sheet any keywords, concepts, and ideas that are in your mind, 144
Upgradability (computer) means that you are able to buy internal parts, such as additional memory, that can run newer software, 231
Used computers, 232–233
Usenet, 245–246

Values are principles by which you lead your life. They are important beliefs or attitudes that you think "ought to be" (or "ought not to be"). Moreover, they are

beliefs that you feel strongly enough about to take action on and that you have consciously chosen, 24–28
  characteristics of, 24–25
  on higher education, 25–27
  on persistence, 27
Verbal memory aids, 106–108
Visualization is a procedure in which you essentially daydream an image or desired change, anticipating that your body will respond as if the image were real, 261
Visual learners like to see pictures of things described or words written down, 80
Visual memory aids, 108
Vocational Preference Inventory, 291
Vocational-technical education, 2 *See also* Higher education
Vocational-technical student, 2–3 *See also* Practical student
Vocational tests, 289–292
Voice mail digitizes incoming voice messages and stores them in the recipient's "voice mailbox" in digitized form. It then converts the digitized versions back to voice messages when they are retrieved, 242
Voice Of Judgment (VOJ), 124

Waiting time, 71
Web browser is software that enables you to "browse through" and view Web sites, 246
Web directories are search tools classified by topic, 246
Web search engines allow you to find specific documents through keyword searches, 246
Weekly timetable, 57–60
Wellness services, 324
Word processing software allows you to use computers to create, edit, revise, store, and print text material, 235–236
  features of, 237
Work. *See also* Career; Employment
  balancing study with, 12–13
  interview for, 300, 302
  online tools for finding, 299–300
  part-time, 276, 278
  process of looking for, 293–303
  time needed for, 63
Working title is a tentative title for your paper, 190

Work-study programs, 276, 278

World Wide Web (WWW, or simply "the Web") is the Internet's most graphical and usable service. It resembles a huge encyclopedia filled with thousands of topics or sites (called "pages"), which have been created by computer users and businesses around the world, 246

Worriers, 70

Writing
career skills and, 6, 170
documentation for, 194–195
environment for, 188
essays on tests, 151–158
fine-tuning, 194
first drafts, 190–191
information retention and, 107
paragraphs in essays, 156–158
personal vs. expressive, 171
proofreading, 195
reorganizing, 194
résumés, 296–298
term papers, 173–195
tips on, 191–192
transitions, 194

Written examinations require the student to write essays, either short or long, 151
long-answer essay, 151, 152–158
short-answer essay, 151–152